THE SOCRATIC WAY OF LIFE: XENOPHON'S *MEMORABILIA*

T0385620

# THE SOCRATIC WAY OF LIFE:
# XENOPHON'S *MEMORABILIA*

## THOMAS L. PANGLE

THE UNIVERSITY OF CHICAGO PRESS

CHICAGO AND LONDON

The University of Chicago Press, Chicago 60637
The University of Chicago Press, Ltd., London
© 2018 by The University of Chicago
All rights reserved. No part of this book may be used or reproduced in any
manner whatsoever without written permission, except in the case of brief
quotations in critical articles and reviews. For more information, contact the
University of Chicago Press, 1427 E. 60th St., Chicago, IL 60637.
Published 2018
Paperback edition 2020
Printed and bound by CPI Group (UK) Ltd, Croydon, CR0 4YY

29 28 27 26 25 24 23 22 21 20    1 2 3 4 5

ISBN-13: 978-0-226-51689-9 (cloth)
ISBN-13: 978-0-226-75426-0 (paper)
ISBN-13: 978-0-226-51692-9 (e-book)
DOI: https://doi.org/10.7208/chicago/9780226516929.001.0001

Library of Congress Cataloging-in-Publication Data

Names: Pangle, Thomas L., author.
Title: The Socratic way of life : Xenophon's Memorabilia /
    Thomas L. Pangle.
Description: Chicago ; London : The University of Chicago Press, 2018. |
    Includes bibliographical references and index.
Identifiers: LCCN 2017026964 | ISBN 9780226516899 (cloth : alk. paper) |
    ISBN 9780226516929 (e-book)
Subjects: LCSH: Xenophon. Memorabilia. | Socrates. | Justice. |
    Philosophy, Ancient. | Political science—Philosophy.
Classification: LCC PA4494.M6 P36 2018 | DDC 183/.2—dc23
LC record available at https://lccn.loc.gov/2017026964

♾ This paper meets the requirements of ANSI/NISO Z39.48-1992
(Permanence of Paper).

To My Daughters
Heather and Sophia

The *Memorabilia* of Xenophon give a really true picture, that is just as spiritually rich as was the model for the picture; one must, however, understand how to read this book. The philologists believe at bottom that Socrates has nothing to say to them, and therefore are bored by it. Others feel that this book points you to, and at the same time gives you, happiness.

—Nietzsche, posthumous frag. 18 [47] (1876)

# CONTENTS

A keynote of the study that follows is struck by the aphorism *"Socrates"* in Nietzsche's most humane and sober, least shattering and visionary, work, *The Wanderer and His Shadow*. There (aph. 86) Nietzsche declares that in "the *Memorabilia* of Socrates"[1] we find "the simplest and least perishable of mediator-sages," to whom "the pathways of the most diverse philosophic ways of life lead back" inasmuch as they are "at bottom directed to joy in living, and in one's own self." Xenophon's Socrates, in contrast to "the founder of Christianity," possesses "the joyful kind of seriousness" and "that *wisdom full of roguish trickery*"[2] that "express the best condition of soul of the human being."

For today's readers, Nietzsche's stress on the Xenophontic Socrates's "roguish trickery" is particularly helpful. Nietzsche lifts the cloak of boy-scout-like earnestness[3] with which Xenophon playfully envelops his, and his Socrates's, radically free spirits. Since nowadays there prevails a loss of comprehension of the reasons necessitating the employment, by ancient philosophers, of such jocoserious veils,[4] late-modern conventional scholars have, with some notable exceptions,[5] failed to penetrate to Xenophon's deeper, jovial, Socratic message and teaching.[6]

Yet Nietzsche's appreciation for Xenophon's "roguishly wise" Socrates does not lead Nietzsche to become Xenophontic-Socratic. The "best condition of soul of the human being" exemplified in Xenophon's Socrates ultimately remains, for Nietzsche, "human, all-too-human." Nietzsche has much greater cultural hopes for and from, he makes much greater cultural demands upon, the potentially "super-human" philosophic soul and its creative uniqueness.

The fact is, Nietzsche's evocation of the Xenophontic Socrates as a model occurs in unusual authorial circumstances. At this stage in his life, Nietzsche presents himself as a somewhat disheartened "Wanderer" who is preoccupied with the possibility that he is living during a cultural "age of darkness" that may take a long time to wane. In this deflated mood the Wanderer has for the first time in his life been addressed by, and then has held a long conversation with, "his Shadow." As a result, the Wanderer has given to his Shadow a promise to "become again a good neighbor to the nearest things." Previously, and more characteristically (the Wanderer confesses to his Shadow), he has been inclined to overlook "the nearest things," and has been given to "slandering" all shadows. Previously, the focus of Nietzsche's intellectual gaze has been on "that still distant state of things" in which philosophy must undertake "unspeakably great and bold" cultural responsibilities extending far beyond ambitions so modest as those exhibited by Xenophon's Socrates.[7] Does all this show how Nietzsche, looking from the superior vantage point of "the historical sense,"[8] has surpassed Xenophon and his Socrates in depth and breadth of understanding of the most complete, because "creatively legislative," philosophic life? Or has Nietzsche in crucial respects been misled by "the historical sense" into a distorted understanding of the most truly philosophic life? Could the Wanderer's appreciation of Xenophon's Socrates have been Nietzsche's most perspicuous moment?[9] This question, of the relative merit of peak ancient and modern conceptions of the philosophic life (and of that life's proper relation to civic life), will hover over our study.

In following Xenophon and his portrait of Socrates, we shall remain for the most part in what Nietzsche calls the realm of the shadowy "nearest things." Xenophon's Socrates, unlike Nietzsche, finds in the wrestling with the perplexities found in the nearest and dearest prephilosophic opinions the essential source of liberation—the only path to an adequate answer to the most important question confronting human life: "By what standards ought one to live?" Reason's attempt to answer this question encounters its biggest challenge in the widespread human testimonies to revelations of supreme commandments from mysterious, suprarational, providential divinity (cf. 1.4.15–16).[10] Xenophon spotlights the experience of Socrates himself in this regard by way of his famous *daimonion*. Xenophon tells us that Socrates "engaged in conversations always about the human things": "What is piety, what is impiety?" "What is noble, what is shameful?" "What is just, what is unjust?" "What is moderation, what is madness?" "What is courage, what is cowardice?" "What is a city, what is a statesman, what is rule of human beings, what is a skilled ruler of human beings?" (1.1.16). Xenophon thus indicates that the primary "human thing" that is puzzled over in Socrates's conversations is piety (and impiety). To puzzle over this "human thing" as Socrates did entails intense reflection on being as a whole, viewed from a perspective that conceives the critical study of moral opinions and human psychology as the key to unraveling the universe's greatest mystery. Xenophon indicates that for Socrates, perplexity about piety and impiety is closely connected with perplexity about the noble and the base, the just and the unjust, virtue and vice, and skilled political rule. This points us to the crucial distinction between Socratic philosophizing and Nietzschean philosophizing—nay, between Socratic philosophizing and modern philosophizing as a whole.

As Nietzsche is acutely aware, the Socrates of both Plato and Xenophon takes piety so seriously that Socrates comes to sight as "a divine missionary"—though with "a perceptible whiff of Attic irony and a delight in jesting."[11] And Nietzsche judges "the precise religious task to which Socrates feels himself assigned"—"putting the god to the test in a hundred ways to see if he has spoken the truth"—is "one of the finest compromises between piety and freedom of spirit that has ever been thought up." Nietzsche nevertheless decisively concludes that "now we have no more need for even this compromise."[12] For Nietzsche, as for his predecessors, modernity—through its progressive philosophic and scientific secularization of civic culture—has adequately disposed of the challenge posed to rationalist philosophizing by purportedly revealed, suprarational, divine commandments and teachings: "God is dead!" What is needed now is a "creative" enrichment of the successfully God-destroying but (alas!) humanly soul-destroying shallowness of modern rationalism. For Nietzsche, political philosophy's highest mission has become the creative legislation of a future, world-historical culture that will incorporate while surpassing—in spiritual wealth and depth, and in earthbound intellectual probity—the once-enchanting but irrational and antinatural religious cultures that humans created for themselves in the past. Philosophic questioning must now give way to philosophic commanding.[13]

This vast project of Nietzsche's may be viewed as the fullest development of the enterprise uniting all the philosophers who, since Machiavelli, have broken with classical (Socratic) philosophy. Modern philosophy as such has been dedicated to taking over, and reshaping, by rationalizing, humanity's culture—thereby mastering by eliminating the anti- or suprarational theological challenge. Through Xenophon's Socratic writings we are given precious access to the character and way of life of the philosopher who is the fountainhead and paradigm of the alternative, premodern political rationalism, and its radically different, far less ambitious, response to the challenge of suprarational revelation.

Xenophon makes it obvious that Socrates does not seek to revolutionize the pious, participatory-republican culture that environs him. Rather,

Xenophon shows Socrates undertaking, on the basis of a mixture of doubt and appreciation,[14] a cautious if often imaginative interrogation of his civic culture's foundational opinions, in order to assist a few others as well as himself to assess better the degree of truth and coherence in those opinions— and, on that basis, to make both their society and themselves, their own lives, more reasonable. What most obviously and decisively distinguishes Socrates from his "pre-Socratic" predecessors is that he engages in a never-ending series of encounters with a variety of nonphilosophic interlocutors, whose attachment to foundational civic opinions is more or less gently and convivially brought to full expression and critical scrutiny. As a consequence of being subjected to, and witnessing in others, these encounters, some of Socrates's companions, especially among the young (most notably Xenophon), are converted, in varying degrees, to the restlessly skeptical and meditative Socratic mode of existence—not least as regards piety. The Socratic life thus presupposes, while transcending, through critique, the moral and religious horizon of republican virtue.[15] As a result, the Socratics inevitably attract moral and religious suspicion. Socrates strives, through his art of rhetoric, to dispel or to mitigate this distrust, and to prevent potentially subversive political consequences that might flow from his critical questioning. Eventually, however, the Athenian democracy indicts, convicts, and executes Socrates for impiety and corruption of the young. This sad outcome evidently does not come as a surprise to Socrates. He declares, as the day of his trial approaches, that throughout his life he has been concerned with, and preparing, his defense (4.8.4). And in Xenophon's *Apology of Socrates to the Jury*, Socrates's defense speech in court succeeds just as he has planned: not in preventing his execution, but in turning that execution into a kind of martyrdom that was to contribute crucially to a lasting defensive legacy for Socratic philosophizing.

Yet Socrates's own lifelong self-defense, and then his courtroom speech, were not in themselves enough to bequeath a sufficiently accurate, while sufficiently protective, legacy of access to Socratic thinking and living. Needed in addition were the complementary writings of Plato and Xenophon, Socrates's two greatest and closest students. Xenophon left it to Plato to construct a poetically sublime and even quasi-religious version of the more scientific and "metaphysical" dimensions of Socratic thought and life. Xenophon for the most part even left to Plato the portrayal of Socratic refutative dialogues focused on the "What is . . ." questions. Xenophon chose to continue, and to perfect as literature, the dimension of Socratic rhetoric that combines piously and moralistically defensive edification with subtle

and often humorous provocation to questioning thought about the foundational opinions that govern prephilosophic human existence.

The *Memorabilia*, the longest and deservedly most popular of Xenophon's
four Socratic writings, is divided into two parts of very unequal length: in
the first, Xenophon rebuts the charges of injustice in the official indictment
brought against Socrates; then in the second, he explicitly transitions to a
much longer account of how Socrates "seemed to benefit those who had intercourse with him" (1.3.1). As is made more evident in the conclusion to the
whole work, the unifying focus is thus on defending the memory of Socrates
by demonstrating his virtue of *justice*, or his being "so just as to harm no
one, even a little, but to benefit in the greatest ways those who made use of
him" (4.8.11). Accordingly, the last words of Socrates quoted in the *Memorabilia* are these: "I know that it will always be witnessed on my behalf that I
never was unjust to any human being nor made one worse, but tried always
to make better those who had intercourse with me" (4.8.10). The *Memorabilia* may thus to some extent put into the background, but certainly does
not neglect, Socrates's virtues in relation to or as concerned with *himself*: as
Xenophon also says in the conclusion, the work has presented Socrates as "so
self-controlled as never to choose for himself the more pleasant instead of the
better, and so prudent as not to err in judging the better and the worse things,
nor to be in need of another in addition, but to be self-sufficient in knowing these things" (4.8.11). Xenophon's three other Socratic writings allow the
more self-concerned dimensions of Socratic virtue to come to the fore, and
thus to a greater extent present "Socrates even if he transcends justice."[16]

The perspective from which, through Xenophon, I will be analyzing
the import of Socrates's founding of political philosophizing is one that has
tended to be subordinated, even neglected, in modern scholarship. This is
an angle of approach to Socrates—and to philosophy in general, especially
ancient—whose recovery has been notably advocated by Pierre Hadot, as
expressed in the very title of his book *Philosophy as a Way of Life: Spiritual
Exercises from Socrates to Foucault* (1995). Influenced by, while influencing,
Foucault, Hadot looks to philosophic texts less with a view to studying and
explaining systems and doctrines, and more in order to illuminate and to
revivify, as vibrant models or guides, what Hadot calls "spiritual exercises"
leading toward, and constituting, deliberately paradigmatic ways of living
that philosophers have enacted and promoted, in deed and in word. It is "the
figure of Socrates" (Hadot stresses) that "causes" such exemplary spiritual
exercises "to emerge into Western consciousness." "The point" of Socratic
dialogue "is not to set forth a doctrine, but rather to guide the interlocutor"

(and, indirectly, the reader) "towards a determinate mental attitude"; it is "a combat, amicable but real"; or, in the apt turn of phrase that Hadot repeatedly quotes from Victor Goldschmidt, the "dialogue's goal is more to form than to inform" (Hadot 1995, 89, 91).

But, strange to say (given this approach), Hadot, in striking contrast to Foucault,[17] attends very little to Xenophon, and focuses almost exclusively on Plato's portrayal of Socrates. Moreover, Hadot downplays the dialogues in which Plato has his Socrates wrestling most persistently with *political* questions (*Republic, Gorgias, Crito*, etc.). Hadot's focus is on dialogues like *Phaedo, Theaetetus*, and, above all, *Symposium*. As a result, Hadot obscures Socrates the *citizen*-philosopher, the critical teacher of civic politics, the (cautious and gingerly) critic of contemporary civic religion and civic ethics. It is striking that it is only when Hadot treats (and only very briefly; 1995, 23 and 155) Socrates on *justice* that he turns to the portrait of the Socratic life given in Xenophon's *Memorabilia*. Hadot's neglect of the Xenophontic portrait leads him to go too far in conceiving the exemplary Socratic way of life as a forerunner of (especially Christian) Neoplatonism and its apolitical spiritual exercises. Departing still further, in my judgment, from authentic Socratism, Hadot winds up assimilating the Socratic way of life to Kierkegaard's existential-Christian way of life: "Kierkegaardian consciousness is identical to Socratic consciousness."[18]

Some of the needed corrective is provided if we return to key relevant comments of Nietzsche (referred to by Hadot). As we saw in our opening quotations from Nietzsche, he stresses the contrast between Socrates and Jesus. More than that. "If all goes well, the time will come," Nietzsche prophesies, "when one will take up the *Memorabilia* of Socrates rather than the Bible as guide to morals and reason."[19]

Xenophon's *Memorabilia* is to replace the Bible?! Xenophon's Socrates is to replace Jesus, as a guide to morals?! Can Nietzsche be serious?

More so than one might at first imagine, I believe. The massive objection, of course, is that Socrates is so extraordinary a human being, with so superior a mind and heart, advised by so unique a "daimonic" voice, and dwelling in a historical context so alien to our own, that only a foolish vanity would propel any of us to think that we are imitating him, or could ever do so. There is doubtless truth in this.[20] But Nietzsche does not have in mind imitation in the sense of reproduction. Even as Christians of many stripes in vastly diverse cultural circumstances have down through the centuries made Jesus the polestar, shining far above them, by which they have tried to steer their admittedly inferior soul-journeys, it is not unreasonable to suggest that rationalists might some day orient their moral compasses by the lowlier star of Xenophon's portrait of Socrates, *mutatis mutandis*.[21] In the American tradition of political and moral thought we have an outstanding example: Benjamin Franklin. His down-to-earth *Autobiography* presents his life as a model, for future Americans—and explicitly indicates that he took as one of his own main models Xenophon's portrait of Socrates in the *Memorabilia*.[22]

# PART I

# Socrates's Innocence of the Injustices for Which He Was Executed

## CHAPTER ONE

# Socrates Was Not Guilty of Impiety or Disbelief as Regards the Gods of Athens

Xenophon commences his *Recollections*[1] by expressing his frequently recurring wonder at what could ever have been the arguments of the prosecutors by which the Athenians were persuaded that Socrates was deserving of the death penalty. Xenophon's first sentence does not declare any amazement at the bringing of the charges, nor even at the fact that the Athenians were persuaded to convict Socrates on those charges. It is the death penalty that he says makes him marvel (see also 1.2.63–64). The "whiff of Attic irony"[2] in this opening sentence becomes apparent when we read our author's *Apology of Socrates to the Jury*, and there find that it was the trial speeches and strategy of Socrates himself that, in the words of I. F. Stone (1988, 187), "according to Xenophon, left the jury no alternative to the death penalty."[3]

But the second sentence, beginning with a "For" (*gar*), shifts the focus from the death penalty to the official indictment (which, as quoted here, omits the mention of that penalty[4]). Xenophon now gives the impression that it is rather the formal *charges* that have incited his amazement: he speaks as if the citizen-jury must have been bamboozled by cleverly deceitful prosecution speeches in order for them to have swallowed such nonsense as is stated in the indictment. Among other things, Xenophon thus helps to prepare the ground for the Athenian public to absolve itself of its sense of guilt by blaming the prosecutors, if and when the public mood should morph into regret about the conviction and execution of Socrates.[5]

Xenophon does not, however, proceed to give any critical analysis, or even indication, of the content of the speeches and arguments of the prosecutors. He lets us gather that he was not present at the trial;[6] but did his wonder never prompt him to find out what the prosecution's arguments actually were, and in what consisted their rhetorical power—if for no other reason than so that he could respond to them, and expose their hollowness and trickery? Eventually Xenophon does report, in direct quotation, impassioned arguments by someone accusing Socrates of corrupting the young (1.2.9, 12, 49, 51). Yet these do not seem to be quotations from the prosecution speeches at the trial (pace Taylor 1911, 4). Having highlighted the amazing persuasiveness of the prosecution speeches, Xenophon avoids contending with them.

## HIS PIETY PROVEN BY HIS WORSHIP

Responding to the first and most fully elaborated of the two charges in the indictment[7]—"Socrates commits injustice, in that those whom the city believes in (nomizei) as gods he does not believe in (nomizōn), but he carries in other strange/novel, divine things (kaina daimonia)"—Xenophon proceeds, in the fashion of a good defense lawyer, to exploit an ambiguity in this wording. The verb nomizō, when applied to humans in their posture toward divinities, can mean either "believing, according to lawful custom" or "worshipping, according to lawful custom"—or both.[8] Xenophon rejoins as if "not worshipping" were the gravamen. This allows him to dismiss the charge as absurd: what possible evidence could be used to suggest that Socrates failed to worship the gods in a lawful manner? For Socrates "manifestly performed sacrifices often at home,[9] and often on the public altars of the city; and his employment of divination was not un-evident!" In this way Xenophon begins by eclipsing the much more serious issue that was doubtless uppermost in the intention of the prosecutors, and in the minds of the jury: whether Socrates believed in the gods in whom the citizenry believed—the gods, such as Zeus and Athena and Apollo, whose customary ritual worship he conspicuously, but perhaps disingenuously, performed.[10]

## HIS BELIEF PROVEN BY HIS *DAIMONION*

Our advocate does not, however, entirely duck the truly serious question of his mentor's religious beliefs (see also 1.1.19). For he next confronts the fact that as regards Socrates's employment of divination, "there was much talk" about Socrates's unorthodoxy, as expressed in his "asserting that the divine thing (daimonion) gave signs to him."[11] Indeed, Xenophon opines that it was on this basis especially that "they charged him with carrying in strange/novel divine things (daimonia)" (1.2.2). Xenophon proceeds to show that by Socrates's asserting his power of divination through the private daimonion, he made himself stand out—first and foremost to his companions—in the idiosyncrasy of his piety, as regards both his practice and his proclaimed belief.[12] We can see that Socrates thus provoked especially his companions[13] to ponder, in all seriousness, and with wonder, how Socrates understood, and how they were to understand, his and other people's (perhaps the companions' own) unique and powerful religious experiences of prophetic revelations from providential and monitory divinity. Socrates certainly did not present himself in a way calculated to attract atheists, or those casual about religious belief and purported religious experience. Socrates seems rather to have wished to attract those who were seriously perplexed, or capable of becoming seriously perplexed, about divine revelation and (personal) religious experience. And Xenophon in his *Memorabilia* continues, or resuscitates, this Socratic allure. Xenophon both begins and ends the work (see 4.8) by spotlighting Socrates's controversially unorthodox claim to have received prophetic, guiding revelations from a private *daimonion*.

By such a self-presentation Socrates broadcasted through the city his deviation from customary piety, and gave considerable purchase to those suspiciously hostile to him and his companions on religious grounds. Socrates incurred grave risks—for himself but also for his followers—in headlining his claim to unique experiences of divine revelation (so this aspect of his self-presentation must have been of great importance to him: Guthrie 1971a, 81–84). As a result, in the wake of his conviction and execution, his companions now are in need of a defense that goes beyond what Socrates himself offered—a defense of their hero's proclaimed, extraordinary, prophetic experiences. Xenophon takes it upon himself to deliver that defense. He does so in a way that continues and enhances Socrates's own provocation to ponder and to puzzle over the character and meaningfulness of divine revelation and religious experience.

Xenophon begins by insisting that, in relying on the prophetic power of "the divine thing," Socrates "carried in nothing stranger than others—as many as, believing in an art of divination, have recourse to (*chrōntai*) birds and voices and symbolic portents and sacrifices." For "they don't conceive that it is the birds and other things they encounter that possess knowledge of what is beneficial for those having recourse to divination"; rather, they conceive that "the gods signal *through* these." And Socrates "believed thus" (1.1.3). Xenophon initially makes Socrates's belief sound perfectly traditional.

"But," Xenophon continues (in an apparently slight, but significant, qualification), whereas most "declare" that they are admonished "by birds and other things they encounter," Socrates "spoke even as he judged, namely that it was the *daimonion* that signaled."[14] Xenophon implicitly indicates that Socrates did not, like others, rely on divination through birds or other omens and portents—or through sacrificial victims (Socrates's sacrificing was in this crucial respect very different in spirit or belief from the customary, lawful, performance of sacrifices). What is more, Xenophon's formulation leaves open the following pregnant questions:[15] Did Socrates believe, as is believed by the rest who employ divination, that his *daimonion* was the *intermediary* of "the gods"? Or did Socrates believe that his *daimonion* was, in itself, the (single, ultimate, unmediated) source of beneficial prophetic knowledge? And how would this latter not then be a major departure from the city's belief about the gods?[16] On the other hand, if Socrates believed that his *daimonion* was merely an intermediary, then the question is mooted: Was it "the gods whom the city believes in and worships" that Socrates believed were communicating with him through the *daimonion*? Or could he have believed, as charged, that the divinities communicating with him through the *daimonion* were "strange/novel *daimonia*"?

These crux questions continue to loom unanswered in what follows. In fact, on close inspection we see that (pace Vlastos 1991, 166n41) nowhere in his defense against the indictment does Xenophon actually ever even deny, let alone argue against, the accusation that Socrates did not believe in the gods in whom the city believes.[17] Nor does Xenophon in his defense of Socrates ever refer (except in two profane expletives quoted from an accuser) to "Zeus and Hera and the gods associated with them" (to quote Socrates as reported in *Apology* 24). Xenophon bends his efforts to proving that Socrates was not an atheist—as if that were the real issue; as if that were the question the thoughtful reader needs seriously to ponder.[18]

That Socrates must have believed in "gods" follows, Xenophon contends, from the fact that Socrates had an excellent record in benefiting his companions through accurate practical predictions, which Socrates declared came from the *daimonion*. Xenophon's argument is formulated in the logically weak but forensically effective device of anaphoric questions.[19] The crucial questions in the sequence are based on the dubious premise that no one could ever "trust in" anything except "a god" (sing.) to be able to "trust" that his practical predictions about and for his friends were true.[20] Xenophon then jumps to the concluding question: "And if he trusted in gods [pl.], how could he not believe that gods exist?"[21] Xenophon reproduces the thought-provoking Socratic combination: intense seriousness about the experience of divine revelation interwoven with subtly ironic questioning of the official, traditional belief about the source of such experience.

## HIS BELIEF PROVEN BY HIS TEACHING ON DIVINATION

Xenophon turns, from Socrates's *daimonic*-divinatory guidance of his "companions" (*tōn sunontōn*), to "the things he did in regard to" his "serviceable associates" (*tous epitēdeious*) (1.1.6). These latter Socrates counseled, concerning matters whose outcome his reason disclosed to be evidently necessary, "also to do what he believed would be best done." But, concerning contingent matters whose outcomes were not rationally evident, Socrates sent these "serviceable associates" off to consult divination of the normal sort, to learn what needed to be done. (The eccentric prophetic power of Socrates's *daimonion*—whom, we later learn, Socrates may not have needed to consult[22]—was limited, in its application, to Socrates himself and his "companions.") Xenophon does not explain what counsel Socrates gave to his "serviceable associates" as regards that vast intermediate range of practical matters whose outcome his reason disclosed to be, not "necessary," but only more or less probable. But Socrates's view in this regard becomes clear, by implication, from what follows next.

Xenophon segues to Socrates's general doctrine on the sound employment of conventional divination (1.1.7–9). This "art of divination is needed in addition," Socrates declared, by all those who are "undertaking to manage households and cities in noble fashion."[23] Socrates taught, however, an uncustomarily restricted, rationalized recourse to such divination (Kronenberg 2009, 50–51). He insisted that to ask for divinatory advice in practical matters that the gods have granted to humans to know or to learn through their own artful, rational expertise is not only crazy, or "to be possessed by the divinely uncanny" (*daimonān*—the verbal form corresponding to the adjectival substantive *daimonion*) but can be "grave violation of divine law" (*athemista*). According to Socrates's gospel, in order to conform to divine law, piety must take care to exhaust fully the capacities of practical human reasoning before seeking guidance from conventional prophecy—which is a needed supplement, but never a replacement, for rational art. On the other hand, Socrates also taught that to suppose that everything in practical affairs belongs to human judgment, and that there is not anything "divinely uncanny" (*daimonion*) in these matters, is also crazy, or "to be possessed by the divinely uncanny" (*daimonān*).[24] For although Xenophon reports Socrates going rather far in assessing the power of rational artfulness, he has Socrates insisting that "the greatest things"—namely, whether or to whom successfully expert human practice will turn out to prove beneficial or harmful—are matters that remain, in the final analysis, unknowable by human judgment.

This theological doctrine of Socrates, as reproduced by Xenophon, stresses the need for ordinary divination specifically in the artful practice or employment of farming, house building and other crafts, generalship, statesmanship, marrying a beautiful woman for the sake of delight, and securing (through marriage) kin who are powerful in the city (1.1.8). The doctrine seems to take for granted the goodness of all these endeavors. One is goaded to question why, then, Socrates engaged so little in these gentlemanly pursuits (Xenophon does not have Socrates refer to fathering children). If Socrates had been asked this question, one suspects that he would have said—perhaps with a barely visible twinkle in his eye—that his *daimonion* forbade him (cf. Plato, *Apology* 31c). This response would enable Socrates to dispense entirely with seeking guidance from conventional divination, without contradicting his own doctrine concerning the (qualified) need for such guidance.

We now see that Socrates not only was widely known to employ, for his companions and himself, an unorthodox mode of divination; in addition, he taught, for the benefit of other associates, a far-reaching and untraditional, rationalistic, theological doctrine regarding the divine law that governs recourse to conventional divination. Xenophon's account leaves unclear whether or to what extent Socrates himself publicly promulgated this innovative creed. What is clear is that Xenophon, by writing these pages, does make the novel theological doctrine more widely and permanently known. This is a somewhat assertive aspect of Xenophon's own "apology of Socrates" (1.2.13). The assertiveness becomes more evident if we stop to consider what is pointed to by Xenophon's use of the verb "to be possessed by the divinely uncanny"—as meaning to be crazed by divinity, in a self-destructive way. This reminds us of a dark element in traditional piety, made vivid by the great tragedians: the conception of divinity as being capable of manifesting itself by driving humans to self-destructive madness and infatuation. Xenophon incites his readers to wonder on what basis Socrates was so confident that divinity does not intervene in human existence in such ways that are radically mysterious, alien to reason, only ambiguously friendly, and even apparently envious or capricious.[25] In other words, Xenophon points to all that is at stake in the controversial, new, Socratic doctrine of divine law (*themis*). How do Socrates and Xenophon *know* that divinity legislates such massive reliance on rational, artful, human expertise? How do the Socratics *know* that this doctrine will not appear to the divinity as an assertion of prideful hubris deserving severe, possibly endless, punishment (consider the opening of Euripides's *Orestes*, esp. line 10)? Certainly the Socratic doctrine of divine law as regards divination intensified, for Socrates's followers, and in Xenophon's presentation intensifies for his serious readers, wonder as to the philosophic *basis*, the philosophic *ground*, of Socrates's new theology.

## HIS BELIEF PROVEN BY HIS ATTITUDE
## TOWARD NATURAL SCIENCE

At this point (1.1.10) Xenophon seems to anticipate a warily hostile reader's suspicion having been aroused, by the distinction that has emerged between what Socrates communicated to his "companions" and what he taught to others who associated with him: might this not be a sign that Socrates had a private, esoteric, religious doctrine, based on long private study of astronomy and of nature as a whole—as was portrayed by Aristophanes in *The Clouds*?[26] Xenophon rushes to rule out the possibility: Socrates, Xenophon insists, was "always out in the open"; he was in public all day, from "early morning," in the gymnasia and the "crowded marketplace" and "where the greatest number of people would be gathered." There, Xenophon alleges, Socrates was mostly talking (not asking questions or engaging in dialogues), and in such a way that anyone who wished could *listen* (not respond) to what he had to say. Socrates is thus depicted as a kind of preacher. Xenophon here in effect asserts that Socrates never engaged in private conversations, and still less in any private study or reading groups with students and close friends, or anything of that sort at all. This will soon be flagrantly contradicted.[27] What could be the reason for this initial, exaggerated, defensive diatribe? To what is Xenophon somewhat comically alerting us? We see the answer when Xenophon suddenly discloses the key presumption or suspicion that he is here rhetorically combating, with a sort of overkill. "For" (Xenophon continues) "he never carried on dialogues in the manner of most of the others about the nature of all things, inquiring into how what is called by the sophists the 'cosmos' holds,[28] and by what necessities each of the things in the heavens comes into being" (1.1.11).

Living as we do today in the scientific culture brought into being by the Enlightenment and its political philosophy, we are cut off from an understanding of why a healthy society, and especially a healthy classical republican citizenry, would regard such inquiry into nature as criminal. We thus suffer from an ignorance that Xenophon could not have foreseen in his readers. To begin to recover the understanding of what is at stake—an understanding that the classics could presume shared by all readers—we are in need of some illuminating help given by Plato in his *Laws* (967a). There the Athenian Stranger declares: "Most people think that those who deal with such matters, by astronomy and the other necessarily conjoined arts, become atheists, having had the insight that, to the greatest extent, matters come into being through necessities and not by the thoughts of a will aiming at completed goods."[29]

As we are provocatively reminded in Xenophon's *Symposium* (6.6–8; see also *Oeconomicus* 11.3) Socrates was widely known, by foreigners as well as Athenians, through the notorious image of him painted in Aristophanes's *Clouds*: as a "thinker" who, on the basis of study of the nature of the trans- or subhuman whole, denied the existence of the gods. Against this, Xenophon here defensively gives the superficially strong impression that Socrates did not *at all* concern himself with the study of nature as a whole: Xenophon goes so far as to say that Socrates "even showed that the ones thinking[30] about such things are foolish."

This strong initial impression is contradicted by subsequent reports in the *Memorabilia* of conversations that indicate Socrates's deep reflection on, and conversation about, the nature of all things and the causal structure of the whole, including the heavens (4.7.4–7; see also *Symposium* 7.4). In fact, the very first serious and sustained conversation that Xenophon depicts in the *Memorabilia* has Socrates elaborating a comprehensive teleological-theological cosmology, which he is later presented as restating (1.4 and 4.3). It is these passages of the *Memorabilia* that constitute the first written records we have of the elaboration of a philosophic, teleological cosmology and biology, and these passages were a major inspirational influence on the Stoic and all later cosmological tradition.[31]

The gross contradiction is dispelled, however, when we notice, on closer inspection (and helped by Smith and XS ad loc.), that what Xenophon actually says can mean that Socrates "*did* converse about the nature of all things, but *in a manner different* from that of most others." The distinctive manner in which Socrates conversed and thought about the nature of all things is adumbrated in the three criticisms Xenophon reports Socrates making to show the "folly" of the *manner* in which his philosophic colleagues conversed and thought about the nature of all things.

The first criticism (1.1.12) suggests that other philosophers are foolish to proceed to the study of the transhuman nature of the whole (or, to use the term Xenophon suggests that Socrates employs in referring to the dimension of *nature* beyond the human, "the divinely uncanny things" (*daimonia*) *before* "knowing adequately the human things." And by "the human things," Xenophon soon explains, are meant the matters addressed dialogically by way of Socrates's "What is . . ." questions: first and foremost, "What is piety and impiety?"—followed closely by the questions, "What is the noble and the base?" "What is the just and the unjust?" and What are the moral and political virtues or excellences? (1.1.16). Socrates, we may conclude, held that it is only by reaching, through dialogues, agreed-on *answers* to these "human" questions that access is gained to a related, dispositive knowledge that gives the best available answer to the most fundamental and important question of cosmology, of metaphysics, and of existence: the question, *Quid sit deus?* For the most powerful empirical evidence of providential divinity, the evidence most in need of critical testing and purification, is found not in transhuman nature but in the purported revelations from divinity, and kindred religious experiences, attested by numerous human beings (including some, like Socrates himself, who seem to be among the wisest and most honest).

Socrates's second criticism of his predecessors (1.1.14) indicates the deep doubt at which Socrates arrived, as to the availability to the human mind of adequate evidence giving access to the causal roots or sources or grounds of the natural order that we experience. The "folly" of other philosophers in claiming to have achieved such access is manifested in the crazily extreme opposition of their theoretical contentions: some of them "opine that being is one only—and others, that there is a limitless plurality"; some opine "that always all things are in motion (changing)—and others, that nothing ever moves (changes)"; some opine that "all things come into being and pass away—others, that nothing ever comes into being or passes away." Xenophon has Socrates prefacing this synopsis of his predecessors' opposed ontological extremes with an analogy of the opposed follies of certain common madmen. Some of them "fear nothing of the things that are terrible, while others fear things that are not frightening." Some of them "opine that it is not shameful to say or to do anything in public, while others opine that one ought not to go out among humans." Some of them "honor neither temple nor altar nor any of the divine things (*theia*), while others show pious reverence to stones and chance pieces of wood and wild beasts." These opposite forms of nonphilosophic folly point to and surround a sane middle outlook. Xenophon prompts us to deduce an analogous sober middle outlook as regards the philosophic understandings of the nature of all things. This sober Socratic middle ground can be defined as follows, in contrast to the opposed extremes (see XS ad loc.): intelligible being is to be understood as plural, but finite in number (the kinds, or species, of beings); some beings move or change, and this includes coming into being and passing away, while some beings are immovable or unchanging, and some even eternally so. In other words, Socrates's manner of studying and conceiving the intelligible nature of all things was not to proceed by asking "by what necessities each of the things in the heavens comes into being"; instead, Socrates's manner was to study the natures of the beings in their present actuality, as they are directly experienced by and through us. The beings, including most importantly ourselves, come to sight as mutable and mortal individuals whose existence is structured by evidently unchanging, and some even eternal, species or forms, including the logical and the mathematical forms.[32]

Socrates's study, in this distinctive manner, of the nature of the beings, thus articulated, does not seem to be among the "human things" about which Xenophon says Socrates asked his characteristic, dialogic, "What is . . ." questions. Even the question, "What is a human being?" (or "What is human nature?") Xenophon does not include among "the human things." On close inspection, we see that the "human things" are not beings. They are, rather, moral and political qualities or relationships (including the association that is the polis) that belong to or characterize human beings and their life. But we must not overlook the pregnant if obscure addition Xenophon makes: he says that Socrates carried on dialogues not only about the "human things" but also about "other things"—that is, things beyond the human (beyond the moral and political). To be sure, Xenophon rarely portrays Socrates engaging in dialogues about such matters (about the beings, or about nature). But Xenophon "rarely presents Socrates engaged" even "in raising 'what is' questions regarding the human things: at most 3 chapters out of the 49 chapters of the *Memorabilia* present Socrates engaged in this pursuit."[33] Xenophon fosters his readers' education by challenging us to think out by ourselves the Socratic dialogues about the "What is . . ." questions that are embedded in or pointed to by the sorts of Socratic conversations that Xenophon actually does depict. Xenophon challenges us still further to think out by ourselves (as we have started to do in the preceding) the Socratic dialogues about the nature of the beings, dialogues embedded in or pointed to by the Socratic dialogues about the "What is . . ." questions.

The massive, primary reason why Xenophon and his Socrates are so unforthcoming about the Socratic ontology and study of nature is indicated in the analogy that Xenophon presents of unphilosophic sorts of insanity. Xenophon circumscribes a sane middle ground that consists in caution—as regards especially one's public actions and utterances, and most particularly as regards expression of pious reverence for temples, altars, and all the rest of "the divine things." This moderate middle position expresses a specific understanding of the permanently powerful religiosity of human civil society—of humanity's social nature—which every prudently responsible thinker must always bear in mind (see Melzer 2014). The "pre-Socratics," Xenophon seems to indicate, were somewhat deficient in this prudent responsibility, and thus in the understanding of human nature. No wonder none of their works survive, while every single writing of Xenophon (and of Plato) has come down to us.

This implicit suggestion of the political immoderation of the pre-Socratic philosophers of nature takes on a dramatically enlarged dimension when we proceed to Socrates's third criticism (1.1.15). For Xenophon reports Socrates expressing a wonder whether what is partly animating (and distorting?) his predecessors' study of nature may not be a "hope" for a radical enhancement in their *power*, as scientists, over nature—and consequently over or within civil society. Socrates "inquired about them in addition" whether, "even as those who learn the human things" consider that they will thereby be able to "do what they wish for themselves or another,"[34] so the philosophers of nature "believe that by inquiring into the divine things, once they know by what necessities each of the things comes into being, they will make, when they wish, winds and rains and airs and whatever else of such things they need"; "or do they hope for no such thing, and does it suffice for them only to know?" By characterizing the objects of meteorological science as "divine things" (*theia*) Socrates underlines the hubris involved in such study aimed at mastery over nature. But he seems also to point to the danger that this "hope" for mastery over nature may becloud the clear-eyed philosophic desire simply and truly to understand. The "Baconian" turn that so defines modern, technological science seems to be a possibility that Xenophon's Socrates descried—as dubious.[35]

## HIS BELIEF PROVEN BY HIS FIDELITY
## TO HIS SACRED OATH

Introducing his final rebuttal argument and evidence concerning Socrates's religious beliefs, our advocate concedes that much of what his client really thought about divinity was not manifest (1.1.17). The full thrust of this concession becomes apparent when one reflects on what Xenophon soon says was Socrates's expressed teaching concerning the gods' knowledge of "the things deliberated about in silence," in addition to the things declared and done (1.1.19). We are reminded that it is only the silent and private inner thoughts that determine what a person truly believes—possibly in sharp contrast to the beliefs to which he thinks it prudent to give expression, in speech and deed. Xenophon points to the fact that, contrary to what he suggested shortly before, Socrates's spiritual life is far from being an open book.[36]

Yet our apologist makes this momentous concession while adducing something "everybody knows," which he claims renders astounding the imputation of impiety. On the fraught day of the illegal trial of the admirals from the battle of Arginusae, Socrates, as presiding chair of the Assembly, defied, at great risk to himself, the angry populace and its threatening leaders, by insisting on following the lawful process—which he had sworn a sacred oath to uphold. This clinches Socrates's pious belief, Xenophon submits, because it shows him to have been motivated by fidelity to the oath that he had sworn to the gods, "since he believed that the gods exercise providential care through knowing everything" (1.1.18–19; see also 4.4.2).

But this is an *interpretation* of what motivated Socrates to take his stand on that fateful day; and it is an interpretation that is by no means the only possible or even the most likely or most noble—as becomes clear from the account of the very same event later in the *Memorabilia* (4.4.2), as well as in Xenophon's *Hellenica*. In the last we find our wily author, speaking as a historian, telling quite a different story. Socrates is not depicted as the presiding chair, but only as a dissenting member of the presiding committee.[37] And the *Hellenica* version includes a report of Socrates's own express declaration of what motivated him to dissent: "that he would not do anything except in accordance with the law"—without any reference to the sacred oath.[38] We see that Socrates's motive could have been predominantly or even entirely his justice, as obedient respect for law, rather than his pious oath and concern for divine, providential punishment.

We may also observe that the *Hellenica's* account shows that the popular passion that chiefly allowed the demagogues to goad the populace into carrying out the illegal trial and execution of the generals was fanatic piety: in other words, the *Hellenica* presents Socrates's heroic action as an insistence on lawful justice *against* and in the face of (fanatic) civic piety.

## CONCLUDING THE DEFENSE AGAINST THE CHARGE OF IMPIETY OR DISBELIEF

Xenophon concludes by reformulating his ironic opening expression of amazement. Now what Xenophon says he finds astonishing is the Athenians' being persuaded that Socrates was not "of *moderate* mind (*sōphronein*) concerning gods"—given the scrupulous attention to piety that he exhibited publicly, or in everything that he said or did. Immediately previous to this, Xenophon has disclosed a major facet of Socrates's inner religious belief that Xenophon does not say Socrates himself ever declared—namely, that "he believed that the gods exercise providential care for humans not in the way in which the many believe."[39] Socrates himself was apparently too much of "moderate mind concerning gods" to broadcast this profound disagreement with his fellow citizens' conception of divine providence.

## CHAPTER TWO

# Socrates Was Not Guilty
# of Corrupting the Young

In the case of the charge of impiety, Xenophon opened his exoneration by proceeding, with a straight face, on the assumption that the prosecutors aimed to charge Socrates with not being a "regular churchgoer," or worshipper in the conventional fashion; Xenophon was then able to dismiss the indictment as preposterous, given the well known fact of Socrates's regular, public, participation in conventional worship. Xenophon thus initially aroused sympathy for Socrates among ingenuous readers, while provoking thoughtfully bemused readers to a wryly suspicious attentiveness. In a similar vein, Xenophon launches his exculpation as regards the indictment's second charge—"and he is unjust through corrupting the young"[1]—by proceeding, with a straight face, on the assumption that the arraignment aimed to charge Socrates as being, and as encouraging the young to be, lascivious, gluttonous, bibulous, flabby and soft, or a luxurious spendthrift who flaunts fancy, delicate clothes and footwear. Xenophon is then able to protest the preposterousness of such an imputation, given the barefoot, threadbare Socrates's well-known "great skill in endurance"[2] and austerity in all carnal and monetary matters (see also 1.6.2–3). "How then," our advocate expostulates, "could such a man corrupt the young?!—Unless, of course, the caring for virtue is corruption!" (1.2.8).

These last words contain a subtly comic-paradoxical formulation of the seriously intended meaning of the indictment. This becomes more evident if we recall what Xenophon spotlighted earlier but now keeps offstage. Socrates's peculiar, and unprecedented, "caring for virtue" consists in a ceaseless questioning of what is piety and impiety, noble and base, just and unjust—accompanied by an insistence that only those who can give knowledgeable answers to these Socratic questions are gentlemen (noble and good), while those who cannot do so are justly to be called slavish (1.1.16.). This relentlessly

skeptical and judgmental questioning may well strike serious citizens as cor-
rosive of traditional, habitual, unquestioning, civic virtue, with its inbred respect for conventionally taciturn gentlemen, whose chief care is not for themselves, but for others and for their city, and who exercise their virtue not in
skeptical dialogues questioning what virtue is, but in virtuous civic actions,
orations, and deliberations.[3]

Socrates, Xenophon here says, "made many *desire* virtue," and instilled
in them "hopes, that if they cared for themselves, they *would* be gentleman."
So what Socrates convinced many of, was that they were *not yet* gentlemen,
and *lacked*, desired, virtue. "Virtue," and "gentlemen," *in what sense*? The true
meaning of Socrates's self-mastery as regards carnal and monetary matters
depends on Socrates's understanding of the *reasons for* such self-mastery;
and Xenophon allows us to see that Socrates did *not* regard his self-mastery
(*enkrateia*) as being a virtue in the sense of a noble end in itself.[4] Instead,
Socrates declared his approval of self-mastery as a "habitual disposition" on
the grounds that "this was sufficient for health, and did not *impede* the care
for the soul." The question then becomes, How did Socrates understand the
care for the soul? What were the spiritual ends for the sake of which Socrates
practiced severe restraint as regards money and the body?

Xenophon obliquely trenches on a gravely serious intended meaning of
the indictment when he gives, as a leading instance of Socrates's "not making his companions erotic lovers of money," the fact that Socrates not only
refrained from charging any fee for his companionship, but decried those who
do so, as enslavers of *themselves*, because they thereby become compelled to
converse with those who pay them. Xenophon makes visible his keen awareness of his need to rebut the opinion that Socrates belonged among the sophists, or that he taught the young, for his own profit, a dubiously sophistic
meaning of virtue and of gentlemanliness. Xenophon reports that Socrates
was amazed that someone professing to teach virtue would charge a fee; for
Socrates conceived that the truly greatest profit, for anyone professing to
teach virtue, was the acquisition of a good and very grateful friend in the student. Before this last can ring an alarm bell, Xenophon rushes in with a fire
extinguisher: but Socrates "never professed (to teach) any such thing to anyone." Or, as Xenophon has put it shortly before, "Socrates never promised to
be a teacher" of gentlemanliness—except "by manifestly being such."[5] But
Xenophon adds: Socrates "trusted that those of his companions who were
receptive to the things that he judged favorably would be good friends with
him and with one another for the whole of life." So Socrates was indeed a
teacher, in some sense, of (a nontraditional) virtue—that was learned not so
much by way of "teachings" as by example.[6] Through this innovative educa-

tional process, Socrates carefully cultivated a lasting circle of chosen, grateful friends. Serious citizens might well ask, "What is the relation of this circle to the wide friendship among the citizenry that is essential to, and prized above all by, the city?"[7]

The life together of the Socratic friends is a key dimension, and a profoundly distinctive dimension, of what Socrates meant, and practiced, and inspired in others, as "virtue." His refraining from charging money was part of what enabled him to be highly selective in forming his community of lifelong friends.

## ANSWERING A NAMELESS ACCUSER'S CHARGE THAT SOCRATES PROMOTED CONTEMPT FOR THE ATHENIAN REGIME AND LAWS

At this point (1.2.8), Xenophon has completed his direct rebuttal of the official indictment's charge that Socrates corrupted the young.[8] Yet Xenophon has said nothing about Socrates's posture toward youthful political ambition, and self-mastery over that dangerous passion. Now, suddenly (1.2.9), Xenophon ventriloquizes a cursing accuser, whose bellicose eruption sounds like an exasperated reaction to this massive inadequacy of Xenophon's rebuttal of the corruption charge thus far.[9] "The accuser" (whose words and tone remind of Aristophanes's *Clouds*[10]) yells out, "But by Zeus!"[11] Socrates "made his companions look down on the established laws!"—and did so, by deriding the foolishness of the egalitarian-democratic mode of selecting rulers according to lot, instead of on grounds of proven expertise and competence.[12] Through such speeches, the accuser charges, Socrates "aroused the young to have contempt for the established regime!"—*and* "made them violent!"

Xenophon responds only to the latter denunciation, of promoting violence. He archly (and provocatively) acts as if he has failed to hear the first and most substantial part of the shouted accusation that he has put into the mouth of his character.[13]

Moreover, the argument Xenophon gives for the implausibility of Socrates promoting violence is based on the much greater political efficacy, safety, and self-sufficiency of a prudent employment of persuasive rhetoric: "For who would wish to kill someone rather than make use of him alive, persuaded?" and "The one capable of persuading needs no one—for he would hold himself capable, even alone, of persuading" (1.2.11). Xenophon presents this argument in his own name; but he tacitly reminds readers of the widespread imputation, made vivid in Aristophanes's *Clouds*, that Socrates employed and taught effective, manipulative rhetoric, "making the weaker argument the stronger."[14]

If we look more closely at what Xenophon is saying, we notice that he in fact attributes nothing to Socrates here. Instead, speaking repeatedly for himself, in the first person singular, Xenophon refers to unnamed persons who "cultivate prudence and believe that they will be capable of teaching the citizens what is advantageous." Xenophon's use of the first person singular will continue to be a feature of his defense of Socrates against the charge of corrupting the young. Xenophon thus quietly reminds his readers that he is himself a preeminent exemplar of Socratic education (or "corruption") and that there is much to be discovered about the nature of Socrates's didactic influence by reflective attention to Xenophon's unobtrusive self-revelations.

## STARTING TO EXPLAIN HIS ASSOCIATION WITH CRITIAS AND ALCIBIADES

Xenophon contrives to have the nameless accuser focus his rejoinder on the corruption exhibited by two notorious youthful intimates of Socrates: Critias, whom the nameless accuser characterizes as "the most thieving, murderous, and violent of all those in the oligarchy," and Alcibiades, "the most unrestrained and hubristic as well as violent of all those in the democracy" (1.2.12). That these Socratic associations are very much in need of an explanation—and that the explanation is not easy—is indicated by the length of Xenophon's response. Yet we see that Xenophon would not have had to enter into these troubled and troubling waters if he had confined himself to rebutting the official indictment, instead of conjuring up a nameless, impassioned accuser.[15] Xenophon evidently wants to make us puzzle over the question, How and why—for what important purposes—did Socrates attract, and befriend, and spend time and energy upon, young men of such extreme and questionable political ambition?[16] Association with these young men was (predictably) costly: it obviously involved Socrates and his other friends in grave political dangers; it has never ceased to tarnish the Socratic legacy.[17] And neither Critias nor Alcibiades sounds like a very promising candidate to join Socrates in his philosophic way of life, with its minimal, defensive engagement in political action. Why did Socrates not focus his educative efforts on youths resembling himself when he was young, like the "young Socrates" whom we meet in Plato's *Statesman*—youths who were ambitious scientifically and philosophically? Why did Socrates expend his educational efforts on youths who were "by nature the most ambitious for honor, wishing that all things be done through them, and that they might become the most renowned of all" (1.2.14)? We have learned from following Xenophon's stress on Socrates's talk of his *daimonion* that the philosopher sought, at some risk, to attract youths who were skeptically perplexed as regards traditional religion, without being simply unbelievers. Now, Xenophon shows us that the young men whom Socrates sought out were also such as he could "exhort to desire the noblest and most magnificent virtue, by which cities and households are well managed" (1.2.64). Why did Socrates put before himself the challenge of converting, to his transpolitical outlook on life, young men (like Xenophon) of such an unusual "theologico-political" spirituality? Was it not because Socrates understood that there was something of the utmost philosophic, even cosmic or theologico-political, importance that he could learn best through observing the sometimes successful, sometimes unsuccessful outcomes of attempts at such unlikely conversions?

However this may be, Xenophon's exculpatory response explicitly focuses not on the motives of Socrates, but on the motives of the young pair of miscreants (1.2.13–16). They were attracted to the master not only by their knowledge of his economic self-sufficiency, and his self-control over pleasures, but by their knowledge of a momentous fact that Xenophon only now allows to come to the fore: speaking with perhaps some slight overstatement, Xenophon declares that Socrates "in speeches dealt as he wished with all who conversed with him (*tois de dialegomenois autōi pasi*)" (1.2.14). It was this extraordinary dialogical power of Socrates that made the pair believe that "if they associated with him, they would become most competent to speak and to act."[18] Xenophon insists that they were so far from being drawn to adopting Socrates's way of life, with its moderation, that if a god had given them the choice, they would have chosen to die rather than to live their whole lives as they saw Socrates living! This is made clear, Xenophon avers, by the fact that as soon as in and by their association with Socrates they "considered that they were superior to their companions, they immediately left Socrates, to do the political things—which is why they had reached out to Socrates."

Xenophon here implicitly concedes that Socrates did teach, and very effectively, the political things.[19] This becomes more explicit when Xenophon goes on to reply to another possible criticism (which he no longer ascribes to any accuser—one does not have to be an accuser of Socrates to voice this animadversion): "Socrates ought not to have taught companions the political things before moderation." Xenophon says that he does not contest this (cf. 4.3.1). But he insists (with first person emphasis) that Socrates, like other teachers (see also 1.2.27) presented himself to his students as a model, in action, of what he was teaching—namely, "gentlemanliness" and "conversing most nobly about virtue and the other human things." Indeed, Socrates made himself exemplary with such success that "I know," Xenophon asseverates, that even and precisely Alcibiades and Critias did in fact become "moderate" when they were associates of Socrates; and this because they became convinced "at that time that this was the superior way to act" (1.2.17–18). Or as Xenophon puts it a bit later, Socrates brought about moderation in the pair, just as successful teachers of music or of other arts bring about in their students skill in practice (1.2.26–27). This disclosure stands in stark tension with or contradiction to Xenophon's immediately previous claim, that the two would have chosen to die rather than to live as Socrates lived—and it stands equally in tension with or contradiction to the claim Xenophon will subsequently make, that the pair could have gained no education from Socrates because he never was pleasing to them.[20] Here, on the contrary, Xenophon reveals that the two came to believe that Socrates lived a superior way of life—the example of which impressed them so much, that it induced a major change in their own outlook and even to a considerable extent in their active lives. In other words, Socrates succeeded in effecting in the young men a dramatic, if incomplete and temporary, spiritual conversion. And it becomes clearer that Xenophon is using his explanations of Socrates's relation with Critias and Alcibiades to arouse the reader's puzzled reflection on controversial facets of Socrates's educative activity in general.[21]

If we put what Xenophon has said so far together with what we will find him saying much later, at 4.3.1–2, we may draw the following conclusions. By the example of his way of life and not least his ceaseless, provocative questioning about the "human things," including the "political things," Socrates induced in his young companions political "moderation." He did this as the first stage in his guiding them toward a deep understanding of the human things, an understanding that eventually included knowing how "skillfully to speak and to act and to contrive." "Moderation" (sōphrosunē) means, then, much more than self-mastery (engkrateia) over the bodily and economic passions. Moderation as the opposite of hubris (XS 12) entails a spiritual conversion that curtails or diminishes political ambition (the ambition to rule), on account of coming to emulate the philosophic life, as led by Socrates and his friends—who continue, as good citizens defending philosophy, to engage in "moderate" or unhubristic public speech and action, especially about divinity.[22]

## IN WHAT SENSE VIRTUE IS KNOWLEDGE

At this point Xenophon digresses somewhat, in order to respond to an imagined phalanx of "many" critics among "those claiming to philosophize," who challenge the very possibility that the spiritual influence of Socrates could have *temporarily* induced Critias and Alcibiades to become actually or in fact moderate (*sōphrōn*) or virtuous. The challengers invoke a general philosophic-psychological proposition: someone who has become just cannot become unjust, nor can someone who has become moderate become hubristic, even as someone who has learned anything learnable cannot ever cease to be a knower of it (1.2.19). The criticism sounds like a half-baked or commonly misconceived version of the famous Socratic thesis that virtue is (a kind of) knowledge.[23] Xenophon exploits the occasion to correct this common misunderstanding of the Socratic thesis.

Xenophon begins the rectification by focusing on the parallel that obtains between the capacity for physical accomplishments and the capacity for spiritual accomplishments. Both require for their acquisition and maintenance habitual practice that includes associating with others who are exemplars—as is attested by poets, whom Xenophon adduces as possessing a psychological wisdom that is lacking in "the many claiming to philosophize."[24] In his characteristic fashion, Xenophon leads off sounding as if he is treating morals on a rather low level, insofar as they are chiefly a matter of self-mastery (*engkrateia*) involving habituation of the bodily appetites. But the context is of course the explanation of the acquisition and then loss, in Alcibiades and Critias, of Socratic-induced *moderation* (*sōphrosunē*), that for a time supplanted its opposite, including above all the spiritual hubris of overweening ambition to rule and to win civic honor. Besides, the poetry whose testimony Xenophon adduces warns that bad companionship can "destroy also the intellect (*nous*) within." And when Xenophon proceeds to offer his own testimony (based on personal experience?), he reports his observation that even as poetry, though once known, can be forgotten if it is not regularly recalled, so a "forgetting of the instructional reasoning in speeches"—"the admonitory reasoning in speeches"—occurs to those who "neglect," or fail to keep repeating and mulling over in their minds, such reasoning. When this forgetting occurs, then "the soul has forgotten those things that it experiences [the things that the soul undergoes] when it desires moderation"—and with the loss of those spiritual experiences or passions, "it is no wonder that moderation is also forgotten." Xenophon adduces two leading examples of what causes such "forgetting": fondness for intoxicating drink, and erotic love—the latter of which he stresses. Again, Xenophon puts in the foreground virtue insofar as it is self-restraint of bodily appetites. But then Xenophon extends this teaching to the *entirety* of nobility and goodness (gentlemanliness): "To me at least it seems therefore (*men oun*) that *all* the noble-and-good (gentlemanly) things are matters of practice. For in the same body there grow together with the soul the pleasures persuading it not to be moderate, but instead to gratify them, and also to gratify the body, as quickly as possible." Both the soul, and the pleasures that persuade the soul not to be moderate, "grow in" the body—but are not, then, *simply* bodily or "physical."

We may summarize Xenophon's Socratic teaching here as follows.[25] Moderation, as the opposite of hubris—moderation as a key ingredient of virtue in its entire range—lives or dies depending on success or failure in the constant revitalization of Socratic reasoning that entails fervent psychic experiences essential to the continuing strength of the desire for moderation. All this is threatened by the experience of the various pleasures of erotic intoxication, which expresses powerfully persuasive, quasi-rational opinions of its own—and is by no means *simply* "physical" (see also 1.3.6). But the "success" of which we are speaking varies, in degree, as is illustrated in and by the cases of Critias and Alcibiades. So long as, and to the extent that, their souls held perspicuously in view certain Socratic reasonings, which they were hearing from and in the company of Socrates, the two youths were initiated by Socrates into a life of moderation. But just as "knowledge" of wise poetry can range from mere rote memorization to an ever fuller and more deeply taken-to-heart understanding of the poet's teaching—and this "knowledge" can become arrested at various intermediate points along this range—so something similar is true of the acquisition of knowledge of Socratic reasoning (consider Plato, *Theages* 130). Critias and Alcibiades never *fully* understood—and, to the extent that they did understand, the disposition of their passions prevented them from holding firmly in view and taking fully to heart—the decisive Socratic-refutational (1.2.47, 1.4.1) reasoning that entails disenchantment with hubristic political ambition.[26] Even during the time when they admired as superior the Socratic life with its moderation, their souls continued to experience the strong lure of their pre-Socratic enchantment. They lived, we may surmise, in a kind of blurred psychological mixture: of emulation of Socrates, and of his questioning analysis of the political things, together with a political ambition that was dampened but lingering, still hopeful; as Xenophon now says: "So long as they kept company with Socrates, they were able, *by using him as an ally*, to *restrain* the ignoble desires" (1.2.24).

This leaves us eager to learn, with the help of all that will follow, what specifically constitutes the elenchic reasoning in speeches that is the key to conversion to Socratic virtue, and what exactly are the powerful passions that the soul undergoes insofar as it grasps, and continuously revitalizes, this reasoning.

## THE BIG DIFFERENCES BETWEEN CRITIAS AND ALCIBIADES

As Xenophon turns back, in light of the preceding, to tell the story of how the two black sheep were drawn away from Socrates, and as a consequence from the virtue that they had acquired in his company, a significant change emerges. Previously, Xenophon treated the duo almost as twins;[27] now, a divergence opens up, and expands.

### CRITIAS

Xenophon reports in a half sentence that Critias became detached from Socrates and his influence by being sent into exile, among lawless people who corrupted him (1.2.24). Xenophon remains primly silent here on what was the alleged crime on account of which exile was imposed on Critias—while, be it noted, Critias was still associating with Socrates. Writing as a historian in his *Hellenica* (2.3.15), Xenophon informs us that it was the *dēmos* or democratic element that imposed exile on Critias—and that this was a cause of Critias's later killing "many" honored by the populace, when he subsequently became a leader among the Thirty oligarchic tyrants. We also find that the banishment of Critias evidently occurred when he was a mature man in his fifties[28]—contrary to the impression Xenophon gives here in the *Memorabilia* (cf. BD ad 1.2.47). But before the reader can puzzle over the very brief account given here of Critias's separation from Socrates, Xenophon rushes on to a more elaborate and arrestingly vivid recounting of what detached the young Alcibiades—after which Xenophon returns for a while to treating the two as nigh twins (1.2.25–28).

Eventually, however, Xenophon focuses our attention on a dramatic narration of the incident that brought Critias to "hate" Socrates (1.2.29–31). It is not entirely clear how this elaborate story is consistent with our elusive author's short, first explanation of Critias's apostasy. Apparently some time after returning from his period of exile,[29] Critias was still in the company of, and being admonished by, Socrates—who exhorted Critias to master his physical lust for his beloved boy Euthydemus. When Critias ignored the admonition, Socrates "is said" to have pronounced before "many" a harshly humiliating censure of Critias (not for anything political, but) for his failure to heed Socrates's previous, gentlemanly exhortation regarding Critias's private lust. Socrates is said to have brutally characterized Critias as a pig-like lover, and to have done so (worst of all!) in the presence of Critias's beloved Euthydemus. This was a Socratic intervention that was obviously calculated to infuriate Critias. (Since, as we later learn at length in book 4, Socrates was himself intent on educating the beautiful young Euthydemus, we may surmise that it was chiefly out of concern for the latter, more than with a view to trying to improve the mature, and probably pretty hopeless, Critias, that Socrates behaved in such an aggravating fashion.)

Xenophon proceeds (1.2.31–38) to tell us that it was this private insult (and not anything political—Dresig 1738, 106–7) that led to the targeting of Socrates by Critias when the latter became a legislator during the reign of the Thirty. Critias couldn't get at Socrates in any other way (Socrates was not easy prey for the Thirty, even though—we learn from Xenophon's *Hellenica*—they were rounding up, putting on trial, and executing numerous partisans of democracy), and so Critias went after Socrates by outlawing "teaching the art of speaking." Critias's aiming in *this* way at Socrates, Xenophon expostulates, was a "calumny," since "I at least never heard this from Socrates, nor perceived another claiming to have heard it!"[30] Yet that this law was indeed aimed at Socrates became manifest when word of Socrates's private, ironic criticism of the destructiveness of the Thirty's rule reached the ears of the ringleaders Critias and Charicles. For they thereupon summoned Socrates and impressed upon him, in a threatening way, the relevance of this law to him, to his conversational engagement with the young. But they thus left themselves open to becoming trammeled in the sly master's deliciously impish and insolent dialogic questioning—which confounded them and their law. (In this, the very first Socratic dialogue[31] that he depicts, Xenophon contrives to bring Socrates's roguish sophistic skill to vibrant life in the most respectable sort of context—challenging oppressive rulers and their laws.) When we inspect this first Socratic dialogue, we receive the distinct impression that Charicles as well as Critias knew Socrates rather well, and, while angered by him, was not altogether surprised, nor totally outraged, by his insolence—and was disinclined to hurt him. To be sure, Xenophon leaves no doubt as to Socrates's (muted, indirect, and ironic)[32] criticism of the rule of the Thirty. At the same time, Xenophon lets us see that despite Socrates's power with words, he lacked the politically essential *coercive* power to check or to weaken the Thirty—or even to criticize them to their faces.[33] Xenophon makes it evident that if the Thirty had been more brutally tyrannical, and less concerned with the appearance of lawfulness, Socrates would not even have gotten away with embarrassing them in conversation.

## ALCIBIADES

Xenophon "gives no example of Socrates rebuking Alkibiades, to say nothing of a conflict between Socrates and Alkibiades."[34] What corrupted Alcibiades, Xenophon tells us, was the latter's rapid political success on democratic terms: the self-forgetting or self-alienating allure of his popularity, combined with flattery by individual men (and women) powerful in the democracy. Xenophon compares Alcibiades to an athlete for whom victory in competition comes easily, and who as a consequence slips into believing that he need not care for self-discipline—and, thereby, for himself. By implication, it was Socrates's attempt to teach Alcibiades virtue, and the political things, and thus to lead him toward the greater contest and victory that consisted in cultivation of his own excellence—above and beyond a career serving the Athenian populace—that would have saved the young man from this democratic depravation.[35]

Xenophon gives us our deepest insight into Socrates's relations with Alcibiades only indirectly.[36] In concluding his account of Critias's fraught association with Socrates (1.2.38–39), Xenophon insists again that neither Alcibiades nor Critias associated with Socrates because he was pleasing to them, but rather because, from the outset, they sought preeminence in the city. Yet then Xenophon suddenly reveals that during the time when they were companions of Socrates, they imitated the master by engaging in his distinctive kind of refutative dialogues (although, Xenophon insists, not with other sorts of interlocutors more than with those deeply engaged in politics; but is this so very different from Socrates?). Xenophon illustrates by depicting the still-teenage Alcibiades carrying out, with great skill and success, an elenchic Socratic dialogue[37] with no less an interlocutor than Pericles (his legal guardian as well as the acclaimed leader of Athens), on a most fundamental and momentous "What is . . ." question: "What is *law*?" Xenophon shows us Alcibiades making manifest, step by step, to Pericles himself, that and how the great statesman has a profoundly confused conception of law and thus of what he regards as virtue. Since we find in the *Memorabilia* no other explicit presentations of a thorough Socratic dialogic refutation effected through pursuing "What is . . ." questions (BD 1: CXVIII), we do well to follow attentively this singular and highly competent[38] example.

Xenophon says that the dialogue was *reported* to him as having been begun by Alcibiades asking Pericles, "Would you be able to teach me what is law?" The refutation apparently took place before very few witnesses. Alcibiades acted with greater discretion than did the Platonic Socrates in his Delphic mission (Plato, *Apology* 21c-d).

When Pericles unreservedly answered his first question in the affirmative, Alcibiades asked to be given the teaching as to what law is—expressing his keenness with an oath that invoked the gods in general. (In addition to suggesting Alcibiades's mood of irreverence, not to say impiety, Xenophon, and perhaps his Alcibiades, may by the oath signal that, to grasp the full import of what follows, we would need to consider the implications for our understanding of divine rule and divine law.) Alcibiades then explained to his august interlocutor the reason for his eagerness. He had heard some "praised" for being "lawful men," and he supposed that one would not "justly" happen upon such praise if one did not know what is law. Alcibiades spoke as one concerned to know what law is because he is concerned with the public honor that justly attends a man of lawful virtue, on the understanding that such virtue depends on one's knowing what is the lawful, as the standard and the substance of virtue.

Pericles unhesitatingly accepted this outlook and starting point, this premise or basis for the discussion. What is more, Pericles manifested supreme confidence that he knew, and could teach his young ward, what is law—thereby conveying to his ward knowledge that is essential to possession of the high virtue of lawfulness. Pericles declared (with consummate complacency) that what Alcibiades "desired" was "an affair of no difficulty," as regards the "wish to know what is law." Whatever his shrewdness as a politician, mastering rivals who were not educated by Socrates, the great Pericles did not have an inkling of what would be proven by his young ward in the next few minutes: that Pericles cannot give a coherent explanation of what law is, and therefore, by the moral principle that he explicitly accepted, is not justly honored as a man of lawful virtue. In sharp contrast to the Socratically educated Alcibiades, Pericles is a babe in the woods as regards the perplexities involved in law as a concept—and is also naively ignorant as regards the psychological disposition, as well as the dialectical power, of his young Socratic questioner (and potential political rival). And this despite the fact, disclosed by Pericles near the end, that he recalls being in his youth one of those who (he claims) were "terrific" at practicing such dialectics (which he now regards as sophistry).

Pericles, the great democratic statesman, defined law as all things that the assembled multitude has decided on and promulgates, as to what ought and ought not to be done. Alcibiades responded with a boyishly simple-minded question: Is it *good* things that they lawfully hold ought to be done, or *bad*? Pericles emphatically, and patronizingly, answered: "The good—by Zeus!—my boy, and not the bad." Now, this obvious answer raises two other more acute questions: The good *for whom*? And: what becomes of the multitude's law and lawfulness when the multitude, out of unwisdom, legislates something bad? Alcibiades did not proceed to enter into an elaboration of these complex, profoundly troubling, typically Socratic questions about the coherence of democratic law (consider in this light the Socratic sequels to this dialogue, 1.2.49–51, 53–55). Instead, having confirmed what he presumably expected Pericles would answer, naively and thoughtlessly, when the great man was asked about the relation between the democratically lawful and the good, Alcibiades took a shorter route to his goal—of exposing, to Pericles himself, the great leader's incoherent ignorance.

Alcibiades asked a question that immediately awakened Pericles to the inadequacy of his previously stated definition of law. The question compelled Pericles to see that the definition he had given fits only law in democratic regimes governed by assemblies where the majority always predominates; Pericles knew that there are other types of regimes in which not the assembled majority, but some minority, predominates and legislates. So a somewhat uneasy Pericles declared, with a slight note of hesitation, that what "is called" law is rather all the things that the dominant power in a city, having deliberated (scil. about the good), promulgates as to what ought to be done.

But then Pericles had to agree that it necessarily follows, from this drastically revised definition, that whatever things a ruling tyrant promulgates as to what ought to be done are also to be called laws. And then Pericles also had to agree that force, without law, is expressed when the stronger, through violence or its threat, coerces the weaker, without persuading or getting consent, to behave in a way that accords with the opinion of the stronger (scil. about what is good). Pericles further had to agree that such promulgations, characteristic of a tyrant, are lawlessness. His contradiction and confusion now stared him in the face: what he had said are to be called laws can constitute the antithesis of what he holds to be law. Pericles attempted to escape his self-contradiction by changing what he had said was the meaning of tyrannical law: he added the crucial qualification that any command promulgated by a tyrant *without persuading* those to whom it is promulgated, or getting their consent, is *not* law.

In response to this, Alcibiades asked Pericles about how "we are to speak" about the promulgations of a regime where the few, a minority, rule without persuading or gaining the consent of the many: Are we to say, or to deny, that this is violent, that is, lawless? In response, Pericles made more explicit his changed articulation of the meaning of law in general, conceived now in contrast to violence or lawlessness: "All things, whether promulgated or not, that someone compels another to do without persuading, constitute violence rather than law." At this point Alcibiades asked a question that compelled Pericles to contemplate how this conception of law must be applied to democracy: "So then, whatever the entire multitude promulgates for the few rich without persuading them and gaining their consent would be violence rather than law?"

In order for Pericles to overcome what had now transpired to be his incoherence as regards the meaning of law (and the meaning of lawfulness, as a virtue), he had to abandon one or the other (or both) of two contradictory conceptions of law that he had shown himself to hold: (1) that whatever the majority in a democracy promulgates as good, and to be done, is law (and accordingly, to abide by such promulgations is the virtue of lawfulness, while to disobey is the vice of lawlessness); (2) that law must rest on persuasion or consent of all who are to be subject to the law (and, where consent is missing, lawlessness prevails—in which a man of virtuous lawfulness will not join).

Pericles refused even to try to clarify his thinking on this momentous matter, and broke off the conversation with a dismissive quip—to which Alcibiades replied with a deserved, if insolent, put-down. This final word of Alcibiades allows us to descry what he aimed at, and achieved, in this private conversation. He indisputably confirmed for himself what he previously surmised: his own decisive superiority, over the greatest political figure in Greece, as regards coherent understanding of the most important political things—upon whose understanding, virtue and its true honors are agreed to depend.

It is more difficult to determine, from this short exchange, what is Alcibiades's own, Socratic-instructed, conception of law and the virtue of lawfulness. We can glimpse this much.[39] The Socratic Alcibiades sees with penetration that the unexamined respect for law and lawfulness veils the truth that all law has an essential element of coercive violence, made necessary because law is always at bottom the expression of a conception of the good held by a factional regime (of the one, few, or many, or some mixture of these) that is opposed by other factions having antagonistic conceptions of the good. We may add that this insight either arises from, or puts us on the threshold of, the critical Socratic inquiry into the political good—and into the extent to which the competing factions' and regimes' conceptions of the political good approach or veer away from the truest political good.[40] Xeno-phon will give us some adumbration of this inquiry in the pages that im-mediately follow. Alcibiades, for his part, apparently failed to complete this inquiry with Socrates. His failure was less demeaning than the failure he exposed in Pericles, because Alcibiades did not shrug off his own failure. In the very next sentence Xenophon tells us again that Alcibiades and Critias left Socrates and went back to the affairs of the city—but now Xenophon adds, for the first time, that Socrates was not pleasing to them because they "were *pained* by *being refuted* as regards their *errors*" (1.2.47).

Xenophon concludes his account of Socrates's association with Alcibia-des and Critias by contrasting this errant pair with seven others who associ-ated with Socrates not in order to become adroit popular or forensic orators, but so that, by becoming gentlemen, they might nobly use household and household servants and kin and friends, and also city and citizens.[41]

## EXPLAINING THE TEACHING OF SOCRATES
## THAT WISDOM IS THE TITLE TO RULE

But what precisely was it that Socrates taught as "gentlemanly and noble use" of others? This immediately becomes a question because once again Xeno-phon ventriloquizes the nameless accuser, now vociferously responding[42] with a series of incriminations to the following effect. Socrates taught his companions that it is neither fathers nor other relatives nor well-intentioned friends who as such deserve respect and heed, but instead only those who are wisely capable of benefiting—who, as wise, have a lawful right even to chain up the ignorant! What is more, Socrates persuaded the young that *he* was both the wisest and the most capable of making others wise, and thereby disposed his companions to regard others as "nothing" compared to him (1.2.49–52).

Once again Xenophon replies as if he has not heard the worst part (this time it is the last part) of these charges that he has put in the mouth of the nameless accuser. Xenophon concedes, however, that he himself knows that Socrates did indeed say, as regards fathers and other relatives and friends, much if not all of what the accuser reports; and Xenophon adds still more teachings of Socrates along the same lines (most provocatively, about what respect one should have for the bodies of one's closest relatives after their death[43]). Xenophon offers as a defense a fuller articulation of the Socratic teaching about family, and about honor, that is implicit in all this. Socrates demonstrated that lack of prudence is dishonorable, and he urged that one take care to be most prudent and most beneficial so that if one wished to

be honored by relatives, or anyone else, one should not be neglectful, trust-
ing to kinship, but should try to be truly beneficial to those by whom one
wished to be honored (1.2.50–55). This Socratic teaching makes no reference
to filial obedience, or to love, or to the wish to be loved, even or especially
within the family.[44] Xenophon places only a thin veil over Socrates's radical
departure from traditional conceptions of paternal authority and filial obedience and devotion.[45] Xenophon can avoid dealing with questions concerning
Socrates's piety, and influence on the piety of his young companions, as regards parents because he has separated the charge of corrupting the young
from the charge of impiety (even though he has acknowledged in passing
that the two charges overlap—1.2.2; see also 1.3.1).

Xenophon presents the nameless accuser lodging a further, more directly
political charge—but no longer expressed in direct discourse, and thus less
dramatic (1.2.56–61): Socrates "picked out from the most esteemed poets
very wicked passages, on whose authority he taught his companions to become evildoers and tyrannical." In particular, Socrates employed a line in
Hesiod's *Works and Days* (311) praising industry and blaming idleness to
teach that in the pursuit of gain one need not refrain from anything unjust
or shameful; and he "on many occasions" employed lines from Homer's
*Iliad* (2.188–91, 198–202—in which Odysseus is indeed described by Homer
as treating leaders with great respect, and men of the people with contempt)
to teach that it is praiseworthy to beat the populace and the poor.

Xenophon does not deny that Socrates appealed to these poetic passages
as authorities supporting his teachings. But he insists that what Socrates
taught using the Hesiod line was that those who do something good are
thereby industrious, and good workers. Now this certainly sounds innocent—
indeed, to the point of banality. How could anyone find this teaching objec-
tionable, let alone corrupting?[46] We may descry an answer when we notice
that Xenophon does not deal with the question pointed to by the accuser:
What does Socrates teach, invoking Hesiod, about the relation between
"good work" and the "gainful," the "just," and the "noble?" Surely this was
exactly the kind of question that thoughtful students were prompted to ponder by Socrates—and that we are here prompted to ponder by Xenophon and
his contrived nameless incriminator.

Xenophon hastens on, to insist that Socrates used the Homer passage to
teach that those who do not benefit army or city or populace—especially if
they are in addition bold—must be checked in every way, even if they are
very rich. This leaves unexplained, and indeed bewildering, why Socrates
would have chosen so arrestingly "elitist" a Homeric passage to illustrate
and to authorize so conventional a teaching.[47] As Stone alertly points out,

the puzzle at first grows, but then the solution comes into view, when one looks at the Homeric context, and especially the lines that continue the passage, in the original. For one sees that the quotation as presented here "is so carefully truncated by Xenophon that its significance is hidden from" the casual reader—and revealed to the alert.[48] In the lines immediately following those quoted by Xenophon, Homer has Odysseus declare: "It is not good that many rule; there is to be one ruler, one king."[49]

To be sure, Xenophon goes on to contend that Socrates was *dēmotikos*—well disposed toward the democratic populace—and a lover of mankind in general, foreigners as well as fellow Athenians. The proof Xenophon offers is that Socrates refrained from charging a fee for his teaching, and thereby unreservedly helped everybody (contrast *Apology* 26). This is in considerable tension with Xenophon's previous indication of the exclusivist reason why Socrates thought it was imprudent to charge a fee for teaching virtue.[50] However that may be, Xenophon adds that Socrates "adorned the city in the eyes of the rest" (of humanity) by "spending what he had, throughout his entire life, in benefiting, as regards the greatest matters, all those who were willing."

## TRANSITION TO PART 2 OF THE *MEMORABILIA*

This last statement prepares the ground for the second and much longer part of the *Memorabilia*. After concluding his explicit defense against the charges—that is, after showing how Socrates was *not unjust* (1.2.64)—Xenophon turns to recalling "how in my opinion Socrates benefited companions"—that is, how Socrates was *actively* just.[51] While this division of the *Memorabilia* into these two unequal parts is manifest[52]—as is the twofold subdivision of the first part, which we have now completed—Xenophon has put before his readers a challenging puzzle as regards the subdivisions of the much longer second part of the whole work.[53]

The very first sentence of the second part is playfully-defensively misleading: Xenophon declares that he will write as much as he remembers of "how indeed it seems to me that he also benefited those who had intercourse with him, by showing in *deed* what sort of person he was, and also by conversation/dialogue." This gives the strong impression that what follows will focus primarily on the beneficially self-revealing deeds of Socrates, and only secondarily on his conversation or dialogue (which is conspicuously not said to be self-revelatory). In other words, Xenophon introduces the second part as if he were going to write recollections of the sort that are impressive in the terms of the city, or in accord with the prejudices of the citizenry (recollections that would feature, for example, the deeds of Socrates as a citizen-soldier); only gradually and insensibly does Xenophon reveal that "the plan of the whole work" is "based on the assumption" that, in the case of Socrates, "speech" is superior to "deed." And accordingly, Xenophon will never say a word about Socrates's deeds as citizen-soldier (the contrast with Plato's presentation of Socrates, not least in Plato's *Apology*, is vivid).[54]

Leo Strauss sets us on the path to a further deciphering of the puzzle of Xenophon's design by pointing out[55] that the thematic divisions of the second part of the *Memorabilia* emerge when one first gives due attention to passages[56] that indicate the Xenophontic Socrates's understanding of the list of the areas of serious concern of a normal gentleman. One can then recognize that the rest of the *Memorabilia* is divided into four major sections, the first three of which show how Socrates benefited others as regards three of the most important items from that list of normal gentlemanly concerns: (1) good character, particularly the virtues of piety and self-mastery, which Socrates exemplified (1.3–2.1); (2) loving friendship or *philia*, beginning with family relations (2.2–10); and (3) reaching for the noble or beautiful (*kalon*), understood primarily but by no means exclusively as political honor and office (3.1–14). The fourth and last major section of the second part (4.1–7)—set off by Xenophon through an elaborate, distinct introduction (4.1)—focuses more thematically and explicitly on what most obviously sets Socrates apart from "normal" gentlemen: his singular conduct as educator of close or "beloved" companions, exemplified in his tutelage of Euthydemus. Yet this focus comes after three major sections treating what one may call the "overlap" between Socrates's gentlemanly concerns and the "normal" gentleman's concerns.

Only if we consider what is missing from the overlap, or which among the major concerns of "normal" gentlemen are not at all concerns of Socrates, do we begin to see more starkly how Socrates is not your normal gentleman—though he tirelessly exhorts others to normal gentlemanliness (and, by the contrast with his own peculiar gentlemanliness, provokes critical thought). Strauss spotlights for us the fact that Socrates is not depicted by Xenophon as having among his major concerns servants or slaves (one may even wonder if Socrates owns any, despite 3.14.1), whereas we hear from the "perfect gentleman" of the normal sort, Ischomachus, teaching Socrates in the *Oeconomicus*, that slaves and the rule over slaves (treated as gentlemen) is a very great gentlemanly preoccupation and concern. Indeed, Ischomachus's teaching of Socrates concludes and culminates in an awed salute to the divinely mysterious character of kingly rule over willing slaves as the peak of virtuous human fulfillment: "This good—to rule over willing subjects—is not altogether a human thing but, rather, divine; it is manifestly given only to those who have been genuinely initiated into the religious mysteries of moderation" (*Oeconomicus* 21.12). Socrates, in *his* distinctive moderation, is not at all concerned to engage in the activity that the normal gentleman regards as the mysteriously divine peak of moderation and indeed of active virtue—as an imitation of the rule exercised by divinity itself.

We further observe that among what Socrates regards as the main concerns of "normal" gentlemen, but missing from his own chief concerns, are also "elevating one's paternal house"; guarding for others their "wealth, or sons, or daughters"; winning lawsuits; gaining and leading "allies," while "subduing enemies" (not least, "enemies of the fatherland"); "doing good deeds for, and enlarging, the fatherland"; being honored and considered worthy of trust by one's city and fellow citizens.[57] All these major areas of normal gentlemanly concern are in Socrates's life eclipsed by the three areas of concern that he does share with normal gentlemen. The deepest level of the Socratic conversations that we will study concerning the last of these three areas of concern—the noble—will be of great help in our understanding of the decisive reasons for the superiority of Socrates's "abnormality."

# PART 2

*Socrates's Active Justice,
as Benefiter of Others*

## CHAPTER THREE

# How Socrates Benefited through
# His Piety and His Self-Mastery

The first division of the second part of the *Memorabilia* consists of seven subsections (1.3–2.1)[1] showing how Socrates benefited his companions in regard to, and through, piety and mastery over his appetites. Sections on Socrates's piety alternate with sections on his self-mastery. The plan thus continues, for a time, to be governed by the defensive response to the twofold official indictment[2]—for Xenophon rather comically persists in proceeding as if the issue of whether or not Socrates was a corrupter of the young turns on whether or not he controlled his carnal and monetary appetites, and influenced others similarly.

## HIS TEACHING ON PRAYING AND SACRIFICING

Regarding the gods (Xenophon now solemnly assures us), Socrates manifestly conducted himself, in speech and in deed, and gave advice to others to act, in accordance with the Delphic oracle's reply to those who ask it what they ought to do in regard to sacrifices, and care of ancestors, and such: "Doing what is in accord with the law of the city is doing piously" (1.3.1). Xenophon once again starts out giving a massive impression of the conventionality of Socrates's piety.[3] So of course we hear nothing now about Socrates's idiosyncratic *daimonion*.[4]

But Xenophon adds that Socrates went beyond the oracle (contrast 4.3.16 and 4.6.2–4): Xenophon now attributes to Socrates the "belief" that as regards piety, "those who do in some way otherwise than as the law of the city directs are excessive, and vain." Since the law obviously says not a word about the peculiar *daimonion* of Socrates, this makes Xenophon's silence about the *daimonion* here all the more impish. We further note that Xenophon never indicates that Socrates was manifest in exercising pious care for *his* ancestors (recall the Socratic teaching at 1.2.53). On the other hand, Xenophon certainly has Socrates making oblations to the gods.

Before elaborating on Socrates's performance of sacrificial rites, however, Xenophon "inserts" (XS ad loc.) for the first time a brief statement about Socrates's praying, and understanding of prayer (1.3.2). Socrates "prayed to the gods simply to give the good things," on the grounds that "the gods have the most noble knowledge" of what the good things are. The eschewing of prayer for any specific goods is a further momentous step in what we learned earlier (1.1.8–9; see also 4.2.35) was Socrates's radically untraditional doctrine on the unknowability, by human means, of "the greatest things" regarding the future—namely, whether any specific good may turn out to benefit rather than to harm its possessor. Here, however, Socrates is no longer said to have advised others to consult divination regarding the future (BD ad loc.); is this because here Xenophon is speaking of how Socrates benefited his *"companions"* (*tous sunontas*—1.3.1)? What is more, there is now an implicit suggestion that Socrates regarded as intrinsically dubious the various goods that many pray for: specifically, gold, silver, tyranny, and victory in gambling *or in battle* (Socrates's contemning of the last would seem to put him acutely at odds with prayer dictated by the law of the city).[5] Socrates's novel, austere understanding of truly pious prayer—and of wise providential divinity—provokes the question (cf. 4.2.35), Does not divinity's noble knowledge insure that it will *always* do what is best for us, within its power? If so, then what is the point of our praying to the gods even to give us the good things (XS 83)?

A possible answer implicitly appears as Xenophon proceeds to explain Socrates's teaching on the meaning of religious sacrifice: he "believed that the gods especially enjoyed honors, from the most pious" (1.3.3)—and of course, the gods may be honored by prayers, as well as by oblations. But the latter more definitely express an honoring that is devotional or self-abnegating, since it involves a cost or loss to the devotee. And, in a striking statement, Xenophon informs us that such self-sacrifice Socrates declared to be noble in relations not only with divinity but also with humanity in general: "In relation to friends and strangers and in regard to the rest of the conduct of life, he declared it to be noble advice 'to make sacrifices (*erdein*) in accordance with one's capacity'" (1.3.3). At the start of his account of Socrates's justice in benefiting others, Xenophon spotlights the Socratic declaration that the noble for humans entails primarily self-sacrifice.

The gods, of course, do not offer sacrifices: Socrates teaches that they "enjoy" (*chairein*) receiving them (1.3.3). The gods' "nobility" is expressed in their knowledge—of what is truly good and pleasant (1.3.2). Does not Socrates imply that the gods' very noble knowing is higher in rank than the humans' noble sacrificing? Could Socrates imply that wisely pious humans, partly as a consequence of their noble offerings, hope to share in the higher divine nobility—the enjoyable divine good of knowledge (see 4.3.17)?

Xenophon adds that Socrates believed that, by offering the small sacrifices to the gods that he could afford, he did not fall short of those who made many grand sacrifices, from great wealth—because, "he declared," it "would not be noble for the gods to be pleased more" by the latter, since that would imply that "they would be pleased often by the wicked more than the upright"; and in that case, "life would not be worth living for humans!" (1.3.3). This fervid expostulation provokes the question, What was the firm basis for this conviction of Socrates that the gods are honorable upholders of strict justice? An answer here is seen in Socrates's invocation of a great traditional authority: Hesiod's *Works and Days*. Yet we can assume that Socrates encountered some who denied this, including some who did so on the basis of what they believed to be direct experience of the gods.[6] Could it be that one important purpose and outcome of Socrates's study of, and his dialogues concerning, apparent religious experience in others as well as in himself was the testing of such denials, and the consequential repeated discovery that the denials were never consistently maintained—that some version of self-abnegating nobility and justice (however perverse or peculiar) always was detectable as crucial to religious beliefs and purported religious experiences?

From our study of this first section of Xenophon's presentation of how Socrates benefited others, we begin to see that Xenophon will helpfully guide and stimulate our grappling with the perplexities that arise from Socrates's "What is . . ." questions, beginning with the first—"What is piety?"

## SOCRATES'S SELF-MASTERY VS. XENOPHON'S SEXUAL INDULGENCE

Turning to the more mundane topic of Socrates's exemplary "regimen" (1.3.5), Xenophon tells us first about the master's extraordinarily limited expenditures, which practically freed him from having to work for a living. The reason the philosopher could live without regular income[7] was that he restricted his diet (even when he accepted invitations to feasts, where he "very easily kept up his guard") to what his wisdom indicated to be pleasant to eat and pleasant to drink so as to satisfy hunger and thirst without any superfluity. So, in regard to food and drink, Socrates did not deny himself pleasure (see also 1.6.5); he was abstemious, but not ascetic. Accordingly, when he exhorted others to achieve similar self-mastery, Xenophon says, Socrates took pleasure in jokes that were "simultaneously playful and serious" (1.3.6–8).[8] Xenophon gives us a single example. It is a takeoff on a Homeric tale that is of great philosophic significance because it contains the sole mention, in Homer, of nature (*phusis*).[9] In Socrates's comic version, the goddess Circe is enabled to enslave Odysseus's men because they succumb to the temptation of a banquet into whose dishes she has insinuated poison that miraculously transforms the diners into pigs; Odysseus is immunized, because he possesses mastery of his appetite for food, and, in addition, receives from the god Hermes a crucial "clue" (unspecified by Socrates, but in Homer, this is the secret of "nature"). If we put this together with Xenophon's arresting statement at the outset of this section, to the effect that the purpose of Socrates's continence was to "educate his soul," as well as his body, and to live not only "securely," but "boldly" (*tharraleōs*)—"If," that is, "there were no sort of *daimonion*" (1.3.5)—we may venture to state Socrates's most serious point as follows. The failure to master one's physical appetites, and one's consequent need for money, renders one a hostage to fortune, and thereby more subject to becoming spiritually enslaved to a conception of divinity imagined as having supernatural powers of assistance—in contrast to divinity conceived in accord with nature. By the same token, one's becoming and remaining clear-sighted about divinity in accord with nature is promoted by a life of Socratic austerity. The Socratic virtues of piety and self-mastery are complementary.[10]

But, as is well known, while the Homeric Odysseus was immune to becoming enslaved through food, he nonetheless became entrapped by Circe's erotic charms. Does Socrates's joke not also hint that it is above all the enchantments of eros that threaten to captivate the minds of even the otherwise self-controlled—subjecting them to needs that engender illusions about divinity (see 1.3.11)? And, given that Odysseus appears in this jest as "in some sense the double of Socrates" (BD ad loc.; XS 19–20), the reader is instigated to wonder about Socrates's conduct and teaching as regards sex. To this Xenophon immediately turns (1.3.8–13).[11]

There is a striking contrast between Socrates's teaching on self-discipline as regards food and drink, and his teaching on sexual abstinence: "On the other hand, in regard to things of Aphrodite, he advised that one severely abstain from those who are beautiful" (1.3.8). This Socratic teaching on sexual pleasure would seem to be ascetic. Yet the reason Socrates gave for the teaching was this: "For one who touches such [beauties], to be *moderate* is not *easy*." Socrates did not say that it is "not possible." Was his conduct (and his subtler teaching) in regard to eros quite as ascetic as the first impression he gave?[12] To be sure, Xenophon informs us that Socrates thought that "those who were not out of danger in regard to the things of Aphrodite" ought to indulge only "with such as the soul would find intolerable if it did not feel great physical need"—and with such, moreover, "as would not cause trouble" (1.3.14). And Xenophon makes it plain that Socrates judged that his disciples, such as Xenophon, were by no means "out of danger." But Socrates himself "in these regards was manifestly so prepared that he more easily refrained from the most beautiful and blooming than others refrained from the ugliest and least blooming."[13] It sounds as though Socrates was largely out of danger. At any rate, Xenophon concludes that as regards sex, as well as food and drink, Socrates "thought that he had no less satisfying pleasure, and much less pain, than those who are much troubled by such things."[14]

Xenophon's previous report of Socrates's mode of teaching by way of joking sets the mood for Xenophon's own jocoserious story here of his personal dispute with Socrates about sexual desire. Since this is, as Strauss repeatedly spotlights (XS 20–21; XSD 90–91), Socrates's "only conversation with Xenophon that occurs in Xenophon's Socratic writings," its importance can hardly be overestimated. Yet it is *the* least serious, *the* most boisterously comic, Socratic dialogue in Xenophon: as Strauss observes, "Xenophon is the only character in his writings who is ever apostrophized by his gentle and urbane master" as "you wretch!" (*tlēmon*); "you fool!" (*mōre*)—or "anything like this." Our author here presents Socrates speaking to his wayward student Xenophon in the manner in which Aristophanes (*Clouds* 398, 687) presents Socrates speaking to his wayward student Strepsiades. And Xenophon is here portrayed as, like Strepsiades, swearing "Heracles!" (*Clouds* 184). Strauss warns us not to rest satisfied with the "easy" assumption that the clash over eros depicted here pertains to the "young Xenophon who had not yet undergone the full weight of the complete Socratic training." We should not rule out the possibility that we are shown here Xenophon as "the finished product," who nonetheless engaged with his philosophic mentor in a mutually bantering and affectionate, but by no means insignificant, disputation over eros. Strauss here characterizes Xenophon as "the light-hearted Xenophon rebuked by Socrates"—suggesting that the friendly disagreement may go with (or be traceable to?) the fact that Xenophon was, in contrast to Socrates, somewhat less grave at heart.

Now in what exactly does the bantering disagreement consist? Socrates is mock-enraged because Xenophon fails to acknowledge what Socrates insists is the enormity of the danger from the "poisonous infection" that is contracted from kissing, touching, or even gazing upon the erotically attractive

(1.3.11; see similarly *Symposium* 4.27–28). Socrates declares that this infection renders one "a slave instead of free"—a slave spiritually and mentally:
one becomes "compelled to take seriously things that not even a madman
would take seriously" (1.3.11); one is driven "mad" (and here Socrates refers
to the divinities called cupids, *erōtes*—1.3.13). If we put this together with
our interpretation of the Socratic joke that Xenophon reported just previously, and if we bear in mind the *Symposium's* opening, as well as its later,
scenes and conversations (esp. 1.8–10, 4.24–29), we may surmise what is
the most serious point of this Socratic declamation. Socrates is warning
not chiefly about the temporary mindlessness brought on by indulgence
in "the matters of Aphrodite." He is warning chiefly about the illusory
"sweet hopes," and the forgetfulness, involving some kind of belief in transcendence of necessitated mortal limits, that naturally begin to well up in
one who starts to experience the spiritual enchantment of "the things of
Aphrodite."

Xenophon here portrays himself, in contrast to his teacher, as being dis-
tinctly more willing to suffer some (more or less temporary) erotic cloud-
ing of his vision. As Xenophon's *oeuvre* as a whole makes clear, he knows
that he is by nature less single-mindedly philosophic, more human-all-too-
human, than that man whom he understood to be "the best and the happiest" (4.8.11). The life that is best and happiest for even so fine a speci-
men as Xenophon is inferior to the more ascetic life that is simply best and
happiest—but that is appropriate only for the very strongest souls, such as
Socrates. In this comic dialogue with his teacher, Xenophon portrays himself
as more analogous to Pheidippides than to Strepsiades or Aristophanes.[15]

## SOCRATES'S TEACHING ON DIVINE PROVIDENCE

Returning again to Socrates's benefiting others through his piety, Xenophon
next reports a dialogue "about the divine" (*daimonion*) that, he notes, he
himself witnessed. This first serious Socratic dialogue in the book is introduced in a curious way (1.4.1): Xenophon presents it as his "first" contribu-
tion in response to the belief "some" may hold, on the basis of what "some
write and say about Socrates," that while Socrates "became very strong at
turning humans *toward* virtue, he was *not* capable of *leading* them *to* it." In
the immediate context, this criticism would imply that while Socrates succeeded in making people seriously concerned and thoughtful about piety,
he was not able to lead them toward actually becoming pious. Xenophon's
response is surprisingly and puckishly tentative and heuristic.[16] Xenophon
asks the critics to "test" Socrates's capacity in this regard by "investigating"

not only how Socrates used refutative questioning to chastise those who thought they knew everything, but also how he spoke on a daily basis to those who spent time with him.

But it is not easy to fit the dialogue that follows into either category. For Socrates's interlocutor is Aristodemus, whom Xenophon identifies more precisely by adding, "the one called Shorty."[17] Xenophon indicates that we have here the rather notorious character who, we learn from Plato and elsewhere, was one of the most fervent lovers of Socrates, following and imitating his adored master in every possible respect, almost to the point of fanaticism.[18] This makes rather startling what we now learn about Aristodemus: he not only habitually failed to engage in religious sacrifice (except when "fighting in battle"),[19] and failed to use divination, but "mocked those who did so" (1.4.2). This would imply that he mocked Socrates! Or—if that seems implausible[20]—that he expressed openly what he perceived to be his hero's tacit, ironic ridicule and self-ridicule when engaging in public sacrifices or in making reference to experiencing divination through his *daimonion*. In the dialogue that now follows, Aristodemus is certainly presented as skeptical about the truth of Socrates's claim to have communication from the gods through the notorious *daimonion* (1.4.15).[21]

Xenophon of course presents Socrates deploying a rich argumentation to try to convince Aristodemus to abandon his (obviously dangerous—XS 102) open impiety, and to "serve the gods." After presenting the dialogue, Xenophon opines that by such discourses Socrates made his companions refrain from impiety not only when they were being observed by humans, but also when they were alone—since, or if, they held that nothing they did could escape the notice of the gods. But Xenophon gives no indication that Aristodemus in particular was convinced by Socrates's argumentation to this effect (XS 21, 26). Xenophon has Aristodemus remain stubbornly silent throughout the last half of the dialogue—except for an expression of doubt about Socrates's claim to receive divine guidance (1.4.11–18).

Xenophon has Socrates open the dialogue by establishing that Aristodemus admires certain humans for wisdom, and by eliciting their names: first Homer, and then other great poets such as Sophocles, as well as plastic artists.[22] This surprises us, given that Aristodemus ridicules worship of the gods whom Homer and other poets and artists present as the sources of their inspired wisdom and as the chief actors in the drama of life. On reflection, we may surmise that Aristodemus admires poetic wisdom as entailing artful religious deceptions. However that may be, by bringing to the fore that what Aristodemus admires as wisest is powerfully influential artistic making, rather than philosophic-scientific discovery and contemplation of natural necessities, Socrates finds the crucial material for laying the foundation of his subsequent dialectical argumentation (Powers 2009, 252). For he next (1.4.4) elicits agreement that the living beings must be the result *either* of "chance, luck" (*tuchē*) *or* of "making," by "design" (*gnomē*): the only two, exhaustively alternative, sorts of causality recognized in this conversation are chance versus productive art. Totally disregarded is the third, philosophic-scientific, category: causal necessity (*anangkē*—recall 1.1.11). Socrates's strategy is to proceed to show the implausibility of ascribing to chance or luck some of the most obviously beneficial, functional organs of human and animal anatomy. Aristodemus's response makes it evident that, despite his skepticism and mockery of traditional piety and belief, he is open, and perhaps even somewhat hopefully inclined, to recognizing anatomical evidence as grounds for believing that animals, including humans, are "very likely" (*panu eoike*) the products of "some wise, animal-loving craftsman" (1.4.7). This does not, however, entail his conceding that such evidence suggests any *particular* providential concern for humanity (BD ad 1.4.11). And in reply to Socrates's reminder of the mortality that attends all life forms, and of the attendant reproductive eros—the fear of death, and the longing to leave behind offspring—that pervades all conscious existence, Aristodemus steps back, to the more austere and minimal concession that this "certainly bears resemblance to contrivances by someone intending that animals exist" (1.4.7).

When Socrates proceeds to question the plausibility of, first, attributing to luck or chance the human possession of intelligence, and, second, denying the existence of prudent intelligence outside of humanity—intelligence governing the well-ordered body of the universe—Aristodemus again shows that he is far from unsympathetic, but frustrated by the absence of visible evidence: "By Zeus!—I don't see the Lords, as I do the craftsmen who bring about the things here!" (1.4.9: Socrates had made no mention of "Lords"). To this Socrates replies by pointing out that Aristodemus's own intelligence, which is the "lord" (sing.) of his body, is not visible. This suggestion of a world-mind strikes a chord. Aristodemus suddenly confesses his belief in a kind of divinity and divine order: "I do not (he said),[23] oh Socrates, look down on the divine (*daimonion*), but I hold that it is too magnificent (*megaloprepesteron*) to need my service in addition" (1.4.10). We thus see that Aristodemus's impiety has never been atheistic.[24] Indeed, his impiety as regards the gods of the city may be said to be rooted in a transcivic, and even trans-Hellenic, cosmic piety. Socrates has succeeded in bringing this naturalistic piety to emphatic expression; one can even go so far as to say that Socrates is here shown to be a teacher of "a piety which emerges out of the contemplation of nature and which has no necessary relation to law"

(OT chap. 7, para. 3). This is a piety that is in deep tension with the piety Xenophon attributed to Socrates in 1.3.1, the beginning of the long second part of the book. It is precisely this cosmic piety that leads Aristodemus to conceive of divinity (which he calls the *daimonion*) as being too sublime, too self-sufficient, to have any need for human worship or service. Against this, Socrates tries to argue that precisely the "magnificence" of the *daimonion* should make its providential care for Aristodemus more deserving of honor (but would this entail worshipping the gods *of the city*?). Aristodemus's rejoinder makes even plainer than what he has said before that he does not believe that the true divinities exercise any particular providence for humanity, as a species or as individuals: if he thought they cared at all, he assures Socrates, he would not neglect worshipping them (1.4.11).

This is practically Aristodemus's last word. He listens in silence as Socrates responds by elaborating an impressive list of ways in which our human species has been privileged in body and soul above all the animals—not least in our ability spiritually to "serve the gods" (1.4.13). For us humans, in our relation to the other animals, the gods have made a "life like gods" (1.4.14): a life that resembles that of the gods, in their relation to us humans. So, are the divine shepherds, as Socrates is here presenting them, naturally needy—at least of honor? Does Socrates see this as essential to making intelligible the requirement that we serve and honor them? But how does this avoid clashing with the pious Aristodemus's conception of the "magnificence" of divinity? And is this Aristodemian conception not more consistent with the Socratic conception of the divine that we will hear of shortly—"To need nothing is divine"?[25] Besides, Socrates has given no argument implying that the gods attend to humans as individuals, rather than as members of herds.[26] Certainly Aristodemus gives no sign of being won over by this argumentation. When Socrates concludes the dialectical part of the conversation with the nigh exasperated question, "But what will they have to do, so that you believe they care about you?" Aristodemus sharply replies, "When they send, as you *claim* they send to you, counselors as to what to do and not to do!" (1.4.14–15). In effect, Aristodemus suggests that the sole convincing evidence for divine particular providence would be one's own personal experience of divine intervention and guidance. Aristodemus evidently sees in everything that Socrates has said only further confirmation of the absence of any other cogent evidence, in nature and in human experience, for particular providence (and, having been nicknamed "Shorty," as Xenophon tells us, Aristodemus evidently has found no sign in his own life of being cared for by divinity!).

At this point Socrates is clearly being challenged, by Aristodemus, to articulate a convincing account of his own religious experience with the *daimonion*. Socrates dodges the challenge (thereby doubtless confirming Aristodemus's disbelief in his master's claims about the *daimonion*).[27] Instead, he launches into a plea that Aristodemus take to heart the testimony of the Athenians, and then of the Greeks, and then of mankind at large, claiming and believing to receive guidance through divination and prophetic revelation (1.4.15–16). Surely (Socrates pleads) this widespread witness, by "the wisest of humanity, cities, and nations," to experiences of divine intervention and guidance, is massive and powerful evidence that must be taken seriously by any skeptic.

Yet this makes more conspicuous Socrates's failure to mention, let alone to argue for the existence of, any of the Olympian or the infernal deities and heroes whose worship is commanded by the law of Athens and other Greek cities (Zeus's absence from Socrates's theology is underlined by the naming of Zeus in profane expletives by Aristodemus here). Instead, Socrates exhorts Aristodemus to conceive of divinity's rule over the cosmos as that of a single, intelligent, cosmic soul analogous to Aristodemus's own psychic intelligence in its rule over his body.[28]

Finally, Socrates proposes to the ever silent Aristodemus that he make trial of the gods (as if Aristodemus has never done this?!). In effect, Socrates says: even as you experience reciprocal service and gratification from humans whom you serve and gratify, and even as you recognize others as prudent by taking counsel with them over mutual needs, try this with the gods, to see "if they are not willing to give you advice about matters unevident to humans." Socrates assures Aristodemus that if he does, he will recognize that "the divine is such as to see all and to hear all and to be everywhere while caring for all simultaneously" (1.4.18). The stubbornly mute Aristodemus, with his belief in the "magnificence" of true divinity, is likely not only to find the suggestion of the god's human-like neediness unattractive, but also to have noticed that Socrates's last words do not quite entail particular providence. As a consequence, Aristodemus may be left wondering—along with the silent auditor Xenophon, who has stressed that he was present—whether Socrates has been urging more than that they imitate Socrates in sagely trying to conform outwardly to public, lawful practices of worship and belief, as regards the civic divinities, in speech as well as in deed. Certainly Xenophon does not claim, at the end of the presentation of this dialogue, that by such discourses Socrates made his companions pious, but only that he made them refrain from impieties along with injustices and shameful things (1.4.19). Since Socrates "in speeches dealt as he wished with all who conversed with him" (1.2.14), we are inclined to conclude that

Socrates succeeded as planned, in at least getting Aristodemus to refrain from openly mocking those who sacrifice and employ divination.

## SOCRATIC SELF-MASTERY VS. CONVENTIONAL SELF-MASTERY

Circling back to Socrates's benefiting others through his self-mastery, Xenophon continues the previous chapter's remarkably tentative, heuristic, and inconclusive response to the criticism that Socrates was incapable of leading others to virtue.[29] "Let us investigate" whether Socrates "in some degree" led to self-mastery, "when he said some such things as the following" (1.5.1). Xenophon proceeds to quote a short, evidently typical, Socratic oration, consisting largely of anaphoric-rhetorical questions, addressed to an unspecified group of mature males (andres) whom Socrates addresses rather formally. Here we witness for the first time Socrates in his more public persona: the citizen-philosopher, who comes to sight exhorting fellow gentlemen-citizens to self-mastery.

Accordingly, the sermon begins by pointing out that lack of control over one's appetites disqualifies anyone from being elected by "us" as "our" military commander in wartime. In the second place, Socrates applies the same to anyone whom "we" would choose to be executor of "our" estates, and guardians of "our" children. In the third place, Socrates preaches, the same holds as regards "our" slaves: and it is, curiously, on this last basis—the unacceptability of lack of self-control in "our" slaves—that the oration insists to the gentlemen that the very same is applicable to "oneself." (Socrates speaks from a perspective that views the slaves and their gentleman-masters as on a moral continuum. Xenophon presents Socrates as learning this, to his surprise, from the consummate gentleman Ischomachus.[30]) The oration proceeds to stress that lack of self-mastery is harmful not only to one's household, but to one's own body and soul; then, that lack of self-mastery obstructs the intercourse of friends (recall 1.2.7–8). Finally, the oration speaks no longer of the lack of self-mastery, but of its possession—as essential for learning, and for taking care of something good. We discern an ascent,[31] from concerns that Socrates shares with the entire citizenry to concerns that he shares, but less and less, with conventional gentlemen, and finally to priorities that give a glimpse of his distinctive kind of gentlemanliness. This distinctiveness is visible also in Socrates's peculiar characterization of self-mastery (here even more plainly than before—recall 1.2.4): self-mastery is not virtue, but only the "basement" or footing or foundation (krēpis) for virtue (1.5.4; L. Strauss 1939, 514).

In the oration's rather ardent conclusion, Socrates proclaims to his manly audience that "a free real man (*anēr*)" ought to wish not to acquire a slave lacking self-mastery—and then Socrates adds, amazingly, that if a real man is himself a slave, to such pleasures, he "ought to beseech the gods to let him happen upon good masters, for only in that way would such a one be saved" (1.5.5). Socrates reinforces this proclamation by swearing his first oath in the *Memorabilia*; but the oath he swears (tongue in cheek) is a conventional woman's oath—"By Hera!"[32] That there is a gulf between conventional manliness and Socratic self-mastery, that Socrates's conception of what constitutes the possession, or lack, of self-mastery entails demands that would be hard for conventional manliness to incorporate is quietly made still clearer by Xenophon's closing comment. He declares that this homily shows Socrates to be more self-controlled in his deeds than in his speech, since he mastered not only the pleasures of the body but also those of money, believing that through moneymaking one sets up a despot over oneself, and enters into an enslavement second to none in shamefulness (1.5.6). Socrates's public oration that Xenophon has here reproduced prudently says not a word about this far-reaching and distinguishing "economic" dimension of the Socratic conception of self-mastery. Xenophon, by making this dimension plain only in his own, supplementary words, tacitly points to its radicalism.[33] In the *Oeconomicus* (20.22–29; cf. 12.15–16, 14.9–10), Xenophon presents Socrates being taught by Ischomachus that a perfect gentleman, following his father and thus tradition, prides himself on his love of, and success in, ever increasing agricultural moneymaking. Putting these texts together, it would seem to follow that in Socrates's eyes normally "manly" gentlemen are in need of good masters, in order to counter or control their enslavement to love of moneymaking.[34] The oration's closing recommendation of prayer points to how and where gentlemen may believe that they find such masters. Again we see that Socrates's teachings on piety and on self-mastery are complementary, with a view to the preconditions of attaining inner human freedom, or at least of escaping the worst sorts of (spiritual) enslavement.

## THE VIRTUE THAT SOCRATIC SELF-MASTERY SERVES

The biggest unanswered question provoked by the preceding is, What is the virtue, the virtuous life, that Socrates built for and within himself, and encouraged in others, on the "footing" that is self-mastery? Xenophon next provides glimpses of the answer, by portraying a series of three exchanges in which Socrates responded to "the sophist Antiphon's" unvarnished critique of the Socratic way of life, primarily on account of its austerity. The wording of the introductory sentence (1.6.1) prepares us to see that at this point, although he is supplementing the immediately preceding account of Socrates's self-mastery, Xenophon loosens somewhat the bonds with which he has tied his recollections thus far to rebuttal of the official indictment. Here, Socrates is presented responding to accusations of a very different kind from the city's accusations. Here, he responds, in the first place, to the accusation of being a betrayer of the true purpose of "philosophizing"—conceived as the cultivation of one's own happiness—and of, in this way (i.e., from the point of view of philosophizing), being a corrupter of the young.[35]

Antiphon in effect asks: What good do you gain, Socrates, you and your followers, from this way of life of yours—which is of such poverty and abstemiousness that even a slave wouldn't tolerate it! "Philosophizing" is supposed to make one happier, but you are a teacher of "unhappiness!"[36] More specifically, Antiphon shows that the happiness that he conceives philosophizing properly leads to, and that Socrates impedes, consists most manifestly of fine food, drink, and clothing, together with much money, "whose acquisition delights, and which makes possible freedom as well as pleasure" (1.6.2–3).

Xenophon thus places his hero in a position to take the high moral ground, as the citizen-philosopher refuting the hedonistic and money-loving sophist. Yet Xenophon presents Socrates implicitly accepting the sophist's major premise, that philosophizing, correctly understood, should make one happier—indeed, that becoming happier oneself is *the* philosophic criterion for the good life. What Socrates takes issue with is Antiphon's conception of what becoming happier consists in.

Xenophon stresses that the sophist laid down his challenge in the presence of Socrates's "disciples,"[37] with a view to drawing them away. The sophist was doubtless shrewd enough to choose to speak before a group of "disciples" that included some, or maybe even most, whom he had detected were "convertible"—not yet entirely or irreversibly immersed in the abstentious Socratic life. Socrates's reply must be seen in this context. In other words, Socrates is here defending his austere way of life with a view to helping a mixed company of his followers resist the temptation of the sophist's hedonistic conception of the aim of philosophizing.[38]

The first and longest part of Socrates's response (1.6.5–7), proceeding anaphorically through seven rhetorical questions, vividly expresses what we have come to see is a major theme of Socrates's more public teaching on the reason and goal of self-discipline as regards money, food, drink, clothing, and physical conditioning. Through abstemiousness one achieves, in regard to the aforementioned, maximal independence and self-sufficiency, consistent with humanity's natural limits and needs. The sole element of this proto-Cynic picture that does not show the mind preoccupied with regulating the body and external goods is the first thing mentioned: by abstaining from accepting money, Socrates says, he "is not constrained to converse with anyone he does not wish to talk to" (1.6.5). The weakest or most contestable element is the only one that mentions pleasure, and is parked in the least exposed, fourth and central place: the (dubious) claim that the most pleasant dining is experienced by one who least needs meat or tasty food, and that the most pleasant drinking is experienced by one who least desires some absent drink.[39]

From this rather exoteric opening Socrates moves to a more revealing level when he suddenly indicates that he does not regard maximal self-sufficiency and freedom in relation to one's physical needs and pleasures (and he now includes sex and sleep) as the main goal of, or motive for, self-discipline—nor even as the main motive for avoiding enslavement to bodily pleasures. In truth, for Socrates avoiding such enslavement is properly understood as a *means* to acquiring *other* things that are *more pleasant*, as well as more lastingly beneficial, than the pleasures that are foregone: "Do you think that there is *anything else* that is more responsible for not being enslaved to stomach or sleep or lust than having other things *more pleasant* than these—things that not only delight in their employment, but also provide hopes that they will be of benefit always?"[40] To give a pointer to these "other things," Socrates appeals to observations about human nature that he is sure Antiphon has made: unless humans think that they are "doing well" (*eu prattein*), they lack joy; and it is when humans "hold that they are *progressing* nobly in whatever they happen to be working on" that they experience the joy of doing well. But then Socrates adds: outweighing all the aforesaid, in pleasure, is the awareness that one is progressing in becoming better, and in acquiring better friends—and, Socrates asseverates, he spends his entire conscious life believing this of himself (1.6.8–9).

Socrates thus makes it clear that while he does not simply identify the human good, or "doing well," with enjoying pleasure, he does understand the aura of this specific intellectual pleasure—the self-consciousness of steady progressive improvement in oneself and in one's friends—to be a central component of the happiest life for a human being (see OT chap. 6). This of course leaves tantalizingly open the question, What exactly for Socrates constitutes the truest improvement of himself, and of his friends? What is Socrates's "work," or what leisured activity takes the place of "work"? And why did Socrates first mention prominently, then drop (when he spoke of himself and his friends) the good things as providing "*hopes* that they will be of benefit *always/forever (aei)"*? And why did he first mention and then drop *"nobly* progressing in work"? (see L. Pangle 2013, 29–30).

Continuing his response, Socrates finally takes the high moral ground, turning attention away from the question of what constitutes his own, and his friends', personal improvement—and thus his and his friends' pleasure and happiness. He submits that "if it should be necessary to benefit friends *or city,"* then his way of life, in contrast to the one that Antiphon "calls blessed," provides greater leisure to exercise *this* care, and better conditioning for the unpleasant trials of military campaigning and of holding out when besieged (1.6.9).

Leaping finally to the highest ground, divinity, Socrates declares his "belief" that "to need nothing is divine, and to need the least possible is nearest to the divine, and the divine is most superior *(kratiston),* and what is nearest to the divine is nearest to what is most superior" (1.6.10). He thus returns to his proto-Cynic beginning, now deified or expressed in religious terms. To Socrates's noble disciples, Antiphon's "happiness," of "luxury and extravagance," must appear petty and vulgar in contrast to their master's ascent toward divinity in its autarchic strength. Besides, the roguishly tricky Socrates may confound or stymie Antiphon by throwing in his face here a famous comment about the divine that in fact is a quotation from the beginning of the sophist's own treatise entitled *Truth.*[41]

But despite this confounding of Antiphon, there is visible a certain tension between Socrates's introduction of the divine standard and his previous evocation of the supreme human pleasure. Would divinity, as Socrates here conceives it, experience the joy of progressing? Would it need any friends? Is not the joy of continually progressing necessarily intertwined with the painful awareness of one's continuing deficiency—not to mention the ultimate finitude of all human progressing? Does not the divine standard cast a shadow of insuperable imperfection, incompleteness, limitation, over Socrates's human, all-too-human joys?

At a later time, Xenophon reports, Antiphon returned to the attack, this time sardonically charging Socrates, on the basis of his being just, with self-confessed total lack of wisdom. (We see again how radically different from the civic are the standards by which the sophist condemns Socrates.) The justice that Antiphon wryly imputes to Socrates is that of quid pro quo—honestly demanding, in recompense for any good one gives away to another, no more and no less than the commodity is worth; and since Socrates demands nothing for his association, he must "know" that his associates gain no worthwhile wisdom from it (1.6.11–12).

Socrates's response makes completely explicit his activity as a teacher of wisdom, framed in what we may call an articulation of the code of Socratic gentlemen.[42] "Among us" bestowing the beauty of wisdom is customarily regarded as analogous to a youth's bestowal of physical beauty: "If someone sells the latter for money to whomever wishes, they call him a whore (pornon)"; "but if someone makes a friend of a lover whom he knows to be noble and good (a gentleman), we customarily believe this person to be moderate (sōphrona)." Analogously, "those who sell wisdom for money to whomever wishes, they call 'sophists,' like whores"; but "he who by teaching whatever he has, to someone he knows to be of a good nature, makes a good friend, we believe does what befits a noble and good (gentlemanly) citizen" (1.6.13).

Switching to the emphatic first person singular, and sharply addressing Antiphon by name, Socrates expresses the un-needy delight he takes in good friends, and adds: "And if I have something good, I teach it; and I bring them together with others from whom I hold they will be benefited in some way with a view to virtue." Then Socrates discloses a key activity in and through which occurs his teaching, which is simultaneously his own learning: "The treasures of the wise men of old, which they left written in books, I go through with the friends, scrolling together; and if we see something good, we pick it out; and we believe it a great gain if we become friends[43] to one another."

Xenophon here interjects himself with singular alacrity: "To me, on hearing these things, he seemed to be blessed himself, and to be leading his hearers to gentlemanliness."[44] Xenophon has said nothing like this when describing Socrates's self-discipline, or his piety, or his various other speeches. Xenophon will never say such a thing again. Xenophon thereby indicates that learning from the study together of old books, that are great because they contain treasures of wisdom, is a peak activity of Socratic life and friendship (XS 29–30). Here, finally, we see virtuous activity that Socrates did not merely turn his companions toward, but effectively led them into (recall the challenge at 1.4.1).[45]

The wisdom in which Socrates deals is a truly common good for those few select friends of "good nature" able to share in it. Thus the peak justice in which Socrates participates with his friends is crucially different from the vulgar justice Antiphon deployed in his sarcasm: the peak justice among the Socratics involves no giving away, or sacrificing, of what is good, and therefore results in no obligation to make recompense (recall, in contrast, Socrates's first, more conventional, word about sacrifice and friendship: 1.3.3). Yet Xenophon's comment also underlines the inequality in rank (in happiness) that continues to distinguish the "blessed" Socrates from his close friends; the good that is common is not equally shared or enjoyed, given the vast inequality among even "good natures."[46]

We note that the "wise men of old" to whom Socrates refers would be the "pre-Socratic" philosophers and poets. The study of their books would therefore be interwoven with, but also would sometimes transcend, Socrates's "ceaseless" dialogues about the "human things," his pressing of the "What is . . ." questions, beginning with "What is piety?"

We further note that Xenophon evidently intends to become himself, in the future, and indeed "for all time," one of the wise men of old whose books are studied for their treasures of wisdom:

> It does not escape my notice that someone will probably declare things written with beauty and order to be written without beauty or order. For it will be rather easy for them hastily to blame, incorrectly. And indeed things have been written in this way so that they would be correctly written, and would form those who are not sophistic, but wise and good. For I do not wish the writings to be reputed, rather than to be, useful—in order that they be irrefutably so, for all time. (*The Skilled Hunter with Dogs* 13.6)

Even brief reflection suggests that Xenophon's spotlighting of Socrates's small, elite "reading groups," preoccupied with studying old books, runs a considerable risk: of arousing or confirming the suspicion that Socrates seduced the best and brightest young away from civic and familial or household engagements.[47] Xenophon counters this danger by immediately showing that the master's joyful didactic activity included a very large practical-civic dimension. For in the third and shortest exchange with Antiphon, Xenophon has the latter demand how Socrates "can hold that he makes others skilled statesmen without himself engaging in politics—if indeed" (Antiphon snidely adds) "you do understand it." This, we note, is a rather odd, not to say incredible, challenge to be voiced by a "sophist," since it would recoil immediately upon the sophist's own educational profession. However that may be, by attributing this challenge to Antiphon, Xenophon is able—seemingly in contradiction to his own earlier emphatic defensive claims made in a very different context[48]—to present Socrates as in no way denying that he teaches political skill; on the contrary, Xenophon here has Socrates rejoin by asking whether he would engage more in politics if he did so only by himself, or if he made it his care that as many as possible become capable of engaging in politics skillfully (1.6.15). Xenophon has his hero give here the impression of making a very big claim as to his successful devotion to the task of affording civic education to many of the citizenry. It is no accident, then,[49] that immediately after this, Xenophon presents Socrates's dehortation from boasting.

## SOCRATES'S DISCOURAGEMENT OF BOASTING

The pattern that has hitherto been established is now suddenly interrupted—temporarily, and all the more conspicuously. Instead of a third account of how Socrates benefited by his piety, we get a report of the monologue by which he turned his companions away from boasting (*alazoneia*, 1.7). This is then followed by a return to the pattern, with a third account of how Socrates benefited by his self-mastery (2.1). To what educative thinking is our playful author-teacher directing us? "Could the speech against becoming a boaster deal in a disguised way with piety?" (XS 32)—that is, with the piety peculiar to Socrates, inasmuch as he claims to receive privileged divine guidance from a special *daimonion*? We recall that Xenophon first used the term "boaster" (*alazōn*)[50] in reference to how Socrates would appear if he were detected lying when he claimed that things were made manifest to him through a god (1.1.5).[51]

Xenophon here quotes Socrates describing, first, the elaborate and costly lengths to which one would need to go in order to create a false reputation as a talented musical performer, only to be exposed, the minute one performed, as a laughable *alazōn*. Then we hear Socrates pointing out the disastrous as well as disgraceful dangers, to others as well as to oneself, that would accrue from one's succeeding in creating a false reputation for skill as a general or a pilot. Xenophon adds in his own name that Socrates further showed that creating a false reputation for being rich or courageous or strong is "unprofitable" (to the boaster, that is, if or once he is detected). Then Xenophon oddly (and thus provocatively) adds that Socrates also decried two *successful* swindles, one of which—conning people out of their property—he called "fraud on no small scale," and the other of which—conning the city into thinking one is capable of leading it—he called "much the greatest fraud." The companions who listened to all this might well have been prodded to wonder what the master was pointing to by delivering a speech that moves from warning against laughably imprudent boasts to deploring successful and harmful swindles of the city. The shrewder among them might have discerned that Socrates, "with a whiff of Attic irony," was circumscribing an intermediate possibility: a mildly comic, prudently boastful deception of the city that does substantial (defensive) good and little if any harm or offense—at least to humans.[52] But then, must the shrewd companions not also have been incited to wonder how Socrates can be so sure that there do not exist punitive gods who will be infuriated at his hubristic *alazoneia*, and so will respond by inflicting upon him grave punishment? The Xenophontic Socrates partakes to a modest extent in the boldness (*tolma*) exhibited by leading characters in Aristophanes, including the Aristophanean Socrates.

Our author introduced this section by proposing that "we investigate" whether Socrates, in turning his companions away from boasting, turned them toward care for virtue (Xenophon in this case does not even suggest that we investigate whether Socrates actually led his companions to become virtuous: 1.7.1; recall in contrast 1.4.1). Xenophon concludes by declaring that it seems to him that by such conversation Socrates did turn his companions away from boasting (1.7.5). Xenophon cannot bring himself to say that it seems to him that Socrates thereby turned his companions toward (let alone led them to adopt) the virtue relevant here, of truthfulness.

## HIS TEACHING OF SELF-MASTERY FOR THE SAKE OF A LIFE DEDICATED TO POLITICS

What is most obviously important about the seventh and final subsection (2.1) is that it presents Socrates in dialogue exhorting to self-control and endurance as necessary preconditions for *a life dedicated to politics*—a life which Socrates now defends and advocates in opposition to Aristippus, who contemns the political life, and advocates instead an apolitical, private life, on the grounds of the latter's being far superior in pleasure, and therefore prudence.[53] Xenophon here richly elaborates the point of the last of the three conversations that Socrates had with the sophist Antiphon (1.6.15)—correcting a misconception that one might contract on the basis of the culmination of the second and central of those conversations (1.6.14). Now Xenophon makes it indelibly manifest that the citizen-philosopher Socrates conveyed to his companions great respect for the life dedicated to politics, and taught them that the transpolitical, philosophic life should and could never leave behind civic engagement (recall also 1.2.64).[54]

### THE SETTING OF THE DIALOGUE

Xenophon introduces the dialogue as exemplifying the sort of things said by Socrates that turned his companions toward self-discipline as regards sensual desire and comfort. The occasion is further specified as brought about by Socrates "knowing that one of his companions was rather unrestrained in these regards" (2.1.1). Since our author then proceeds at once to present Socrates addressing and conversing with Aristippus, one is at first led to assume that it is the latter who is the wayward companion whom Socrates intends to influence.[55] But when Aristippus reappears later in the *Memorabilia* he seems to be differentiated from the companions of Socrates (3.8.1). Moreover, in the course of the present dialogue, Aristippus seems to be as yet rather unacquainted with the way of life led by Socrates, and believed by Socrates to be happiness (2.1.17). Above all, even though Socrates "in speeches dealt as he wished with all who conversed with him" (1.2.14), there is no sign that Socrates's elenchic speech here moved Aristippus: the latter's last words are stubborn (2.1.17; see also 3.8.1), and Xenophon ascribes to him no reaction to Socrates's rendition of the brilliant speech of Prodicus. This last is hardly surprising, since a speech aimed at inspiring emulation of a heroic warrior like Heracles seems comically inapt and inept as meant to attract an effete voluptuary like Aristippus.[56] So with good reason a number of readers[57] have suggested that Aristippus is not the companion whose lack of restraint Socrates here seeks to counter, but that there is likely to be some silent listening companion(s) for whose benefit and in whose presence Socrates performed the dialogue with the (predictably) stubborn Aristippus. Now the sole listener explicitly indicated here is our author; and we know from before (1.3) that he incurred Socrates's (somewhat histrionic) disapproval on account of insufficient restraint in sexual matters—without giving any indication that he changed his ways. In that earlier passage Xenophon quoted himself emitting the manly-heroic expletive "Heracles!": the present conversation culminates in a depiction of Heracles at the moment when he is deciding whether to lead a life of virtue or a life of (sensual) vice. If Heracles is a figure that would be a most unlikely model to put before Aristippus, Heracles might well be a boyhood hero of Xenophon.[58] In that earlier passage Socrates apostrophized Xenophon, in mock rage, as "wretch!" (*tlēmon*); here Virtue apostrophizes Vice as "wretch!"[59] So we may have to fear the worst about our author. That Socrates's intended target is not so much Aristippus as it is a politically ambitious companion like Xenophon (or Alcibiades) helps explain the otherwise seemingly maladroit Socratic starting point. For Socrates at first (2.1.1–7) questions Aristippus as if it could be assumed, as the premise of the discussion, that the education and life of one capable of ruling are superior to the education and life of one who does not even lay claim to rule; but Aristippus soon makes it plain that he does not at all, and will not ever, accept such a premise: *au contraire!*

## Self-Discipline as Crucial to Education for Ruling

Through his initial series of seventeen questions (the ninth, and central, per-tains to learning) Socrates gets Aristippus to agree quite emphatically that an education that makes one capable of ruling must include severe self-discipline in regard to food, drink, sleep, sex, and the endurance of labori-ous toil in cold and in heat.[60] What is surprising is the way Socrates here conceives the attractive challenge of political life: as a ceaselessly danger-ous competition to become dominant, and to avoid becoming dominated. In his central question, Socrates proposes that the "learning" needed for a political career is "that which is useful with a view to dominating the adversaries" (2.1.3). Socrates goes so far as to assimilate the political life to the life of animals who hunt one another as prey: he who aims at rule needs to be educated in self-control so as to be "less subject than are other animals to becoming prey of adversaries" (2.1.4). In contrast to Aristippus, Socrates does not say a word about rule as doing the city's business, as pub-lic service, as a common good or an enactment of justice and lawfulness (the silence on the just is pointed to when, as the culmination of the series of questions, Socrates asks Aristippus if he has considered in which tribe—those seeking to rule, or those failing to compete—he should "*justly*" place himself: 2.1.7).

But the strangest feature of Socrates's initial series of questions is his cu-rious drift away from his manifest theme, of how self-discipline is essential for one who is competing to rule. Socrates's lengthiest question portrays how lack of self-control can lead to "unhappiness" in one's *private erotic* life—if or inasmuch as one is led to risk foolishly breaking the law against adultery, leading to one's getting caught, and then paying the shameful legal penalty as well as being harshly used. (Socrates here reminds of the culmination of the debate between the Just and Unjust Discourses in Aris-tophanes's *Clouds* 1083–86.) Aristippus does not hesitate in agreeing that such lack of self-restraint is a mark of a life of "unhappiness" (2.1.5); soon we hear Aristippus declaring that it is "great work to provide what is needed for oneself" (2.1.8). The dialogue thus gestures toward a life that is private and erotically hedonistic, while being shrewdly self-disciplined—a way of life left unexplored here. Socrates concludes his series of questions by speaking as if the choice of how one should live is between only two alter-natives: joining those who become self-disciplined so as to seek to be com-petent rulers, or joining those who, lacking self-discipline, make no claim to rule (2.1.7).

## WHY ONE MUST SEEK TO BE ONE OF THOSE WHO RULE

This framing of the choice suits the self-indulgent hedonist Aristippus, who gladly numbers himself among "those wishing to live most easily and pleasantly" (2.1.9). Seeking to rule, Aristippus submits, is foolish, because rule is public service or voluntary servitude, and even dangerous servitude: not only does the ruler neglect his own needs while attending to the needs of the other citizens, but "having presided over the city, if he does not accomplish all that the city wishes, he undergoes a judicial penalty for this." Cities treat their rulers like masters treat their slaves—"like," Aristippus says in emphasis, "I use my slaves": "the cities think that their rulers ought to provide them with as many goods as possible, but that their rulers ought to refrain from the goods themselves!" (2.1.8–9). But Aristippus also makes another strong preliminary point: he first declares that it is foolishness to think that the care for one's own needs is not a "sufficient" work, and that one should take on in addition the task of providing the other citizens with what they need. This reminds us of Xenophon's earlier criticism of Alcibiades for having "neglected himself" and having thereby become lost in political life (1.2.24–25). It reminds us even more of a teaching that Cyrus heard from his semi-Socratic father (*Education of Cyrus* 1.6.7). In other words, there is a grain of the Socratic-Xenophontic in Aristippus's outlook.[61] The most obvious break with Socrates is in Aristippus's identification of his true happiness with enjoying what is most easy and pleasant. Aristippus is ignorant of or deaf to the Socratic admonitions about the difficulty of discovering one's deepest needs and hence truest happiness—and about the obstacles to such discovery posed by indulgence in the most obvious desires and pleasures. Above all, we see that Aristippus has not begun to engage in serious thought about what should be for him, as a hedonist, the most profoundly puzzling fact about the human concern with the good, a fact that Xenophon and his Socrates often focus upon (recall 1.3.3): those who are most ardent about virtue are attracted to politics in large part precisely because it does come to sight as public *service*, as a *noble* life devoted to the good of *others*, rather than—and even at the sacrifice of—one's own good.

Xenophon does not, however, show Socrates trying at first to get Aristippus to reflect on such noble attraction to politics. In Aristippus, Xenophon and his Socrates have chosen an interlocutor who is not a good candidate for such a dialogue. And Xenophon has Socrates here argue for the superiority of the political life primarily on Aristippus's own ground: greater pleasure, less pain, for oneself. (This is a tactic that is calculated to arouse at least as much surprised thought in the reflectively nobler-minded onlookers and readers as in Aristippus.[62])

Socrates's initial, hedonistic argument for the life of rule does not attempt to refute directly Aristippus's characterization of rulers as "slaves" of "the cities." In speaking thus, Aristippus was evidently thinking especially of the officeholders in republican and perhaps primarily democratic regimes (like the Athenian); and Socrates tacitly concedes some truth to Aristippus's characterization. Socrates implicitly (but only implicitly) proceeds on the more precise premise that in republican regimes it is not "the city" that rules, employing as its servants the elected officials, but instead the dominant portion (be it few or many) of the citizenry: that is, the regime (politeia—recall the basis of Alcibiades's refutation of Pericles, 1.2.41–46). Certainly Socrates makes it clear that he thinks Aristippus has failed to take into account the pleasures of political domination, even when one has only a small share in the dominating, and conversely, the great pain of being among those politically dominated. He asks Aristippus to consider the empirical evidence, in international relations, of what it is like to live belonging to a people who mainly dominate others, versus belonging to a people who are mainly dominated by others: "Which," Socrates asks, "seem to you to live more pleasantly?" (2.1.10).[63]

Aristippus dodges the question, and the dilemma in which an answer would involve him (2.1.11; XS 34; BD ad loc.). He no doubt recognizes that the pleasures of domination and the pains of being dominated that are seen so clearly and felt so strongly in foreign affairs are reproduced in domestic politics, and not least in democratic politics, in varying degrees. But he submits that there is a third way, which individuals like himself can "try to follow": a way of "freedom" *from* politics or from *both* ruling *and* slavery, a way "that especially leads to happiness" (this freedom is not itself happiness, but presumably allows indulgence in personal pleasures that Aristippus thinks are greater, and less alloyed with risk and pain and service, than the pleasures of political domination, whose sweetness he does not deny).

Socrates's rejoinder begins curiously: "but if" this third way "also avoids humans, there might be something to what you say" (2.1.12). Is Socrates thinking of the way that might be attributed to the truly divine? However that may be, he proceeds to aver that he thinks that Aristippus cannot have failed to observe that in human society, in private life as well as public, if or to the extent that one is not ruling, one is ruled; and if, as one who is ruled, "you will not willingly court/minister to (therapeuseis) those who are ruling," then "the stronger know how to inflict suffering" until the weaker are "persuaded" to a "voluntary slavery" in which "the manly/courageous (*andreioi*) and powerful" reap a harvest from the "unmanly and weak" (2.1.12–13). Courting or ministering to the stronger who rule (say, the Athenian popular majority or its servant-leaders like Alcibiades or Nicias or Laches) is not as bad as being enslaved to them, and even allows room for some influence over them; but there is nothing rosy about Socrates's view of the domination that pervades human, including republican and democratic, society.[64] What is more, we are invited to think out for ourselves what this implies about Socrates's and Xenophon's understanding of their own political choices (XS 38). One must start from here to understand in the proper light Xenophon's quitting Athens in order to serve Cyrus, as well as everything that the ironic Xenophon later published in regard to Sparta, the brutally hegemonic power of his era under whose sway he wound up living, in exile (cf. Buzzetti 2014, 196n43).

Aristippus concedes the grim facts of political life as Socrates has stated them. Indeed he makes it clear that it is precisely on this basis—"in order not to suffer these things"—that he has chosen to live as an itinerant "stranger," not "enclosing myself in any political order" (2.1.13).

Socrates responds by portraying in stark terms the grave vulnerabilities to which this gambit exposes Aristippus, as a stateless person. Bearing in mind the "stranger's" way of life led by Xenophon himself, in exile,[65] as well as by his wise Simonides,[66] not to mention the lives of the itinerant sophists, we may say that the unstated implication of Xenophon's Socrates is that if one lives as a traveling stranger, one becomes all the more compelled to seek protection from, and therefore to court and to serve, some among the ruling powers in each city or territory in which one sojourns (as, indeed, the historical Aristippus wound up doing—courting the tyrant Dionysius; Diogenes Laertius 2.65–66).

What is most interesting, however, is that in the process of thus admonishing Aristippus, Socrates points out key ways that citizens who are free—not in Aristippus's sense, but as active participants in patriotic republican politics—mobilize and unite in forging defenses against being dominated and suffering injustice (2.1.14–15). Here, for the first time in this conversation with Aristippus, Socrates describes politics in terms of collective self-government, civic friendship, fatherlands and patriotism, the rule of and by laws preventing injustice—though, to be sure, all this as grounded in, and for the sake of, an only partially successful mutual defense. Still, Socrates here speaks the language of citizens who understand and express themselves as seeking not domination or empire, but civic freedom.

But in the next breath Socrates adds a long section on the harsh slavery that is essential for enabling citizens to have the leisure necessary for their extensive participation in self-government and collective self-defense (2.1.15–16; see also 3.10.1–2). The primary reason for Socrates's almost lurid talk here about slavery, in its discipline of violent punishment, is to bring home more vividly how politically naive and inconsistent Aristippus is (XS 34): Aristippus has spoken in such a way as to reveal that his whole life, and its enjoyment of pleasure, depend on his owning and being able to exploit slaves (2.1.9, 17)—without his ever having appreciated, apparently, how totally the success of this exploitation is dependent on the support of the citizenries and laws of the (slave) political communities he wanders through (Nichols 1979, 132). What is worse, and what Socrates now exposes in its nakedness, is Aristippus's failing to realize that he too, as a stateless person, may easily be enslaved, and, despite his luxurious past life, whipped into shape as an efficiently exploited slave worker. Socrates makes it clear that the republican practices and laws of slavery by no means exclude the violent enslavement of a noncitizen, be he ever so spiritually independent as Aristippus, and however much he considers himself "*deserving* neither to rule nor to be ruled nor to court voluntarily the rulers" (2.1.12). Socrates thus implicitly brings to light the underbelly of participatory civic freedom: republican citizenries, however modest their claims to empire, owe their freedom under law and their claimed justice, as collectively defensive, to a basis in harshly exploitative collective domination of nonmembers, regardless of the latters' qualities.[67] A defensive-minded republican citizenry can certainly mitigate, among its members, but does not escape, the iron law of human society that dictates only two alternatives (with varying degrees): being among the rulers who dominate, or among the ruled who are dominated.

## Why the Active Political Life Is the Good Life

Aristippus refuses to enter into the self-critical discussion and reflection to whose vestibule Socrates has led him. Instead of attempting to defend further (or to begin to modify) his own life plan, he mounts a counteroffensive. Addressing Socrates by name, he asks how the painful laboriousness and risk of the education to "the kingly art, which you seem to me to believe to be happiness," differs from violent compulsion by others—except that, being self-chosen, this shows stupidity (2.1.17).

Socrates counters by asking Aristippus (addressing him by name—2.1.18) if he does not agree that he who voluntarily endures hunger and thirst is able to eat and to drink when he wills (Socrates characteristically continues to refrain from defending self-control as a virtue or an end in itself). Then Socrates introduces a new consideration (2.1.18–19). He declares that one who is voluntarily suffering hardship delights in thinking[68] on his good *hope* for *future, consequent,* prize acquisitions—as is illustrated by the hopeful hunting of prey. This example of hunting would seem to suggest that the type of hardship Socrates has in mind is a pain not unalloyed with a certain pleasure, found in meeting the challenges involved. But Socrates at once admits, apologetically—and thus draws attention to—the lack of dignity of this example of hunting;[69] he rushes to list more worthy prizes for which serious gentlemen toil, beginning with the acquisition of good friends.[70] Socrates asks Aristippus whether he doesn't agree that serious gentlemen toil in order to become able to handle enemies, and, beyond that, to become powerful in body and soul so as to manage nobly their own households and do good to friends and fatherland (*patris*). "How can one not think," Socrates asks, that they "both toil pleasantly with a view to such things and live delightfully, admiring themselves and being praised and envied by the rest?" Prior to this, Socrates's argument for the self-controlled political life has focused mainly on somewhat dark or defensively necessitated aspects. Now he has stressed more positive dimensions. Even in the preliminary toil necessary for acquiring the capacity to rule there is already some pleasure, especially because of the pleasing hope for the rich gratification that is eventually found in using one's spiritual and physical powers not only to master enemies but to generously help those one cares for—friends and family and sharers in a fatherland—reaping praise and envy, and experiencing self-admiration, in the process. (We have to note that these gratifying activities do not require a republican form of rule, and are compatible with "the kingly art" which Aristippus presumes Socrates has in mind, in arguing for the political life of ruling. Consider *the Education of Cyrus* as a whole.)

Despite having been addressed by name with these questions, Aristippus remains silent; he refuses to agree. He has spoken his last word, and will remain strikingly silent even when addressed at the end of this episode (Richter 1893, 88).

But Socrates is by no means finished with articulating the full case for the self-controlled political life and its animating hopes. Transitioning to a quasi-oratorical monologue (2.1.20), Socrates next declares, appealing to the authority of experts in gymnastic, that the easy and ready pleasures are not sufficient to effect good condition for the body, and—he affirms on the basis of his own expertise and life experience—are not sufficient "to bring about in the soul any scientific knowing worth mention"; whereas—he declares on the authority of "good men (*andres*)"—"the cares exercised through endurance accomplish the gentlemanly deeds." This sinuous formulation quietly but incisively prompts the following questions: What is the relation between, and the relative ranking of, (1) the goal consisting in "the gentlemanly deeds," and (2) the (Socratic) goal consisting in "scientific knowing in the soul"? If or since these two goals are distinct, and require selection of either one or the other of them as having priority in a life plan, what is the basis of the prioritizing? And how does each of the two distinct goals become modified, in its meaning for one's life plan, when it becomes subordinated to the other? How does self-mastery, over physical appetites and money, differ, depending on which of the two goals is given priority in one's life (cf. XS 38)?

In the rest of his monologue Socrates quotes, and in effect asks his audience to contemplate the coherence of, three famous writings that articulate varying versions of the case for the life devoted to gentlemanly and heroic deeds (the quotations are silent about scientific knowledge, or about the joyfully virtuous activity of studying great old books with friends, though of course by having Socrates quote famous writings Xenophon indirectly reminds us of that virtuous Socratic activity: recall 1.6.14).

The first quotation, initially setting the tone, is from the venerable Hesiod, who testifies in his *Theogony* that he was miraculously transformed from a lowly, ignorant shepherd into a mellifluous and wise poet by the Muses, who revealed themselves to him in a dramatic epiphany. The second, briefest, and central quotation is from the fountainhead of comic drama, Epicharmus of Cos.[71] The third and most eloquent and elaborate of the quotations is from "Prodicus the wise" (as Xenophon's Socrates likes to call him: see also *Symposium* 4.62), a prominent sophist[72] contemporary with Socrates.

Through the quotations from this triumvirate of authorities, there floods into the discussion a massive consideration on the side of the life dedicated to gentlemanly deeds that has not previously been mentioned by Socrates when speaking to Aristippus in his own name (XS 35b–36t). We now hear of providential divinity, holding out the promise of rewards and punishments deserved in proportion to how each of us deals with the requisite sacrifices, sweaty toils, and deprivations that divinity (Hesiod stresses) has assigned to the life of gentlemanly action—the life that divinity commands us to pursue (the life to which, throughout his *Works and Days*, Hesiod is calling upon his cheating brother to return).

The quotation from Hesiod teaches, even more emphatically than does Socrates, that the practice of self-restrained, toilsome endurance does not itself constitute virtue, let alone happiness. For the poet teaches that the life of virtue, once attained, is "easy." It is only the *ascent to* that life which is "hard"; and this is the case, in substantial part at least, because of "sweaty" obstacles placed by "the immortal gods." (To understand the full poetic teaching that underlies this rather cryptic characterization of virtue, we would need of course to follow Xenophon's prompt and to study the *Works and Days*, which was doubtless one of the books of the wise men of old in whose study Socrates led his close friends.)

A cruder, not to say blasphemous, teaching is expressed in the line quoted from the comic poet Epicharmus (or as is likely, from a character in one of his comedies): "The gods sell us all good things at the price of our labors"—adding that the gods punish attempts to elude this market relationship: "Oh rogue! Don't desire the soft things, lest you get the hard!" Epicharmus (as presented by Socrates) seems not to agree with Hesiod about the possibility of eventually ascending, through toil and endurance, to a life of easy virtue: the comic poet implies that our life is one of unceasing, if recompensed, toil for and under ruling divinity. Does this disagreement between Socrates's poetic authorities reflect a basic tension, even a summons to decision, within the case for virtue that Socrates is presenting in this long section?

## HERACLES'S CHOICE

What Socrates dwells on, however, is his toned-down[73] reproduction of an allegorical parable from the wise Prodicus depicting "the education by Virtue of Heracles" (the hero-demigod glorious for his divinely ordained, terribly trying "labors"[74]).

The tale begins in a disconcerting way. When Heracles had reached the age when young Greeks are conventionally released from their educators, and are regarded as having "become self-governing" (BD ad loc.), the future hero went off by himself, "to ponder in perplexity"[75] whether he should live the life of virtue—or, instead, the life of vice! Prodicus-Socrates teach that a noble youth's exalted and even divine parentage, fine nature (*phusin*), and traditional education (*paideia*; see OT chap. 5, n. 33)—all stressed by Virtue in beginning Her address to Heracles (2.1.27)—do not at all leave an extraordinary lad's heart and mind settled as regards the question of whether he should lead a moral or an immoral life. There is required an additional education, effected through an encounter with the personifications of Virtue and of Vice, each making its case in debate.

When this encounter is responsibly portrayed, as by the sophist Prodicus, mediated and modulated by Socrates, the choice, for any manly and ambitious youth, would seem to be pretty much foreordained from the outset. For Vice expresses, by Her very appearance, a life totally given over to soft, sensual, and especially sexual pleasure, proffered by a voluptuous femininity that is absurdly given to meretricious vanity.[76] In Her speech, Vice promises Heracles an effeminate life—"to begin with, without thought about war or action"; a life licensed to support its sensuality by profiting from every possible source and by all possible means (2.1.23–25). Vice in no way suggests a life of warrior and political contests leading to victorious tyrannical domination, imperial rule, and consequent fame. No wonder Heracles does not at first recognize this allegorical Vice, at least in Socrates's version of the story:[77] after seeing and hearing from Vice personified, Heracles asks for Her name. She evidently does not embody the vice whose temptations Heracles has been pondering in his perplexity.[78] This is not to deny that in asking for Her name Heracles betrays interest in Her. Sensual vice is a powerful draw for even the manliest of men.[79] But however sensually alluring She may at first appear, the "Vice" that is here allegorized as the rival to Virtue does not incarnate the most powerful temptations that lure manly, ambitious youths (such as Alcibiades or Critias—or Xenophon?): *political* vice, tyranny or injustice on a grand scale, is not allowed to present itself in this scenario.[80] The dice are thus so loaded, in favor of the life of political virtue, that demanding listeners with intense political ambition (such as Xenophon) are prodded to think for themselves how and to what extent the case made here by Virtue disposes of the much more serious temptations to *political* crime and corruption. Xenophon's presentation of the attractions and the repugnance of such vice is his *Hiero, Or One Skilled in the Tyrannical Art.*[81]

Vice responds to Heracles's request for her name by saying that She is called "Happiness" by Her friends, while it is those who hate Her who have "bad-mouthed" Her as "Vice" (no man calls Her "Misery"—XS 36). As soon as Socrates has had "Happiness" (as She likes to be called) thus admit Her infamy, Socrates has Virtue alertly intervene, to remind Heracles of his glorious parentage, his nature, and his education, and to express Her hope that the lad will become "a very good doer of noble and august deeds," thereby bringing greatly increased honor, as well as distinction for good things (2.1.27). Heracles does not need to ask Virtue for Her name; She, at any rate, is immediately recognizable to him.

## Virtue's Call to Self-Transcendence

But the honor, and the distinction for good things, for which Virtue hopes, is *Her own;* it is *not* that of Heracles. What Virtue calls to, at the outset, is a life inspired by devotion to the greater glory of Virtue, Who is encountered or envisioned in Her pure beauty and grace—of moderation (*sophrosunē*), of reverent modesty (*aidōs*), and of generous freedom or liberality in accord with nature (*eleutheria phusei*). Virtue demands of the best men self-transcendence, even or especially as regards their concern for their *own* honor and distinction. Virtue does not, however, issue this call to self-transcendence in the name of or for the sake of the gods, or *their* honor. Initially, Virtue stands forth as the sole, resplendent end or purpose of human existence—though not as a or the perfect good in itself, since Virtue seeks and needs human service to achieve Her full glory.[82]

## Virtue's Turn to the Gods

Of course, Virtue does *turn*, emphatically, to the providential gods,[83] and to what She stresses is a "truthful" account of the way that *they* have disposed "the beings" (*ta onta*; 2.1.27–28; was there something less than truthful in Virtue's prelude?). Virtue initiates this turn to the divinities by declaring that She will not deceive Heracles with preludes about pleasure (does She betray an uneasy awareness that some of Her advocates do practice such deception?). Vice, whose speech was one long prelude to pleasure, and Who is named Happiness by Her friends, is silent on the gods,[84] and ignores their disposition of the beings. Virtue for Her part did not mention happiness in Her "prelude" about Her "hope." Does Virtue, as here presented, turn to the gods, and subordinate Herself to their disposition of the beings, as an expression of the fact that She by Herself cannot provide what is requisite in order to make the virtuous life—of toilsome and dangerous transcendence of both enjoyment and self-glorification—fully choice-worthy, as happy, for humans?

Certainly the divine ordering of the beings, as Virtue proceeds to explain it, puts the virtuous life in a framework that is quite different from the initial one. For in Her prelude Virtue said that She "hopes" that Heracles will become a very good doer of noble and august things, greatly enhancing Her glory. Now, however, Virtue teaches (2.1.28), going beyond Hesiod and Epicharmus, that it is the gods who give "the beings that are *good and* noble," including one's personal glory—and give none to humans without toil and trouble, such that humans have to wish that the gods be gracious, and, to that end, humans must serve the gods in order to gain the good and noble things. What's more—Virtue goes on to explain—the gods have ordered the beings so that this sort of *quid pro quo* pervades human existence, defining what is "wished, desired, claimed as deserved": "If you wish to be cherished by friends, then the friends are to be done good; if you desire to be honored by some city, then the city needs to be benefited; if you would claim to deserve being admired for virtue by all Greece, then an attempt must be made to benefit Greece"—and so on, through succeeding at farming and at getting wealthy through cattle,[85] and, by means of war, achieving imperial "growth" while helping friends and harming enemies, as well as gaining physical power. (Ironically but revealingly, Xenophon thus contrives to have Virtue, in explaining the divine ordering of the beings, advert obliquely to the temptations to political injustice that are most likely to corrupt an ambitious youth like Heracles; Virtue is surprisingly silent on law, lawfulness, and justice: contrast the debate between political virtue and political vice as Aristotle articulates it in *Politics*, bk. 7, chap. 3).

## Vice Strikes

Socrates shifts to Prodicus the responsibility for having shrewd Vice jump in at this point, to take advantage of what Virtue has said.[86] Vice in effect asks Heracles if he does not understand that "this woman here" has now presented the practice of virtue as a "hard and long path" to "enjoyments" that are *extrinsic consequences* of the *intrinsically un*enjoyable cares and risks and toils that are the acts of virtue. In contrast, Vice proclaims, "I will lead you on an easy and short path to happiness!" (2.1.29). Vice thus concedes that the manly goals Virtue has proposed are indeed enjoyable, once they are attained; but Vice in effect denies that these are the enjoyments that constitute happiness,[87] especially given the enormously toilsome and care-ridden and dangerous virtues required for their achievement. (Vice continues to ignore the gods and their ordering of the beings.)

## Virtue Indignant

Virtue's response is remarkable (2.1.30). She loses Her temper. The advocate of self-control is presented as being unable to control Her indignation. The same name-calling in which Socrates had earlier indulged, in mock fury, at Xenophon, Virtue (who is here for the first time named such[88]) now employs in earnest rage at Vice: "Oh wretch (*O tlēmon*)! What good do you have?! Or what pleasure do you know, being unwilling to undertake any action for the sake of these things?!"[89]

Virtue's anger seems to betray Her frustrated sense that there is some truth, or at least plausibility, in Vice's characterization of the virtuous life (as ordered by the gods). At any rate Virtue, having become an advocate of the ordering of the beings by the gods, does not attempt to repair, in dignity, to Her magnificently austere and self-sufficient opening statement and self-presentation. She is now silent on the noble and august. In Her anger,

Virtue attacks Vice on the grounds of the latter's lack of the good, *and* lack of *pleasure*—thus conceding that a crucial criterion of a choice-worthy life is its acquiring and enjoying, for oneself, the good and especially the pleasant.[90]

Virtue does not stop here. She proceeds to the tendentious argument that Vice, or the life to which Vice beckons, lacks experience of real *carnal* pleasure, because Vice indulges in everything before having strong desire—as evidenced in Vice's dining, on "contrived" gourmet meals; in Her drinking, of expensive wines and ice-chilled potations in summer; in Her sleeping, on soft beds; and especially in Her sexual pleasures, since Vice engages "by compulsion, prior to need, contriving everything, and using men like women"—"spending the night in hubristic insolence, and the most useful part of the day asleep!" (2.1.30).

## Virtue Recovers Her Footing

But just as we, in astonishment (and Vice, in satisfaction), may think that Virtue has conceded the need to make Her case by claiming to provide greater carnal pleasures, and especially better sex, than Vice, Virtue pulls up out of Her angry tailspin, and ascends to a higher level, of spiritual pleasures, where she finds a surer footing. Virtue confronts Vice with the fact that although Vice is admittedly "immortal," you have been "cast out by gods, and are dishonored by good human beings"—with the consequence (Virtue asserts) that you "do not hear the most pleasant of all sounds, praise of oneself." Since Prodicus or Socrates does not allow us to hear any rejoinder from Vice, we do not hear Her reiterate that She is called "Happiness" by Her "friends" (Smith ad 2.1.32); if She were allowed to speak here, would Vice not be likely to add that, in Her view, it is *Her* friends who are the "good human beings"? In a moment, Virtue Herself will refer to "the troop of worshippers" of Vice (*tou sou thiasou*, 2.1.31).[91]

Virtue spotlights in addition, however, a more incontrovertible deficiency in the life of Vice: "You do not see the most pleasant of all sights": for "you never see any noble deed of your own" (2.1.31).[92] Virtue returns to the noble, now attended by the greatest visual pleasure—which is not, to be sure, the self-transcending pleasure of contemplating Virtue Herself, in Her glory, but rather the pleasure of contemplating one's *own* noble deeds. The human life of virtue is not without this very great, distinct pleasure of its own (though this is not to concede that this *pleasure* is the *chief motive* of the virtuous life in its noble actions).

If Vice were allowed a hearing, we might suspect that, given Her previous intervention, She might question whether these "noble" deeds are truly good, or choice-worthy, except as *intrinsically* unpleasant, and therefore unattractive, *means*—to good *extrinsic* consequences, the hope for which is the source of the pleasure taken in contemplating the otherwise ugly deeds. If Virtue could keep Her temper in the face of such blasphemy, She would doubtless dismiss this as patently contrary to what all decent humans experience in witnessing noble deeds.

Still, Virtue certainly recognizes the importance of consequences: She proceeds to stress the bad consequences of following Vice, and by implication, the good consequences of following Herself. Virtue asks, anaphorically and rhetorically: Who would trust what Vice says? Who would supply Her when She was in need? Who would join Her troop of worshippers? For (Virtue asserts) the latter are physically weak as youths, lack intelligence when elderly, and, despite living their youthful prime in comfort without toil (Virtue concedes), they pass their old age in toil and discomfort, ashamed of what they have done and weighed down by what they are doing. Conceding that the followers of Vice "run through pleasures in youth," Virtue insists that they "lay up harshness for old age" (2.1.31).

In saying this, Virtue ignores Vice's earlier promise that She will license Her follower Heracles to engage in successful because unscrupulous profit making, thus avoiding financial need (recall 2.1.27). Yet the fact remains that Virtue has spotlighted the insuperable vulnerability and neediness that pervade our mortal human condition. Contemplation of old age, presaging the end that awaits us all, is not something that Vice encourages, to say the least.

## Virtue's Decisive Superiority

The full significance of Virtue's drawing attention to mortality becomes manifest in her peroration, with which she evidently turns to address Heracles again.[93] She first proclaims: "I am in close association with gods, and I am in close association with good humans. Without me there does not come into being a noble deed whether divine or human. I am honored, beyond all, both by gods and by humans whose honoring is fit" (2.1.32). Virtue here re-ascends to a height, now of Her supreme honor from the gods. Yet Virtue, in Her ambiguity, proceeds to give as reason for (*gar*) this honor the manifold *utility* of the assistance She gives humans, in meeting their needs—in the crafts, in masters' guarding of their households, in slaves' work within the households, in toils of peacetime, as well as in deeds of war, and, last but not least, in friendship. In addition, Virtue insists once again that it is *Her* friends who enjoy "trouble-free" the *carnal* pleasures, of food and drink, and of better sleep (She ceases to mention sex). Yet Her devotees' enjoyments go together with their capacity to endure sleeplessness, when it is required, in order to do "what ought to be done." And it is their enjoyment of honor for having endured thus, for having done their duty, however unpleasant, that Virtue stresses above all[94]—explaining that Her adherents take pleasure in remembering their past deeds as well as in doing their present deeds since, through Her, they are not only admired by human friends and honored by their fatherlands, but they become "friends of the gods." This has the consequence that "when they arrive at their fated end, they do not lie forgotten without honor, but they flourish, being remembered in song for all time," and thus "acquire the most blessed happiness."[95]

Here is Virtue's "golden trump":[96] by Her supremely honored association with divinity She offers Heracles, in return for his heroic labors and his honoring of Her, the consequently deserved award of wings for the flight into immortality—and the austerity of the promised immortality very much enhances its plausibility.[97] It is thus that sensual Vice is definitively refuted, Her claim to offer happiness proven hollow; She tries to ignore humanity's deepest erotic longing and hope; and insofar as She might be forced to confront that longing and hope, She can fall back only on ultimately pathetic escapism—"Let us eat and drink, for tomorrow we shall die" (Is. 22:13; Eccl. 8:15).

## Heroic and Socratic Virtue

As we contemplate this victory of heroic Virtue, we cannot but look back, in comparison, to the glimpses that Xenophon has given us of Socratic virtue in peak action: Socrates's ceaseless pressing of the "What is . . ." questions, his conversing about nature in a manner different from that of most others, and his joyful study, together with friends, of great old books. The life given over to this kind of (unheroic) virtue exhibits no core ambiguities or waverings. Its pleasure and its goodness, in satisfying the mind's needs, are inherent, and not claimed or bestowed as deserved. We recall that Xenophon judged this life and virtue "blessed." At the end, Xenophon will opine that Socrates was "the happiest man" (anēr eudaimonestatos, 4.8.11; see BD ad loc.). But he does not claim that Socrates "acquired the most blessed happiness." He does not show that the blessed Socratic life and virtue satisfy the human soul's profound longing, and inextirpable natural need, for a share in immortality. Socratic virtue lives always unflinchingly bearing in mind, and understanding ever more fully, the melancholy significance of the truth that "from the moment I came into being I was by nature condemned to death" (Apology 27). Paradoxically, a major component of the supreme good and virtue of the Socratic life is this specific understanding; this is not the least of the reasons why Socrates does not identify the good, or wisdom, with the pleasant, though he lives in serenity.[98] Xenophon prods us to ask: What exactly is the knowledge, of the truth about "the beings," that provides the solid ground for Socrates's confident choice of his kind of virtue, over the heroic Virtue, with Her promise and hope, that was chosen by Heracles?

## CHAPTER FOUR

# How Socrates Benefited in Regard
# to Family and Friends

From the heights of the "grand words" describing Virtue's defeat of Vice, we are plunged down into a dialogue between Socrates and his eldest son, Lamprocles, aimed at repairing the lad's infuriated estrangement from his mother. What didactic purpose dictates this roller-coaster drop?[1] Ought we not reasonably to expect that the allegory of Virtue establishing Her predominance in the soul of the hero Heracles might be followed by an account of Socrates's own heroic military services? And, if or since friendship is to be the next theme, why not start with Socrates's courageous saving of his friends' lives in battle?[2] But, except for one very brief allusion (4.4.1), Xenophon will *never*, in any of his works, refer to Socrates's military service or experience (XSD 87–89). Could our puckish author be suggesting that Socrates's closest approach to the heroic labors of Heracles was his endurance of his tempestuous wife?[3]

In trying to figure out how Socrates's conversation with his son fits into or reveals the track upon which Xenophon is conducting us, our first thought is naturally the pattern that we have observed unfolding—alternating sections, first on self-mastery and then on piety; and, given that the immediately preceding speech of Virtue culminated the third of the segments on self-mastery, and given further that Socrates now emphasizes to his son the close connection between filial duty and piety, we are first inclined to see in this paternal conversation yet another exhibition of Socrates's beneficial piety. But this segment is not followed by another that exhibits, yet again, Socrates's beneficial self-mastery. The hitherto prevailing pattern ceases. Instead, this conversation in which Socrates tries to start patching things up between his wife and their son is followed by a conversation in which Socrates attempts to start repairing the angry estrangement of two brothers. Then there follows a series of presentations showing Socrates's concern for and teaching about the fraught nature of friendship (*philia*)—a term and a relationship that, for the Greeks, applies not least to family relations.[4] So we may more fully and accurately characterize this report of the conversation of Socrates with his son as a transitional overlap. Here Xenophon loosens the tether by which he has hitherto tied the second part of his *Recollections* closely to the first part. Xenophon now segues into a second division of the second part, a division whose theme is Socrates's beneficial wrestling with, and teaching on, the problematic of *philia*—first familial, and then extrafamilial (H.-R. Breitenbach 1967, cols. 1778 and 1797).

## ATTENDING TO HIS SON AND WIFE

Through the previous conversation, with Aristippus, Xenophon dispelled any false impression the reader might have received from the account of Socrates's blissful study of books in private with friends that this implied that the philosopher disparaged the political life; now, Xenophon dispels suspicion that Socrates was unalive to paternal duties.

Granted, this is the one and only episode in which Xenophon ever depicts Socrates concerned with managing his family and household. And by the abruptness of his turn to the father-son colloquium, Xenophon omits any claim to have been present at, or to have heard from Socrates or Lamprocles a report of, this conversation. Father and son evidently spoke in private—as is quite natural; but this provokes the question, How did Xenophon come to be able to repeat the conversation verbatim? Doesn't our author quietly indicate that this familial conversation (along with the next—cf. XS 39) is to a special degree his own invention? Certainly Xenophon has Socrates begin the dialogue in a rather improbable way.

For Xenophon does not have Socrates address at first his exasperated son's problems with his mother. Instead, Xenophon has Socrates begin by evoking from his son abhorrence at the "pure injustice" of ingratitude *in general*; then we hear Socrates decrying ingratitude above all when it is exhibited by children toward parents—for "who (he asked) would we find receiving from anyone greater benefactions than children receive from their parents?" (2.2.3). And this is the launching pad for an eloquent reminder by Socrates to his son of the great goods and concern that "we fathers" and "our" wives bestow on "our children." "The man," Socrates says, "supports his partner in child-making" and "provides in advance, to the maximum that he is able, everything he thinks will benefit the future children in life"; much more extensive are the benefactions on the part of "the woman," once she has conceived; and "when the children seem to be capable of learning something,

the parents themselves teach whatever things they know that are good for
living, and they spend money to send the children for instruction in whatever things they think someone else is more capable of teaching" (2.2.4–6).

To this general sermon Lamprocles replies by saying, in effect, that none
of this bears on the present situation, since "even if *she* has done all this, *and*
much else besides, no one would be capable of tolerating *her* harshness!"[5]
One wonders why the adept Socrates should think that such an expansive
homily would be effective in these particular circumstances; in fact, one
may well wonder whether this Socratic speech would not be, for Lamprocles,
an irritating reminder of what are likely to have been his mother's insulting
and unremitting complaints of his ingratitude toward her. No wonder some
readers[6] have concluded that Xenophon is exploiting this chapter "apologetically" (and, we would add, rather wryly): taking the opportunity to put into
Socrates's mouth an edifying, but uncharacteristic, declamation on devoted
paternal as well as maternal parenting.

This is not to detract from the importance of the fact that Xenophon
begins the series of his Socrates's disquisitions about *philia* by bringing to
the fore that form of *philia*—parental and especially maternal love—that
is most indisputably and universally understood to be self-sacrificial, and
therefore deserving of gratitude and honor in return.[7] In addition, and in
the first place, Xenophon has Socrates highlight the broader, universally
agreed-upon moral duty of grateful proportionate reciprocity. Xenophon vividly reminds that neither loving benefaction (and most emphatically parental benefaction) nor gratitude can be conceived or experienced as primarily
in the interest of the agent, and that any attempt to so reduce love and
gratitude would be a distortion of the phenomena: our recognition that the
benefactions have *not* been chiefly for the sake of the self-interest of our
benefactors is the essential basis for our conception that the gratitude we
feel is *deserved* by those to whom we feel grateful. But Xenophon goes further. He indicates a variation in the understanding of the justice of gratitude. For he has Socrates ask his son whether it is not the case that it is
opined that while ingratitude to friends is unjust, ingratitude to enemies
is just, even as it is just to enslave enemies, but unjust to enslave friends.
The high-minded young Lamprocles agrees, but adds: "And in my opinion,
it is unjust to fail to try to enact reciprocal gratitude to anyone, friend or
enemy, from whom one has received a benefit." To which Socrates responds
with a question: "Then, if this holds, in this way, would ingratitude be a
*pure* injustice?" When Lamprocles agrees, Socrates asks another question,
elaborating the implications, to which Lamprocles again agrees (2.2.2–3).
By "pure" (*eilikrinēs*), Socrates and Lamprocles evidently mean, unalloyed

by personal considerations: proportionate gratitude is *always* a demand of justice, even if the benefactor hates and is a threat to you, even if he is seeking (justly) your enslavement, and is an object of your hatred and of your threats, a target for (just) enslavement by you; the duty is diminished neither by consequences for your well-being nor by your feelings for the benefactor. Gratitude as a dimension of justice in its "purity" is, we may say, *categorically* imperative.

But of course the homily on deserved gratitude, especially to parents, takes up only the first half of the dialogue. Socrates is finally forced, by his son's angry insistence on the singular intolerability of his mother (in relation to his mother, Lamprocles forgets his high-minded principle), to descend from moralizing generalities to address the specific problems within the (peculiar) Socratic household. Socrates starts by pointing out to Lamprocles that his mother does him no physical harm. But this only provokes from the youth a cursing expostulation that it is her verbal insults that so deeply wound his spirit. To this, Socrates suggests that his son try to conceive his mother's tirades as similar to those one sees actors emitting on stage: Socrates gets his son to agree emphatically that his mother does not truly intend to wound his spirit; in fact, Socrates then adds, she wishes him well, more than does anyone else; her raging is not therefore an expression of her deepest intention, and her truest concern, for her son. She is not really *herself*, she has in a deep if temporary sense forgotten herself, when she loses her temper, be that ever so often. Not only does she nurse the boy when he is sick, not only does she try to see that he lacks nothing, but— Socrates stresses—she prays to the gods, and fulfills burdensome vows that she makes to the gods, in order to gain (as thereby deserved) "many good things" for her son (2.2.7–10).

We thus see that through his wife and to a lesser extent his son, the Socratic household and family life are steeped in traditional piety, which meets here with Socrates's unqualified endorsement.[8] Presumably Socrates's wife and son are aware of his widely bruited religious eccentricities; but Socrates has no more sought to reform his son's and his wife's traditionally pious beliefs than he has tried to reform the city's. Xenophon's Socrates aims at no rationalizing general "enlightenment" of society at large, or even of his own family; he is in no way a prophet, armed or unarmed; he is as far as can be from Nietzsche's philosopher-lawgivers. Socratic rationalism and the Socratic way of life as presented by Xenophon are, to an even greater degree than in Plato's presentation, uncontaminated by subphilosophic ambitions and hopes. In this crucial respect, Xenophon's Socratic philosophizing in no way foreshadows modern rationalism.

After having reminded Lamprocles of his mother's underlying goodwill, and of her past benefits and prayers and laborious vows, and of the enormous moral and pious debt of gratitude she is therefore deservedly owed, Socrates adds prudential considerations. He turns his son's attention to the youth's future welfare: he reminds him of his need for assistance and goodwill from others, and hence of his need to serve, to satisfy, and even to obey many others. All of this the son readily grants. Socrates then protests: "But so you are prepared to care about these, while you do *not* think you need to serve your mother, who is the one who most of all loves you?!"

But of course the mother's very love for her son makes unlikely her ever ceasing to help him, and hence diminishes her son's needing to serve her. Lamprocles evidently feels strongly that his mother's failure to show him the respect that he deserves, as her faithful son, outweighs her moral right to (otherwise deserved) gratitude from him. So Socrates immediately adds to the scales a very substantial counterbalance in terms of the son's future dignity or respect, as well as his future benefit: Socrates reminds Lamprocles that while the city's legal system overlooks other forms of ingratitude, it punishes with public disgrace those whom it perceives failing to serve their parents—on the grounds that such ingratitude is impiety, which will bring down the wrath of the gods. Here, for the first time in the *Memorabilia*, Socrates invokes Zeus in an oath (2.2.13). We may reasonably surmise that Xenophon means us to understand that Lamprocles took this oath as an expression of the solemnity of his father's admonitions. But we may with equal reason surmise that Xenophon intends us, the audience of this vignette, to take the oath as signaling a different spirit.[9]

"Child," Socrates admonishes, "if you are sensible, you will beg the gods to be forgiving if you have in any way neglected your mother," and "as regards humans, you'll watch out lest, perceiving you to be one who neglects his parents, they all hold you in disgrace, and you find yourself bereft of friends": for "no one," god or human, "if they conceive you to be ungrateful toward your parents, would believe that they'll receive gratitude from you if they do you good" (2.2.11–14).

Thus, in trying to manage his own household and family, Socrates relies, like any normal patriarchal gentleman, finally on the city's law and piety and standards of reputation, and on every citizen's need for his fellows and their gratitude—as well as on lawful piety's menaces of sanctions, human and divine. Even for a Socratic household, the city and its laws and retributive gods are needed to regulate and to restrain family relations, on account not least of conflicts that inevitably arise out of relatives' perfervid moral claims and counterclaims upon one another, on grounds of what they believe they deserve.

The conversation between Socrates and his son bespeaks a cordial relationship. Socrates's arguments seem to make a definite impression (Lamprocles's last four responses are calm assents). One may infer that, at the end of this conversation, there is a fair prospect of the lad's being persuaded to repress his anger and to try, at least, to follow his father's wishes as regards his mother.[10] But is she likely to change her harridan ways? Xenophon leaves the upshot unreported. The problem that both father and son confront in their wife and mother would seem to be an extreme version of the problem Socrates wrestles with in his son: moral indignation at perceived denial of the respect which is believed owed, as a matter of rightful desert, in return for loving, selfless devotion. With his son, Socrates sees some prospect of dampening this destructively reactive moral passion through arousing constructive, unimpassioned, but by no means undignified, prudential calculation of one's true future needs and concerns.

What is strikingly missing from Socrates's deportment as father and husband is the issuance of any authoritative command, or any threat of personal force. This deficient patriarchy is more pronounced in Socrates's pliant attitude toward his wife. Socrates does not at all dispute his son's characterization of the terrible ways that his mother reviles and shames him. But Socrates does not offer, and his son shows no sign of expecting, any effort to compel or to command or even to try to persuade "Mrs. Socrates" to alter her termagant ways (XS 41–42). Socrates does not appear to be willing or able to *rule* his household (cf. OT 211–13). Though he "in speeches dealt as he wished with all who conversed with him," he was pretty powerless with those, starting with his wife, whose passions made them refuse to listen to him (Strauss 1989, 145–46).

## ATTEMPTING TO RECONCILE FEUDING BROTHERS

In witnessing the second of Socrates's exercises in what we may call family therapy, we ascend: from his attempt to repair damage done by his tumultuous wife's hectoring, to his effort at repairing broken relations between a pair of gentlemanly brothers, Chairephon and Chairecrates. These two were listed back at 1.2.48 as among seven examples of Socrates's "associates" (*homilētai*; but here they are demoted to "acquaintances"—*gnōrimō*) who, in contrast to Critias and Alcibiades and their ilk, "kept company with him, not in order to become assembly or courtroom orators, but in order that, by becoming gentlemen, they might be able to make use in a noble fashion of household and household slaves and relatives and friends and city and citizens"—and who never did, nor were accused of, anything bad. Yet this aspiration to gentlemanliness that the brothers shared did not prevent a serious falling out. The heart of the reason seems to be indicated in Chairecrates's outburst here against his brother: "This, Socrates, is why he *deserves* my hatred—that he is able to be pleasing to *others*, but to *me*, wherever he is present, everywhere, in deed and in word, he is a pain rather than a benefit!" (2.3.6). And Socrates subsequently indicates that he knows that Chairephon—given how intently he "loves honor" (2.3.16)—is even less disposed to reciprocal brotherly friendship (2.3.14). As in the previous conversation, but now on a higher level, Xenophon points to the source of family rupture (even or especially among gentlemen) that consists in moral indignation at the failure of close relatives to give one another the respect and assistance that each one claims to *deserve*, as a consequence of his or her love (*philia*) and adherence to family right. Is there some connection between Xenophon's provoking the reader's meditation on the problematic of unreasonable human claims of deserving and Xenophon's previous presentation of the sublime peroration of Virtue?

In contrast to the depiction of the preceding father-son conversation, here Xenophon does not show Socrates leading off with a maladroit stress on the gratitude that his interlocutor owes to his alienated relative (which would be likely to exacerbate rather than to cool the fire of indignation in Chairecrates, who, like Lamprocles, is angrily certain that whatever debt he owes his kin is eclipsed by the indignity he suffers from that kin). Here, Xenophon has Socrates start out by ignoring the special moral ties (and claims) of brothers;[11] instead, Socrates immediately introduces prudential calculation, of a more shrewd sort than that into which Socrates eventually drew his own son. Socrates asks Chairecrates to view the value of brotherhood almost cold-bloodedly: first, in terms of a brother's superiority over wealth, in general utility; and then, specifically, in terms of a brother's usefulness as an ally for mutual protection of the private property of each, through a utilitarian "friendship"—like that among fellow citizens. Socrates points out that however emotionally distant and mutually envious citizens may be, they must stick together for mutual protection. Socrates does indeed adduce also the special bonds between brothers, of fraternal kinship and shared upbringing; but he adds this as something seen also in wild animals, and as valuable in strengthening and making more intimidating to outside competitors a fraternal defensive alliance (2.3.1–4).

This rhetorical strategy of Socrates is not without some initial success: Chairecrates concedes the utilitarian points, and their implication for action; he agrees further on the prudential wisdom of therefore enduring at least minor evils from a brother. But Chairecrates insists that Chairephon is a special case, in the simply *intolerable* degree of his harmfulness as a brother (2.3.5–6).

Socrates does not respond, as he did with his son, by trying to get his interlocutor to see his relative's truer goodwill underneath the hostility expressed—that would in this case not be credible (BD ad loc.). Socrates takes an altogether different tack, suggesting that Chairecrates may not be employing the "knowledgeable handling of a brother"—which is analogous, Socrates suggests, to the "knowledgeable" handling of a horse! When the somewhat puzzled Chairecrates shows that he thinks such "knowledgeable handling" consists of speaking and acting in a beneficial way *in response to the same* from one's brother, Socrates expresses wonder at such psychological naiveté. In effect Socrates says: to be "knowledgeable" in this regard means to look upon your alienated and troublesome brother as you would a fierce dog that you owned and that you could use profitably, if or once you tamed the creature. You should "disregard his anger," and "manipulate" him, with gifts (2.3.7–9). Socrates suggests to Chairecrates a rather cunning perspective that puts him on a manipulative level far superior to his brother: a vantage point from which Chairecrates can view himself as his intolerable brother's needed trainer (and owner). Socrates thus begins to try to induce in Chairecrates a calculative fraternal attitude that will be at once more mutually beneficial and less subject to wounded pride—because it will (initially at least) lead Chairecrates to respect his brother much, much less.

When Chairecrates in his gentlemanliness shows that he is bewildered by what Socrates is suggesting, Socrates softens somewhat his outré suggestion, by leading Chairecrates to reflect on what the latter already knows he needs to do in order to get a *non*brother to do him favors. It's not complicated: first you do for the fellow the favors that you will later want him to do for you. The art of these inducements of gratitude is what Socrates calls, with some irony, the "knowledge of love-charms for humans" (2.3.10–14).

But Chairecrates's conventional, gentlemanly self-respect—which goes hand in hand with his antagonistic respect for his brother as an equal—stands in the way of so radical a change in outlook: "You hesitate," Socrates observes, "to start, lest you find yourself in a shameful position, by doing good to your brother before he does?" Socrates tries to counter this conventional gentlemanly prejudice with another conventional gentlemanly prejudice: he reminds Chairecrates that custom holds praiseworthy anyone who takes the lead in hurting enemies and benefiting friends.

The problem with this Socratic gambit is obvious. Chairecrates now views Chairephon as an enemy!

So Socrates adds the flattering reflection that he *would* have spoken to Chairephon if *he* seemed more capable of taking the lead in benefiting; but that honor—the honor of being teachable by Socrates—Socrates says belongs to Chairecrates (2.3.14: Chairecrates does not observe the implication, namely, that Socrates has indicated that he would be quite ready to make Chairecrates the "victim" of the proposed psychological maneuver).

Chairecrates now expresses amazed puzzlement, at what has become Socrates's rather complex teaching, that veils manipulative psychological craftiness with conventional gentlemanly opinion: "The things you are saying are extraordinarily strange (*atopa*), Socrates!" What's more, they are "also not at all like you—in that you bid me, who is younger, to take the lead; this goes contrary to what is conventionally believed by all humans—which is, that the elder should lead, in every speech and deed." Evidently Socrates in his relations with Chairecrates has always before stuck closely to conventional gentlemanly moral opinion. And here again Socrates quickly finds a way to massage traditional custom so as to make it appear to support and indeed to enhance his "extraordinarily strange" innovation: "Isn't it conventionally believed, everywhere, that the younger, when he meets the elder, should make way on the road; and, when sitting, to stand up; and to honor with the soft couch; and to give way when speaking? Good fellow, don't hesitate (he said), but try to tame the man!"

Then Socrates adds yet another dimension of psychological caginess, focusing on distinctive proclivities of conventional gentlemen: Socrates teaches that whereas, to capture vile types, you actually have to give them something, you can best beguile gentlemen very cheaply—merely by using them in a friendly fashion—since they are such lovers of honors, and are so generous. In effect, Socrates submits, Chairecrates need not actually do or give all that much to his elder brother, in order to "tame" him, but need only make a big point of practicing, in very conspicuous ways, all the conventional marks of respect due to an elder brother (2.3.15–16).

Chairecrates still hesitates, his vanity worried: in effect, he asks how he will look to the public if he does such things, and then his brother fails to act better. Socrates responds by taking his psychological manipulation of Chairecrates to a new level: "What do you risk, except to display that *you* are noble and have brotherly love, and that *he* is base and undeserving of good treatment?" Our wily sage thus holds out to Chairecrates the prospect of an unprecedented public triumph over, and humiliation of, his infuriating brother; but then Socrates immediately switches tack, declaring that he thinks the likely outcome will be quite different: "I believe that when he perceives that you are calling him out to this competition, he will be intensely animated by love of victory with a view to *triumphing over you* in good treatment by word and deed" (2.3.17).

Socrates aims, we may say, to execute a kind of psychological judo-throw with the two gentlemanly brothers' proud, antagonistic passions: what is now a dead end of resentful reciprocal hurt and alienation can become a closely joined contest to outdo one another in mutual outward shows of respect—and, perhaps, eventually, gradually, this may evolve into a mutually beneficial and respectful, if still intensely competitive, brotherly partnership.

It is this ultimate goal, of a fraternal partnership, that Socrates in his closing words evokes, and to which he lends awesome religious support and adornment and inspiration (2.3.18–19). The nobly competitive, if manipulative, self-assertion that has been disclosed as the heart of Socrates's prescription for reconstructing a beneficial friendship between the estranged gentlemanly brothers is by itself incomplete. In order to support and to sustain the naturally fragile directness of human nature to brotherly love, there is needed, in addition, the supplement of an aspiration to a divinely intended and sanctioned partnership (see also *Education of Cyrus* 8.7.15 and context). But the gulf, between the brotherhood aspired to, and actual brotherhood, seems indicated by Socrates's account of the divine purpose; for, in his telling, divinity seems to intend that all brothers be sets of twins! Obviously, this divine purpose is very rarely realized in nature (cf. XS 43).

## SOCRATES ON THE VALUE OF EXTRAFAMILIAL FRIENDSHIP

The two episodes that have depicted Socrates attempting, through subtle psychotherapy, to repair broken relations of *philia* within families give way to a series of seven episodes showing Socrates promoting and analyzing and assisting friendship outside the family (the exception being the fourth and central episode). The disproportion in length of the treatments of extrafamilial versus pious,[12] familial *philia* reflects Socrates's distinctive "priorities"— whose abnormality[13] is immediately indicated. Xenophon reports that Socrates deplored the undervaluation of extrafamilial friendship that he saw all around him in people's actual conduct—conduct that contradicts their words: "This (he said), he *heard* from many: that a clear and good friend would be superior to all acquisitions; but, he said, he *saw* the many concerned with everything" that belonged to them (Socrates obviously meant, including family) "rather than with acquiring friends"; and this, to such an extent, that while people know the number of the rest of their possessions, even when those are numerous, when it comes to counting their few friends, they don't know the number; and, knowing that they don't know, they waver, at one time including, and another time dropping, the same names (2.4.1–4).

Xenophon here has Socrates spotlight a nigh-universal failing, familiar to and shared, ruefully, by us all. Xenophon thus provokes the question, Why is it that we have so highly praised a vision of a "clear and good friend," and yet we expend so little of our time and energy trying to realize that vision, and wind up remaining so terribly uncertain and changeable in counting who among our so-called friends really are our friends? Can this be explained simply by our carelessness? Or does this not express a quiet, deep despair that signals the profound gulf between what, on one hand, we hope and wish for, and even demand, as a "clear and good friend," and what, on the other hand, we find that we humans are capable of being for one another, and can reasonably expect from one another?

The Socratic speech proceeds, suddenly in direct discourse, through a series of four anaphoric-rhetorical questions, stressing the superior utility, over a horse, and then over an ox team, and then over a slave, of "a good friend," that is, "a useful (*chrēstos*) friend"—as "*property (ktēma),*"[14] useful for the *owner* (2.4.5). The speech goes further: "*The good friend* orders himself with a view to *every* lack of *the friend*, as regards both private equipment and communal actions; and if it should be necessary to do good to someone, he helps; and if some fear disturbs, he takes the field—with expenditures, or acting in concert, or helping persuade, or using forceful violence; and when *they* fare well, he most rejoices, and when *they* fall, he sets *them* aright" (2.4.6). The "good friend" serves "the friend(s)"—who do *not* necessarily reciprocate, who need not be "good" friends. This formulation prompts the question, Is it then some kind of a cross between a faithful dog and a demigod-genie that we are looking for, in "the good friend?" Is not Xenophon having his Socrates hold up to us a mirror, in which we may see the unreasonable demands we may be making in our uncritical, implicit, normative vision of "the clear and good friend"? At the very end, the speech will say that what has been described is "what is *called* friend" (2.4.6).[15]

But first the speech continues by reinvoking the analogy that was introduced at the end of Socrates's speech to Chairecrates: the partnership of the twin hands, eyes, ears, feet. Before, these were analogies for the aspired-to, reciprocally beneficial partnership of a pair of (quasi-twin) brothers; now, this analogy and aspiration seem to be applied to a pair of mutually helpful, extrafamilial friends. This lays the ground for the next Socratic speech, whose message is the following: in order to have or to acquire a friend, consider how to be one; and learn that you ought reasonably to demand and to expect from a friend only as much as you enable him to expect from you. Here in the present speech, the introduction of the image of friendship as a twin-partnership is followed by a considerably toned-down statement on the efficacy of a "friend" (no longer a "good" friend): "Often [not always] things that one either has not done or has not seen or has not heard or has not accomplished *for oneself* a friend *suffices* for doing, for his friend" (2.4.6). In this formulation, a friend sounds like a supplement to one's imperfect self-sufficiency (BD ad loc.), rather than like an omnicompetent devotee.

Yet there is a further complication. In the formulation here of the twins analogy, the pairs of cooperating, twin, bodily organs are *not* described, as they were in the speech on brothers, as helping *one another*; they are here described as *both serving* the *single owner* (2.4.6). Similarly, the helpful action of friends is compared, not to what one of the pair of hands, and so on, does for the *other* of the pair, but rather to what the pair *together* do for "each" person who is their possessor. After all, this is the way it is: hands, eyes, ears, feet—even or precisely in their mutually helpful cooperation—serve not one another, but their possessor. So, on a closer look, the analogy would seem to suggest that friendship as a mutually helpful paired partnership exists to serve someone or something above and beyond, in some sense possessing the two friends, who *together* are like a "friend" *to* that higher entity. Who or what is that higher entity? Could it be divinity? But while divinity in its purposefulness was crucial to the twins analogy as it was employed in the speech about brothers, divinity is conspicuously absent here. In fact, extrafamilial friendship is never by Socrates linked to divine support and sanction, as is family friendship.[16] Could the higher entity be the Virtue that we heard allegorized by Prodicus? Or could it be the nonallegorical virtue of Socrates and of Xenophon, to which the oration of the allegorical Virtue silently pointed us? The twin analogy here adumbrates friendship as a partnership dedicated to something beyond the partners. What might that be?

The more carefully one looks at this speech that opens the series on extrafamilial friendship, the more it seems to be meant to table questions or puzzles that stimulate our meditation. Reflection on those questions is enhanced if we attend to two striking stylistic idiosyncrasies, first in the way this episode is introduced and then in the way it is unfolded.

At the start, Xenophon says, using a phraseology almost identical to that which he used in introducing the dialogue with Aristodemus (1.4.2; see also 1.6.1), and even closer to that which he uses in introducing the dialogue that is the *Oeconomicus*, that he "heard Socrates once carrying on a *dialogue* about friends" (2.4.1). But what follows is *not* a dialogue; it is a monologue![17] Or could this monologue be, in some sense, simultaneously a dialogue? How so? Who is the interlocutor-partner? Could it be someone present, who is in some kind of unobtrusive but actively helpful interaction with Socrates as he speaks here?

As for the oddity in the way the speech unfolds, Xenophon begins the speech as emphatically *indirect* discourse: "He said that he heard . . . but he said that he saw . . ." (four repeated "he saids"). However, at about the center (2.4.4 end–2.4.5 beg.), our author switches to *direct* discourse—leaving it unclear whether the speaker remains Socrates, now being quoted directly, or whether Xenophon as author has unobtrusively taken over, and now is the one speaking in the first person. What could be the point of this arrestingly singular maneuver? How might it go with the arrestingly eccentric manner in which our author introduces this speech (and the next)? How might both these eccentricities be clues to the higher "possessor" being served by a pair of Xenophontic friends?

I suggest this answer: at the start of the series of segments on extrafamilial friendship Xenophon subtly and wittily reminds us that his own friendship with Socrates flowered into a meeting of minds that was so complementary that on every page, in almost every sentence, of this book Xenophon has spoken for and through Socrates, whose thinking and living have thus been continued through and by Xenophon as author (who may have communicated to Socrates foreknowledge of his authorial plans). The friendship of Xenophon and Socrates has succeeded in a grand shared project, of giving the gift of this book, the *Memorabilia*, to the ages. The pair of friends have thereby succeeded in doing together as much as they could to stimulate the continuation, into the indefinite future, of the peak activity of Socratic virtue and friendship—the study together of great old books. In and through this achievement, as well as in other respects, theirs is *the* normative friendship. Given this friendship's height and unconventionality (or pure naturalness), Xenophon and his Socrates can share with us its character, and invite us to join, only through clues didactically arranged so as to inspire and guide our protracted self-critical meditation and our serious self-experimentation.

## PROMOTING REFLECTION ON ONE'S OWN WORTH AS A FRIEND

Xenophon next tells us that he witnessed another Socratic speech, occasioned by the master having noticed that one of his companions was ignoring a friend who was in financial straits. Socrates contrived a short therapeutic-didactic dialogue, in the presence and primarily for the benefit, it seems, of the neglectful companion.

The companion's neglectfulness evidently expressed a view that the value of the needy friend was outweighed by the expenditure that would be required to keep up the friendship; so Socrates started the dialogue by making brutally explicit the delinquent companion's premise. Socrates asked Antisthenes, at some length, if it was true that "some friends are worth certain amounts, as are slaves?" (2.5.1–2). Socrates knew that he could count on Antisthenes (a fervently enamored follower—see 3.11.17 and the *Symposium*) to go along with the implicit lesson: swearing by Zeus, Antisthenes replied that yes, he valued different friends at different prices; but— Antisthenes predictably added—there was one friend whom he valued more than all money, and all toils. Thus Socrates in effect solicited from Antisthenes a reminder to the company that the most valued friend is priceless. Socrates then drew from this a "noble" conclusion: "Well then, what would be noble would be to examine oneself as to how much one might be worth to one's friends, so that they would be less likely to betray one" (2.5.4).

It may be said that "Socrates and Antisthenes allow it to be clearly understood by their negligent companion" that "he would do better to examine himself as to his true value," and "that he risks, if he continues to show himself useless here to a friend in need, being abandoned by his other friends, in the first rank Socrates and Antisthenes" (BD ad loc.). But this is at best only half the story.

For Xenophon has artfully written this episode in such a way as to make it twofold: in the Greek, "He asked Antisthenes in the presence of the very one who was neglectful" also means "He asked Antisthenes in the presence of the very one who was neglectful of *him*." Taking the latter meaning, it is upon *Antisthenes*, as the neglected pauper friend, that Socrates brings to bear the sobering lesson—and this fits better with Socrates's final two sentences. For Socrates says that when he hears people complaining that they have been betrayed by a friend for money, this causes him to look to see whether such betrayal is not due to the "wickedness" of the friend who is betrayed—"for I don't much see the finely useful slaves being sold, or friends being betrayed" (2.5.5; XS 45). Xenophon does not report any response or reaction from Antisthenes: was he shocked into doing some self-critical thinking?

We have proceeded far enough into Xenophon's presentation of Socratic speeches on friendship to enable us to rise up to a bird's-eye view, retrospectively and prospectively. What Xenophon is presenting, as regards extrafamilial as well as familial *philia*, is not Socrates elaborating a full and thematic teaching, such as we find in Aristotle's *Nicomachean Ethics* or Cicero's *On Friendship*; instead, Xenophon is giving us a series of portraits of Socrates as therapist, and diagnostician, of key, ever recurring problems or tensions inherent in *philia*, especially among gentlemanly types. Socratic therapy consists largely in trying to help his associates become more self-conscious about their own and others' needs from and for friendship—and about what, consequently, they can and cannot expect or demand from others, as well as from themselves, as generous but also needy and thus by no means selfless friends. Xenophon doubtless intends to extend this therapy to those of his readers who are receptively self-reflective. In exercising this therapeutic individual enlightenment, Xenophon and his Socrates find it necessary to downplay, or even to abstract from or to draw into question, the nobler (as well as the affectionate), the apparently need-transcending, dimensions of friendship—as part of a chastening of the demands of desert that are fueled by somewhat self-deceiving noble and loving passions. The resulting Socratic speeches can appear on their face to express a rather plebeian or bourgeois utilitarianism. This impression is to some extent counteracted in the next segment.

## SOCRATES ON THE POWER AND PROBLEM OF FRIENDSHIP AMONG GENTLEMEN

This peak and central of the nine segments on *philia* is introduced as an example of Socratic speeches that seemed to Xenophon to teach about what sort of friends are worth acquiring. The interlocutor is Critobulus. We met him earlier, as "the son of Crito" whom Socrates in mock horror advised to go into exile for a year, while describing him to Xenophon as "a great hothead and one who will stop at nothing"—all on account of Critobulus's having dared to kiss a beautiful boy. It was Xenophon's avowal that he would share in such rashness that led Socrates to lower the boom on our author (1.3.8–15): Xenophon presents himself as having a streak of Critobulus in him. In the present dialogue, Critobulus's lighthearted erotic proclivities continue to be evident—and Socrates's disapproval appears much less severe.[18] If we step back and take a synoptic view of Xenophon's Socratic writings, we see that Critobulus plays a recurring, surprisingly large role in them. The long discourse that constitutes the *Oeconomicus* is the subtly risible depiction of Socrates's rather fond[19] attempt to educate the devil-may-care young Critobulus in his yet unmet responsibilities and financial needs as a wealthy gentleman-farmer and household head.[20] The present conversation, here in the *Memorabilia*, would seem to be another chapter in this ongoing, comically Sisyphean, labor (consider especially 2.6.38). With an eye to what we learn from Plato (*Euthydemus* end), as well as from Xenophon's *Symposium* (4.24), we may presume that Socrates undertook this task out of friendship to his old comrade Crito, in response to the latter's anxious concern about his elder son's lack of moral education—and, we are compelled to add, the young man's erotic escapades (XSD 101, also 90–91). But we also learn from the *Symposium* (3.7, 4.9–29, 5.1–6.1) that Socrates found the handsome young scamp to be attractive and amusing; we learn from the *Oeconomicus* (3.7) that Socrates was drawn into long, early morning treks to attend comic dramas with Critobulus; we even learn (again from the *Symposium*, 4.22) that Socrates allowed himself to be "dragged around" by Critobulus to wherever the latter would be able to see his beloved beauty, Kleinias. As for Critobulus's attitude toward Socrates, "we are free to suspect" that "he admired Socrates more, much more than his own father," a possible reason why Crito's "influence on his son" might "have been altogether insufficient" (XSD 101). We may conclude that Socrates's intimacy with Critobulus mixed duty with affectionate pleasure: Critobulus was a rather good-looking and amiably witty young ne'er-do-well with whom Socrates had fun, while trying to give the young fellow some help.[21] As Xenophon has made abundantly clear, Socratic fun is interwoven or leavened with Socratic provocation to thought, for onlookers such as Xenophon himself—and not least in the present conversation.

In what we may designate a first stage of the dialogue (2.6.1–5), Xenophon presents Socrates questioning Critobulus in order to bring him to agree on the criteria that the two of them should bear in mind as they seek "a good friend" (for Critobulus[22]). The latter first assents to six disqualifying vices, and then to four "contraries"—qualities that, Socrates says, "result in a person's being profitable to those who use (or deal with) him." Socrates thus begins by putting the utilitarian, profit-seeking dimension of friendship in the foreground; he thereby indicates what he thinks the future farmer and household manager Critobulus needs to hear, at least in the beginning. Accordingly, three of the six disqualifying vices pertain to monetary relationships, having as their contrary the quality of "being good to do business with" (*eusymbolos*). But a nobler dimension suddenly appears when Socrates articulates the last of the four good qualities—the one that is contrary to the sixth vice, of "giving no thought to reciprocating good deeds": they should seek as a friend for Critobulus someone who has "a love of victory with a view to not being bested in doing good to those who have done good to him." This is a purer version of the gentlemanly competitive ardor that Socrates told

Chairecrates he could probably count on in his brother Chairephon, and which could be manipulated as a basis for reconciliation. What exactly does Socrates have in view by invoking here this passion for victory? Is Socrates implying that Critobulus ought to seek a friend whose passion for triumph in generosity he can gratify (and exploit) by gracefully accepting defeat in the contest, thereby reaping the greater benefit? Or isn't Socrates (also) testing Critobulus—to see whether he will respond by expressing his ambition to *be* such a friend, to compete for victory in gentlemanly generosity? If this latter, the trial result is negative.

For a second stage (2.6.6–7) is initiated by Critobulus asking, "So how then would we test for these things, Socrates, before we make use [of the person]?" Socrates's response is provocatively twofold. First, he invokes an arresting analogy: "Sculptors (he said) we test not by the evidence of words, but instead, he whom we see having previously worked beautifully on the statues, this man we trust will do well making the rest." By this analogy, Socrates points to the idea of the sought-for "good friend" as being like an artist of beautiful (nonutilitarian) gifts. When Critobulus responds in a way that indicates his failure or refusal to take note of, let alone to be invited to thought by, this higher perspective, Socrates invokes an entirely different analogy, speaking now in the first person singular: "For also as regards horses (he said), when I see someone who has previously made use of them in a noble fashion, I think this man will also make use of others nobly." By this analogy, Socrates implies (no doubt with a twinkle in his eye) that what Critobulus may need in a friend is someone who will nobly train and use him (along with others), as something like a fine horse (recall Socrates's similar suggestion to Chairecrates, regarding the perspective he should assume toward his brother: 2.3.7).[23]

Critobulus responds by asking—ignoring or oblivious to Socrates's unflattering jest—*how* they should make a friend of someone who seems to them worthy; and this starts a third stage in the conversation (2.6.8–16). Socrates answers that, to begin with, the signs from the gods should be consulted, to see if the gods advise that the person in question should be made a friend. On the basis of Socrates's doctrine on the narrow reasons why such consultation is ever needed (recall 1.1.8–9), the implication is that the eligible good friend (or "horseman") might turn out to "make use" of Critobulus in a way that is harmful. But the insouciant Critobulus shrugs off or is heedless of the danger: "So what then? (he said). As for the one who suits us, and whom the gods do not oppose,[24] can you say how this one should be hunted?" The introduction of the hunting metaphor evokes from Socrates an emphatic, but obviously playful, semidemurral (2.6.9): "By Zeus! (he declared) not by chasing, as is the hare, nor by deceptive trapping, as are the birds, nor by violence, as are the enemies!" Friends are better hunted by what are said to be "incantations" (*epōdai*) and "love-charms" (*philtra*) that are sung and wielded by "knowers." And the knower-poet Homer, as he is in this instance inventively interpreted by Socrates, teaches the seductive power of the Sirens' song, as a song of great praise—but only as directed to the very few who, like Odysseus, are in love with being truly honored for their virtue, and for this reason are repelled by any false flattery.

Does not Socrates here implicitly disclose a key opening or early gambit in his own poetic art of seduction (consider 4.2.9)? We recall that Plato has Alcibiades compare Socratic seduction to the enchantment/entrapment by the Sirens.[25]

Critobulus, however, resists Socrates's elite narrowing of the range of potential friends. Critobulus is interested in incantations of a more vulgarly wide applicability; and Socrates concedes that less noble versions of praise—such as praising someone for his stature, or looks, or strength—can, if the praises are not preposterously flattering and thus a form of ridicule, be more widely successful (2.6.12). Critobulus wants to hear more along this line: "And do you know some other incantations?" Socrates answers in the negative; but he adds that he has heard that Pericles knew many incantations by which he seduced the city as a whole (the incantations that Socrates knows and employs are aimed at a small elite, taken one by one, in contrast to the crowd incantations of the popular leader). Critobulus is impressed by the allusion to Pericles. He wants to hear more about leaders who make themselves loved by the city as a whole: "And Themistocles, how did he make the city love him?" Socrates replies, with an oath, that Themistocles made the city love him not by incantations, but instead by actually bestowing something good on the city (2.6.13): incantations, and certainly Periclean incantations, are not in themselves good for the seduced (Socrates leaves "love-charms" otherwise unspecified: recall 2.3.11).

At this point, apparently stirred to greater seriousness by the consideration of the love or friendship that statesmen can arouse, the mildly mercurial Critobulus finally recognizes and acknowledges something of Socrates's implicit lesson for him: "You seem to me to be saying, Socrates, that if we are going to acquire some good friend, it is necessary that we ourselves become good at both speaking and doing." Socrates indicates that this is on the right track; but he descends (with some evident irony) to Critobulus's level: "And you supposed (said Socrates) that it was possible to acquire useful friends by being wicked (*poneros*)?!" (2.6.14). Critobulus confesses that his view of friendship has indeed been influenced by observing comradeships between paltry orators and good public speakers, and by observing political alliances (*hetairoi*) between incompetent and competent generals: Critobulus's attitude toward friendship has been shaped by his rather disillusioning observation of friendship in public life (2.6.15). Still, the young man now expresses his awareness that Socrates is seeking to invigorate in him a higher aspiration, to making a truly "beneficial" friend from someone among those who are the *gentlemen*, "the noble and good" (*kaloikagathoi*)—and, with that end in view, to strive to distance himself from what is not gentlemanly.

But standing in the way of Critobulus's embracing this aspiration, he now discloses, are his observations of how fraught are the friendships between or among precisely "the noble and good" (as we have earlier had occasion to be reminded, by Socrates's conversation with Chairecrates). It transpires that what has appeared to be Critobulus's reserved and even rather low or vulgar view of the "good friend" is not so much a result of his having failed to wish or to hope for and to think about securing a noble friend, as it is a result of his deep discouragement (*athumia*) occasioned by his reasoning about (*logizomai*) the strife commonly dividing proud gentlemen—and similarly the wars dividing the civic regimes that most care for gentlemanliness. This grave problem is the subject of a fourth stage in the conversation (2.6.17–28).

It is Socrates who elaborates, with arresting power, the evidence that so troubles Critobulus: the latter has "observed" that "often" (not always) "real men (*andres*) who practice the noble things and refrain from the shameful, instead of being friends, are in fractious strife with one another," to the point where "they have greater difficulty dealing with one another" than do "worthless humans" (2.6.17). The core of the difficulty is, as Critobulus somewhat crudely expresses it, "those who cultivate virtue are in fractious strife *over being first in the cities*, and, out of envying one another, hate one another" (2.6.20). Speaking in more gracious and gentle terms, we may say that it is precisely the noble ambition of those who cultivate civic virtue that renders so elusive a common good shared among them, as regards the good that is noblest and that matters most to them. For each dedicates his life to becoming maximally virtuous, and, as such, seeks to be the supremely generous source of benefit, through ruling and public service, to all others in the city, including not least his fellow votaries of virtue; each of these understands acutely that it is nobler to give than to receive, that it is nobler to rule and thus to care for all the rest in the city than to be among the ruled and cared for; but then, even if envy is avoided, how can each, in striving to maximize his generously virtuous activity, avoid depriving his peers of their maximally virtuous activity?[26]

Socrates's lengthy response is complex, nuanced, and thought-provokingly ambiguous. He begins by listing four sources of friendship found in human "nature" (*physis*)—that is, in all humans, regardless of their degree of concern for virtue or for the noble (BD ad loc.; Gigon 1956, ad loc.). In the first place, humans by nature simply "*need* one another" (apart from any utilitarian benefit[27]). This is reinforced by the fact that, secondly, they naturally "have *compassion*" for one another. Then in the third place, Socrates highlights (as we have come to expect) the fact that by nature humans *benefit* one another by working together; and finally, as a consequence of the third, they are drawn toward friendship by mutual *gratitude* (2.6.21).

Over and against this, Socrates lists sources of war found in human nature. First and foremost, when humans conventionally hold the same things to be noble and pleasant, they fight over these (this would seem to apply also, and maybe especially, to the gentlemen); and when they disagree over what is noble and pleasant, this too makes them fight. More generally, war is caused by strife, together with anger; and the erotic passion to gain more than others entails ill will; and envy breeds hatred. These sources of war in human nature would seem to be at least as strong and effective as the sources of friendship (2.6.21). "Nevertheless," Socrates continues, "friendship[28] slips through all these, to draw together" (not all, but) "those who are the gentlemen [the noble and good]" (2.6.22). For, Socrates submits, gentlemen—on account of their virtue—choose to acquire in measure, and without toil, rather than to dominate everything through war; they are capable of painlessly sharing food and drink even when they are hungry and thirsty, while they are restrained as regards their indulgence in sexual pleasure with those in bloom; they are able, as regards monetary property, lawfully to resist being greedy, and instead to share and to assist; they are capable of engaging in rivalry in ways that are painless and mutually beneficial, restraining their anger from making them later regretful; they entirely eschew envy, and regard their goods as communal among friends (2.6.22–23: the central of the five qualities highlights the fact that gentlemen live in accord with conventional lawfulness, *nomos*).

Socrates here briefly limns the animating spirit that would uphold what Aristotle calls the "best regime," the regime of wish or prayer—a regime in which the gentlemen would rule without having to compromise with the nongentlemen.

One hesitates to raise any questions in the face of so impressive an assemblage of factors promoting friendship and community among gentlemen. But there is a serious difficulty left on the table. Does all this add up to an entirely adequate solution to what we have seen Socrates and Critobulus so lucidly expose: the deeply troubling competitive tension, supervening over partnership, as regards what is the greatest good, in the eyes of the civically virtuous or "the noble and good" (cf. Gigon 1956, 148)? In response to such a question, Socrates offers thought-provoking questions (2.6.24–26): "How therefore is it not likely that the gentlemen can be sharers also in political honors/offices, in a way that is not only harmless, but even beneficial to one another?" For "if someone were wishing to be honored in a city so that he would not be done injustice, and so that he would have the power to help friends in just matters, and so that he would, through ruling, try to do something good for the fatherland—what would make such a one incapable of harmonizing with another such?" Would it be because "he will be less able to benefit the friends when the gentlemen are with him?" (The wording of this question, and to a lesser degree of the preceding, shows that it is doubtful whether the friends that can be helped are the gentlemen who are corulers or cobenefactors: XS 49.) Or "will he be less able to do good to the fatherland when he has the gentlemen as coworkers?"

The deep problem is made comically visible as Socrates invokes the analogy of gymnastic competitions to illustrate his questions: if, among those competing for individual victory in gymnastics, it were possible for all the strongest competitors to team up against the weaker, then the former team would clearly win all the contests and take all the prizes. Wonderful; but then how would the members of the team of winners establish the ranking in gymnastic excellence among themselves—except by starting, among themselves, a new, and indeed the only true, gymnastic contest? As Socrates laconically and ironically remarks about his hopeful proposal, "they don't allow this to be done" in the gymnastic competitions. The arrangement that Socrates suggests would obviously make of the competitions a joke; *the point* of the competitions is to have them take place between those who are the strongest competitors, to test which of *them* is *the* best (cf. *Hiero* 4.6). Nonetheless, Socrates concludes by asking: "In the political contests, in which the gentlemen are the strongest," why "would it not be to one's advantage to engage in politics after having acquired the best as friends, using them as partners and fellow workers in the actions, instead of them being antagonistic competitors?" Socrates does not suggest that gentlemen can become friends *while* or *through* engaging in political contests (friendship must *precede* the contests); and he gives Critobulus no opportunity to respond to this series of questions.

Socrates abruptly adds a declaration of what he says is "clear" in the dynamics of *warlike conflict* (2.6.27): "If one makes war on another, one will need allies"; this is all the more the case, he adds, "*if one's opponents are the noble and good.*" Now (he continues), to win eager allies, one needs to benefit them; but it is more effective to benefit the best, even if they are fewer in number, than it is to benefit the worse, even if they are more numerous, because the wicked need to be given many more benefits than the worthy.

It is on the basis especially of this last declaration, highlighting key facts of actual, faction-ridden political life, that Socrates concludes by exhorting Critobulus to take heart, and to try to become good, and, becoming such, to undertake the "hunt for the gentlemen [the noble and good]" (2.6.28).

Socrates's conclusive point may be elaborated as follows. The inevitable competition among the civically virtuous gentlemen for superiority or victory in generous rule and honor must be seen as only the highest level of a much broader and cruder contest for rule that takes place in the political arena—where the gentlemen are in the distinct, and threatened, minority; and it is more prudent for each gentleman to secure some, at least, of the other gentlemen as allies, before he enters the political arena, than it is for each to oppose all the other gentlemen while seeking allies (only) among the much more numerous but more grasping, more expensive, nongentlemen.[29]

So the higher, virtuous grounds that support or promote friendship among gentlemen find crucial supplement in each gentleman's need for other gentlemen as allies in the broader class struggle. That struggle, whose varying outcomes determine the regimes (*politeiai*) that truly define the diverse and mutating and clashing characters of the cities, is nobly and beautifully cloaked by stress on the "fatherland" (or "country": *patris*), and on patriotism, or service to the fatherland (or to "our country")—a veil that Xenophon has Socrates readily employ (see XS "Appendix"). The alloyed nature of the civic common good that is possible between or among politically virtuous gentlemen thus becomes manifest. But this lightning glimpse of the political realities of friendship among gentlemen is overshadowed by the remarkable last and longest stage in the dialogue—where the gulf between Socrates and Critobulus as regards friendship becomes yawning (2.6.28–39).

Socrates turns away from the contemplation of friendship among gentlemen in *political* life—as if he detects that this has not entirely succeeded in convincing Critobulus of the need to bend his efforts to find a friend among the gentlemen—and suddenly turns to his own, less competitive (XS 50), friendships: "On account of being erotic, even I, perhaps, might be able to assist you in some way in the hunt for the gentlemen [the noble and good]." For, Socrates confesses, "as regards those humans whom I desire, I totally strive, to a terrific degree, to be cherished as a friend even as I cherish them as friends; to be longed for as I long for them; to have my companionship desired as I desire their companionship." This consuming passion, Socrates boasts, has given him experiential expertise in knowing how "to please one who is pleasing to me."

Since Socrates articulates this striking self-characterization in the context of offering to help Critobulus in *his* quest, for gentlemen friends, Socrates leaves tantalizingly unexplained what motivates his own zealous quest for friends, as well as what precise type of person erotically attracts him. He does apply to the latter the broad term "humans" (*anthrōpoi*) rather than the restrictive and conventionally honorific term "real men" (*andres*: for the distinction, see *Hiero* 7.3 and 7.9); and he speaks as if his own "hunt" is not, as Critobulus's should be, a hunt for friends among mature gentlemen, "the noble and good." It is easy to understand why Xenophon "apologetically de-eroticized"[30] the picture of Socrates back in the early part of book 1, where he was defending Socrates against the charge of corrupting the young. Now Xenophon prods us to put the present revelation of Socrates's ardent, experience-based expertise in seduction together with that earlier, more restrained portrait of Socrates's relations with distinguished young men of great ambition, above all Alcibiades—but also Xenophon (while Socrates has experience in his successful seductions, Xenophon has experience of being successfully seduced by Socrates).

We do learn more here about Socrates's distinctive erotic preferences, from the bantering dispute that now breaks out between him and Critobulus. The latter, who is evidently diverted to his stronger passionate proclivities by Socrates's introduction of eroticism, declares his "long-standing desire" to learn the knowledge of hunting that Socrates has—"if," that is, "the same knowledge will suffice, to me, for those good in their souls *and* for those beautiful (*kaloi*) in their bodies!" (2.6.30). Socrates replies by protesting, in no uncertain terms, that *his* erotic knowledge of seduction does not permit touching—whose repulsiveness, Socrates says with mock horror,[31] is depicted in the figure of the Scylla. Socrates once again invokes by way of contrast, for the allegorical portrait of his own knowledge and practice of seduction, the figure of the Sirens—but this time no longer as presented by Homer: "people say" the Sirens employed song, from afar, to enchant "all" who heard them (Socrates lowers drastically his "elite" standards in order to help Critobulus: cf. XS 50.)

Critobulus agrees to abide by the prohibition on touching—with his hands; when Socrates makes explicit that the prohibition also applies to touching with the mouth, Critobulus impishly rebels. Socrates retorts with the assertion that the "beauties" (at least those who are such in Socrates's eyes) do not themselves tolerate being kissed.[32] Critobulus makes it clear that he does not agree with this chaste assessment, at least as applied to those whom *he* hunts.

Despite or because of this sharp divergence that has come to sight in how the two of them define the contrasting "beauties" who are the different sorts of prey of their erotic "hunting," Socrates offers his services to Critobulus as a (mildly accusatory) go-between: "When you wish to become a friend to someone, will you allow me to accuse you to him of being an admirer of him and desiring to be his friend?"—"Make your accusations!" gaily replies Critobulus, "because I know that nobody hates those who praise them!" (2.6.33). As Socrates proceeds to elaborate on the further "accusations" he is seeking Critobulus's permission to make, on the latter's behalf, we at first wonder why Socrates is capitulating to and offering to serve the un-Socratic erotic tastes of Critobulus (2.6.34)—until we see that this is the lever by which Socrates is trying to get his young friend to agree that matches will be made for him, by Socrates at least, only with beauties who are attracted by hearing a prospective lover praised for his gentlemanly qualities, culminating in his "knowing that the virtue of a real man (*anēr*) is to be victorious over friends in benefiting, and over enemies in harming" (2.6.35).

But Critobulus hesitates to give his assent, and instead asks, with a note of arch suspicion: "Why then (said Critobulus) are you saying this to me—as if it isn't up to you to say whatever you wish about me?" Swearing by Zeus, Socrates appeals to the highest knowledgeable authority in vulgar, sexual seduction: Aspasia, the most famous of all courtesans. From her, Socrates says, he has learned that "the good matchmakers" always speak truthful praise, since deception leads to hatred, not only in and of the match, but of the matchmaker (2.6.36).

Critobulus sees that Socrates is sportively saying that he will deploy his capacious knowledge of seduction on behalf of the erotic Critobulus only if the latter truly strives to be a gentlemanly friend to those whom Socrates approaches on his behalf. Critobulus wryly protests: "So this is the sort of friend you are to me, Socrates!"—"You would not be willing, for my benefit, to say something fabricated!" In response, Socrates turns a bit more serious: "But how (said Socrates), oh Critobulus, would I seem to you to benefit you more—by praising you falsely, or by persuading you to try to become a good man?" (2.6.37).

Apparently the answer Critobulus would give to this question is by no means obvious, for either he remains silent or Socrates offers him no opportunity to answer. At any rate Socrates takes a new tack: "But if it is not evident to you in this light, consider it in light of the following." Socrates proceeds

to point out how much destruction Critobulus would cause, and would himself suffer, if Socrates succeeded in matching him with someone on the basis
of the false claim that Critobulus knew how to pilot a ship skillfully, or to
serve as a general, or to act as a juryman, or as a statesman; and how not only
harmful, but, in addition, laughable Critobulus would appear if Socrates succeeded in matching him with someone on the basis of the false claim that
Critobulus could manage a private household and care for belongings. Critobulus does not in the least contest any of this.[33] On the contrary, he concludes
the conversation by declaring that he would be ashamed to contradict what
Socrates has just said, for that would be neither noble nor truthful; Critobulus
accepts with docility Socrates's exhortation to learning and practicing "whatever among humans are said to be virtues." So in the last part of the dialogue
Socrates would seem to have sobered up Critobulus, at least temporarily, and
turned the young man toward thinking about exerting himself to become
eligible as a friend to a gentleman. To this extent the dialogue vindicates Socrates as attempting to lead the wayward son of his old friend Crito toward
conventional gentlemanliness.[34]

One does have to wonder, How long will the edifying effect last? (And
therefore, How serious is Socrates in trying to reform Critobulus?) How
deeply has Socrates disquieted the careless young man? The wealthy Critobulus's life hardly seems to be desperate. He may be incompetent in all
serious gentlemanly skills and virtues, but he nonetheless (or therefore?)
exudes confident experience of joyful success as a fun-loving, witty, uncom-
petitive, erotic lover and friend—though not of mature gentlemen (except
Socrates). Somehow, this makes him the eligible interlocutor in the Xenophontic dialogues (above all the *Oeconomicus*) showing Socrates thematically teaching about, and exhorting to, "normal" gentlemanliness.

## HOW SOCRATES HELPED FRIENDS IN
## SERIOUS ECONOMIC DIFFICULTIES

From the previous, peak dialogue on extrafamilial, gentlemanly friendship
we descend, through four vignettes that show Socrates remedying, with varying degrees of success, baffling economic problems that were plaguing some
of his friends (*tas aporias ge tōn philōn*).[35]

### A SOCRATIC REVOLUTION IN A DESPERATE FRIEND'S HOUSEHOLD

In the lead instance (2.7),[36] Xenophon tells how Socrates persuaded a friend
named Aristarchus, driven to desperation by the civil war that led to the

end of the regime of the Thirty,[37] to undertake a radical expedient in household management that would not have occurred to the friend by himself, as a propertied (if destitute) gentleman—even though the friend's family had been brought to the brink of starvation. Socrates convinced Aristarchus to transform his home into a miniature factory,[38] by setting his thirteen "liberally educated" female relatives to work, on the analogy of barbarians and slaves, producing commodities (2.7.4–5). Socrates not only counseled that the indigent household would thus recover materially; he contended that through being gainfully employed, *humans generally* become more moderate and more just and more mutually loving—and Socrates predicted that especially the last would be the result in this case, resurrecting the harmony of the beleaguered and increasingly fractious home. Socrates clinched his case to his gentleman friend by declaring that if the work in question were "shameful" for the ladies, then of course "death would be preferable"; but the manual labor that Socrates was proposing was baking and sewing, *"knowledge of"* which, he stressed, is "held to be most noble and fitting for women" (2.7.10). Socrates obscured the fact that the actual work that he was suggesting—given that it consisted in producing the maximum of commodities for market sale—was held conventionally to be neither noble nor fitting for free ladies. We recall that Socrates was wont to appeal to a line of Hesiod's that his accusers judged "most wicked": "No work is to be blamed; idleness is to be blamed" (1.2.56–57). In the present instance, Socrates cheerily added that "all, when they work at what they know, do so most easily and swiftly and enjoyably," so that the ladies would "obey with pleasure."

In response Aristarchus declared, swearing an oath by the gods, that Socrates had spoken "nobly"; then, going beyond what Socrates had suggested, Aristarchus added that he would borrow capital (*aphormē*, 2.7.11) with which to buy wool. It sounds as if Socrates unleashed something in Aristarchus.[39]

Certainly Aristarchus proceeded to get his womenfolk toiling—overtime: "working while they breakfasted, and working while they supped, in cheerful spirits instead of downcast." The women wound up feeling *philia* toward Aristarchus "as protector," while "he cherished them as beneficial" (2.7.12).

Aristarchus joyfully and gratefully reported this happy outcome to Socrates—while noting one fly in the ointment: the women were blaming him for being the only one in the (now prosperous without slaves) household who consumed while being idle, without working. The formerly leisured ladies now appeared to believe that justice requires that one earn one's keep (Shulsky, forthcoming). Their conception of the household and its management had changed dramatically and fundamentally—from a leisured, slave-dependent ethic to a slaveless work ethic. The ladies had been converted to a radically un-Greek conception of the household and its management (the "oeconomic art"), based on a newfound respect for the dignity of free commercial labor, beginning with their own.[40]

Socrates did not, as one might expect, counsel Aristarchus to dissipate the blame by stressing to his womenfolk how energetically he was laboring outside the home, as marketer of the clothing product and as purchaser of the wool raw material (Millett 1991, 73–74). Perhaps Socrates did not think he could go quite that far in getting a Greek landed gentleman to transform himself in the eyes of his family into a commercial entrepreneur. At any rate Socrates proposed instead that Aristarchus tell his women "the speech of the dog," as follows: a ewe once complained to "the master" that the ewes had to provide wool, lambs (!), and cheese, being given nothing in return except what they took from the ground, while the dog, who provided nothing, got to share the master's food (including the lamb chops); it was the dog who replied—swearing by Zeus—that he was the one who protected the sheep from being kidnapped by humans, or ravaged by wolves; and "it is said," Socrates added (thus interjecting a note of skepticism), that "even the sheep agreed that the dog should have pride of place." Socrates advised Aristarchus to say to his laboring womenfolk that he takes the place of the dog, insuring that they can work all day without being "done injustice by anyone" (2.7.13–14). This advice seems oddly malapropos, since, as Xenophon has previously told us, the women *already* "love" Aristarchus "as a protector"—and *nonetheless* blame him for not working. How will telling them "the speech of the dog" end this blame? Or does not Xenophon have his Socrates deliver this Aesopian (BD ad loc.) advice in order to incite our thought about implications of the revolutionized household?

Socrates's story has the "dog," and then Aristarchus as the "dog," first eclipsing and then replacing the "master." The Socratically reorganized household is thus assimilated to a very odd shepherding, in which the sheepdog takes over, and the master disappears (XS 52–53; see also Gigon 1956, 179–80). Who is represented by the erased master? We note that the dog in the story swears by Zeus, and, further, that Socrates provokes the gentleman interlocutor Aristarchus to use profane expletives more often than any speaker has in any conversation thus far in the work.[41] Conversely, neither Socrates nor Aristarchus says a word about praying, or sacrificing, or consulting divination, before carrying out the Socratic revolution in the household. Profanity takes the place of piety. In striking contrast, in the *Oeconomicus* (7.7–17), when Socrates is taught by the perfect gentleman Ischomachus how he educated his young wife in what her work should be, the gentleman ex-

plains that of course he did not begin until he had first prayed, and also carried out sacrifices, together with his wife; then, when the young lady asked
him to explain what her work should be, Ischomachus tells Socrates that
he replied: "that which the gods have made you naturally capable of, and
what lawful convention praises." The gentleman goes on to elaborate that
the wife's position in the home is, in accordance with pious belief and convention, to be like that of the ruler in the beehive, supervising the domestic
slaves. Socrates's household-transforming solution of his friend's economic
impasse depends on leaving behind what the ruling gods are held to intend,
for free female nature, and what lawful convention praises, as work befitting
liberally educated, leisured women. Xenophon instigates in his reader a skeptical question: Does not the Socratic revolution remove not only the leisure,
but also the pious, customary protections—and open the door to new forms
of exploitation—of free women and their children (lambs)? To be sure, what
we may, with pardonably Marxist anachronistic exaggeration, venture to call
Socrates's "proto-bourgeois"[42] revolution of the gentlemanly household is
not advanced by Socrates or by Xenophon as a suggestion for societal reform,
but only as a singular response to the peculiarly straitened circumstances
of a gentleman friend and his womenfolk—who do not become wage laborers. Yet the argument Socrates gives is based, in part at least, on implicit
appeal to a universal principle: through being gainfully employed, humans
generally, women as well as men, become more moderate and more just and
more mutually loving. Xenophon's Socrates has obviously meditated on the
limitations of the fundamental economic prejudices governing upperclass
Greek households and their conceptions of the role of women. We can see
in this proposal—making free commercial labor, of women, a respectable
"economic" substitute for slave labor—another instance and dimension of
Xenophon's Socratic "experiment" that "paves the way for certain post-
Machiavellian thinkers."[43]

## Socrates's Advice to a Fellow Economic Misfit

The counsel Socrates is portrayed as giving in the second incident (2.8) is of
more doubtful success, because this time Socrates is up against an intensely
self-reliant "old comrade's" recoil from the dependency entailed in permanent wage-employment.[44] When Socrates points out to Eutheros (whose name
means "sunny,"[45] and who is not downcast, in marked contrast to Aristarchus: XS 53) that the physical day labor by which he now supports himself will soon become unfeasible on account of his advancing age, Eutheros concedes as much (2.8.2). But when Socrates then advises him to find

someone wealthy under whom he could find permanent employment as a supervisor of laborers, the flinty oldster, addressing Socrates by name, labels such a status "slavery" (2.8.3–4).

Socrates counters with an elevated analogy: politicians who serve the public as supervisors of others are "conventionally regarded as more free," rather than as more slavish. But Eutheros—again appealing to Socrates by name—makes it clear that he is too independent minded to be impressed by this conventional way of thinking: "In general, I don't allow myself to be held accountable to anyone" (2.8.5; recall 2.1.9–10). Eutheros evidently looks down upon what he sees as the slavishness of public service—despite, if not because, such service is popularly (and, in Eutheros's view, ignorantly) admired as "more free."[46]

Socrates's response concedes quite a lot to the outlook of Eutheros (does not Eutheros know that in some key relevant respects he and Socrates are kindred spirits?): it is true that it is "not very easy" to find a job that doesn't involve being "blamed" by someone; and even if one makes no mistakes, it is "difficult" to avoid being blamed by some ignoramus boss. But Socrates wonders whether Eutheros escapes such reproaches in his present situation (2.8.5).[47]

We can easily imagine Eutheros thinking, and being on the point of saying, "Yes, but now I change my bosses daily; I don't have to stay with any single one!" Xenophon, however, does not let us hear any reply from the stubbornly free-spirited old codger. Instead, we, along with Eutheros, hear a brief Socratic homily (2.8.6) that ends with another sobering, friendly reminder of approaching "old age"—and that exhorts Eutheros to seek out "bosses" (plural) who are "of good judgment" (or "forgiving"?[48]), and then to work "as nobly and eagerly as possible" under "*them*" (pl.). So what is the upshot? Is, or is not, Socrates suggesting that Eutheros exchange his present, individualistic, and constantly shifting employment under multiple, changing bosses for a permanent job under a single rich boss? Could it be that Eutheros has partly convinced Socrates? Is Socrates not suggesting a middle path: that Eutheros remain, for the time being, a transient day laborer, but use his encounters with a variety of employers to keep an eye out for one who might be tolerable as a permanent boss?

The words of both Aristarchus and Eutheros make it clear that their economic ruin has been the result of the disaster that has overtaken the entire city of Athens. What we almost certainly see here are effects of the defeat of Athens in the Peloponnesian War, and of the subsequent civic upheavals.[49] This would mean that these two conversations are set after 405 BC,[50] or at a time when Socrates himself is elderly—and of course living in the same harsh economic climate as his impecunious friends. Xenophon thus delicately rouses the question: How is it that Socrates, "despite his poverty," never "worried about the source of his livelihood in old age" (XS 53)? However frugal the Socratic household, it could not survive without some income. From where? Socrates reports that the perfect gentleman Ischomachus taught that "he who knows no other money-making art, nor is willing to farm, obviously intends to live from stealing or robbing or begging, or is altogether irrational."[51]

## A Glimpse of Socrates's Own Economic Art

The answer is implicit in the next episode (2.9)—which, Xenophon remarks, with an unusual stress, "I know" took place. We hear how Socrates gave effectively combative economic advice to his wealthy, beleaguered old friend Crito. This conversation, when put together with the conversations in the *Oeconomicus* as well as in the *Memorabilia* through which Socrates tried to aid, by educating, Crito's son Critobulus, allows the reader to discern that "Socrates helps Kriton and Kritoboulos with speeches, while Kriton helps Socrates with more tangible things if and when he needs them." This, however, "means that in his way Socrates possesses the art of increasing his wealth." Accordingly, "that art belongs to the best life."[52]

Crito's bewildered need for help arose from the very opposite of insolvency. As Crito complained to Socrates, a gentleman who minded his own business in democratic Athens was constantly subject to trumped-up lawsuits by certain litigious characters ("sycophants") who expected that the wealthy would provide monetary settlements in order to avoid the trouble and risk of court cases before mass juries (see similarly the complaint of Ischomachus, *Oeconomicus* 11.21–22).

Socrates pointed out to his old friend that just as Crito supported dogs who kept wolves away from his flocks, so he could combat these litigious pests by finding a "real man (*anēr*)," needy of material support, who was "very competent in speech and action," and very ambitious to have the honor of being friends with a Crito. (It was this last quality that Crito had failed to appreciate—a "leash" whose power he had to learn about from Socrates; Crito had given thought to employing a counter-sycophant, but feared that such a person would turn against him.) Socrates proceeded to help Crito find such a man, one Archedemos,[53] who with ease completely turned the tables on the "sycophants"—and eventually did so on behalf of Crito's other, wealthy, "gentlemen" friends as well, thereby winning their honor, along with Crito's friendship, and in addition some money.

Once again Xenophon has the wily and resourceful Socrates manifest his scrappy, "plebeian" capacity to help gentlemen friends escape the economic culs-de-sac in which they find themselves trapped on account of the high-minded limitations of their competitive and acquisitive instincts.[54] Socrates himself suffered no such bafflement and limitations (and, by the way, Xenophon reports at some length Archedemos's moralizing rejoinder to the malicious reproach that he "toadied" [kolakeuoi] to Crito so as to be economically supported by him—2.9.8).

## EXTENDING HIS ECONOMIC ART

The last of the Socratic speeches on friendship (2.10) is again introduced by Xenophon with the emphatic "I know," and is again a conversation between Socrates and a prosperous "comrade," to whom Socrates again teaches the profitability of supporting a needy but able man. The wealthy comrade with whom Socrates converses has the rather common name Diodorus ("Gift from Zeus"), and is otherwise unknown.[55] Xenophon instigates the wonder: How many such rich "comrades" or sugar daddies did Socrates have?

The needy man in question is none other than Hermogenes. He was at the center of the list of seven examples of those who, in contrast to Critias and Alcibiades, kept company with Socrates, "not in order to become assembly or courtroom orators, but in order to become gentlemen," and thus to dwell nobly in their households and cities (1.2.48). Hermogenes plays a notable role in the Symposium, where (4.47–49) Socrates congratulates him on believing himself to be a gentleman who, even in his poverty, is an especial favorite and communicant of the gods. Above all, Hermogenes is shown performing a very considerable and rather complex service of trust for Xenophon and Socrates in the Apology of Socrates to the Jury, as well as, to a lesser extent, in the concluding segment of the Memorabilia (4.8.4–10). In the passage before us, Xenophon lets us see one key part of the reason why Hermogenes can have this function. For Socrates praises Hermogenes as an example of someone who is a "willing assistant, of good intention, constant, competent not only to do what he is bid but capable on his own of being useful, of thinking and planning ahead—and as such, equal in value to many household servants" (2.10.3). We surmise that Socrates speaks from personal experience of these benefits that Hermogenes can provide.

Diodorus is acquainted with Hermogenes, and is not unaware that the current "troubles" have impoverished a number of gentlemen in Athens. But it takes Socrates to point out to Diodorus that "at present, on account of the troubles, good friends can be purchased cheaply" (2.10.4), and that while

Diodorus spends a lot to avoid losing his slaves, he could make a greater profit, with a smaller investment, by saving from destitution a gentleman like Hermogenes. For, Socrates promises, Hermogenes will be much more useful than the slaves—not least because his gentlemanly sense of shame will make him feel impelled to reciprocate with energy any charity. Diodorus responds to this by declaring that Socrates has "spoken in a noble fashion" (2.10.5). But when Diodorus then tells Socrates to bid Hermogenes to come to him, Socrates emphatically demurs, invoking Zeus in an oath, while opining that it would be "nobler" for Diodorus to go to Hermogenes, and then stressing again how mutually beneficial the outcome will be. Diodorus's rather utilitarian sense of the noble renders him insensitive to the shame that would prevent Hermogenes from coming to him for help; but this makes perfectly apt the utilitarian, undeceptive rhetoric by which Socrates persuades Diodorus to a substantial generosity that would otherwise never have occurred to him, nor to his high-minded recipient. Xenophon's Socratic speeches on friendship conclude with an exhibition of how Socrates employed his shrewd understanding of the profitable in order to practice and to promote noble generosity, in and for himself and his friends.

## CHAPTER FIVE

# How Socrates Benefited Those Reaching
# for the Noble/Beautiful (*Kalon*)

Xenophon emphatically marks the turn to what we may designate the third division of the second part of his recollections: "Now I shall show," he announces, "that Socrates benefited those reaching out (*tous oregomenous*) for the noble/beautiful things (*ta kala*)" (3.1.1). Xenophon thus indicates that the previous division, with its nine episodes depicting Socrates benefiting others in regard to friendship or *philia*, is not to be understood as showing Socrates benefiting those reaching out for the noble or beautiful (XS 43). Of course, concern for *philia* and for the *kalon* are far from being mutually exclusive (recall 2.6.22ff. and 30ff.). Still, the core of *philia* is reaching out to kin or a kindred spirit; and the central and peak of the nine episodes dealing with *philia* brought out the tension, for the virtuous, between reciprocal friendship and striving for shining excellence in nobly generous action (recall esp. 2.6.16ff.). Throughout the speeches on *philia*, within and outside the family, Xenophon showed Socrates stressing how attachments of *philia* draw strength from friends' attentiveness to the usefulness, the mutual benefit, of their friendship and love. We learned how very attentive Socrates was to the cooperative satisfaction of material needs, as a foundation for love and friendship. Indeed, the last four of the nine speeches have taken us down to a level so materially utilitarian that even sympathetic readers, especially if they have been inspired by Aristotle's more elevated account of noble friendship, may express "*un certain malaise*"[1]—and greet with some relief the beginning of a new ascent preoccupied with striving for the noble or beautiful.

It is political offices and honors that turn out to be the noble things reached for by those whom Xenophon shows Socrates engaging in the first seven conversations. These interlocutors are thus more akin to the dubious Alcibiades and Critias than to the seven politically less ambitious, gentlemanly associates whom Xenophon named as evidence that Socrates did not corrupt his companions (recall 1.2.48: all four of the Athenians among those companions were featured in the previous set of speeches on friendship, but are absent from the speeches directed to those reaching out for the noble; Xenophon of course remains present throughout, as a silent observer and learner and recorder—he has a place in, while transcending, both groups).

The specific way in which Socrates benefited those reaching for the noble things was by making them "take care about" or become "attentive to" (*epimeleis*) what they were reaching for. Those who were thus benefited were not limited to the interlocutors, and those *most* benefited may even have been certain thoughtfully reflective onlookers (Lorch 2010, 192), such as Xenophon—who, in his capacity as author, makes those among his readers who reach for noble things members of the audience, so to speak, and thus potential recipients of the benefit (*if* we activate our critical interpretative thinking and questioning).

There is an obvious affinity, but also obvious differences, between Socrates's (largely dialogical) beneficial activity in this part of the work and Virtue's (oratorical) education of Heracles—the victorious peroration of which we do well to keep in mind.

## HIS PLAYFUL TEACHING OF NOBLE GENERALSHIP

In the opening episode, we witness what was manifestly a rather comic Socratic drama. To and through a nameless young "companion" who was animated by thoughtlessly immature ambition—to become elected a general—Socrates gave a roguishly tricky, bantering, semipublic, and thus all the more indelible lesson in the full demands of that high office.

In the process Socrates exposed (among friends) the dubious pretensions of a sophist, named Dionysodorus, who purported to teach generalship for money, in a few easy lessons, by educating solely in the art of *taktika*—that is, arranging troops in the proper order. The practical joke that Socrates played on his young follower, by inducing him to become a student of this sophist, obviously cost the youth or his father some money—no doubt making the lesson more memorable. Presumably the family was wealthy enough not to have suffered any serious economic damage.[2] Did Socrates also show his beneficial humanity by helping the sophist to make a living? Does this episode to some extent continue the previous episodes inasmuch as Socrates is here shown once again managing to relieve the financial distress of an acquaintance? In Plato's *Euthydemus*, Socrates and Dionysodorus are portrayed as on not unfriendly terms.

The way in which Socrates persuaded the young man to seek out lessons
in generalship was by stressing to him how shameful, and justly punishable
by the city, would be a failure to seek instruction, while attending only to being elected—given the enormous goods and evils that can accrue to the city
from a generalship performed either correctly or erroneously (3.1.3). This
implies that all those who attend to being elected to crucial offices, without
first seeking instruction in and acquiring the necessary wisdom, are justly
punishable by the city.

When the young man returned to Socrates, after "having learned" from
the sophist, Socrates "poked fun" at him by asking a group of mature men
whether it was not the case that the youth "by learning" had acquired the
"majestic appearance" that Homer ascribed (through the mouth of King
Priam, conversing with Helen—*Iliad* 3.170) to the actually ruling king, Agamemnon. Socrates explained that if or since the youth had completed the
education in generalship, he would "continue as a general from this point
on, even if no one elects him" (3.1.4). "The Socratic joke implies" that someone who has learned the knowledge requisite for generalship "need no longer care to be elected general nor to desire to practice generalship."[3] (Would
Homer, or his Priam, agree?) This of course does not exclude the possibility that a Socratic who has learned the knowledge of generalship might in
certain circumstances feel impelled to seek to practice generalship—as did
Xenophon in the *Anabasis*. Socrates himself here referred to the possibility
that he might sometime need to become a leader of a squadron or a company.

Turning to address the young man, Socrates admonished him that generalship involves much more than *taktika*. "Doing well as a general" requires
a distinctive "nature" (XS 57: "Generalship is not simply knowledge") that
enables the acquisition of specific "knowledge" (*epistēmē*). This knowledge comprises not only a wide range of complex practical arts and powers,
but also extraordinary moral flexibility and capacity: one must be not only
"skilled at equipping the army for war, and skilled at provisioning the soldiers," but also "skilled at cunning contriving, and skilled at working, and
supervisory (*epimelē*), and skilled at enduring, and shrewd in mind, and both
kind (*philophrona*) and cruel/savage (*ōmon*), and both forthright and deceptive, and both skilled at guarding and thievish, and lavish and rapacious, and
fond of giving gifts and greedy, and cautious and aggressive, and many other
things."[4]

Without allowing the youth to respond to this amazing pronouncement,
and without offering any assistance to the youth's learning these essential
"moral"[5] and practical skills, Socrates continued: "And the artful arranging in orders is *also noble*" (all of the preceding skills are noble). Socrates

evinced, however, a curiously idiosyncratic perspective on the "art of ordering." He focused laser-like on a single aspect of the art, while simultaneously viewing this single aspect as a key ingredient in a broad genus of constructive arts. The Socratic focus was on the need, in constructing something—be it a house or an army—to place *in the middle* those parts that are most vulnerable or weak, surrounded and protected or carried along by the stronger parts (3.1.7–8; see similarly Xenophon's stress on this matter in *The Skilled Cavalry Commander* 2.3–5, where our author makes the important point that it is what comes last that "saves" the whole when retreat or defense is necessary). L. Strauss comments: it "was a rule of forensic rhetoric to discuss the strong points of the defense in the first part and in the last part," and "the weak points in the center, i.e., when the attention of the listeners is flagging." The "weakest points" are "the most important," in "a speech or book that presents an unpopular or forbidden view in the guise of a perfectly innocent or 'orthodox' view."[6] Socrates eventually added, here, that this rule about the middle does not always hold, in ordering troops (*tattein*) or in *making a speech/logos* (*legein*[7]). It was the sophist's failure to make this variability clear that aroused Socrates's mock indignation: swearing by Zeus, he commanded his young follower to go back and to shame, by interrogating, the sophist into completing his teaching on the rule about the middle, in its variability (3.1.11).

We note that the present episode occupies the exact middle of the *logos* that is Xenophon's *Memorabilia*. Following the rule about the middle, could this section somehow playfully indicate the *Memorabilia's* inevitable vulnerability, protectively guarded? I suggest the following (contrast XS 58). This is the section that brings the *Memorabilia* into a kind of overlap with the other major pole of Xenophon's oeuvre: the *Education of Cyrus*. As many commentators have noted,[8] Socrates's very brief and playful education of his young follower regarding generalship parallels, and in numerous stylistic and substantive ways cries out to be compared with, the Persian king Cambyses's much more elaborate, much more serious and even momentous, culminating education by dialogue of his son Cyrus (*Education of Cyrus* 1.6). The education of Cyrus, including not least his education to generalship through dialogue with his wise father, is vastly more impressive than the Socratic education in generalship—in every obvious respect, and above all in its successful outcome: Cyrus's achievement of vast empire. To be sure, that education and achievement are fictional; they are found in a philosophic novel. But their implicit intrusion at this point in the *Memorabilia* impel a reader familiar with both of these major works to reflect that no one educated by Xenophon's Socrates, including Socrates himself,

succeeds in coming within hailing distance of Xenophon's Cyrus in obvious political importance and impressiveness. Even Xenophon, exercising
actual generalship as the "Socratic Prince" (Buzzetti 2014), is a small fry in
comparison with Cyrus—except, of course, for the fact that it is Xenophon,
the Socratic-philosophic author, who is the *creator* of *his* (fictional) Cyrus,
and "education of Cyrus." All the more does the pointer here, in the exact
middle of the *Memorabilia* (at the start of the sections on seeking the noble), prompt the question, Does not Xenophon's Cyrus, and his *Education
of Cyrus*, deservedly overshadow in "greatness" and therefore in "importance" Xenophon's Socrates, and his *Memorabilia*?[9] We have the affirmative
testimony of Machiavelli, the most prominent and influential philosophic
student of Xenophon: Machiavelli speaks emphatically of what he learned
from Xenophon's *Education of Cyrus* (and *Hiero*) while saying not a word
about Xenophon's *Memorabilia* (or Xenophon's other Socratic writings:
L. Strauss 1958, 291). To be sure, Machiavelli's testimony is that of the first
great "modern"—the philosopher who started the "quarrel between the ancients and the moderns"; and that quarrel is signaled and epitomized by this
very choice, of praise and of silence concerning the two poles of Xenophon's
oeuvre. The eclipse of Xenophon's Socratic writings may be said to be at the
very basis of philosophic modernity.

Here is the most appropriate moment to stress that a full understanding
of the *Memorabilia* remains unaccomplished until we have a complete interpretation of it *together and integrated with* a complete interpretation of
the *Education of Cyrus* (and vice versa);[10] and, what is more, until we have
integrated our understanding of both these masterpieces into what Shaftesbury (1964, 2: 309)—the "ancient" or "Socratic" within modernity—aptly
characterizes as the "original *system*" of Xenophon's corpus.

Returning to our text, let us note that there was one important aspect
of generalship about which Socrates did offer some instruction of his own.
Socrates led the youth to see that the sophist had failed to teach him how to
distinguish which soldiers should be put in the middle, and which distributed
to the van and to the rear—to distinguish, that is, the "best" from "worst" (as
the youth first puts it), or (as Socrates then puts it), "the good ones" from "the
bad ones," who are analogous, respectively, to "the noblest money" versus
"the worst" or "the counterfeit." The youth emphatically drew the conclusion that the two of them needed to establish the grounds for the distinction
between "the good ones and the bad ones" (as he said, correcting himself and
showing that he was learning something). Socrates responded by getting the
youth to agree that if the two of them were to lead a robbery of money, they
would "correctly" put in the van the ones who most loved money. Socrates

then asked: "And what about those who are going to run risks? Shouldn't the ones who most love honor be put in the van?" (3.1.9–10). Despite Socrates's previous stress on the great goods and evils that can accrue to the city from war, he now made no reference to those motivated by noble love of the city: contrast 3.3.2. Nor did he refer to those animated by noble devotion to Virtue: recall 2.1.27. No wonder Xenophon reports the reply of the young interlocutor as slightly hesitant or qualified—or perhaps puzzled.

Why might Xenophon have his Socrates draw such an unexpected and provocative parallel, between leading a gang of robbers, the "good ones" among whom are the most money-loving, and leading the Athenian citizen army, the "good ones" among whom are the lovers of honor? At the start of the series of episodes concerning quest for the noble, conceived primarily as political honor, Xenophon thus has Socrates prod his thoughtful hearers to start puzzling over the key question, How, exactly, is the noble, as zealously sought-after honor, good—for whom? And for what?

## INTERPRETING HOMER ON THE
## VIRTUE OF A GOOD LEADER

The disconcerting levity of the first, dialogic, Socratic lesson on the noble is compensated for by the edifying gravity of the second, monologic lesson (from which, accordingly, Xenophon excludes profane oaths). Having "chanced upon" one who had actually been elected general by the Athenian citizen-soldiers, Socrates spontaneously delivered a homily that explicated what it is that the great traditional authority Homer teaches to be the heart of the virtue of an actually commanding general—and of an actually ruling king.

Since he was explicating not his own, but Homer's teaching, it was easy for Socrates to avoid having to express to his interlocutor, the elected general, the Socratic teaching that puts into question the legitimacy of elected generals on the grounds of the need to possess the "nature" that has enabled "learning" of the "knowledge" of generalship. And Socrates now made no reference to the multifaceted and morally flexible specifics of that knowledge. In the particular manner that he here "examined what might be the virtue of a good leader"[11]—that manner being, to examine what *Homer* teaches—Socrates (Xenophon concludes, in his own name) "put aside the other things," and left, as the heart of the matter as Homer saw it, "making happy those who are led" (3.2.4).

Socrates began by asking: Why do you think Homer (speaking on numerous occasions, in his own voice: BD ad loc.) characterizes Agamemnon as "shepherd of the people?" And Socrates immediately suggested the answer, in the form of another question. Isn't it because, even as a shepherd should take care that the ewes be safe and have what they need, and that the purpose, for which they are nourished, be achieved (scil. furnishing lamb chops, wool, and profit for the shepherd and owners—recall 2.7.13), so a general should take care that the citizen-soldiers be safe and have what they need, and that the purpose for which they campaign be achieved? "And" (Socrates added, no longer in the form of a question) "they campaign so that, dominating the enemies, *they* might be happier" (3.2.1). Homer, Socrates seemed to be suggesting, defines the virtuous leader (in contrast to the actual shepherd) in terms of his nobly selfless care for his *followers'* well-being (contrast *The Skilled Cavalry Commander* 1.1). At the same time, Socrates implicitly indicated that the selflessly virtuous leader thus wins from the poet the deserved honor of becoming famous, as such a "shepherd of the people."

But Socrates did not leave it at this. He ascended to what he called Homer's "praise" (on a single occasion, through the mouth of Helen, in the conversation with Priam quoted in the previous episode: *Iliad* 3.179) of Agamemnon as a "good king" as well as a "strong spearman" and again asked what Homer meant. Didn't he mean that Agamemnon would be a strong spearman "if he not only contended well *himself* against the enemy, but *also* were *the cause* of this in the entire army"; and that he would be "a good king, not if he *only*[12] presided *nobly* over his *own* life, but if he *also* were *the cause* of the happiness of those over whom he ruled as king?" (3.2.2). Socrates now suggested that Homer (when speaking through Helen) recognized that the virtuous king does also care, nobly, for his own life, and his own virtuous combat, as well as his virtuous responsibility for his followers' happiness.

Socrates proceeded to add several more general propositions—no longer in the form of questions. First, with an odd inconsequence: "For a king is elected, *not* so that he would care for *himself nobly*, but so that *also* the electors will do well through him." (The *electors*, at any rate, focus solely on their *own* well-being: Smith ad loc.) Second, "*all*" (the leader as well) "campaign militarily so that life for *themselves* will be the *best* possible." Third, "they elect generals for the sake of this, that with a view to this, the latter would be leaders of them." On this final, very ambiguous, basis Socrates concluded that "therefore the one who is general ought to provide *this* [which?] to those who elected him"; and, Socrates added, "to find something nobler than this, is not easy" (i.e., it can be done).

Xenophon's own concluding and apparently bland and clear intervention is rendered ambiguous by his preceding quotations of Socrates's for-mulations of Homer's thought. For those formulations subtly circumscribe the question: Does the virtuous leader as understood by Homer, in focusing on making his electors happy, have as his ultimate and guiding goal *their* good, for which he nobly subordinates or even neglects his own good; or does he aim ultimately at his *own* greatest good, accomplishing it through making his followers happy (thereby enacting his own *virtue*, through his generosity, and thus nobly achieving for himself the very best, because vir-tuous, life—a good that he cannot share with the followers, even or pre-cisely in their inferior, because less virtuous, merely receptive, "happiness" of which he is the cause)?[13] How is the noble related to the good? What is (the) noble?[14] And Xenophon stirs us to ask: Does a Homerically guided leader—unless and until he acquires the Socratic knowledge of generalship and leadership, through having been incited to seriously pursue and answer the question, "What is noble?"—possess a coherent answer to these basic questions about his goal? Is he even aware of these basic questions? Or does he live in a kind of fog, which is essential to his motivation?

## ON THE GOAL AIMED AT BY A NOBLE COMMANDER

The next episode begins with Socrates explicitly confronting an elected leader with the question, "Would you be able (he said), young man, to ar-ticulate for us *what it is, for the sake of which*, you desire to command?" (3.3.1). This time Xenophon has his Socrates orchestrate a real dialogue. It is rather amazing that the interlocutor is a "young man" (*neania*): we do not expect one so youthful to be elected to the highly responsible office of Athenian cavalry commander (see *The Skilled Cavalry Commander* 7.1); what's more, as Socrates proceeds to show, this particular young man is sin-gularly ignorant of obvious practical demands of the office. Xenophon here gives a somewhat comical portrait of the gulf between an elected ruler and a true ruler. To be sure, the young man does exhibit a kind of virtue in this regard: he shows himself capable of listening in docility to Socrates, as the latter points out to him key dimensions of what he must start attending to. But is all this plausible? Seeming to anticipate (and thus to point to) such doubt, Xenophon begins his report of this episode with the unusually strong (or defensive?) affirmation, "*I know* he once also carried on a dialogue as follows. . . ." One of the other writings of Xenophon is a treatise on the art of the cavalry commander—some of whose contents overlap with the pres-ent dialogue,[15] and which is addressed, using the second person singular, to an "apprentice cavalry commander."[16] Xenophon's more serious and sober and practical lecture to his young addressee highlights by contrast the more playful but also (or thereby) profoundly allusive Socratic dialogue.

Not unsurprisingly, the young commander did "not have a ready answer" (XS 60) to Socrates's profound opening question as to his goal. So Socrates went on to disparage and to discard two rather shallow answers that might well have occurred to the young commander but that would not have expressed or done justice to his deepest concern. The goal that animated the young man's desire to command, Socrates submitted, was neither riding in the "deserved" forefront, nor "becoming known." The goal was rather returning the cavalry to the city in "better" shape, and, if the improved cavalry needed to be used, "to become, as leader, the cause of some good *for the city*."[17] When the young commander responded affirmatively, Socrates swore by Zeus that this was a "noble" animating goal—*if*, that is, the young man "was able to do these things" (3.3.2). And then Socrates proceeded, through questioning, to bring the astoundingly (or comically) ignorant young commander to appreciate all the matters to which, for the sake of this goal, he should *start* "giving thought"—and to which he had never before paid any heed!

"First"[18] Socrates showed that as commander the young man ought not to assume (as he was assuming) that the knight-owners would contribute horses that were in good condition for cavalry service; instead, he should himself attend to "making the horses better." For the knight-owners, thinking that they had better things to do for themselves, including better uses for their horses, might well neglect to make their horses "better" for civic cavalry service (cf. *The Skilled Cavalry Commander* 1.13–15). In which case, Socrates asked: "What benefit *for you* will the cavalry be? Or, how will you, as leader of such, do some good *for the city*?" The young man replied: "But you are speaking nobly too (he said), and I will try as much as possible to attend to the horses" (3.3.3–4). These formulations of Socrates, and the young commander's response, brought out the fact that the latter was assuming that what would be of "benefit" for himself, from the good cavalry that he led, would conform with or even be identical to what made him better at "doing some good for the city" (even as the horses' "being made better" meant, "better" for their service to the city—and not necessarily for their owners' private interests).

Next Socrates elicited the young commander's agreement that he would try to make the riders "better." When Socrates specified that this meant in the first place making them more skilled at mounting, the young interlocutor in agreeing gave as the reason, "In this way, if one of them falls off, he would more likely be saved" (3.3.5), apparently thinking, primarily, of the personal security or safety of each individual whom he commanded. Socrates then felt compelled to remind the young commander that he and his horsemen "might have to run risks," and asked if therefore they shouldn't practice on "terrains where the wars take place," rather than on the terrain where they had been accustomed to practicing—sandy (safer) places. The young commander declared that this would be "better, at any rate" (i.e., even if, or precisely because, it would be less safe for the individuals while practicing). He further agreed that it would be "better, at any rate," if he attended to making his men practice throwing to hit as many of the enemy as possible (and practice risking or suffering being hit in return, of course). Then Socrates abruptly turned to "the souls" of the cavalrymen. The young commander affirmed, with some slight hesitation, that even if he had not previously, he would now commence, "at least trying," to make his men "more stouthearted" by "sharpening their souls" and "arousing rage (exorgizein) against the enemy" (3.3.6–7). But this time the young interlocutor did not say that this would be "better." Was it dawning on him that there is a profound tension between what is good for his cavalrymen as individuals, and what serving the good of the city requires of them, which includes not least a major and not unambiguously healthy modification of their souls? This would help explain why Socrates's next lesson finally induced real perplexity in the young commander.

Socrates pointed out that if the commander did not instill obedience in his men, there would be "*nothing* of *benefit* from good and stouthearted men and horses" (the goodness and stouteartedness of his men are not themselves the benefit aimed at by the commander, anymore than are the goodness and well-being of the horses; since Socrates was no longer interpreting Homer's view of leadership, Socrates in this dialogue did not speak of the happiness of the men as the leader's aim; see similarly *The Skilled Cavalry Commander*, esp. 8.5–8). Agreeing with Socrates, the young commander asked how one might especially turn the men toward "this" (3.3.8). For the first time, he had become acutely aware of his own ignorance, and of his consequent need for Socratic education, at least in military leadership—but maybe in much more.

Socrates's elaborate answer was not without ambiguities. He began by successfully appealing to the young man's "awareness" that "in every matter of practical concern (*pragma*), humans are especially willing to obey those whom they hold to be best"—and Socrates adduced as illustrations the sick obeying one they hold to be best at doctoring, sailors obeying one they hold to be best at piloting, and farmers obeying one they hold to be best at farming (all instances of humans obeying those whom they hold to be most knowledgeable in achieving the well-being of those obeying). Socrates then submitted that it was "likely" that similarly, in cavalry service, "the others would especially be willing to obey the one who especially appeared as knowing what needed to be done" (3.3.9).

The young commander responded with a question that ignored Socrates's stress on knowledge, and especially knowledge with a view to the well-being of those obeying. The youth asked only if his being evidently the best would suffice for inspiring obedience to himself. So Socrates made his point more elaborate, thereby bringing out its complexity: "If, at any rate, in *addition* to this, he said" (i.e., in addition to being best), "you teach them that obeying you will be, *for them*, both nobler, *and* more conducive to security." Socrates spotlighted the fact that a cavalry commander's gaining obedience through "appearing as knowing" is distinguished from other sorts of leadership by requiring the rhetorical skill to somehow persuade his troops that in commanding action that is more noble in mortal combat he will be commanding what is safer, for his followers as combatants. The young man's response showed that he was not unaware of how great, not to say staggering, is this challenge: "Now how (he said) will I teach this?" Socrates avoided answering this key question.[19] Instead, he responded with a surprising, not to say jarring, jest, leavened with a profanity: "A lot—by Zeus! (he said)—more easily than if you had to teach that the bad things are better and more profitable than the good!" (3.3.10). Was not Socrates hinting that the "teaching" that a commander must instill in his troops comes to sight as a milder version of this seemingly impossible rhetorical challenge?

In any case, the young commander's response showed that he was starting to realize that a commander of cavalry needs to attend to oratorical rhetoric about the noble, depicted as somehow combined with the good or beneficial, including not least what conduces to security—for the troops who will risk making the ultimate sacrifice in battle. But suddenly (3.3.11) Socrates vastly enlarged and deepened this perplexing lesson in ruling, by asking his interlocutor to "ponder" the fact that it is through speech that "we have learned all the things that are most noble according to lawful convention"—"the things through which we know how to live." The challenge a cavalry commander faces, in teaching his troops about the noble, in its relation to the good or beneficial, including personal security, partakes of the challenge the law faces, in teaching us all about how we ought to live in accord with what is lawfully noble. There is no mention of happiness in this dialogue, even as there was no reference to law in the preceding monologue, which culminated with a stress on happiness.

Socrates took a further step. He asked his young interlocutor to "ponder," in addition, the fact that it is through speeches that one may learn "something else noble"—that is, something noble beyond what the law teaches;[20] and he asked the youth to ponder how "those who are the best teachers especially use speech," and how "those who especially have knowledge of the most serious matters carry on *dialogues* most nobly."[21] We are becoming more open to the idea that we have here the closest Xenophon ever came to giving a taste of what happened when he first met Socrates.

But, having provided this glimpse of the blissfully wise nobility achievable through dialectics, Socrates abruptly switched this present, blissfully noble, dialogue of his back to "pondering" two distinctive lawful customs of Athenian civic piety (3.3.12). Specifically, Socrates reminded that Athens is unrivaled in the competitive choruses that it sends to Panhellenic religious festivals, and also in the beauty contests that it holds among its male citizens (*euandria*[22]) during the Panathenaean and Thesean religious festivals at home. Then Socrates declared, no doubt with due gravity, that the reason Athens is unsurpassed in chorus contests and male beauty contests is not because Athenians are distinguished by better voices or by bigger and stronger male bodies, but because Athenians are distinguished "by love of honor, which especially spurs to the noble and the honored things" (3.3.13; honor and love of honor are *not* themselves the noble and honored things, *not* the goals to which honor spurs). And "do you not think (he said) that if somebody were to attend to the cavalry here, that they would in this respect also far surpass the others," even "in readiness to run risks against the enemies," if "they held the lawful belief" that they would thereby "obtain praise and honor?" Socrates thus finally explained the theme of the rhetoric the young commander needs to deploy: you should "try to turn the men to these things" (3.3.14–15): to desire for praise and for honor—like that won in singing-dancing and male beauty contests at festivals, that is, in the presence of and with devotional sacrifice to the gods.[23] But of course, in those contests of music and of male beauty, no contestant risks sacrifice, of his very existence; in those music and beauty contests, the victors always live to enjoy their honors, unscathed—and even the defeated remain perfectly safe. The nobility of warriors is heroic; and their deserved civic honors, especially if and when they die, are accordingly much, much greater—as we will see vividly in the following episode (3.4.3), *and* as we recall from Virtue's victory in Her debate with Vice. Socrates concluded his dialogue with the young commander by promising that "from" such rhetorical success "you yourself will reap benefit, and the other citizens through[24] you." The dialogue concluded with the young commander passionately swearing by Zeus that he would try to execute the rhetoric that Socrates had now suggested to him.

Socrates did not specify the benefits he promised would accrue from this rhetorical success. Xenophon thus spurs us to try to do so, and to encounter and to ponder the puzzles that thereby arise. The most obvious benefit for those "*other* citizens" who are *not* cavalrymen is their safety, procured by the fighting, sometimes dying cavalrymen. But for the latter, who are also among the "other citizens," safety is precisely what they, along with their commander, sacrifice (the cavalry, as a distinct minority of the citizenry who fight and risk their lives for the rest, bring to light a major dimension of the problem of the goal of leadership that was veiled in the Homeric teaching). The cavalry's most obvious "benefit" will be to have some share in "praise and distinction"; and one might go so far as to say that these "constitute the specific happiness of the military commander" (XS 60–61). But are not the cavalrymen, together with their commander, hoping to be distinguished and honored above all for having subordinated, risked, or even sacrificed their safety, and thereby their happiness (their prospect of *living to enjoy* their distinction and honors), for the sake of nobly achieving what is good, not for themselves, but for the city and the other citizens (recall 3.3.1–2 and see 3.5.3), under the gods? Is not the honor or glory that they receive to be rightly understood as a deserved, compensatory reward for their selfless risk and sacrifice? Or, alternatively, is it possible that their nobility is to be rightly conceived as their own greatest good, because the enactment of their own excellence of character, and hence their nobility, is not, in the final analysis, a self-sacrifice? And are the consequent distinction and honor to be rightly conceived as no more than the shining forth of their superior flourishing, and the expression, from others, of congratulatory admiration for their success in life, much like the congratulations accorded winners of beauty contests, and the admiration accorded those who "carry on dialogues most nobly" (see 4.8.6–7)? Which of these two alternative conceptions correctly articulates what truly constitutes the noble, the honored, the ultimate goal coherently animating and guiding virtue, and in particular the virtue of the commander and his cavalry?[25] Or does successful command depend on no one asking and pursuing this question?

## ASSIMILATING MILITARY-POLITICAL RULE TO HOUSEHOLD MANAGEMENT ("OECONOMICS")

The contradiction within the conception of nobly virtuous rule or leadership becomes blatant in the next reported confrontation. A veteran named

Nicomachides (meaning "son of a victorious fighter"),[26] accosted by Socrates, expressed with passion, and profane invocations of Zeus, the view that what constitutes the virtue of generalship is proven ability such as his own: that is, capacity as leader to "have worn myself away" (*katatetrimmai*) in service, suffering repeated wounds—whose ugly scars the veteran dramatically displayed, by stripping. Such a dangerous, painful, and mutilating service record entails, as the veteran's anger indicates, a moral claim of entitlement to election by the other citizens, as his just desert and recompense.

But the Athenians, the scarred veteran indignantly reported, all too typically (he bitterly remarked), elected "Antisthenes"[27]—someone who had never done any military service of note, and who "has knowledge of nothing except accumulating money," for himself (3.4.1).

Although Socrates had refrained from even attending the electoral assembly, he defended as "good," in this particular case,[28] the electors' choice. For, Socrates asked, won't Antisthenes's economic expertise make him competent to procure provisions for the soldiers? Moreover, Socrates added, this winner of the election has the character of a "contentious lover of victory"[29]—a "trait suitable for a general"—as evidenced especially by his spending his money often in sponsoring contestants who always win the choral contests (3.4.2–3; one wonders: did Antisthenes also spend his money to win the election to generalship?).

To this, the understandably exasperated veteran rejoined: "But there is *nothing* similar in presiding over a *chorus*, and over an *army*!"—invoking Zeus's name in a curse. (In referring to Antisthenes's choral triumphs, Socrates did not mention the gods, and gave no indication that Antisthenes was motivated by piety, or by anything except his enjoyment of public victories.) Doubtless the battle-scarred Nicomachides was thinking of what most dramatically differentiates chorus competition from battle: no need for the capacity to risk sacrifice of life and limb.

Socrates blithely responded by pointing out that although Antisthenes, as an expert knower of moneymaking, himself "lacks experience in guiding song and dance," he "nevertheless has become competent to find those who are the strongest at these things."

"So then," Nicomachides scornfully retorted, "he will find in the army *others* who give the orders, instead of himself, and *others* who fight?!"

Socrates answered: "If, at any rate, he does find and choose the strongest in contests of war, as he did in the choral contests, then it is likely that he would be the one who carries away the victory also in this." Besides, Socrates added, Antisthenes was likely to be willing to spend even more of his money on the grander victory—in contests of war, with the whole city—than he had spent on the lesser victories in choral contests, with only his tribe (3.4.3–5).

Nicomachides could not believe his ears.[30] His response expressed his completely contrary conception of the virtue of generalship, his doubt of the very possibility of such a virtue of generalship as Socrates was advancing and defending: "Are you really saying (he said), Socrates, that it belongs to the same man nobly to sponsor *choruses* and to be a *general*?!"

Socrates had certainly staked out a provocative position: without denying that men with the capacity and spirit of the veteran are essential to the city's army, he was contending that the superior virtue of the general consists solely in knowing how to provide and to effectively use whoever and whatever is needed to maximize the likelihood of the general's enjoying his own victorious preeminence (which requires and entails, as a condition, but *not* as the purpose, the victory also of the general's followers and city). What is more, in response to the veteran's incredulous question, Socrates next "doubled down" and vastly broadened his contention, applying his thesis not only to leadership of an army and of choral contestants, and not only to the pursuit of victory, but to leadership of a city and of a household—without specifying the latters' goals (3.4.6).

The veteran's incredulity turned to shock, seeing the implications of thus reducing what he regarded as noble public service to what is concerned largely with amassing and spending one's own money, primarily for one's own interests: "By Zeus! (he said), Socrates, I would never have thought to hear from *you* that the good household managers (oeconomists) would be good generals!" Evidently Socrates had never before disclosed to an acquaintance such as the veteran his "oeconomic" conception of the virtue of generalship (and of statesmanship). Yet a version of this unpopular conception of rule and statesmanship Xenophon depicts Socrates learning from the perfect gentleman—who teaches this conception as the truly wise, inspiring and inspired, rule over slaves (even gentlemen-slaves) that in its wisdom partakes of the rule exercised by divinity itself (*Oeconomicus*, esp. chap. 21). Here, in confrontation with the "worn-away" veteran, Socrates articulated his own, more provocative version,[31] in which what is at issue is not primarily wise, inspiring mastery over slaves versus republican freedom expressed in popular election,[32] but rather rule as self-sacrificial service versus rule as prudent self-aggrandizement (contrast XS 63).

Socrates proceeded to put his case to Nicomachides, through dialectical "examination." The veteran agreed that both a manager of his own estate and a general must render the ruled "heedful and obedient"; must order each of them to do his suitable tasks; must punish the bad and honor the good among them—and that it is "noble for both"[33] to make their subordinates well disposed. Nicomachides further concurred that it is "advantageous for both" to draw in allies and helpers; that both ought to be guardians of property (Socrates refrained from specifying to whom the property belongs; the veteran's agreement was emphatic—he presumably had in mind private property; consider *Hiero* 10.5 and 11.1–4); and that both ought to be attentive, and fond of labor, as regards his own tasks (3.4.8–9). In short, the veteran did not and could not deny the need in a leader for all these sorts of shrewd practical knowledge, including the capacity for persuasive rhetoric. But the veteran was sure that the heart of the virtue of generalship is something else altogether.

That distinguishing core of the virtue becomes obvious, the veteran believes he knows, in actual combat: while the preceding skills "all similarly belong to both," it is "the *fighting*"—Nicomachides insisted—that "no longer belongs to both" (3.4.10). Conceding to Socrates that both the general and the household manager have enemies ("That's for sure!") and that it is advantageous for both to prevail over their enemies, Nicomachides nevertheless accused Socrates of "passing over" the decisive consideration: "If it would be necessary to fight (*machesthai*), of what benefit would the art of household management be?" (3.4.10–11). With these, his final words, reaffirming his basic view (recall 3.4.4), Nicomachides surely had in mind the fighting that takes place in the city's wars; but by speaking of "fighting" rather than "making war" the oft-wounded veteran indicated that he was thinking not so much of strategy, supply, and so on (the managerial aspects of generalship) but rather of the horrors of hand-to-hand, bloody, phalanx combat—which Greek generals lead, literally in the front line, and frequently at the cost of their lives.[34] He was thinking that there is no way to derive, from expertise at household management with a view to amassing and spending private wealth (even if spending it on winning victories), the key virtuous capacity: the readiness to put life and limb on the line for the city.

But the pertinacious Socrates insisted that it is precisely in this respect that is found "the greatest" claim of the art of household management to be *the* art of rule and leadership. For the "good householder," since he "knows" that "nothing is as profitable and gainful as being victorious in fighting the enemy, nor as profitless and costly as being bested," will "with an eager spirit (*prothumōs*) seek out and provide the things advantageous with a view to victory," and will "attentively inquire into and guard against the things that conduce to being bested"; and "if he sees the preparations such as to be victorious, he will fight, and energetically (*energōs*)." (So Socrates by no means denied that the household manager, in order to be a good general, must be ready and able to fight energetically, to risk death—when, that is, the odds of victory are good.) And besides, "what is not the least of these things (Socrates stressed)," if he should be unprepared, he will guard against joining battle" (3.4.11).

Addressing Nicomachides by name, but no longer appearing to seek agreement, Socrates exhorted him "not to despise the oeconomic men." For "the attentive care of the private interests differs only quantitatively from the attentive care of the public interests," above all because "those who attentively care for the public do not use humans who are different from the humans whom the oeconomists use in attentively caring for their private interests"—and "it is those who are knowers of how to use the humans" who are the ones who "carry out nobly both the private and the public affairs," while "it is those who are not such knowers who err in both" (3.4.12).

The veteran remained stonily silent. There was no sign that he had budged from his original thesis, and from his revulsion at the Socratic thesis. Since Socrates "in speeches dealt as he wished with all who conversed with him" (1.2.14), it is not likely that Socrates intended to convert this interlocutor. In all likelihood his aim was instead a provocatively confrontational display for onlookers, including the reporter Xenophon—who has reproduced the educational display, in all its provocation, for us.

The veteran's dramatic role, in this display, is to make it unmistakably manifest that Socrates is here embracing one alternative within the contradictory commonsense conception of the nobility of virtue and virtuous rule—while the veteran stands up for the contrary alternative. Socrates takes his stand on the priority of the goodness, the benefit, of nobly virtuous rule *for the nobly virtuous.* Do we not mean, by the goodness of noble virtue and the nobly virtuous, not merely or mainly goodness "for" something or someone else, but goodness that constitutes the virtuous person's superiority, in regard to his own greatest personal good—his good character, and the life expression of that character? Does not nobly virtuous ruling enact the nobly virtuous ruler's own greatest good, precisely through leadership that benefits those whom he leads?

But, by here defending his thesis by way of an example that contains a mercenary element and even allows a somewhat mercenary connotation (Antisthenes the expert oeconomist), Xenophon's Socrates insures that we listen with sympathy and respect to the veteran's obstinate, anti-Socratic stand. The battle-scarred veteran insists on the priority of sacrificial service, entailing just compensatory desert, as the core of a noble leader's virtue. In ignoring this, does not Socrates abstract from, and thereby circumscribe, the nobility of virtue as *selfless or self-transcending devotion*, to the lawful and just good of the *others* in the city? Is it not this that induces our awed reverence, that arouses our sense of obligation to and compassion for the nobly virtuous, that moves us to honor them, in imperfectly just recognition and recompense for all that they have suffered and given? Does not the Socratic thesis remove noble virtue's moral claim of deserving?

But can we rest on the conception that noble virtue in and by itself is *not* good for the nobly virtuous person? Is the choice of noble virtue a choice to render oneself worse off, in the most important respect? In seeking to raise one's children as nobly virtuous, is one seeking to make their lives worse, for them? Or in what dimly but powerfully felt way can noble virtue be conceived as in a deep sense supremely good for the nobly virtuous person precisely because it is so obviously not good for that person? Or are we, is "common sense," not deeply contradictory and confused? Is this not something of the greatest importance that we desperately need to sort out if we are to know what we live (and die) for, at our best?

## HIS EARNEST TEACHING OF NOBLE GENERALSHIP

The preceding, deeply provocative, fourth or central of the speeches on the politically noble is followed (and superficially veiled) by a dialogue that portrays Socrates in his finest hour as a serious adviser to his city's leadership (naturally then, this conversation, unlike so many in the *Memorabilia*, is unsullied by any profane oaths). "In dialogue with Pericles—the son of *the* Pericles" (*tou panu Perikleous*—3.5.1), Socrates is shown trying to uplift the spirits of the disheartened general. Socrates does so by showing Pericles the Younger insufficiently noticed potential roots of civic spirit in the demoralized Athenians, and by arousing an aspiration to make the citizenry lay claim to their ancestors' drive to "be first, with virtue" (a more elevated version of the passion Socrates attributed to Antisthenes: 3.5.7–8, 3.4.3–5). Then, Socrates is shown finally suggesting, more concretely, a shrewd strategic innovation that, if executed, would substantially enhance the security of Athens and all its inhabitants (including, of course, Socrates and those he loves).

In this episode Socrates continued to maintain his thesis that knowledge (*epistēmē*), which has been "learned" (*manthanein*), is the core of true generalship (3.5.21)—and he gave fuller indication of how this thesis can be applied in practice. Socrates taught Pericles that, as elected general, he needed to begin to attend (as Pericles had previously neglected to attend) to studying "many" (not all) of "your father's strategies," and "many things from elsewhere." More generally, Socrates taught Pericles the Younger that he ought, having become aware of his ignorance, "to spare neither gifts nor favors" that would enable him "to learn from others what one doesn't know, and to acquire good helpers." Pericles eventually declared that he had become "not unaware" that Socrates was here subtly "teaching me" (3.5.22–24). Only after thus gaining Pericles's explicit acknowledgment of having become Socrates's student, aware of his own ignorance, did Socrates as teacher and thus possessor of the science of generalship elaborate his specific strategic suggestion (3.5.25–27). The stratagem Socrates advised was not derived from the great Pericles, nor from any ancestral Greek or Athenian source; it came from study and application of the shrewdness of certain barbarians—who happen to be mentioned repeatedly in the *Anabasis*.[35] We are reminded of the most famous general who was a student of Socrates: Xenophon, who, applying what he had learned from Socrates, led a great escape from barbarians, in large part by shrewdly using barbarians and their ways. Socrates, as true general, did not need to seek or to hold the office or rank of general; instead, he employed his knowledge of generalship—which included the dialectical art of "in speeches dealing as he wishes with all who converse with him" (1.2.14; see again 4.5.12)—to educate those among the elected, so-called generals who were capable of listening to and learning from "General Socrates."

In closing, Socrates told young Pericles that whatever he might accomplish of the things Socrates had advised "will be both noble for you, and good for the city; and if you are unable to do any of them, you will neither harm the city, nor bring shame on yourself." Socrates did not promise that failure would be harmless for Pericles, nor that success would be beneficial for him (3.5.28; XS 68). Socrates at the end seemed to step back toward a "Nicomachidean" view of the noble. Yet Socrates did not attempt to provoke Pericles, as he unsuccessfully tried to provoke Nicomachides, and as he successfully provoked us, to problematize this notion of the noble, or to reflect on the profound tension within our conception of the nobility of virtue. Pericles would not have been helped in his generalship by being educated in that profound tension.

Xenophon, however, does not allow *us* to forget that tension. At the outset, Xenophon has Socrates say to Pericles: "I for my part, oh Pericles, have hope that with you as general, *the city* will be better and more reputed as regards matters of war, and will overpower its enemies" (3.5.1). Accordingly, when Pericles responded to Socrates by introducing the goal of "rearousing erotic passion for ancient virtue" as associated with "happiness" as well as "glory"—*for the virtuous*—Pericles spoke of all this as belonging *not* to himself, but to the citizens whom he leads (3.5.7). Socrates replied by drawing one of his jarring analogies: this time, between (a) the two of them leading the citizen-soldiers to lay claim to money that is in the possession of others, by claiming that the money belongs to them by inheritance; and (b) their leading the citizen-soldiers to strive "to take first place, *with/through* virtue," thereby becoming "mightiest of all" (3.5.8; Socrates here repeatedly referred to civic virtue in terms of achieving superiority over others). Socrates soon added the consideration that their forefathers' "great deeds" went with the forefathers "acquiring" unprecedented "power and resources" (3.5.11). Pericles was impressed; but what moved him to "wonder at how the city ever declined to the worse" was Socrates's reminder that Athens once was renowned for its arbitration of foreigners' judicial disputes, and for taking in, as refugees, many victims of injustice (3.5.12–13). When, in response to Pericles's asking what the citizenry "might do to recover the ancient virtue," Socrates proposed their imitating, if not the pursuits of their ancestors, then at least the pursuits of the best of their contemporaries, Pericles presumed that Socrates referred to the pursuits of the Spartans—in light of whose standard Pericles excoriated contemporary Athens as "far from gentleman-liness" (3.5.14–15). We see that Pericles was self-forgettingly and ardently civic-minded: his eros longed for happiness, virtue, and gentlemanliness *as belonging to the citizenry*; he admired his own ancestral community's generosity to the needy more than its acquisition of power and resources for its own benefit; and he looked from afar, with admiration or longing, at what he conceived to be Spartan *communal* virtue or gentlemanliness.

Socrates did not deny Pericles's indictment of contemporary Athens—as, in contrast with Sparta, woefully pervaded by contempt for elders, disdain for physical exercise, and disobedience; and as riven with febrile envy, public disagreement, private litigiousness, and predatory fighting over public property. Athens had become a sick society. Nonetheless Socrates demurred from Pericles's gloomy conclusion: "Do not at all, oh Pericles, consider that the Athenians are sick with an *incurable* disease!" Socrates appealed to the examples of two most un-Spartan Athenian institutions: the discipline in the navy, and the discipline among the choral contestants. Socrates appealed as well to something in a sense shared with Sparta, though in a more individualistically honor-loving spirit: the discipline exhibited by Athenians competing in gymnastic contests (3.5.15–18; the gravity of this dialogue precludes mention of discipline among the male beauty contestants). Early on, Socrates had gotten Pericles to agree, grudgingly, that the Athenians are the "most honor-loving of all peoples," which is "not the least spur to run risks, for the sake of repute and fatherland"; and Socrates had linked this love of honor with the emulation of noble deeds of ancestors, which can

inspire "many to turn toward caring for virtue and becoming brave" (3.5.3).
We see that Socrates appreciated better, because he was more in syncopa-
tion with, the distinctively individualistic, competitive, civic virtue native
to the Athenian (vs. the Spartan) spirit.

But in response to Socrates's invocation of the Athenian discipline in the
navy and among gymnastic contestants, Pericles bemoaned how all the more
deplorably amazing it was that "the heavy infantrymen and cavalry, who are
held to be preeminent among the citizens for gentlemanliness, are the most
disobedient of all!" (3.5.19; cf. *Regime of the Athenians* 2.1). Socrates rejoined rather evasively by reminding of another distinctive, and gentlemanly,
Athenian institution: the Areopagus (an ancient senatorial and judicial body
whose originally powerful constitutional role was drastically weakened first
by the father of the great Pericles and then by the latter's more radical democratic reforms). Socrates asked Pericles the Younger a question that, given
the contemporary Athenian constitutional circumstances, inherited from
the great Pericles, verged on the plaintive: "Do you know of any who judge
cases and do other things in a more noble or lawful or august or just manner
[than the members of the Areopagus]?"[36] Pericles's reply—"I am not blaming
(he said) these"—was laconic in every sense. When Socrates drew the conclusion that "therefore one should not be disheartened on the grounds that
the Athenians are not well ordered," Pericles stubbornly reasserted that "in
what concerns the soldiers, where especially is needed sensible moderation,
and good order, and obedience to commanders, they pay attention to none of
these!" (3.5.19–21).

The Socratic reply to this last was long, but not very strong. "Maybe
it's because, said Socrates, in these matters, those who are least knowledgeable rule them"—and Socrates proceeded to his thesis that knowledge is the
core virtue that constitutes a true general; and then Pericles acknowledged
Socrates as teacher. But, having achieved this, Socrates gave as his only substantive new practical lesson the limited, if very important, strategic suggestion of instituting a new corps of youthful, light-armed, mountaineer guards
of—and raiders setting out from—the outer borders of Attica (3.5.21–27).
Could it be that the most seriously intended practical function of the whole
preceding, broad and hopeful, Socratic exhortation (to the project of rekin-
dling something of ancient virtue), was to serve as a "pep talk" that would
put Pericles in a mood willing to listen, with somewhat reenergized ambition, to this final, quite restricted, concrete proposal?[37]—a proposal that, "by
suggesting that the whole territory be defended against enemy incursions,
tacitly opposes the whole strategy of the great Perikles: Thucydides 1.143.4–5
and 2.13.2" (XS 68; see also *Ways and Means* 4.43–48).

None of this is to deny that at the end of the conversation Xenophon has Pericles speak approvingly of the usefulness of *all* that Socrates has taught him (3.5.27). Looking back over the conversation, we see that Socrates had suggested a specific *rhetorical* strategy for Pericles to follow, in attempting to inspirit his troops with some sparks of the old-time virtue. Socrates had sketched a publicly inspiring perspective on the whole history of Athenian political development. As numerous commentators have noted, this sketch repeatedly evokes, and calls out for comparison with, the perspective presented by the great Pericles in his famous and inspiring Funeral Oration, as reported by Thucydides. What commentators have largely failed to appreciate, however, is how *anti*-Periclean is this Socratic antistrophe—whose endorsement by Pericles the Younger is thus ironically delicious.

For the great Pericles opened his speech with a criticism of the law of "the ancients" and proceeded to present the history of Athens as one of progress: from the modest virtues of the ancients to the greater virtues of "our" forefathers, and finally to the supreme virtues of *us*, the Periclean generation—"we here now, yet living, and very much in the prime of life," who have most *expanded* the empire (Thucydides 2.35–36; XS 66). The Funeral Oration made no reference whatsoever to the closeness of the ancestors to the gods, or, for that matter, to any divinity whatsoever: in his famous Funeral Oration the great Pericles spoke a-theistically.

Socrates, with the essential assistance of Pericles the Younger, portrayed an Athenian development whose peak was in the beginning: the citizens around the first, demigod king had such "virtue" that the citizenry was qualified to judge a contestation between gods. Under the subsequent king, Erectheus (who was born from Earth Herself), the citizenry fought victoriously to defend and to restore the refugee offspring of Heracles after his apotheosis (see *Hellenica* 6.4.47). Then, under Theseus, the Athenians defeated semidivine marauders (Centaurs and Amazons) as well as human foes, "demonstrating themselves the best among humans of their time" (3.5.10). Only with hesitation ("and, if you will, . . .") did Socrates leave the ancestors and descend to the more recent forefathers, who in the Persian Wars, allied with Sparta, admittedly did grander deeds, and acquired more power and resources, and who later became internationally recognized for equitable judging of human disputes, and who afforded refuge to victims of injustice—*but* whose *virtue* got no mention from Socrates, so overshadowed was it by the *real* virtue seen in the ancestors (3.5.11–12). Power, wealth, grand deeds, including just judgment and affording refuge to the oppressed, do not yet add up to ancestral virtue, which peaks in judging, under a demigod-monarch, and which is of such purity that it gives humans moral authority even among gods. In the light of this history of Athens, Pericles the Younger could not but wonder in amazement, "How have we declined so low?" Socrates did not hesitate to give the answer. In effect, he tacitly adduced the evil consequences of the successful imperialism of the great Pericles: "I for my part think that even as some others,[38] on account of their great preeminence and overpowering strength, have fallen into soft-ness of spirit and become inferior to their competitors, so it is with the Athenians—who, having become very preeminent, neglected themselves and through this became worse" (we recall Xenophon's judgment on how Athenian public life corrupted Alcibiades). Pericles the Younger responded by asking what the Athenians might "do to recover their ancient virtue" (tēn archain aretēn—3.5.13–14). Pericles the Younger did not for a minute look to the recent, so-called virtue of the great Pericles and his imperialism: whereas the oration of the great Pericles peaked in a call for Athenians to become erotic lovers of the imperial power of Athens (Thucydides 2.43.1), Pericles the Younger asked Socrates how Athenians might recover erotic love for ancient (nonimperial) virtue and glory and happiness (3.5.7). But Socrates's reply pointedly did not endorse even this more tradition-oriented version of the great Pericles's political eroticism, or erotic passion for glory and happiness (3.5.8). On a lower but more solid plane, Socrates earlier had responded to the younger Pericles's initial report of the "humbling" of the Athenian citizenry on account of the perceived superiority of enemy Thebes by pointing out that "this makes the city's disposition more acceptable to a ruler who is a good man": for "whereas boldness instills carelessness and softness of spirit and disobedience, fear makes people more attentive and more obedient and more orderly, as is seen also from what happens on the ships."[39] A humbler and more fearful and unerotic Athens is a better Ath-ens, in the eyes of a ruler who is a good man. This implies that the Great Per-icles was not such a man, and that "the self-confidence of the Periklean age was already a sign of decline" (XS 66).

We must observe, however, that the reference to the discipline in the ships goes with Socrates's subsequent favorable reference to the disciplined Athenian navy—evidently a strongpoint of the contemporary Athenian re-gime, in Socrates's eyes. But was not the navy the key instrument of the great Themistocles in launching the empire? And then, as a consequence, was not the navy, empowering the dēmos, key to the democratic, imperial-ist transformation of the Athenian regime and the spirit of its laws, includ-ing eventually the desuetude of the Areopagus (see Regime of the Athe-nians)? Yes, but the navy and the empire it allowed to be launched, and thus the beginning at least of the democratic regime change, were absolutely

essential to the successful Themistoclean effort to liberate Athens from sub-
ordination or enslavement to Persia and Sparta. The ancestors and their
gods were not preventing this enslavement, in Themistocles's eyes; would
Socrates disagree? Strauss (XS 65–66) draws our attention to the fact that
"the only mention of the gods that occurs in this section" is by Pericles the
Younger, not by Socrates; and Strauss also asks us to recall "the earlier contrast" that Socrates drew, "between the spellbinder Pericles and the solid
achievements of Themistokles—2.6.13." An underlying tension is visible in
Socrates's implied evaluation of Athenian political development: the conversation with the younger Pericles affords a bird's-eye view of Socrates's
understanding of the problematic dialectic of foreign and domestic policy in
republics (see Montesquieu, *Spirit of the Laws* 9.1).

## ON WHAT A STATESMAN NEEDS TO KNOW

In another one of his roller-coaster drops, Xenophon plunges us, from the
height of Socrates's politically most serious educative dialogue with the
elected general Pericles down to a conversation in which we watch Socrates
managing to "put a stop to" the megalomaniacal political ambition of a
teenager whose ridiculously embarrassing antics could not be controlled by
"anyone among his other kin and friends."[40] Not surprisingly, this comical conversation contains more profane expletives (eight, four of which are
sworn by Socrates) than any previous episode.

The jocundity in the setting and the tone of this dialogue (Smith ad loc.)
is rather astounding, given that, as regards subject matter, "in the present
section we observe without difficulty an ascent from purely military matters
to the political in the comprehensive sense." In order to bring home to Glaucon the depth and breadth of his delusions of grandeur, Socrates takes the
young man through the key dimensions of public policy that an Athenian
statesman must understand—and about which Glaucon is forced to confess
he does not have a clue. More than anywhere else, "we see here Socrates
'teaching the political things'" and thereby delineating "the scope of political knowledge or rather of the political knowledge required of an Athenian
statesman"(XS 69, 71). Why does Xenophon present *the* portrait of Socrates
in the act of teaching practical statesmanship in so unserious a frame?

The statesman's knowledge, as Socrates lays it out, comprises the following: revenues and expenditures; offensive and defensive military policy;
policing crime; exploiting natural resources (for Athens, that means the silver mines); and managing the food supply, domestic and foreign. As Strauss
says, "Political knowledge thus understood has, so to speak, nothing in

common with the core of Socratic knowledge, with the raising and answering of the 'what is' questions, for instance, of the questions 'What is the city?'; "What is a statesman?'; 'What is rule over human beings?' (I.i.16)." In other words, Socratic "political science" or "political philosophy" proceeds on two levels. There is the teaching on the practical knowledge needed by a practicing statesman, knowledge that Socrates delivers when apt and that he and his students deploy when needed—but that is not his most serious concern. Then there is the dialectical heart of Socratic political philosophy: a skeptical inquiry into the "What is . . ." questions, and especially into the questions about the politically noble—an inquiry such as we have been following in the preceding conversations. The major practical outcome, for the inquirer, of this latter, most profound dimension of Socratic political science is manifest in the radically distinctive Socratic way of life.

In this particular case, the practical Socratic education in politics is employed not for the sake of protecting the city—the febrile Glaucon is, mercifully, in no danger of becoming a leader of Athens—but rather out of goodwill for the self-destructively deluded lad, on account of two elite students of Socrates: Charmides and Plato,[41] who are respectively the lad's uncle and brother. Xenophon thus tacitly (and all the more effectively) spotlights the type of students for whose philosophical-political education, and for whose welfare, and therefore family well-being, Socrates is above all concerned. They, or their souls, are the beauties Socrates loves.

## SOCRATES EXHORTING TO A CAREER AS A DEMOCRATIC LEADER

The playful (and so, fittingly, profanity-laced) but effective dehortation of Glaucon from politics, for the sake of Charmides and Plato, is followed by an exhortation to politics, much more serious in tone and intention (containing no profane oaths, of course), directed at Charmides. Socrates is shown trying to "teach" Charmides to overcome his reluctance to "compete" to become a popular leader in "the Assembly."

The fact that, as we have seen, Xenophon names Charmides in the same breath as Plato, as objects of Socrates's concern, pays Charmides a very high compliment. Xenophon's *Symposium* makes it clear that Charmides was a member, in some sense, of Socrates's inner philosophic circle:[42] Charmides was even vouchsafed a glimpse of Socrates "dancing alone" (see T. Pangle 2010). The present hortatory conversation is thus a striking indication that Socrates judges his own, politically marginal, more purely philosophic, way of life to be unsuitable even for some of his intellectually most gifted students—especially if they have manifested political-dialectical skill and interest. We see here Socrates urging upon Charmides the gnomic command "Be not ignorant of yourself" (mē agnoei seauton—3.7.9)—which in Charmides's peculiar case means "Do not neglect the things of the city, if in some regard it can become, through you, better off." For (Socrates concludes) "not only the other citizens but your friends, and you yourself not least, will be benefited." Socrates in his generosity as a teacher is not self-forgetting, and does not in the least urge Charmides to be so;[43] on the contrary: "Do not err as most err; for the many (hoi polloi) in exerting themselves to look after the affairs of others, do not turn to examining themselves; do you not therefore be soft in spirit about this, but instead stretch yourself to attend to yourself" (3.7.9).

The reluctance to compete politically that Socrates is seeking to get Charmides to overcome is not caused by the latter's preoccupation with philosophy, or by his deep attachment to Socrates and his ways. This is not a conversation in which Socrates tries to turn one of his followers from (Socratic) philosophizing to engagement in politics. For Charmides is already quite engaged politically.[44] Socrates has already observed Charmides's superior political skill, exhibited in conversations with leading politicians who have sought Charmides's counsel—politicians whom Charmides "nobly advises," and, when they make mistakes, Charmides "correctly censures."[45] And the present conversation begins with Socrates bringing out how strongly Charmides believes that it is "soft and cowardly" to be "unwilling to compete" when one is capable of "winning victories in contests that bring honor to oneself and repute to one's fatherland" (3.7.1). What holds Charmides back from becoming himself an actual competitor for preeminence in Athenian politics is the democratic character of the Athenian regime. Charmides is by nature suited to excel as a leader in aristocratic or oligarchic, rather than democratic, politics. For while Charmides "easily converses with" those who are first in the city, even though some of them "hold him in contempt" (3.7.7–8), he evidently feels with singular force the social "shame and fear" that he insists is "implanted by nature in humans" and is "much more present" when one is before "mobs" than when one is "in private gatherings" (3.7.4).

"I am engaged in teaching you," Socrates says, the following absurdity: that you, who are "not abashed before the most prudent," nor "fearful of the strongest," and show yourself to be "much superior to those who are concerned to dialogue with the city," are yet "ashamed to speak before the most imprudent and the weakest!" Think concretely, Socrates implores, of the kinds of people who actually make up the Athenian assembly: craftsmen, farmers, tradesmen, "who have *never* thought *prudently* about matters of political skill"—and who besides "do *not* hold you in contempt" (3.7.5–7).

Yet Socrates does not dispute Charmides's assertion about human nature, intertwined with Charmides's implicit claim of insight into his own peculiarly, and, yes, irrationally, crowd-averse nature. Charmides's very response here expresses this particular nature of his: he voices his anxiety that he will be one of those who are "often" laughed at in the Assembly, while telling the ignorant crowd what is "correctly spoken" (3.7.8).

Socrates protests his "amazement" that Charmides is so troubled by this: after all, though often laughed at when conversing with the few who lead and who know something about politics, you "handle it easily!" To this Charmides makes no reply; and he listens in silence to the rest of Socrates's exhortation to greater self-knowledge as the key to overcoming his shyness in approaching the crowd, and then using his powers to "make the city better" (3.7.8–9). Does not Xenophon show us here a limit case of Socrates's ability "to deal as he wished with all who conversed with him?" Is Socrates not rather desperately trying to reason Charmides out of his distinctive and instinctive political nature—a gifted political nature that needs to, and might, in some circumstances, push dangerously toward a nondemocratic, elitist regime? Overshadowing this conversation, but thereby illuminating its import, are the facts recorded in Xenophon's *Hellenica* (2.4.19): Charmides later (in 404) became a leader in the regime of the Thirty oligarchs, a regime that he died in battle defending (in 403), against the successful democratic counterrevolution. Xenophon of course did not mention or so much as allude to the case and career of Charmides when he earlier presented his rebuttal of the charge that Socrates corrupted the young by leading them to look down upon the democratic regime. We conclude that Xenophon means to show here that Socrates seriously tried to reconcile the politically gifted Charmides with the democratic assembly—but failed in this attempt. We further conclude that this particular case exemplifies a more general and profound problem for democracy, and for Socrates, or indeed for political philosophy: a problem caused by and rooted in a certain type of gifted political nature.

## HOW IS THE BEAUTIFUL/NOBLE RELATED TO THE GOOD?

Immediately after depicting Socrates exhorting one of his closest and best followers to engage in Athenian democratic politics, Xenophon presents a renewal of the debate between Socrates and Aristippus. We recall the latter, from 2.1, as the advocate of the apolitical, hedonistic life, in opposition to Socrates's advocacy of the life of political rule and virtue—an advocacy culminating in Virtue's victorious edification of Heracles. Yet Xenophon does not, as one might expect, now present Socrates enlarging upon his earlier advocacy of the political life. The series of conversations showing how Socrates helped those reaching out for the noble as high political office has been completed. At this point we leap, from the theme of the politically noble, to the theme of the beautiful or noble as such, in its relation to the good as such. Xenophon makes the leap conspicuous by effecting it through a renewal of the debate between Aristippus and Socrates, and then surprising us by *not* having Socrates reprise or continue his defense of the nobility of political life; instead, the renewed debate with Aristippus initiates a series of conversations showing how Socrates "helped his companions" (3.8.1) in their understanding of the beautiful in its entire range, from dung-baskets to divinity.[46]

Aristippus was to become famous as a disciple of Socrates who founded his own (hedonistic) school, the "Cyrenaics."[47] As the earlier encounter between Aristippus and Socrates made vividly clear, Xenophon presents Aristippus as a philosopher manqué, lacking in self-knowledge. Now, Xenophon makes Socrates's second conversation with Aristippus a wry substitute for a conspicuously missing conversation between Socrates and Plato: "The peak is missing" (XS 73–74; this is one of Xenophon's more explicit indications that his oeuvre as a whole presupposes, and complements, the Platonic oeuvre[48]). Xenophon here not only tips his hat to Plato. In the ensuing conversation with Aristippus we are to keep in mind the "missing" conversation between Socrates and Plato (Johnson 2009, 214–25). Here Xenophon points us toward the esoteric teaching of Plato on the beautiful and the good.

"Aristippus tried to refute Socrates, even as he had earlier been refuted by the latter" (3.8.1). Aristippus sought to outwit the maestro at his own game (Rossetti 2008, 118)—"as if he has been stewing away in the wings plotting his vengeance" (Gray 1998, 143). His strategic plan was to ask Socrates to give an example of something Socrates claimed to know to be good, and then to demonstrate that that very thing is sometimes bad. It would appear that Aristippus had received somehow, or from someone (Plato?—Johnson 2009, 214–25), the impression that Socrates conceived of the good, or of what makes the truly good things good, as being unconditionally good—even good-in-itself—and this, Aristippus thought, could be used to trip up the master.

Before giving us Socrates's response, Xenophon goes out of his way to insist that the answer we are about to hear was motivated by Socrates's concern to express what was needed in order to benefit his companions (no doubt by provoking their thought) and was *not* a defensive debating tactic. Xenophon writes as if he thinks his readers might be tempted to view the response in the latter light, and thus not to take it seriously enough.

Socrates spoke of the good things as nothing but remedies for, means to "stop," something that "troubles us." He further declared that "if you are asking if I know something good that is good *for* nothing, I don't know, nor do I need it" (3.8.2–3). In other words, Socrates spoke to the effect that "things are good in relation to needs; something that does not fulfill any need cannot therefore be known to be good" (XS 75).

This exchange, "susceptible to causing scandal,"[49] is obviously not the whole Socratic story. For earlier we heard Socrates tell Antiphon that, in regard to "happiness," "I believe (*nomizō*) that to need nothing is divine, and to need as little as possible is nearest to the divine, and that what is divine is superior (*kratiston*), and that what is nearest to the divine is most superior" (1.6.10). It would seem that in replying to Aristippus, Socrates abstracted from this earlier proclaimed "belief" in the goal of "happiness" conceived as fulfillment, or as unneedy enjoyment (recall "the most blessed happiness" at 2.1.33 end); Socrates certainly abstracted here from the good understood as the happy enjoyment of fulfilled need (cf. Plato, *Republic* 526e1–4). Xenophon contributes, and tacitly points, to this abstraction by failing to report, by leaving it to us to imagine, what was the likely response of Aristippus to this Socratic characterization of the good: it is easy to picture the hedonistic Aristippus protesting that the goodness of enjoying pleasure, even if rooted in response to need, cannot be adequately expressed in terms of a mere remedy, or putting a stop to trouble.

What Xenophon does report is that Aristippus "again" renewed his strategic attack by asking Socrates if he knew something that is noble/beautiful (3.8.4). When Socrates replied that he knew many such things, Aristippus started to press for an articulation of what made them all similarly noble/beautiful. To Aristippus's astonishment, Socrates answered (swearing by Zeus) in the same way that he had answered when asked about good things. People (Socrates referenced wrestlers and runners), and things (Socrates referenced shields and javelins), are variously beautiful or noble, Socrates maintained, "relative, or with a view, to" (*pros*) their various capacities to function well in achieving various needed or desired ends. Socrates went further. On this basis, he challenged Aristippus to agree that as regards virtue, and human beings and their bodies, and all that humans use, there is no discernable or "lawfully believed" (*nomizetai*) difference between beauty or nobility on one hand, and goodness—understood as usefulness—on the other hand.

Socrates made no mention of the soul: he did not attempt to suggest that the beauty and goodness of one's own soul consist in its usefulness.

What's more, in laying down this amazing challenge, Socrates repeatedly and emphatically employed the twofold Greek expression for "the gentlemanly": *kala te k'agatha, kaloi te k'agathoi,* literally, "the noble *and* the good" (3.8.5; see also in the immediate sequel, 3.9.4). This conventional formula gives unmistakable expression to the commonsense awareness of the *distinction* between the noble (beautiful) and the good. This duality and distinction Socrates was here conspicuously and perversely ignoring.[50] We cannot but sympathize when we hear of Aristippus's pert rejoinder: "So then (he declared), also a basket for carrying dung is beautiful?!" Swearing repeatedly by Zeus (thus betraying his ironic exaggeration), Socrates stubbornly maintained his potentially comical[51] thesis, and persisted even when Aristippus proceeded to bring out (with his last words in this dialogue) the more iconoclastic implications of this Socratic thesis: "Are you saying, he asked, that the same things are beautiful and ugly (noble and base)!?" Socrates replied: "By Zeus! I, for my part, am! And likewise (he declared), good and bad!" To illustrate what he meant by the sameness of things good and bad, Socrates adduced the examples of healthy and feverishly sick appetite, pointing out that the same things good for the former may be bad for the latter, and vice versa. To illustrate what he meant by the sameness of things noble and base (beautiful and ugly), Socrates returned to his earlier examples of wrestling and racing, pointing out that what is noble/beautiful in relation to the one contest is often base/ugly in relation to the other. Then Socrates stated his general premise in the following words: "For all things are good, and also noble/beautiful, relative to things for which they would hold well (*eu exē*); and they are bad and also base/ugly, relative to things for which [they would hold] badly" (3.8.4–7). These examples, culminating in this last formulation, pointed to the more sensible, but unstated, dimension of Socrates's thesis, at least as regards the good—the dimension that Socrates in his provocative exaggeration was downplaying here with Aristippus (recall in contrast 2.1.19–20 and our previous discussion of that passage). For in these illustrations there comes to sight as *simply* good (the good that *defines* the *relative* good, and the relative bad, of the means) the achievement or fulfillment of the *ends* (in these particular illustrative cases, recovering or enjoying being healthily nourished; and achieving or enjoying victorious physical fitness).

But where does this leave the beautiful/noble (*kalon*)? Can it be reduced or assimilated to the good (*agathon*), in the sense of either means or ends, or both? If not, what constitutes the distinguishing value of the beautiful/noble?

Xenophon now leaves behind Aristippus, who has evidently served the author's artistic-didactic purpose. Ceasing to speak of "the good," Xenophon himself steps forward, with the words "in *my* opinion" (3.8.8) to defend as "educational," and thus to instigate us to think further about, the seemingly perverse Socratic attempt to reduce or to assimilate the beautiful to the useful (*chrēsimous*)—now, in particular, as regards the mundane art of home building. But precisely this homely topic turns out to reveal that Socrates, by "saying that the same houses are *both* beautiful *and* useful (*chrēsimos*)," and thus "educating as to which sorts of houses ought to be built," did *not* thereby simply identify either the beautiful or the "ought" with the useful.

For Socrates first gets a nameless interlocutor to agree that a house ought to be *both* "most *pleasant* to dwell in" *and* "most useful." And when Socrates proceeds to elaborate the implications, he dwells much less on the usefulness and much more on the *beauty* of a house—insofar as it conduces to (physical) *pleasure*: a house "comes into being in a beautiful fashion (*kalōs*)," if in winter it is *pleasantly* warmer, because sunny and less exposed to north winds, and in summer it is *pleasantly* cooler, because shady.[52] But then, "summing up" his short disquisition on housing architecture, Socrates says that a house in which the dweller "would in all seasons most pleasantly find refuge, *and* would most safely put belongings," would "reasonably be the most pleasant and the most beautiful" (3.8.8–10). Usefulness, in the sense of providing a safe place for belongings as well as the dweller, finally comes in (very briefly, and only implicitly, or without the use of the term "useful") as one of the criteria for how a house ought to be built; and this usefulness now seems to be what makes a house "most beautiful"—in addition to (though overlapping) what makes it "most pleasant." In Strauss's words, "Socrates here first replaces 'beautiful' by 'pleasant' and distinguishes the pleasant from the useful and in particular what affords safety; he then replaces 'useful' (or 'safe') by 'beautiful'" (XS 77). The attempt to replace or to identify the beautiful with the useful is countered by the necessity of conceiving the beautiful as the pleasant. But while the pleasant is what Socrates now makes preeminent (no longer constrained by the need to rebut and to admonish the sensual hedonist Aristippus),[53] Socrates refers only dismissively to what we today (since the eighteenth century) revere as "aesthetic" pleasure or "taste": Socrates declares that "paintings and decorations, however, deprive of more delights than they provide" (cf. *Hiero* 11.2). This by no means entails Socrates's being unappreciative of the serious spiritual pleasure found in contemplating beautifully designed architectural sites—when, that is, they are precincts of divinity and its worship: "But as regards temples and altars, he said that the most becoming site was one that, being most visible, would yet be untrodden; for it is pleasant for those beholding to offer prayers, and it is pleasant for those who hold themselves undefiled to approach" (3.8.10). In the place of what we nowadays hold in respect, or even awe, as the spiritual pleasures found in "art" and "the aesthetic" and "taste," Xenophon's Socrates puts the spiritual pleasures of beholding products of artistic skill created to serve, and to conduce to awe before, and thereby enjoyable worship of, the divine.[54]

But is it really only when artistic beauty is linked to divine worship that Socrates judges such beauty to be spiritually pleasing in a worthy way? Is Socrates otherwise as indifferent to the visual beauties captured or expressed in the fine arts as is suggested by his rather philistine comment about painting and decoration? Or is this also part of Xenophon's exaggeratedly thought-provoking presentation at this point?

As Strauss stresses (XS 76), the Socratic thesis identifying the beautiful/ noble with the good "is contradicted by Xenophon himself."[55] The paradoxical thesis "stems from the attempt to reject the excess of the noble over the good as irrational, just as does the denial of the essential difference between the city and the household (III.4)." The obvious didactic purpose of this "attempt" is to impel the reader to puzzle over, to try to provide, the reasonable basis of the valuing of the noble or beautiful above and beyond the good—the good understood as that which serves our needs and constitutes our enjoyment of fulfillment. As Strauss also observes here, "In the initial enumeration of Socratic themes 'what is noble' occurs in a place of honor and 'what is good' not at all (I.i.16)."[56] *The* place of honor, just prior to "What is noble/ beautiful?" is held by "What is pious?" (cf. XS 78). The Socratic answer to the former provides a key clue to the Socratic answer to the latter.

## THE VIRTUES AS NOBLE/BEAUTIFUL

"From the good and the noble, to say nothing of the pleasant, we are naturally led to the virtues; up to this point the order of subjects" in book 3 "is more lucid than in the enumeration of Socratic topics at the beginning (I.1.16)."[57] In that enumeration at the beginning, the order of specified topics of Socratic questioning was given as "the pious and impious; the noble and base; the just and unjust; moderation and madness; courage and cowardice; city, statesman, rule over humans, and skilled ruler over humans." Here, in Xenophon's account of a part of the execution of the Socratic investigations, overwhelming primacy has been given to the question of the noble and base (in relation to the good and bad). And now we see that the consequences are momentous.

For piety is dropped, and replaced by wisdom (*sophia*), conceived as entwined with moderation (*sōphrosunē*), and therewith as constituting all moral virtue:[58] "And he said that justice also, and all the rest of virtue, was wisdom" (3.9.5). In stressing that Socrates entwined wisdom with moderation, Xenophon indicates that here the term "wisdom" designates *practical* wisdom, prudence or *phronēsis* (XS 80b–81t); Xenophon is here eclipsing or abstracting from *theoretical* wisdom, from science (*epistēmē*)—from that wisdom that characterized the core of Socrates's life inasmuch as he "never ceased examining what each of the beings is" (4.6.1, 4.6.7). Wisdom as *theōria* is contemplative; it is the highest manifestation of "the difference between the good and the beautiful or noble things, among the latter the objects of sight standing out" (XS 81). But here, in contrast, being wise, as entwined with being moderate, means being one who "*puts to use* one's knowing about (*gignōskonta*) the gentlemanly/noble-and-good things." Wisdom in this practical sense culminates in "correctly" choosing, and then enacting, "what one ought to do"—that is, the "noble-and-good things," including "the just things." In response to a questioner, Socrates insisted that to suppose that someone can really know what he ought to do, and thus be wise, but still fail to do what he knows he ought, out of lack of self-control, is mistaken psychology; for the failure to do what one supposedly "knows" one ought to do signals that the so-called knowing, of the ought, is mutilated—occluded or distorted by more or less articulate, strong passion that makes one think, at least temporarily, that what one truly ought to do—that is, what is truly most advantageous for oneself—is not so, that something else is what is most conducive to one's well-being or happiness. "For everyone, I think, choosing from the possible options what they think to be most advantageous for themselves, does these things." True practical knowledge and wisdom is, for Socrates, not merely intellectual; it is knowledge that penetrates, grips, and shapes—that has become interwoven with—the passions, and thus governs the soul in its motions; to achieve this, "practice" (*meletan*) as well as "learning" is essential.[59] By the same token, Socrates holds that those who lack such *effective* knowledge of what is most advantageous for oneself are incapable of doing anything truly virtuous or just or noble-and-good—"If they try, they err" (3.9.4–5). As a momentous consequence of his analysis of the noble, Socrates has a radically unconventional, singularly stringent criterion for what constitutes truly just and noble, virtuous action. We venture to surmise that he is here thinking of his own virtues. Accordingly, courage, which is treated first here, "is not called a virtue" and "is treated separately from the other virtues (cf. Plato, *Laws* 963e)." Socrates "does not say here that courage is a kind of knowledge or even that it presupposes knowledge."[60] Instead of knowledge, Socrates speaks of being "reared" in "laws and customs," and of a kind of "learning" (mathēsis) that is exemplified even by barbarians acquiring skills in specific sorts of weaponry.[61] Xenophon naturally does not wish to spotlight this Socratic downgrading of the "virtue" that is held in very high or even highest honor by cities and by law: Xenophon obscures, and hints at what is being obscured, by having Socrates answer, not the Socratic question (What is courage?), but only the derivative question, "whether courage would be teachable or natural" (3.9.1–3).

The radical unconventionality of Socrates's moral understanding becomes still more visible when Xenophon proceeds to tell us that Socrates defined the opposite of wisdom as "madness," and did not mean by madness "lack of scientific knowledge" (anepistēmē—the opposite of theoretical wisdom). For, Xenophon explains, Socrates had reasoned (logizetai) his way to seeing that what is nearest to "madness" (mania) is ignorance of oneself, in the sense of "opining and thinking that one knows what one in fact does not know." This conception of madness, Socrates pointed out, is widely divergent from what is affirmed by most people—who regard the mad as only that minority who are ignorant of what most people do know; the "madmen" in this conventional sense show their "great ignorance" by exhibiting such beliefs about themselves as that they are as tall as buildings, or strong enough to lift up houses. The fact that most people wrongly think that they know what madness is—that it consists in this sort of "great ignorance"—shows that most people are mad in Socrates's eyes.[62] Socrates connects this with the error most people make in calling only strong desire eros (3.9.6–7). Why this connection? Does not Socrates thus hint that eros is much more pervasive in all human desire than most people realize, and is a or the major source of what Socrates understands to be the nigh-universal madness of people thinking they know what they do not know? Is not understanding eros the key to self-knowledge—and vice versa?

Xenophon abruptly turns to Socrates's teaching on envy (phthonos— 3.9.8). Why should this vice be given such prominence, immediately after the discussion of what is the opposite of wisdom?[63] Why is not Socrates's teaching on the vice of injustice discussed? Or is not envy the one and only form of injustice that is here singled out and put in the spotlight? But then why this singling out and spotlighting of only this peculiar form of injustice? The puzzle intensifies when we hear the peculiarly selective Socratic understanding of what constitutes envy: the envious are "only those distressed by the good fortunes of those they love" (not those who are pained by the good fortunes of enemies, or of people that they do not love). Why this constriction of the meaning of envy? And how many people exhibit envy in this perverse form? Xenophon reports that Socrates had to respond to listeners amazed at the idea that anyone who loved another would be pained by the latter's doing well. Socrates replied that there were "many" such—who, while they could not tolerate seeing their loved ones doing poorly, but would help them, were nonetheless pained at the loved ones' good fortune. Socrates went further. He said that this could not happen to a man of (practical) wisdom, but that the foolish *"always* suffered" (or *"had to* suffer"[64]) from this! The puzzling extremism of this last starts to make sense when we attend to the fact that the overall theme is wisdom, and when we thence recognize what Socrates has in mind as the greatest "good fortune"—and the peculiar envy that such good fortune incurs. The fathers of those gifted few young men whom the Socratic philosopher liberates from paternal authority are quite likely to hate and even to seek to destroy the philosopher for supplanting them in the eyes of their sons. Such paternal envy is a form of injustice that is peculiarly harmful to the Socratic philosopher and his truest beloveds—whose good fortune he is incapable of envying, because their acquiring that good, Socratic education, is for him and them an unqualifiedly *common* good.[65]

The provocatively puzzling character of Xenophon's presentation continues or intensifies when our author makes what a prominent commentator has called an "absurd transition"[66]—from envy to *leisure (scholē)*. What's more, Xenophon has Socrates treat leisure here much less favorably than in his other, more conventionally-gentlemanly mentions of leisure (1.3.11, 1.6.9; *Oeconomicus* 4.3). But by now we have learned that the present passage affords insights into radically unconventional (not to say subversive) dimensions of Socratic nobility or gentlemanliness. Elsewhere, we can now see, Xenophon shows Socrates viewing leisure benignly in its *negative* aspect—insofar as it means being freed *from* needs and labors that impede what is gentlemanly, especially service to friends and city; here, however, we learn that Socrates only regards such negative freedom as a positive good, as truly deserving the honorific term "leisure," insofar as it permits ascent to better things than "fun," than "leisure activities." And if or insofar as "free" time and "leisure activities" attract one away, to a descent, from those better things, one suffers the ill of "lack of leisure"—no matter how much "fun" one may be having. If we bear in mind the immediately preceding context, we see that "leisure activity," insofar as it becomes a preoccupation, is here paired with envy as a threat to the quest for and enactment of wisdom. If we then note the immediately succeeding context, we are prodded to wonder exactly how Socrates viewed political rule in relation to leisure and lack of leisure and wisdom (cf. XS 80–81).

For Xenophon next reports Socrates's assertion that "kings and rulers are not those who hold the scepter, nor those chosen by random electors,[67] nor those obtaining the lot, nor those using force or fraud, but those who are scientific knowers of ruling (*epistamenous archein*)" (3.9.10).[68] The formulation suggests that scientific knowledge of ruling is the sufficient as well as necessary condition for being what Socrates deems a "king and ruler." So did Socrates mean that those he was defining as "kings and rulers" do not typically hold actual office?[69] And that those who do typically hold actual office do not know what they are doing? This paradoxical and puzzling and potentially subversive[70] Socratic teaching we saw implicitly and playfully introduced at the start of, and then looming throughout, the seven accounts Xenophon gave of Socrates helping those who sought nobility in high office. Now Xenophon reports how Socrates made the teaching explicit, and shows how he would defend it dialectically—that is, when someone questioned or doubted the teaching.

Socrates would first get the challenging interlocutor "to agree that it belonged to the ruler to command what *ought* to be done, and to the ruled to obey." Having gained agreement on this normative premise, Socrates would proceed to point out how in other practical arts, beginning with the leading example of piloting (as needed by the ship *owner* and the others on the ship), and continuing through farming (as needed by the *owners* of the fields), and healing (as needed by the sick), and gymnastics (as needed by those in training), those who hold *themselves* to be knowers of what is needed do their supervising themselves, but if they don't hold themselves to be knowers, then they "send for," and obey the guidance of, others who are knowers. Socrates would point finally to the example of wool spinning, in regard to which women "rule" men inasmuch as the women are the ones who know how to spin wool while the men do not (3.9.11). These analogies make vivid how limited is the actual power Socrates was ascribing to many or most practical knowers, serving in the capacity of public and private advisers to those who hold power.

And so, Xenophon reports, a thoughtful interlocutor might reply to the preceding with the following objection or doubt: in politics, "it is possible for *the tyrant* not to obey those who speak correctly."[71] The interlocutor would appear to be deducing that the Socratic thesis implies that many or most actual rulers are "tyrants" inasmuch as they exercise mighty, even lawful, command without knowing what is needed or ought to be done.[72]

Xenophon shows that in response to such an interlocutor, Socrates would not dispute either this deduction or the questioner's assumption that those who speak correctly lack commanding political power. Instead Socrates would question the very *possibility* that the politically powerful might fail to obey the advice of one who speaks "*well*" (rhetorical skill as well as knowledge is needed)—for, Socrates claims, the politically powerful, if they do not obey, incur the "penalty that is laid down" for someone who does not obey the one who speaks "well."

What penalty? Laid down by whom? And how does the threat of this penalty render disobedience on the part of a powerful tyrant practically impossible? Who or what guarantees, through such awesomely threatening penalties, the authority, in politics, of the adviser who is a knower deploying rhetorical skill?

Socrates would explain as follows: "In whatever practical matter someone does not obey the one who speaks well, he will presumably err, and in erring will be penalized" (3.9.12—Socrates implicitly reveals that the knowers of the art of ruling and of speaking will give advice that is beneficial to their powerful but benighted actual rulers, even tyrants[73]).

But Xenophon produces an interlocutor whose reaction shows that he is so far from being convinced that this "penalty" would compel the powers-that-be to obey the silver-tongued knower that (the interlocutor suggests) the "penalty" suffered by someone powerful might well rather infuriate him into exterminating the smarty-pants whose beneficial advice he would not follow: "It is possible for the tyrant also to kill the one who has good practical judgment!"

Socrates would not dispute this possibility. Instead he would ask if the interlocutor thought that one who kills his "strongest allies in battle" would wind up without being penalized, or "would merely *chance* to be penalized"— "for do you think that the one who does this will be saved? Or, will he not thus be destroyed, as quickly as possible?" (3.9.13). Xenophon does not let us hear the interlocutor's answer to this question—which cries out for a counter-question: how does this sudden capital punishment get executed? By whom? Xenophon presents as almost plaintively strained Socrates's argument for the sanctioned and thus guaranteed strength and safety of rhetorically artful knowers who advise, or who try to advise, actual rulers.

Accordingly, Xenophon next tells of someone who was amazed enough to ask Socrates what he opined to be the strongest or most superior (*kratiston*) pursuit for a real man (*andri*). When Socrates delivered the laconic reply, "doing well," he was then asked in return if he believed "good luck" to be also a "pursuit." (The questioner obviously wondered if Socrates meant by "doing well," knowledgeable and rhetorically skillful conduct by itself alone, or intermingled with good luck; in other words: how self-sufficient did Socrates suppose practical knowledge, combined with rhetoric, to be?) Socrates rejoined that he considered "luck," or "good luck," to be *entirely contrary*[74] to "doing," or "doing well"—which he "believed" to be constituted by acting on the basis of learning and attentiveness. The reason why Socrates could thus liberate effective practical knowledge and attentiveness from any dependence on luck appears when Xenophon adds that Socrates "declared that those were the best *and most beloved of god*" who in farming "did farming matters well," who in medicine did medical things well, and who in matters of the political regime did political things well. By contrast, Socrates declared, "those who do nothing well are neither useful for anything *nor beloved by god*" (3.9.14–15). God's love fills, but thereby makes conspicuous, the gap in Socrates's immediately previous teaching on the sanctioned, guaranteed strength and safety of rhetorically skillful knowers who advise, or who try to advise, actual rulers. This teaching contradicts not only common human experience but both Socrates's original teaching on the need for divination (1.1.6–9) and what was taught to him by the perfect gentleman Ischomachus (*Oeconomicus* 11.8).[75] While explicitly encouraging knowers of politics to offer advice (employing artful rhetoric) to those in power, Socrates thus, through obvious exaggeration, implicitly pointed to the risks—to the knower, from those in power.

The full gravity of the risks becomes evident if we follow Xenophon's provocation and reflect, retrospectively, on the *theological* implications of Xenophon's presentation of Socrates's teaching here on the virtues and their contraries or vices (cf. XS 81, 83). If ruling or providential divinity is characterized by intelligible virtue—if providential divinity is wise and moderate (in humanly intelligible terms), and thus free of envy, and thus not leisured in the bad sense (not capriciously playful), then there seems no reason why providential divinity would not care for wise and virtuous humans as much as possible. So, considering the fate of Socrates, is providential divinity then decisively deficient in power? Or, if providential divinity is *not* decisively deficient in power, then . . . what follows?

## SOCRATES AS ARBITER OF THE BEAUTIFUL/NOBLE IN ART

Xenophon begins the next subsection with a Greek particle expression, *alla mēn* ("but, nonetheless, . . ."), that makes the opening of this subsection a qualification of the closing sentences of the previous subsection, which

ended with the word meaning "beloved by god" (*theophilē*). In effect, Xenophon thus says that even though Socrates taught that knowers of practical matters, especially of politics, farming, and medicine, succeed without
any need for reliance on luck, because they are beloved by god, *nonetheless*
Socrates was in general "helpful to those possessing the arts and using them
for business, if on occasion (*ei pote*) he would converse with one of them"
(3.10.1): the philosopher provides otherwise unavailable and needed assistance even to knowledgeable practitioners who as such are without need for
luck because they are beloved by god. The quiet chutzpah is not softened by
any claim that Socrates's helpfulness consisted in his being an instrument of
divine love. And there is no suggestion that Socrates's helpfulness was due to
his *daimonion*. The chutzpah intensifies when Xenophon gives as examples,
of the arts to whose skilled practitioners Socrates gave important help, first
painting and then sculpture: for of course the most important products of
these arts are depictions of divinities and demigods (cf. *On Horsemanship*
11.8). And the particular painter with whom Xenophon reports Socrates conversing, once upon a time (*pote*)—the celebrated Parrhasius—was famous
for his claim to divine visitation and inspiration in his painting of gods and
heroes.[76] Yet the sole references to divinity in the two conversations are pro-
fanities uttered by the painter (expressing his pleasant surprise at what he is
learning from Socrates about expanding the limits of his art). What's more,
Socrates opens the conversation by securing the painter's agreement that the
art of painting is an "imagining" or "making of images (*eikasia*)" of "things
seen" (*not* of things unseen), and that the painter achieves "resemblances to
the beautiful forms" by gathering "the most beautiful things" scattered among
many *humans* (3.10.2). There is no mention of divine inspiration guiding the
painter in his depictions of bodies, even of the bodies of the gods.

    The help that Socrates delivers to the painter through this dialogue
can hardly be overestimated (pace XS 85).[77] For Socrates provides the crucial
instruction that inspires the painter to strive to employ his art in mimetically portraying the "most winning, and pleasing, and loving, and longed for,
and erotically desired character of the soul" (3.10.3: Socrates does not say the
"best" or "most beautiful/noble" character of soul). At first, the painter voices
strong doubt that painting can capture such a thing—since such qualities are
entirely invisible. But Socrates reminds him that human passions, of love
and hate, may be visibly and even dramatically expressed in the eyes and the
face. "So," Socrates asks, "isn't this then imitable, in the eyes?" "Is it not
then possible to make images of these, too?" "Very much so (*kai mala*)!" the
painter repeatedly exclaims in delighted response. Then Socrates takes a big
step. He points out that through the visible signs of such passions—conveyed

not only by the facial expressions but also by the bodily postures, at rest and in motion—there can *also* be expressed virtuous and vicious *characters* of soul. "So," Socrates asks, "aren't these also imitable?" The painter: "Very much so!" But when Socrates further asks if the painter "believes that human beings behold with more pleasure the expressions manifesting the noble-and-good (gentlemanly) and lovable characters, as opposed to those manifest-ing the shameful and wicked and hateful," the painter replies noncommit-tally (but even more excitedly and emphatically): "By Zeus! (he said) there's a big difference, Socrates!" (3.10.4–5). Socrates would seem to have "liberated" the painter to cater to general human taste, which, in the delight such taste takes in beholding imitations of vicious as well as virtuous characters, is at odds with Socratic taste.[78]

To understand the importance for the history of art of this brief conver-sation, we need to consider the named painter-interlocutor. For Parrhasius was so famously distinguished an artist that Xenophon can be assumed to have expected that his name would be at least not unfamiliar to readers in the future. According to Pliny the Elder's history of Greek painters (*Natural History* 35.36.67 and 69), "Parrhasius of Ephesus also contributed greatly to the progress of painting, being the first . . . to make the face expressive (*dedit primus argutias vultus*)"; and "he painted the People (Demos) of Ath-ens with singular ingenuity; representing it in variety: choleric, unjust, and inconstant; easily moved, clement, compassionate, glorious, exalted and humble, fierce and timid—and all these at once." Xenophon would seem to be suggesting that what led to this revolution, so to speak, in the psychologi-cal scope and ambition of Greek painting was these few decisive moments of Socrates's dialogue with the great Parrhasius. We have so few actual remains of classical Greek painting that we cannot tell if Xenophon is speaking with historical verisimilitude,[79] or if this is another example of Xenophon's indul-gence in playful *alazoneia* on behalf of his master.

Much more important is what Xenophon reveals about Socrates, mimet-ically, through this dialogue. For here Xenophon corrects the exaggerated mis-impression he gave previously—when he presented Socrates as apparently so philistine as to see no point in adorning one's home with any paintings. We now learn that Socrates appreciated the pleasure of, and was expert in—that he even understood much better than did the greatest of painters—the beauties, susceptible of being mimetically portrayed in painting, that are the most attractive, most pleasant, and most lovable and moving to behold. (There is in this conversation no reference to the useful as a criterion of the noble or beautiful.) Xenophon's Socrates here embraces, and articulates with unrivaled clarity, the peak of the duality that is at the heart of the Greek word *kalon* (see *Oeconomicus* 6.12–17)—meaning *both* virtuous character *and* perceptible beauty, whose peak is experienced in the beholding of the physical expression of virtuous character, or its mimetic portrayal.

To be sure, Socrates indicates limits to painting's capacity to effect such portrayal. What Socrates stresses primarily are depictions of the facial expressions of the passions of love and friendship (and attendant hostility). Socrates implies that the best taste, such as his own, would enjoy above all the contemplation of such expressions in *virtuous* characters. But there is detectable some Socratic doubt or hesitation as to whether *all* the virtuous (and contrastingly vicious) characters of soul are expressed in such a way as to be imitable in painting. Socrates names four virtuous, and four correspondingly vicious, characters whose expressions are candidates for the painter's art: "the magnificent and the liberal" versus "the humble and the illiberal"; "the moderate and the prudent" versus "the hubristic and the one lacking in experience of beauty/nobility (*apeirokalon*)" (3.10.5). He is silent on the just, the pious, the courageous (or manly), and the wise. But are not the latter four characters of soul represented (and pointed off to) here by kindred characters that are more suitable, in this context, as stand-ins? The magnificent character might be considered the most expressively attractive and lovable (and paintable) extension of the manly character (and of manly piety);[80] the liberal or generous, of the just.[81] On the other hand, however, while we have seen that Xenophon's portrait of Socrates replaces piety with moderation (recall 1.1.20), moderation would seem to be much less expressive, and therefore less paintable, than the former.[82] And, while in the present context it is readily apparent why the wise character would be presented as prudent in the sense of "experienced in beauty/nobility," is this latter character so paintable?[83] Do not these last two, more distinctively Socratic, characters of soul—moderation, and experience in beauty/nobility, indicate the *limits* of painting as a mimetic art—in sharp contrast to the *rhetorical* mimetic art exercised by Xenophon throughout the *Memorabilia*?[84]

From this most revealing account of Socrates's onetime transformative dialogue with a very famous painter, Xenophon descends to a briefer account of a much less dramatic dialogue that Socrates had on one occasion (*pote*) with a sculptor named Cleiton—who is otherwise unknown.[85] This sculptor's work featured runners and wrestlers and pugilists so lifelike, Socrates said, as to "allure the souls" of "human" beholders. Socrates suggested to the "perplexed" sculptor how he might begin to articulate the method by which he brings his athletes' bodies to life; Socrates then led the sculptor to a realization of how important, for inducing pleasure in the beholders, would be his mimetic depiction of his competitive athletes' menacing, and triumphantly joyful, actions (*erga*)[86] of soul, expressed through their eyes and facial expressions (3.10.6–8). Socrates did *not* suggest to this lesser artist, with his talent for lifelike portrayals of menacing and triumphing athletes, that he should attempt to imitate the pleasing expressions of the *characters* (*ēthē*) of the soul—especially the virtues, as seen in love and friendship. Accordingly, there is a conspicuous silence on the beautiful in this conversation.[87] Xenophon and his Socrates thus indicate their very demanding criteria for what is truly beautiful in the mimetic arts—as opposed to what is virtuoso, and alluring to the souls of most people.

From artists we descend to an artisan named Pistias ("Trusty"—a common name; Fraser and Matthews 1987–2013, s.v.), a maker and seller of unusually expensive breastplates, whom Socrates "teaches" to articulate exactly which consequence of the superior "fit" of his products makes him believe them "worth" the exceptionally high prices he charges (3.10.13–14). Socrates and the craftsman agree that not only for breastplates, but for products more generally, "good form" (*to euruthmon*) is not something "in itself" (*kath' heauto*), but is relative to the one using the formed thing, which needs to "fit" the user—whether his body be well formed or ill formed—so as to give him the least physical discomfort (3.10.11–13, 15). The conversation prompts the question, Is the good or bad form of the user's body also relative? To what? To the good or bad form of his soul, that enjoys using his body? And what then of the good or bad form of the individual's soul? Must the form of one's soul not be good (or bad) in another, more intrinsic sense—worthy to be called "beautiful?" While Socrates clearly found the craftsman's breastplates to be well formed, in terms of their usefulness and comfort, he did not therefore designate them, or their fit, as beautiful (contrast Xenophon himself, giving a practical teaching about breastplates in *On Horsemanship* 12.1). What Socrates *did* designate as beautiful, emphatically—swearing the unmanly oath "By Hera!" and addressing by name the artisan—was the *invention* of the breastplate, as protecting what needs protection, while not hindering the use of the hands. What Socrates finds beautiful is the mental action and achievement of nameless, inventive, possibly slave mind(s) sometime in the past (3.10.9). Socrates visited "more than once" (XS 85) this shop whose products, skillfully adapted to the good and bad forms of their users, incarnated and expressed and applied this original mental beauty. The philosopher evidently enjoys contemplating well-wrought work of artful humans responding to the varying needs of humans in their wide inequality, even when the work is of no use to himself as a philosopher. Does this help us to see that for Socrates the beauty of the virtues lies in their efficient functioning to meet the most fundamental human needs?

## THE PROFITABLE BEAUTY OF SOCRATES'S SOUL,
## REFLECTED IN COMIC ALLEGORY

From showing how Socrates helped an unusually successful artisan-producer-entrepreneur, Xenophon descends next to showing how Socrates helped a prosperously successful practitioner of the courtesan's art.[88] This scenario displays Socrates at his most playfully "unbuttoned," and most roguishly allusive (it contains more profane oaths by Socrates than any other single conversation [XS 89], even more than the dialogue with Critobulus, with which this conversation has obvious affinities, in tone, mood, and substance).

Grave scholars have been most disapproving. Xenophon's presentation of Socrates assimilating himself, in his art of seduction, to a beautiful courtesan and her art "has scandalized most commentators, ancient and modern," led by the tight-laced Kierkegaard.[89]

"A woman was once (pote) in the city, a beauty, whose name was Theodote [Gift-of-god]."[90] When Socrates was told both that "the beauty (kallos) of the woman was beyond the power of rational speech (kreitton logou)," and that she was frequented by painters for whom she posed, "displaying as much of herself as would be noble," Socrates immediately insisted that he and his associates should go to behold her, declaring that "it is not possible for those who merely hear to grasp/learn (katamathein) what is beyond the power of rational speech."[91] Socrates did not doubt that the beauty of a woman could be indescribable by rational speech and, as such, something that he was eager to behold;[92] he affirmed by his deed as well as by his speech that only through personally experiencing, seeing with one's own eyes, could one truly know and appreciate such beauty—even or especially if one were a painter (or a philosopher).

Socrates was (perhaps surprisingly) confident that Theodote would be generous enough to allow him and his associates to be appreciative onlookers as she posed for a painter—and he was not disappointed. But when the session of contemplation of beauty concluded, Socrates insisted on raising, to his male companions, a surprising (and spell-breaking[93]) question of justice: Which of us—we contemplators, or "the Gift-of-God" that we have been contemplating—owes more gratitude to the other? Still more surprisingly, Socrates submitted that since Theodote "reaped the profit" of "praise" from "us" onlookers, and stood to "benefit still more" when "we shall spread the word to many," while "we now desire to touch, and we go away excited, and, when we are departed, we will long for the things we have beheld,"[94] it follows that "we serve, and this one is served." Theodote (no shrinking violet), hav-

ing overheard this, broke in with a manly oath—"By Zeus!"—to announce
that from this it followed that she was the debtor, to "you" (pl.). It seems that
Socrates and "the Gift-of-god" agree (but would Zeus?) in discounting, though
not denying, the intrinsic value to the adorers of their sheer contemplation of
beauty such as is incarnate in Theodote. The chief benefit, and thus value, of
her beauty lie in its attracting and transfixing those who subsequently praise
and long for and serve the (needy) being who has the beauty—and who, on
account of being praised and served, comes to owe a justly deserved return to
her devotees (3.11.2–3).

The full human import of this comes to sight when we recognize, from
the episode as a whole, that Xenophon and his Socrates are here presenting
the courtesan, in her monetarily profitable, seductive, chiefly physical beauty,
as a revealing "caricature" (cf. XS 87, 89) of Socrates, in his spiritually profitable, seductive, spiritual beauty.

"After this," Socrates exclaimed—swearing by Hera, the oath of women—
at the luxurious wealth Theodote had obviously amassed, not (he learned by
questioning her) from ownership of any productive property, but solely from
the gifts of her willing friends. These friends Socrates designated a "noble/
beautiful acquisition," and, as a "herd," he judged them to be "much superior" to "herds of sheep and goats and cattle" (3.11.5). But, swearing now
by Zeus, Socrates disclosed to Theodote her woeful ignorance of what we
might call "marketing"—what Socrates calls "hunting."[95] For, he observes,
Theodote simply depends on chance, waiting for potential friends to alight
upon her like flies. Not only does she spin no web-like traps, hunting as does
the spider, but what is worse, she has utterly failed to acquire and to maintain diverse human "hunting dogs," who can be variously employed, some
at night and others after dawn, operating both swiftly and more slowly, to
capture or to drive into well-designed nets "the most valuable prey": eligible potential friends (3.11.5–9).

When the bemused and intrigued Theodote asked what these "nets"
might allegorically stand for, in her case, Socrates explained (3.11.10–14)
that he meant her body, to begin with, but much more her soul, "by which
you grasp/learn how to gratify with a look and to charm with what you
say," and by which you learn "that you need to receive with gladness one
who is attentive, but to shut out one who trifles, and to watch thoughtfully
over a sick friend, and to share intensely in the pleasure of one who does
something noble, and to gratify with your entire soul the one who thinks of
you intently." Socrates softened his criticism of the courtesan's ignorance by
adding the emollient of his confidence that she "knows how to love," and

that she "persuades her friends by deed as well as by speech that they are the best for her."[96] But to this came the expostulation, "By the very Zeus (*ma ton Di'*)!—said Theodote—I devise none of these things!" "And yet," rejoined Socrates, "it makes a great difference if one approaches a human being in accordance with nature and correctly." A friend, Socrates continued, is a "prey, that is caught and kept" by "good deeds and by pleasure." Theodote agreed. But then Socrates elaborated, culminating in his asseveration that, above all, this prey needs to be "hungering," "needy." And "by Zeus!" (Socrates vehemently insisted and promised), hungering can be best induced and enflamed through one's "appearing to the needy as wishing to gratify them, and then running away—until they are as needy as possible!"

We are given here a lively if indirect indication of what it was like to be spiritually seduced by Socrates, acting as a loving philosophic teacher. Moreover, we are afforded insight into the kind of "hungering" interaction that Xenophon himself, as loving seducer-writer-teacher, aims in this book to reproduce, for and with his best and most beloved reader-students.

When the captivated Theodote, sensing herself a tyro in the presence of an expert in the art of seduction, asked Socrates—addressing him by name for the first time—to become her "fellow-hunter of friends,"[97] Socrates "gradually and graciously backed out of the interview" (Grant 1871, 116), making it evident that he did not regard the courtesan seriously. He politely protested that as much as he would like to accept Theodote's invitation to "visit often," he unfortunately lacks leisure, on account of "my public and private business," but especially on account of "female friends who do not allow me to be away from them day or night and who are learning from me love-potions and enchantments." When Theodote then asked, in admiring wonder, if Socrates also knew how to concoct the latter, Socrates responded by asking how else he could have attracted the young men such as she knows surround him—including the absent Simmias and Cebes, as well as the present Apollodorus and Antisthenes.[98] Socrates concluded by first claiming that he wished Theodote would visit him, and then, when she declared her intention to do so, warning her that he could receive her only if "some dearer female than you were not within" (3.11.15–18).

The explicit focus on the neediness and hunger of those who become enchanted, by the physical beauty of the Socratic caricature Theodote, and by the parallel, spiritual beauty of Socrates, obscures, but should not allow us to overlook, the big implicit question all this provokes: what is the neediness, for exactly what profit, that motivates the beautiful magnet Socrates to devote such energetic efforts to attracting and seducing the ardent admirers who are "best for him"? A few pages after this, Xenophon will tell us that Socrates often declared that he was "erotically in love" with someone, "but he evidently aimed at (*ephiemenos*) not those well formed by nature as regards their bodies, with a view to [their] bloom, but those well formed by nature as regards their souls, with a view to virtue" (4.1.2). The parallel drawn between Socrates and Theodote spurs us to ask: What does Socrates himself, as a philosopher, or in his philosophizing, need and "gain," spiritually, from winning the souls of such young admirers? Is it enough to refer to the general intrinsic satisfactions and mutual assistance of more and less deep and rich intellectual companionship? Or has the long series of subsections on Socrates's teachings on the *kalon* (the noble/beautiful) provided the materials for a further answer, to those of us readers "hungry" enough to take to heart these teachings? Does Socrates confirm, through observing the *spiritual evolution* that his admirers who are "best for him" undergo, as a *consequence* of following and truly "drinking in" his analysis of the *kalon*, the validity of his own, earlier, spiritual-religious "conversion"? Is that conversion thus empirically proven to be not idiosyncratic, but essential, in varying degrees, for all rational, critical, self-consciousness? An intimate link between Socratic "hunting" for the friends who are "best for him" and the Socratic teaching on the noble/beautiful may be indicated by, and may begin to solve, a major puzzle in the organization of the *Memorabilia*: namely, why the chief conversation treating Socrates's quest for friends occurs here, in a comically allegorical culmination of the sections on the noble/beautiful, rather than as part of the sections on friendship.

## EXHORTING TO THE CULTIVATION OF BEAUTY OF PHYSIQUE

This much is certain: the allegory of Theodote as a caricature-allegory of Socrates arouses in the reader a hunger to learn more of what it is like, in actuality, and seriously, to be one of Socrates's seduced and beloved tutees. In book 4, the last major division of the *Memorabilia*, Xenophon will provide us with crucial materials for an answer, through depicting Socrates's seduction and tutoring of young Euthydemus. But for now, Xenophon tantalizes us, by recounting how Socrates exhorted another one of his young companions, who had neglected his physique, to train so as to avoid the "ugliness/shamefulness" of "growing old through lack of exercise before seeing oneself becoming *physically* the most beautiful and strongest that one can."[99] Our initial reaction, as we catch on to Xenophon's teasing of us, is a mixture of amusement and mild annoyance: yes, our author does now let us in on what we so wish to overhear—Socrates tutoring, in private, one of his well-known young intimates, Epigenes;[100] but . . . tutoring the young man in what?—the value of calisthenics!

To appreciate the fuller scope and import of Xenophon's leg-pulling here, we need to observe the following.

To begin with, the acolyte's neglect of his physique has occurred *during* the time he has been a companion of Socrates—who seems to have been quite slow to notice this delinquency of his young companion.

Second, when Socrates begins his reproof, he uses pejoratively a word, *idiōtikōs*, that means "untrained"—"in what an *untrained* fashion you maintain your body, Epigenes!"—but that can also mean "as one who lives a private, withdrawn life." Epigenes retorts by seizing defiantly on the latter meaning: "Because I *am* one who lives a private, withdrawn life (*idiōtēs*), Socrates!"

Socrates responds to this by attempting, through the expression of sentiments reminiscent of his warnings to Aristippus, to convince the nerdy-looking student that it is simply not possible to withdraw from the mortal "competition" against enemies that is required by civic-military service in war-prone Athens—and that to enter this competition without a strong physique is to court the risks of death, and shame, and a prisoner's harsh enslavement, or bankruptcy on account of paying ransom. To all this essentially civic[101] admonition Epigenes remains stubbornly silent—even though Socrates alternates between assertions and pointed questions (3.12.1–2). (We have to observe that nowhere does Xenophon ever show Socrates himself training or exercising out of concern for military service—in sharp contrast to what Socrates heard from Ischomachus about proper gentlemanly exercise in *Oeconomicus* 11.17–20. In the *Symposium* 2.17–19, Xenophon presents Socrates fretting a bit about his paunch, and confessing his consequent need for the exercise of *solitary dancing*.)

Epigenes remains tight-lipped when Socrates asks him further if he disdains the superior health, strength, and physical capabilities acquired by those who train (3.12.3). The young Socratic's stony silence persists when his mentor, becoming more assertive, not to say preachy, proclaims (3.12.4) that those with strong physiques can better assist friends and fatherland, thereby becoming "deserving of gratitude and acquiring great fame" as well as "the most noble/beautiful honors," and thus winding up "living the rest of their lives more pleasantly and more nobly," and "leaving to their children more noble resources." (Again we have to observe that this does not fit

Socrates himself. In the next few pages we will learn that Socrates promotes a menu, at the common meals of his associates, that is not suited to those in physical training: 3.14.3)

Finally, after piling on more such general exhortation, Socrates narrows his scope, and provides us another clue as to the source of his student's neglect of gymnastics (XS 90): "In what seems to *you* to involve the *least* use of the body—in discursive theorizing [*tōi dianoesthai*; "in pure thinking": Smith ad loc.]—who does not know that also in this there are many people who falter on account of not being healthy in body?" And (Socrates insists) bad physical condition can affect "the faculty of discursive thinking (*tēn dianoian*)" such as to induce "forgetfulness and dispiritedness and irritability and madness." In contrast, "for those having bodies in good condition, there is much safety, and no risk, that they will suffer such a thing on account of bad physical condition"; and "it is likely (*eikos*)[102] that good physical condition is instead useful with a view to the opposite conditions." And for the sake of these "opposites," "what would one possessing intelligence not endure?"

Epigenes is persistently mute.

We are led to surmise that it is only this last focus, on theorizing, that speaks to the concerns moving the young Socratic Epigenes—and that the youth's experience in being around Socrates has not convinced him of the validity of Socrates's (new or previously undelivered) argumentation concerning the value and need of a strong physique *for theorizing*. We recall that Aristophanes portrays the students of Socrates as looking like starved "prisoners"—pale, bat-like, even like dead spirits or corpses; and the comic poet indicates that this is the way the young followers of Socrates are generally viewed by the physically vigorous young Athenians, typified by Pheidippides (*Clouds* 103, 186, 1112; *Birds* 186, 1296, 1555–64; *Wasps* 1414). Xenophon's effort to invalidate this Aristophanean "slander," by portraying the philosopher's conversation with Epigenes, is of (comically) dubious success.

## PROMOTING EVERYDAY SELF-MASTERY
## AND "LIVING DECOROUSLY"

Xenophon continues to tease us, and continues to exhibit his Aristophanean proclivities, by way of a further delay and descent. In what might be termed a "Tristam Shandyesque moment" of the *Memorabilia*, we are taken down into the thicket of a series of vignettes depicting the master's helping anonymous addressees to overcome their being upset or worried by minor troubles. What Xenophon reports is not without its radical as well as comical dimensions.

Becoming indignant at suffering rudeness is "laughable" (*geloion*), or a subject for comedy, declared Socrates according to Xenophon, because it shows failure to grasp the truth that rudeness is a manifestation of the impolite person's deformity of soul (3.13.1). We have here a rather trivial instantiation of the profoundly radical Socratic thesis that all vice is ignorance and thus deformity of soul, and hence that all moral indignation in response to vicious behavior is absurd; this prepares us for, and helps us to understand the import of, the sole occasion in Xenophon's corpus where he explicitly reports that "Socrates laughed" (*Apology* 28). But this does not mean that merriment is always or solely the reasonable reaction to witnessing moral indignation: upon encountering someone severely and indignantly punishing an attendant slave on account of the latter's purported extreme (Aristophanean) vice,[103] Socrates suggested that the slave owner–punisher might be the one more in need of corrective blows (3.13.4). So there can be "Socratic" corporal punishment, as a coolly rational corrective inflicted without righteous indignation. Is it not in part Socrates's (and Xenophon's) concern with correction (rehabilitation) of us all that makes him (and Xenophon) treat deformity of the soul as sometimes laughable rather than pitiable?[104]

As a remedy for someone dissatisfied with his diet, the superhumanly austere Socrates invoked what he claimed was the prescription of a good doctor: simply stop eating![105] But when someone complained about the tepidity of his home's drinking and bathing water, Socrates tried to arouse shame in the complainer, at his being harder to please than his slaves and the sick (3.13.3): Socrates did not even hint at cessation or diminution of bathing—so can we conclude, on the basis of Xenophon's implicit testimony here, that the repeated, notorious charges by Aristophanes (*Birds* 1282, 1554–55; *Clouds* 836–37), to the effect that Socrates and his followers refrain from bathing, are slanders?

Xenophon devotes considerable space to Socrates's exhortations to those undertaking or undergoing long journeys afoot (3.13.5–6). To someone worrying about a prospective trek from Athens to Olympia, Socrates blithely proposed a schedule of five or six days' travel, with leisurely stops for meals: this would require hiking fifty or more kilometers a day, over partly hilly roads! (BD ad loc.: "tout à fait fantaisiste!"). Is this not a sign of how laughably ignorant Socrates was of travel outside Athens (see Plato, *Phaedrus* 230c-d and *Crito* 52b, 53a)?

Certainly Socrates showed little sympathy for another fellow who complained of being worn out upon returning to Athens: Socrates scathingly elicited from him the emphatic, cursing confession that a slave boy had carried the luggage, and what's more, had endured better! Does not Xenophon indicate that in his eyes there is something a bit (comically) exaggerated and officious in Socrates's preaching about physical exertion and endurance? This brief dialogue about a luggage-toting slave has one of the two densest concentrations of profane oaths occurring in the *Memorabilia* (all uttered by Socrates's interlocutor, not by Socrates). I fear that this may be due to the fact that we are meant to be reminded of the dialogue between the cursing god Dionysos and his beleaguered, luggage-toting slave at the opening of Aristophanes's *Frogs*—where we learn that luggage-toting slaves are a favorite subject of jokes in the comedies of the rivals of Aristophanes (in particular, the comedies of Phrynicus and Lycis and Ameipsias are mentioned). "The *Frogs* is the only Aristophanean comedy at the beginning of which we see and hear a god." It is "the only Aristophanean comedy the action of which proceeds from the design of a god"—"the god of the theater" (and of wine drinking, of intoxication), by whom Aristophanes proclaims he was "bred." It "is the only comedy that opens with the question, what should a character" be presented as doing and saying "with a view to making the audience laugh"?[106] We recall that at the start of the long three-part section on the Socratic-gentlemanly concerns that overlap with "normal" gentlemanly concerns we discerned a deep connection between the austerity of Socrates as regards piety and his jocoserious austerity as regards his physical appetites—especially his erotic appetite.

Finally, and most extensively, we hear how Socrates imposed austere dietary habits on fellow diners (3.14). In Xenophon's account, each of the participants in a Socratic supper brought his own purchased food (the Aristophanean charge—*Clouds* 178–79—that Socrates supplied the food for his circle's suppers from the proceeds of petty theft is, by implication, slanderous). The master led communal meals in which the portions of *opson*— that is, the meat, fish, and relishes accompanying the cereal or bread (*siton, arton*)—were equalized and limited, while wine was apparently neglected. Socrates contended for such a menu on three curiously diverse grounds: to avoid great expense; to prevent the pains that can afflict the luxurious when they must eat simple meals and feel deprived; and (the central, highly incongruous, reason) to avoid the "laughable" or comic failure to take pleasure in the recipes of *opson*-gourmet cooks whom one has procured as the "best knowers" (*aristous epistamenous*) of the culinary art (*technē*). Socrates in this way "attributed feasting also to those living decorously" (3.14.7). Xenophon has Socrates make no reference to health and gymnastic training as a consideration in framing the menu. Could it be that Xenophon tacitly concedes—with tongue planted firmly in cheek—that the dietary regulations of Socrates are not defensible on this score? We recall that according to Aristophanes, the Socratics appear pathetically malnourished. Xenophon does not say that he himself frequented or partook of the Socratic meals and limited menu.

But Xenophon does stress that a part of the philosopher's dietary concern was with the dining *morals* of his young followers. For Xenophon paints a lively picture of Socrates's effective discouragement, in one of his younger associates, of the moral vice of *opsophagia*—of the behavior that makes one, Socrates says, "in my opinion *justly* denominated an *opsophagos*!" (3.14.3). *Opsophagia* is a term that emerges in the debate between the Just and the Unjust Discourses in Aristophanes's *Clouds*, and is common in the fragments of other dramatists of Attic Old Comedy. While there is no equivalent in modern languages, its rough primary meaning is an addictive and insatiable craving for *opson*—succulent morsels, especially of fish, that should properly be eaten only with or upon bread, and sparingly. The comedians, starting with Aristophanes, hilariously inflate *opsophagia*—lust for eating such morsels even without bread—into a leading indicator of, or entryway into, totally dissolute character.[107] In the *Clouds* (982–83), Aristophanes's "Just Discourse" bitterly complains that *opsophagia* is a corruption that was absent from the Athenian youths in the good old days before they were ruined by the influence of Socrates and his "Unjust Discourse." In our present passage, Xenophon has his Socrates join in the burlesque, by deploring the civic impiety to which the young are led by *opsophagia*: "When other humans are praying to the gods for a bounteous harvest, it's likely that the *opsophagos* would pray for more *opson*!" (3.14.3). The massive message of our passage is, of course, that the charge leveled by Aristophanes's Just Discourse—that this vice was spread throughout the Athenian youth by the Unjust Discourse associated with Socrates—is slanderous. On the contrary! Socrates is shown saving a young companion who was teetering on the edge of this "justly" decried moral abyss!

By returning, lightheartedly, to the theme of Socratic self-control, especially as regards eating, Xenophon in a way "bookends" the long three-part section on the Socratic-gentlemanly concerns that overlap with "normal" gentlemanly concerns.[108] Throughout this long section, but especially here at the end, as at the start, Xenophon has stretched himself to do all that he can—within the limits set by his deeper didactic purposes—to make Socrates appear somewhere close to "normal" in his gentlemanliness. Testimony to Xenophon's rhetorical success can be seen in the impression that the Xenophontic portrait has made on most conventional and earnest (not to say humorless) nineteenth- and twentieth-century scholars. Still, even or especially in these opening and closing, *most* "normalized," of Xenophon's presentations, our playful author has given subtly comical indications of how abnormally and controversially austere is the gentlemanly self-control that Socrates exemplifies and promotes. To understand the deeper implications of, and grounds for, Xenophon's indications of some degree of sympathy with the Aristophanean critique of Socratic austerity, one would have to consider Xenophon's *Memorabilia* in light of an exploration of the theme "Socrates and Aristophanes" (see L. Strauss 1966).

CHAPTER SIX

# Socrates as Beneficial Tutor

The fourth and last major section of the second part of the *Memorabilia* starts with a retrospective conclusion, definitive in tone and comprehensive in scope: "And thus, Socrates was, in *every* affair, and in *every* way, beneficial, so that it is manifest, to anyone who investigates and perceives with measure, that there was nothing more beneficial than being together and spending one's time with Socrates, *wherever* and in *whatever* affair" (4.1.1). Xenophon speaks as if Socrates's active justice as a benefiter of his fellowman, in *every* affair and in *every* way, has been established. The overarching, explicit purpose of the second part, and therewith of the whole, of the *Memorabilia* would seem to have been achieved. So why doesn't the work proceed immediately to its concluding chapter? Or, since much more needs to be said, why enunciate at this point such a consummation?[1]

For it soon transpires that the most important of the affairs and ways in which Socrates benefited others—his elaborate, life-transforming, private tutoring of select individuals—still needs its deservedly distinct treatment. But, as Xenophon tacitly reminds us by playfully acting as if he were starting to give in to a temptation to omit this treatment, it was this activity of Socrates that above all, in the eyes of the city, constituted the crime of "corrupting the young." And now, despite the impression our author strove (ironically and defensively) to give in the opening pages, when he claimed that Socrates did not teach,[2] Xenophon undertakes the task of portraying this peak, beneficial, Socratic activity.

This is, if you will, the minefield that Xenophon will now gingerly lead us across, and whose dangers he signals by his provocatively puzzling first sentence.

In his second sentence, Xenophon eases into this most ticklish part of his book with a reflection, adduced as if it were an afterthought, that is quietly but deeply personal: "since even to recollect (*memnēsthai*)[3] that man when he was not present benefited in no small ways the ones who were accustomed to be with him and who were receptive to him" (4.1.1).[4] We are tacitly reminded that Xenophon writes his *Recollections*, and especially this part of them, from the perspective of being a grateful, intimate, former tutee of Socrates—who has not ceased to learn from the master, even after the latter's demise. The writing of the *Memorabilia*, Xenophon here discloses, is an act of important learning on his part.

Our author-tutee immediately submits—as evidence of the benefit from recollecting Socrates—his own recollection of how Socrates profited his companions through his playfulness (*paizōn*). In particular, Xenophon recollects how Socrates would "often" say that he was "erotically in love with someone." This was playfully deceptive, or ironic, inasmuch as Socrates did not mean what he knew he would be taken by most people to mean—given the conventional, upper-class connotation of such a declaration: that he was enamored of "bodies of a good nature in terms of their bloom." No, Socrates made ironic use of this pederastic impression to waft a conventionally acceptable smoke screen for something much more serious and momentous and, from the Greek city's point of view, dubious: his "going after" (*ephiemenos*) "souls of a good nature with a view to virtue." For what Socrates meant by these "good natures," and by their "virtue," was souls that combined "quickness at learning whatever they concerned themselves with, and remembering what they learned, with desire for all the subjects of learning through which it is possible to inhabit (*oikeō*) nobly a house (*oikia*)[5] and city, and, in general, to make good use of humans and human affairs" (4.1.2). This description could fit not only the young Plato and Xenophon, but also the young Socrates of Plato's *Statesman*, and, for that matter, someone like the youthful Anaxagoras or Parmenides or Heraclitus, or the son of the Armenian king in the *Education of Cyrus* (for the range of Socrates's "hunting" was not restricted to Athenians or even to Greeks). Socrates held that such "good natures," if or once "educated, would not only be themselves happy (*eudaimonas*), *and* nobly *manage* their *own* households," but "in addition," they "would have the *potential* to make other humans and cities happy (*eudaimonas*)." Xenophon does not say whether or to what extent, or under what circumstances, Socrates held that the educated good natures would *realize* this *political potential*, through their *action* (XS 92b–93t; consider the last lines of Plato's *Laws*).

Xenophon will not pen a single additional word about "the good natures" (including himself, and Plato), or about Socrates's educative interaction with them—except by indirection, when he will present Socrates declaring that dialectic, and the choices to which it leads, is the key to "becoming best and happiest" (4.5.12).

Instead, Xenophon gives an account of how Socrates (also) interacted educatively with three *defective* types. Xenophon begins by declaring that Socrates "did not proceed in the same way with everyone" (4.1.3). He thus circumscribes the missing account, of the manner in which Socrates proceeded with the "good natures."

The first type of defectives comprises those who "*think* themselves to be good by nature, but despise learning." What Socrates "taught" them was that "those *opined* to be the best natures especially need education." To execute this "teaching," for these defectives, Socrates employed the following rhetorical strategy. He adduced as evidence the need for the youthful "*breaking*" of "the best natured of *horses*," to make them "most *useful*"— without which "breaking," the horses become the most unmanageable; and he adduced the sort of "noble training"[6] of "the best natured of *dogs*," the training that is needed to make them "best for the hunts and most *useful*"—without which "training," they become crazy and intractable. Then Socrates claimed that this was a model for what he told the defectives were "the best natured of humans"—whom he now defined as those "most robust in their souls and most able to execute skillfully whatever work they take in hand." Socrates added that when such humans "are educated and learn the things that need to be done," they "accomplish the most and best good works," but otherwise "they become the worst and the most harmful" (4.1.3–4). As the perfect gentleman Ischomachus taught Socrates, the nature and training of horses and dogs provide sound models for the selection and education of humans suited to work as good *subordinate servants*, but such training is quite insufficient as regards the education of good stewards, not to speak of good masters or rulers.[7]

One has to wonder what Socrates did with the ones among these defectives whom he succeeded in "teaching" this lesson—about *their need* for education on the model of "useful" horses and dogs. Did Socrates himself try to carry out their "breaking" and "training"? Or did he practice for them, in many cases at least, his vaunted skill as a go-between (recall 2.6.36 and see *Symposium* 4)? The analogy Socrates employed implies a dichotomy within this first type of potentially "useful" defectives: one sort, the horsey and spirited,[8] are capable of being educated to become "most useful for the good and even best"; another sort, more doglike or dogged, are capable of becoming "best" for "hunting," and "most useful" (on Socrates's esoteric meaning, in deploying horse and dog analogies, recall also 2.3.7, 2.6.6–7, 3.11.8–9).

The second type of defectives comprises those who pride themselves on wealth, and believe that they hence have no need of education in order to act, and to win honor, as they wish. Socrates "tried to bring these to their senses (*ephrenou*)" by telling them how their outlook was "moronic" (*mōros*) and "silly" (*ēlithios*), in more ways than one (4.1.5). Why is this defective type, and Socrates's treatment of them, mentioned in the central position? Could it be that Xenophon thus hints at the modal type of leisured youths with whom Socrates unavoidably had to deal?

The third type of defectives comprises "those who believe that they have happened upon the best education, and pride themselves on wisdom." It is Socrates's interaction with this type that Xenophon says he will dwell upon (4.2.1). It is easy to see why. This type, so defined, includes those who have encountered a truly philosophic, but still crucially incomplete, education (like certain "pre-Socratics," or even perhaps like Socrates himself, who is presented in Plato's *Parmenides* as a rather overly confident young thinker). In other words, this type comprehends some "good natures" who need to be steered onto a better track (as Plato's Parmenides steered young Socrates).

But our impish author teases us once again. The particular youth whose private Socratic tutoring Xenophon presents as *the* extended example is "Euthydemus the beautiful" (4.2.1):[9] a young man wealthy enough to have purchased a number of books, which he valued more than his money (4.2.9), a youth who was morally earnest (4.2.11ff.), and piously prayerful (4.2.36), having twice already (in his young life) made the pilgrimage to the Delphic oracle (4.2.24), but who was in the lower intellectual and spiritual range of the third defective type. For the young man believed that he had already acquired an education that had launched him well into "philosophizing" (4.2.23), an education that had made him distinguished from his peers in wisdom, *and* that gave him great hopes of becoming distinguished by being superior to everyone in capacity to speak and to act (4.2.1). He believed that all this immense educational accomplishment consisted in . . . his having acquired a private collection of books!—books "of those said to be wise" (4.2.8), books of "poets and the most noted sophists" (4.2.1). There is no sign that Euthydemus had actually read any of these books. Euthydemus comes to sight as a kind of caricature[10] of the good natures.

Still, Xenophon's teasing of his readers here has serious functions—not only protective (let us never forget we are traversing a minefield), but educative. For Xenophon thus puts us to the test of figuring out, by reflectively extrapolating from what Xenophon describes as Socrates's tutoring of this spiritually and intellectually *un*promising beauty, all that we can of what *would have been* Socrates's more thorough or penetrating tutoring of truly promising youths—most obviously, a Xenophon.[11] In addition, we are also prodded to puzzle over the question, Why would Socrates spend time and energy winning over, and then trying to educate, so unpromising a youth as Euthydemus?[12]—whom Plato (*Symposium* 222b) as well as Xenophon testifies was indeed seduced into becoming a student-lover of Socrates. This puzzle grows when we soon learn that Euthydemus was one of "many" such inferior cases, most of which were even inferior to Euthydemus (4.2.40)! Given Socrates's "daimonic" insight into humans and their futures, these surely could not have been the results of numerous grave "mistakes" on his part. Socrates deliberately cast a very wide net. What might Socrates have needed to learn, or to confirm, that he could not learn or confirm by confining himself to the education of the good natures? What philosophic need made him spend so much time and energy on the philosophically unpromising? This reminds us of the puzzle with which Xenophon confronted us as regards the reason why Socrates would invest so much effort in trying to educate the unphilosophic Alcibiades and Critias. And at present we are reminded of those two—not only because we first heard of Euthydemus as the object of Critias's lust, back in the opening pages (recall 1.2.29–30), but because Xenophon says that Euthydemus's book collecting gave the youth "great hopes that he would be distinguished from everyone in the power of speaking and acting" (4.2.1): like Alcibiades and Critias, Euthydemus was moved by political ambition; and it was this ambition upon which, Xenophon shows, Socrates played in his seduction of Euthydemus. What's more, Xenophon makes a point of presenting Socrates confirming that Euthydemus had absolutely no ambition such as Socrates himself had in his youth (see Plato's *Phaedo* 96 and context) to become wise in the sciences—in medicine or astronomy or geometry (4.2.10).

In our study of the series of vignettes in book 3, showing how Socrates helped those reaching for the noble, especially in the form of high political office and honor, we were given—above all through what we ourselves may have experienced as we were being taught by Xenophon—some important clues as to what Socrates might have confirmed by seeking to transform the lives and aspirations of youths of political (nonscientific, nonphilosophic) ambition. We now note that the exchange between Socrates and Euthydemus that initiates their dialogue is marked by profane oaths on the part of each of them,[13] and that the ensuing refutational dialogues are marked by many more profane expletives than we have ever heard before in the *Memorabilia*.

## THE SEDUCTION OF EUTHYDEMUS

It was certainly not the case that the self-satisfied Euthydemus sought out Socrates—even though the young man must have heard of Socrates's renown as a teacher of politics from his lover Critias, as well as from other politically ambitious young men; and even though the young beauty had been the intended witness and object of an unforgettably fraught conversation between Critias and Socrates (recall 1.2.30).

In order to encounter Euthydemus, Socrates had to contrive to start frequenting a bridle-maker's shop where Euthydemus was accustomed to go to transact his business, on account of being too young for the Agora.[14] But Socrates did not go to the shop alone; he went in the company of associates. Nor, once he was there, did he directly approach Euthydemus. (We now get a sample of the Socratic art of coy seduction concerning which Socrates advised Theodote.)

Socrates's "first" move (4.2.2) went as follows. "Wishing to stir" Euthydemus, he arranged for the youth to overhear Socrates's response to a (presumably planted) question—asking about how the great Themistocles became so distinguished. Socrates emphatically announced that it was "foolish naiveté" to think that while it's not possible to become a serious practitioner of lesser arts without competent teachers, humans can nevertheless all on their own come to preside over a city.

But this Socratic stimulus to thinking and conversing about the teaching or teachers of the political art stirred no visible reaction in Euthydemus.

That it was defensive vanity that was motivating Euthydemus's standoffishness became manifest on a subsequent occasion, when Socrates perceived that the young man was holding himself aloof in order to avoid betraying any admiration for Socrates's wisdom. Socrates reacted by delivering, to the company of mature men, in Euthydemus's doubtless mortified hearing, a lengthy and laughter-provoking satire on the vacuity of the lad's political pretensions (4.2.3–5). We see that when he deemed it necessary, Socrates was unsparing of adolescent feelings of self-esteem.

To Euthydemus's credit, he was not simply driven off by whatever hurt feelings he suffered; and eventually—Xenophon does not say how long it took—it became evident that the youth was finally attending to the things Socrates was saying. But the young fellow was still so preoccupied with his own appearance that he maintained his silence, out of the belief that this would give him the "reputation of moderation." Socrates, "wishing to make him stop this," delivered in the lad's hearing yet another speech, this time more serious, stressing to the audience how great and intense is the care that ought to be taken by someone rising to the elite challenge entailed in seeking political preeminence, and how doubtful it is that one can meet the challenge quickly, or on one's own. This time, however, Socrates said nothing about teachers of the arts. He spoke instead in terms of something like apprenticeship with the most reputable practitioners (4.2.6–7). Was this not meant to pique Euthydemus, not only to continue to confront his own ignorance of politics, but also to make him start puzzling over Socrates's intended role—to wonder if Socrates was beginning to withdraw, and was signaling that he meant to try to hand Euthydemus over to some politician (recall the advice of Socrates to Theodote, at 3.11.13–14)?

In any case, Xenophon says that Socrates finally "perceived" that the youth was "more ready to submit" to dialogue, and was listening with greater eagerness. At that point, Socrates for the first time visited the bridle-maker's shop *alone*—and Euthydemus came and sat down beside him (4.2.8).

Socrates's initiation of their first intimate conversation was ingratiating, and even flattering. He asked Euthydemus to confirm his repute as having acquired a collection of books by "men said to have become wise." Euthydemus's response was passionate and manly-profane: swearing by Zeus, and addressing Socrates by name, the young man proudly avowed his intention to keep enlarging his collection as much as he was able. Socrates replied (swearing the woman's oath, "By Hera!") with an expression of admiration for the youth's choice, to "own" a "treasury"[15] of wisdom—of judgments by wise men, leading to virtue—rather than acquiring a treasury of gold and silver, which does not make humans better. Euthydemus was of course elated by what he took to be this ratification of what he regarded as his "correct pursuit of wisdom" (4.2.9).

The young man was thus prepared to take with due seriousness, and therefore to find authentically perplexing, the simple but existential question that Socrates next posed, addressing him by name: "Wishing to become *good in what* (he said), oh Euthydemus, do you collect the writings?" The perplexed youth was then led by Socrates to consider five very challenging sorts of expertise, each of which Euthydemus more or less vehemently (swearing twice by Zeus) disavowed as his goal. But in the process, by being brought to contemplate these demanding arts and sciences, there dawned on Euthydemus something of fundamental importance. For when Socrates put it to him that his aim was nothing less than "that virtue through which humans become statesmen and skilled household managers, capable of ruling and bettering other humans as well as themselves," the lad did not leave it at an expression of agreement. Instead: "Intensely, indeed (he said)—oh

Socrates!—of this virtue I am in *need*." Under Socrates's provocation, Euthydemus became, for perhaps the first time in his incipient adult life, willing to express openly his spiritual neediness. He took the first big and difficult step up the ladder of Socratic wisdom. His vanity began decisively to wane.

Socrates responded by graciously making this neediness appear to be as grand a thing as possible: "By Zeus! (said Socrates): the noblest virtue and greatest art is your aim! For this is of kings, and is called the kingly art!" (4.2.10–11).

## THE CENTRALITY OF JUSTICE, AS A VIRTUE OF SPEECH AND DEED

Socrates next asked Euthydemus if he had turned his mind to the question of whether, in these matters, "one who is *not just* can be *good*." The youth energetically responded that "without justice one could not even become a good citizen!" (4.2.11). Euthydemus understood justice to be an essential requirement of *everyone* in politics, ruled citizens as well as ruling statesmen. And when asked if he himself had achieved justice, Euthydemus expressed his measured, gentlemanly confidence that he shared in this virtue no less than anyone. (Is not every sane person, always, or in all times and places, expected to know what is right and wrong, and to have the capacity to choose to act in accordance with the former, while choosing to avoiding the latter?) When Socrates asked if there aren't deeds/works (*erga*) of the just, even as there are of builders, the young man readily answered in the affirmative. But Socrates then asked a question that pointed to a crucial difference between things built and expressions of justice: "Even as builders are able to *display* their works, wouldn't the just be able to *explain* theirs?" Justice is a matter of speech, and of deeds/works that *need interpretation*. To this question, whose challenging import he divined immediately, Euthydemus responded defensively, rebutting what he thought might be the implied hint that he might not have the capacity to "*explain* the deeds of justice"; then he added, somewhat indignantly: "And—by Zeus!—I for my part can do so for the deeds of *in*justice as well! Since there are not a few such to be seen and heard, every day!" (4.2.12). Euthydemus showed himself to be a youth of some appropriate moral indignation, expressing moral self-confidence. Aren't we all passionately capable of blowing the whistle on injustice? Euthydemus certainly did not think that his "need" to learn the virtue that is the kingly art included any need to learn how to explain what are deeds of injustice, as well as of justice. Accordingly, a note of impatience was discernible in Euthydemus's agreement with Socrates's apparently sim-pleminded suggestion that they write down two separate lists, of just and of unjust deeds (4.2.13).

## THE REFUTATION OF EUTHYDEMUS'S CONVICTIONS REGARDING JUSTICE

Asked successively about, in the first place, "lying/uttering a falsehood (*pseudesthai*) among humans," then swindling (*exapatan*), and maltreating (*kakourgein*), and depriving men of their liberty (*andrapodizesthai*), Euthyde-mus replied that it was "obvious" that these belonged on the list of unjust deeds. To Socrates's seemingly otiose additional question, whether any of these "might for us" be placed on the list of just deeds, the noble-minded youth reacted with horror: "That would be a terrible (*deinon*) thing!" (4.2.14).

But then Euthydemus had to agree that "we" would declare "an elected general who deprived of their liberty the men of an unjust enemy city" to be not only completely innocent of injustice, but a doer of just deeds—"Emphatically so" (*mala*), declared Euthydemus. And what if the general "swindled during the war with them?" "This too would be just." And "if the general stole and robbed their belongings,[16] wouldn't he do just things?" "And this too, emphatically! *But* . . .": Euthydemus's self-contradiction stared him in the face; he tried to escape it by claiming that he had under-stood Socrates to be asking his first questions, about the injustice and justice of the specified actions, in reference "*only* to friends/loved ones" (*philous*—Euthydemus did not qualify the "friends/loved ones" as "just"). Socrates replied by refusing to allow Euthydemus to evade his self-contradiction: it necessarily follows, Socrates insisted, that "as many deeds as we have set down in the list under injustice, these would have to be set down also under justice." Euthydemus gave the uneasy admission that "it's likely" (4.2.15). The youth in effect agreed that his initial or primary understanding, that there is an obvious, absolute distinction—between deeds that are certainly unjust, wrong, and deeds that are certainly just, right—had been decisively refuted. (We for our part are provoked to wonder: are there then *no* deeds that are simply or absolutely unjust—or just? We note that Socrates had ad-duced no example of just lying, of deliberately misleading others in speech.)

Socrates proceeded to ask if, given the new listing—of swindling, mal-treating, and so on—as also among acts of *justice*, his interlocutor wished that "we" add the qualifier "when done toward enemies." And by the same token, in the listing of these same deeds as among acts of *injustice*, "we" add the qualifier, "when done toward friends/loved ones"—to the latter of whom, Socrates emphatically added, we "should be maximally straightfor-ward/honest (*haploustaton*)." Euthydemus heartily agreed (4.2.16). Socrates thus brought the justice of avoidance of lying to the fore, while making it clear what Euthydemus had revealed his fuller conception of justice to be (XS 97): "helping one's friends (and hurting the enemies)." With this latter, major qualification, Euthydemus clung to the view that some deeds are simply right and others simply wrong—and not least, telling the truth, never lying, to a friend or loved one. To use later or anachronistic terminology, the youth clung to the conviction that there exist *categorical* moral impera-tives, or *natural-rational* moral *laws*.

But then Euthydemus was asked how he would classify a general's swin-dling of his *own* troops, in order to remove their sense of hopelessness (*athu-mia*—absence of *thumos*); and then how he would classify a father's use of lying, to his own beloved son, in order to get the son to take medicine that restores the son's health; and then how he would classify the employment of theft and robbery to take away a sword or other dangerous item from a friend/loved one who was in "despair" (*athumia*)—out of the robber's justified fear that this friend might commit suicide. Euthydemus answered in each case (in the last case, passionately swearing by Zeus) that in his opinion the act ought to be listed under justice. "Are you saying," Socrates asked, "that one *ought not* to be straightforward/honest, with friends/loved ones, in all circumstances?" Swearing yet again by Zeus, Euthydemus ardently conceded that it was so, adding that he wished to change what he had said, if that was permitted. Socrates answered that it must be permitted, rather than to make an incorrect classification: for Socrates, to acquire correct understanding of right and wrong is imperative (4.2.17–18).

Socrates had led Euthydemus to become painfully aware that he could not maintain, under examination, the moral code that he had thought he be-lieved in (and, that he had, presumably, believed to be sanctioned by Zeus and the gods).

Insofar as Euthydemus (or we) were to be prodded to meditate on these Socratic refutations, they would open up a path of analysis that leads to-ward the moral principle that the just choice worthiness of every deed must be judged by the standard of what the chooser/doer knows or believes will achieve, in each set of ever different and changing circumstances, the intel-ligibly greatest benefit for those one loves—and in addition, the greatest harm to enemies (presumably so as to defend those one loves). This would imply, furthermore, that the supreme standard and desideratum of moral life is knowledge of what is truly beneficial (and harmful), for those whom one loves, in all their varying life circumstances. This is a very tall order,

especially when one sees that this entails the necessity of prioritizing differing individual loved ones and their changing and differing, even conflicting,
needs. And does it not necessarily follow that sometimes it is just to deliberately harm friends/loved ones? This question looms in Socrates's next step.

Socrates turned the focus to another dimension of the problematic of
justice and injustice: moral responsibility (4.2.19). "Regarding those who
swindle (*exapatōntōn*) their loved ones *so as to cause harm*—so that this we
do not leave aside uninvestigated—who is *more* unjust, the one doing so voluntarily, or the one doing so involuntarily?" (*hekōn, akōn*—Socrates meant
by this latter, presumably, one who mistakenly thought his "swindle" would
*not* cause the loved ones "harm"). The response of Euthydemus revealed how
deeply the previous refutations had undermined his confidence in his primary convictions about justice: "I for my part no longer trust in the things
I answer! For all the things before now seem to me otherwise than as I then
thought!" This exclamation of agonized self-doubt did not, however, indicate
that Euthydemus was starting to follow the Socratic pointer to the moral
primacy of the good, the beneficial. For Euthydemus proceeded to answer
Socrates's new question by voicing (with hesitation) the opinion that "the
one voluntarily lying/uttering a falsehood (*pseudomenon*) is more unjust
than the one involuntarily." His replacement of "swindling" with the less
egregious "lying/uttering a falsehood," and, still more, his dropping of the
*harmfulness* that was crucial to Socrates's characterization of the "swindling" as unjust, along with his dropping of "loved ones" as the targets of
the swindling, all indicate that the young man was slipping back toward
his original, pre-Socratic (and proto-Kantian), gentlemanly conviction that
deliberate lying is in and of itself, or absolutely, more unjust than inadvertently uttering something deceptive.

But Euthydemus also affirmed, when next asked by Socrates, that he
believed there to be "learning (*mathēsis*) and knowledge (*epistēmē*) of the
just—even as of letters" (4.2.20). Thus, in what one is tempted to call a
benevolent "swindle" on the part of Socrates, the youth was led to think
of knowledge of justice as analogous to knowledge of the art of reading and
writing. And in regard to the latter he of course agreed with Socrates that
one who voluntarily spells incorrectly is more knowledgeable, is even "the
one skilled in spelling," in contrast to the one who involuntarily misspells
and is as such "without letters"—"since the former, whenever he wished,
would be able to spell correctly"; and from this he was led by Socrates to
declare that it is "obvious" that, analogously, "the one who knows the just
things is the one voluntarily deceiving and swindling, rather than the one
doing so involuntarily." But when Socrates asked if Euthydemus was also

declaring that, more comprehensively, "the one knowing the just things is more just than the one not knowing," Euthydemus in granting as much nevertheless expressed bewilderment at his own self-contradictory agreement: he sensed acutely that he was missing something. He was dimly aware that "knowledge of justice" is a deeply ambiguous conception.

Insofar as he or we were to be stirred to meditate on this paradoxical Socratic refutation, we would be led to reflect on what is most problematic in the parallel between knowledge of an art such as spelling and knowledge of justice. The knower of an art such as spelling can choose to put into action or not the knowledge, and can choose to enact it correctly or incorrectly—making the choice with a view to some end or good beyond the art; and that end or good would be best known by a more architectonic knowledge. This tables the question, Is not knowledge of justice *the simply* architectonic knowledge—the piloting art of the good life—whose correct enactment no genuine knower can intelligibly choose to abandon? Or is there a higher good, for someone, and an art of achieving that good, that is of such a supreme character that, with a view to it, knowledge of justice, as knowledge of what is truly beneficial (and harmful) for those whom one loves, ought to be employed only sometimes, and, what is more, employed sometimes in order to do what is "incorrect," in terms of the art of justice as helping one's friends/loved ones? What follows in the sequel might suggest that the answer to these questions turns on answering the question of whether it makes sense to conceive of being just to and in oneself, or to and in one's own soul.

For in response to Euthydemus's expression of bewilderment at his own self-contradictory affirmation, Socrates abruptly switched to asking the young man about his self-consciousness, in his experience of having been repeatedly shown to contradict himself as regards his understanding of justice (4.2.21). Socrates gently led the youth to declare, with vehemence, that one in such a condition "does not know what he thought he knew, by Zeus!"; and what is more, that "slavish" is the proper name for "those who do not know the noble things and the good things and the just things" (4.2.22; recall 1.1.16). Then Socrates finally asked, most personally, "Is it not necessary to strain in every way so that *we* not be slaves?" (4.2.23). The Socratic refutations are meant to inspire a fervent, all-consuming *eros* for liberation of oneself from spiritual enslavement to self-contradictory, even if conventionally respectable, moral opinions. And Socrates now seemed on the verge of broadening the dialogue out into an interrogation of Euthydemus's opinions about the noble as well as the good and the just; Socrates seemed on the brink of directing to Euthydemus the sort of questioning about the noble and the good that we were drawn into when we witnessed Socrates "benefiting those reaching out for the noble things."

But in response, Euthydemus burst out—invoking in an oath the gods generally—with an expression of shattered despair (*athumia*). He revealed that he had believed, until these Socratic refutations, that he already was "philosophizing," with a "philosophy through which I believed I would especially be educated in the things fitting for a real man (*andri*) aiming at gentlemanliness; but now, how dispirited [lacking in *thumos*] do you think I am!" The wrenching experience of undergoing the Socratic refutations of his convictions about justice had plunged the youth into the "insight that all the previous toils have left me incapable of answering what is asked about what must especially be known"—and, what is much worse, had fomented in him the reaction of seeing himself as "having no other path on which I might proceed to become better" (4.2.22–23).

To his credit, Euthydemus had recognized the depth of the cave of ignorant incoherence, regarding the supreme moral principles by which to live one's life, in which Socrates had showed him to be lost. But at the same time, Euthydemus now showed that he lacked the heart (*thumos*) to find in this crushing self-discovery anything of an invigorating challenge, eliciting a passionate desire to escape the cave, an erotic quest for a path toward the attraction of a life lived in sunlit clarity.

Having listened[17] to Euthydemus's despondent lament about his "pathlessness," Socrates suddenly introduced the path to divinity.[18] Socrates reminded Euthydemus of his two pilgrimages to the most sacred shrine at Delphi, and of the youth's having read inscribed on the temple wall there the hallowed admonition or commandment (*Education of Cyrus* 7.2.20–21) "Know thyself!" Socrates embarked on an encouraging interpretation of the meaning of this divine injunction—delivered in a more monologic discourse that substituted for the (temporarily postponed) continuation of the dialogic, refutational investigation into the just (and soon the good). Socrates now all but suggested that his previous, deeply disturbing refutations revealing the incoherence of Euthydemus's convictions concerning justice should be understood, after all, as a kind of prelude to the proper interpretation of the divine admonition and commandment.[19] Socrates was apparently serving the god in Delphi.

Euthydemus at first, when asked if he had paid attention to the sacred inscription, confessed with evident chagrin that "by Zeus!" he had failed to do so—that he had failed to undertake to examine himself as to whoever he was, since he had been sure he already knew this, and that he could hardly know anything else if he did not know this. Socrates then asked whether Euthydemus did not opine that the divine injunction "Know one-self" means the following: even as a purchaser of horses needs to investigate whether a horse is obedient or disobedient, strong or weak, fast or slow, and whatever other qualities are suitable or unsuitable, "with a view to the horse's *use/employment (chreia),*" so, the "one who has examined himself, as to what sort he is *with a view to human use/employment,*" is "the one who knows his own power/capacity (*dunamin*)" (4.2.25). This remarkably formulated question tacitly opened the path to conceiving of knowledge of oneself in the very pious terms of knowing one's capacity/power as an employee-servant of divinity—a "horse" to be ridden by divinity. In other words, Socrates tested to see if Euthydemus would react to the devastating discovery that his convictions about justice were incoherent by throwing himself into service to and guidance by suprarational, mysterious, but com-manding divinity. It is certainly conceivable that a person of modest intel-lect, who is not the strongest in heart, would, upon becoming shattered by being shown the incoherence of his moral convictions, respond by, in effect, saying and thinking: "But then, recalling my visits to Delphi, I see with new clarity that I must 'know myself' in the radically humble sense of do-ing whatever God has commanded, despite or because my own convictions regarding justice are ignorantly confused."

But as a matter of empirical fact, nothing like this happened. On the contrary. The youth answered as if Socrates had invited him to seek knowl-edge of Euthydemus's own *power*: "This is how to me at least it seems (he said) that the one not knowing the *power* of himself is ignorant of himself" (4.2.25). It would appear that opening the path of a life of obedient service to divinity, in the wake of the devastating discovery of the contradictory in-coherence of his convictions about justice, produced in Euthydemus a kind of rebound, of renewed will to self-empowerment through self-knowledge (though, as we soon see, this by no means implied an abandonment of prayer-ful piety).

From this launching pad, Socrates generated for Euthydemus a lengthy celebration of the knowledge of oneself as knowledge of one's own power, without any further reference to divinity or service under divine guidance (4.2.26–29). Socrates proclaimed that self knowledge conceived as knowledge of one's own power is the key to "humans experiencing most good things." For "those knowing themselves know what is suitable for themselves, and know the difference between the things they can do and the things they cannot"—thereby "providing the things they need, and flourishing" while "becoming unerring"; self-knowers, in this sense, "being enabled to test others," "provide the good things and guard against the bad through using others"; the self-knowers "become of good repute and honored," since they "use one another with pleasure," while "those who fail in their affairs desire" the self-knowers "to deliberate on their behalf" and "to preside over them"; those who are failures "put their hopes for good things" in the ones who are self-knowers, and, "on account of all these things, admire most of all" the self-knowers. By contrast, Socrates painted in the gloomiest colors the fates of those who are ignorant or deceived about themselves, that is, about their own powers. "And you see," Socrates said in his peroration, "that also as regards cities, those that are ignorant of their own power go to war with those who are stronger, some becoming overthrown, some losing their freedom and becoming enslaved."[20] Self-knowledge as Socrates now presented it culminates in civic freedom, and the avoidance of civic enslavement. His speech as a whole could be understood—and, we soon learn, was understood by Euthydemus—to hold out the promise that self-knowledge, as knowledge of one's own power, is the key to political preeminence.

For the sake of attaining self-knowledge so conceived—as knowledge of one's own power to obtain for oneself most good things—Euthydemus now enthusiastically delivered himself over to the guidance of Socrates (4.2.30). In his speech Socrates had not mentioned the just and the noble things (XS 98), and Euthydemus did not ask to be taught knowledge about them. Along with piety, the just and noble now suffered a partial eclipse.

## THE REFUTATION OF EUTHYDEMUS'S CONVICTIONS REGARDING THE GOOD

Taking Euthydemus in hand, Socrates returned to dialectical interrogation of the youth. Socrates began with the apparently encouraging question, "Now, as regards the good things and the bad—which is which—you presumably know entirely?" Swearing by Zeus, Euthydemus replied with vehement certainty that of course he did—for if he did not, he would be "more vulgar than are slaves." When Socrates asked the youth to specify examples, Euthydemus once again expressed an orientation by belief in an absolute distinction, this time between goods that are unqualifiedly good, exemplified first and foremost by health, with its causes and effects, and things that are unqualifiedly bad, such as ill health, with its causes and effects (4.2.31).

But then he was led by Socrates to concede that there are "many" major civic and private activities—Socrates adduced (swearing by Zeus to make his perhaps intrinsically somewhat weak claim more forceful) disgraceful military expeditions, and harmful sea voyages—with regard to which it may be good (beneficial to oneself) to be disabled by ill health, and bad (harmful to oneself) to be healthy, since the former spares one from participation in these collective actions that ruin one's fellows.

Euthydemus was so disappointed by this refutation that when Socrates asked him if such things, like health, that are sometimes good and sometimes bad, are at least more good than bad, the lad replied with passion: "By Zeus! In no way do they appear so, at least according to this argument at any rate!" (4.2.33). Euthydemus could not abandon his orientation by the hope that what is truly good can and must be unqualifiedly good: and he made it clear that he was sure that Socrates would have to agree that "wisdom" (sophia), at least, is "indisputably" good, "for in what affair would one who is wise not do better than one who is ignorant?" (4.2.32).[21] After all, had not Socrates just before delivered a convincing account of the indisputable goodness of wisdom, as self-knowledge of one's own powers, leading to acquisition of most good things? But Socrates had also quietly pointed to knowledge of oneself as including knowledge of the *limits* of one's power. And Socrates now surprised Euthydemus by reminding that sacred tradition teaches that precisely wisdom (which Socrates did not deny includes knowledge of one's power, or of what one can and cannot do) has led great individuals of the past into misery: slavery under barbarians, and the death of their loved ones as well as themselves. Euthydemus acknowledged, with an oath by Zeus that expressed his surprise, that "so it is said" (4.2.33). Then Socrates asked the youth how many others he thought had been, "on account of wisdom, dragged off" to Persian slavery—thus suggesting that wisdom may be not at all a guarantee of political freedom and rule, in apparent contradiction to Socrates's preceding monologue of promising and hopeful praise of wisdom.[22]

Euthydemus avoided answering, and abandoned the cause of wisdom's indisputable goodness. Instead, he ventured to submit that "happiness (eudaimonia) is most unarguably good." This Socrates did not deny. But it became clear that Socrates and Euthydemus differed radically in their understandings of the meaning or the constituents of happiness—and thus of the meaning of the terms of Socrates's previous, promising monologue in praise of the effects of self-knowledge. Euthydemus was presupposing that one cannot be happy without beauty, strength, wealth, repute, and other such things, which he regarded as "indisputably good." Challenged on this, he stubbornly replied by invoking the highest god: "By Zeus, we will include them! For how could someone without these things be happy?!" In rejoinder, Socrates matched oath with oath, invoking Zeus while pointing to "how many harsh things happen to humans" as a consequence of their possessing beauty and strength and wealth, and "how many, through reputation and political power, have suffered great evils." To this Euthydemus replied: "But then (he declared) if, indeed, I do not speak correctly in praising being happy, I agree that I do not know *for what one ought to pray to the gods.*"[23] In response, Socrates gently suggested that excessive "faith" (*pistis*) had obscured for Euthydemus the need for examination (4.2.34–36).

Euthydemus's life, we now see, had been guided by prayerful piety—which he had by no means abandoned a moment ago, when he submitted himself to Socrates's education in self-knowledge with a view to obtaining happiness or what is indisputably good. Before being interrogated by Socrates, he presumed that he knew what is just and what is unjust, and that he must do the former and indignantly resist the latter; and that he could on this basis hopefully pray to the gods for what he assumed constituted happiness—above all, health and repute and political power and preeminence, if and when guaranteed to be secure and profitable because sanctioned and bestowed by the providence of Zeus and the other divinities, responding to Euthydemus's pious, gentlemanly prayer. His undergoing, through Socrates, the experience of having been refuted and shown to be grossly ignorant, first and foremost as regards his previously confident understanding of justice, and then secondly as regards his previously confident understanding of happiness, or of indisputably beneficial things, had a deep and powerful effect on his prayerful piety. Although Socrates had raised no questions about prayer—had not so much as alluded to prayer—the manifest empirical consequence of Socrates's refutations was that Euthydemus no longer had any confidence that he should, or could, pray hopefully for divinity's granting him, in security, what he had previously been convinced were the human goods. Gripped by the Socratic experience of being refuted and proven ignorant as regards first what is just and then what is good, "it does not occur to him that he could pray to the all-knowing gods to give him what they know to be unambiguously good for him" (XS 99; recall 1.3.2). Euthydemus needs and seeks a good that is to him intelligibly beneficial, fulfilling, and secure. The praying that is likely to have been Euthydemus's most important and vivid regular experience of being in communication with, in the presence of, the gods—whose worship is centered on the Delphic Apollo and his oracle, to which Euthydemus has twice journeyed—this praying had in some measure become paralyzed as a consequence of the Socratic refutations. What's more, we soon learn that Euthydemus's subsequent time spent off by himself, in meditation on the specific refutations by Socrates, led Euthydemus to be in need of, and receptive to, a new

Socratic theology that differed radically from traditional Greek beliefs—and in which prayer seems to play no role. The refutations, that were not about piety or prayer, but about the just and the good, had as their consequence a profound change in Euthydemus's piety and praying, that is, in his religious experience of divinity.

## THE REFUTATION OF EUTHYDEMUS'S CONCEPTION OF DEMOCRACY

But we have gotten a bit ahead of ourselves. What removed the last prop of Euthydemus's pre-Socratic convictions was his experience of being refuted by Socrates in his understanding of the political regime in which he aimed to become preeminent. Euthydemus (whose name, a common one, means "straight from/for the *dēmos*") was ambitious to lead "democracy"—"rule by the people (*dēmos*)." The youth vehemently agreed that—"by Zeus!"—it is not possible to understand "what is democracy" without understanding "what is the *dēmos*" (or "the people"). He declared that he believed "the people" to be the class of the "poor" among the "citizens"—meaning those who lack sufficient spending power, defined over and against the class of the "rich," meaning those with more than sufficient spending power.[24] But then Socrates reminded Euthydemus that "for some who have very little, this not only suffices, but they even make gain from this; while for some, very much does not suffice." This made the young man suddenly realize— expressing his surprise with a "By Zeus!"—that this entails that the *dēmos* as he conceived it overlaps empirically with "tyrants who on account of need are compelled to commit injustice, *even like those most lacking in resources*"; while the class of the rich includes those who possess little, but are skilled household managers (who thus avoid the compulsion to do injustice). Euthydemus judged that it was his "worthlessness" (*phaulotēs*) that "compelled" him "to agree also with these things"; and at this point the youth departed from Socrates—in "despair" (*athumōs*) and filled with self-contempt at his own "slavishness" (4.2.36–39).

Why does Xenophon make the refutation of Euthydemus's understanding of democracy the crushing completion or culmination of the Socratic refutations and their effect? Is this simply the proverbial "straw that breaks the camel's back"? But why would Xenophon need to add *this* straw? Why not make the previous refutations about the just and the good suffice? Why does Xenophon have his Socrates respond immediately to Euthydemus's outburst about prayer with the beginning of the interrogation about democracy (4.2.36)? I believe the answer transpires if we note that this refutation concerning democracy is in effect a return to, and further elaboration of, the refutation of Euthydemus's conception of justice. For now Socrates compelled Euthydemus to reflect on his understanding of the object of righteous devotion to which he planned to dedicate his life—for which dedication he may well have hoped to win from the gods deserved, lasting glory (let us never forget the consideration by which Virtue defeats Vice). Socrates compelled Euthydemus to reflect on the putative justice of the cause of "the people" as the (supposedly deserving) poor, in their purported moral superiority to the "rich." Xenophon does not show Euthydemus being thus led to disenchantment with democracy. Xenophon shows him being led to contempt for himself, on account of his failure to have ever thought critically about the justice and moral character of democracy and the *dēmos*—"the people"—in whose public service he had planned to spend his life proving his worthiness.

"Now many," Xenophon reports, of those who suffered a similarly crushing dialectical experience with Socrates reacted by permanently avoiding his company. The impact of Socratic dialectic was largely negative, and presumably aroused considerable hostility—which must have been intensified to the extent that it became known that, as Xenophon here discloses, Socrates judged these many to be "rather slack" (and recall 1.1.16 end).

In contrast, Euthydemus, to his credit (but not unproblematically for Socrates), became one of the few who were led, by perplexed meditations on Socrates's refutations, to "suppose that he would not otherwise become a real man worthy of note unless he were to be in Socrates's company as much as possible; and he did not leave him any longer except from necessity; and some of his pursuits he even imitated" (4.2.37–40). Euthydemus did not or could not find satisfactory guidance for his life by returning to his pre-Socratic convictions about the just and the good and democracy, or to his pre-Socratic prayerful piety, or by turning to such authorities as "the god in Delphi" and the latter's injunctions (see 4.3.16).

## MAKING EUTHYDEMUS MODERATE
## AS REGARDS DIVINITY

Once Socrates recognized that Euthydemus had become his disciple, Socrates henceforth "disturbed" the young man "as little as possible." Euthydemus was not a promising candidate for anything like a full Socratic conversion through continued, intensely self-critical scrutiny. Evidently, Socrates had learned or confirmed all that he could from the empirical results of his refutational activity with Euthydemus (precisely because Euthydemus was so

unpromising, Socrates had learned what he could never learn from the conversions of truly promising natures). Socrates replaced his "disturbing" in-
terrogations with "very simple and very clear" explanations of "the things
he believed [Euthydemus] needed to know and that would be strongest to
practice."[25]

First and foremost, Socrates judged that he had to reconstruct Euthydemus's religious belief—the disintegration of which, as a consequence of the
Socratic refutations, thus becomes even more glaring.

More precisely (and remarkably), Xenophon interjects the sweeping observation that the attempt to instill "moderation as regards the gods" was
the top item on Socrates's educational agenda *in general* for those who were
converted to become his "companions" (*sunontas*). Xenophon goes so far
as to indicate (4.3.2) that these healing conversations, in which Socrates
made his converts "more pious and more moderate" (*eusebesterous te kai
sōphresterous*—4.3.18), were so frequent, and so often witnessed, that there
have already been other accounts of this (private) endeavor published,[26]
prior to Xenophon's publishing of his eyewitness account here of Socrates's
religious instruction of Euthydemus. Xenophon reveals that a routine part
of becoming a companion of Socrates, as a consequence of undergoing the
experience of being refuted by him, was becoming urgently in need of a personal Socratic conversational education in moderation as regards the gods.
One is tempted to say that it is here disclosed that Socrates had to expend
considerable effort at putting genies back in their bottles, in the wake of the
religious conversions that were a consequence of his shattering refutations—
refutations which, to repeat, were not about religious subjects. We have here
a Xenophontic lightning flash that momentarily illuminates the entire landscape of the refutational-converting project that was distinctive of Socrates—
the project that constituted his divine mission, if you will, or that gave him
the ever increasing empirical evidence that was the basis for his posture toward divinity.

We recall that the very first extended Socratic dialogue that Xenophon
presented was one in which Socrates tried—with uncertain success—to induce moderation as regards the gods in his blasphemous devotee Aristodemus (1.4.2ff.): it was not always or only recent converts in whom Socrates
had to attempt to instill moderation as regards the gods. We further recall
that "moderation about the gods" first appeared in the *Memorabilia* as a substitute for "belief in the gods of the city" when Xenophon closed his defense
of Socrates against the charge of religious dissidence (1.1.20). Xenophon
does not say here, moreover, that Socrates made moderation as regards the
gods his educational priority with his converts *for the sake of piety* (or for

the sake of the gods, let alone for the sake of the gods of the city). It was rather that "he did not *rush* his companions to become skilled speakers and doers and contrivers" (he did eventually make them become such—BD ad loc.), since "he believed that those who, without moderation, acquired such powers were more unjust and also more able to do harm" (4.3.1). Moderation as regards the *gods* was only *part*—if the first and most urgent part—of the moderation that Socrates recognized he needed to try to instill in his converts. As we see presently, Socrates was also concerned to instill moderation as regards humans (i.e., justice, as obedience to the laws of the city).

As earlier with Aristodemus, so now with Euthydemus, Socrates in his theological teaching eclipsed the traditional pantheon with a naturalistic cosmology. The eclipse is circumscribed by the invocations of Zeus in profane expletives, especially in the opening exchanges, and by Socrates's closing appeal, after his teleological argumentation is finished, to "the god in Delphi": "the reference to the Delphic god is noteworthy since the arguments established only the existence of what we may call the cosmic gods" (XS 105). We are again vividly shown that while "he did not converse about the nature of all things in the way most of the others did" (1.1.11), Socrates did (frequently) converse about the nature of all things in his own way. But not always in the same way. The teleo-theological cosmological doctrine that Xenophon reports he witnessed Socrates delivering to the immature and comparatively docile Euthydemus is quite different from the kindred doctrine of whose truth Xenophon showed Socrates trying to convince his mature and much more sophisticated scoffer-follower Aristodemus.[27]

The conversation with Euthydemus began with a rather surprising revelation. Euthydemus confessed—expressing his astonishment with a "By Zeus!"—that it had *never* "occurred to him to ponder how attentively the gods furnish what human beings need" (4.3.3). His prayerful pre-Socratic piety had evidently been addressed to Greek divinities whose providential care he had conceived as uncertain, not to say erratic.[28] Aristodemus, we recall, had—in contrast to Euthydemus—undertaken sustained pondering of this same question, prior to his conversation with Socrates, and had been led to the conclusion that the gods are *not at all* attentive to humans, and hence that belief in and worship of the Greek gods is ridiculous superstition (XS 102).

Socrates induced the young Euthydemus to consider in the first place that light, and then night, and then the visible heavenly bodies—sun, stars, moon—are divinely intended to meet "our" needs. Night Socrates uniquely characterized as "most beautifully" provided, for our needed rest; and it was this assertion that elicited from Euthydemus his only explicit expression of "deserved gratitude" in these opening exchanges (is Euthydemus a youth who especially enjoys sleeping?).

Socrates did not initially make it explicit whether he meant that the heavenly bodies are themselves gods, or only instruments of the gods; but by listing them along with light and night, and then proceeding to fruits and seasons, and so on, he seemed to treat the heavenly bodies, initially at least, as mere unpersonified instruments of the gods. Soon, however, Socrates spoke of the sun, at least, as personified, and indeed punitive; and of the thunderbolt and the winds as "servants" of the gods (4.3.14—*hupēretas tōn theōn*). Socrates had not even attempted to persuade the sophisticated Aristodemus of any of this. One suspects he knew that he would have been laughed at, especially when he got to the thunderbolt (consider Aristophanes, *Clouds* 374–411).

When Socrates proceeded from the sidereal to the earthly, to the earth's products (but not farmer's crops, at least explicitly),[29] along with the seasons, as manifestations of divine generosity attending to our delights as well as to our needs, the response of Euthydemus became more emphatically acquiescent: "Very much are these things too philanthropic!" (4.3.5). Somewhat less enthusiastic was the young man's agreement with Socrates's lengthiest assertion, that water is a divine donation provided "ungrudgingly" (4.3.6; no doubt the youth had heard of, if he had not experienced, droughts as well as floods). What really aroused the youth's fervor, however, was Socrates's assertion that the gods have "procured" fire for humanity—for "without fire, humans equip themselves with nothing worth mentioning of the things useful for life" (4.3.7). How exactly the gods "procured" fire for humans (and how we can be sure that humans did not have to procure it for themselves) Socrates left unstated. "Whether Socrates thus rejects or modifies the myth of Prometheus's theft of fire must be left open."[30] Certain it is that—to the evident gratification or relief of Euthydemus, and, amazingly, without a word of questioning or doubt from him—Socrates broke with a cardinal belief of traditional Greek faith and piety, which expresses the envy and hostility of Zeus toward humanity.[31]

The Socratic gospel about the true source of mankind's acquisition of fire seemed to affect Euthydemus rather strongly. For when Socrates moved back to the sun, and asked Euthydemus to consider now not merely its provision of light, but its causing of the seasons (previously, Socrates had traced the seasons to "the gods"), the youth responded with a tribute, not to the sun (as one might expect was deserved), but to "the gods." He declared that the only thing now making him hesitate to consider "the gods" as having no activity other than taking care of humans was the fact that the other animals also receive their care (4.3.8–9). Socrates removed this source of qualification by convincing Euthydemus that it is for the sake of humans that the other animals come into being and are sustained—and that this holds for animals even more than it does for plants (it holds for plants too). Socrates reached this conclusion by adducing only the evidence of those animal species that humans "domesticate and break in," evidence whose conclusiveness the awestruck young Euthydemus confirmed (4.3.10). Socrates had not advanced such an extreme, anthropocentric teleology when arguing with Aristodemus; instead, he had adduced the functional anatomy and reproductive eros of animals, starting with humans, and thereby gained agreement from Aristodemus that it *looks* like "these exist by the art of some wise craftsman who loves animals," "someone designing that animals exist" (1.4.5–7); then Socrates had tried, with more doubtful success, to persuade Aristodemus that the gods have given humans a privileged place among animals (1.4.11–14).

At this point in the dialogue with Euthydemus, Socrates would seem to have achieved a complete conversion of the young man to the belief that "the gods" (unnamed) have no activity other than arranging the universe to meet humanity's needs—to a belief, that is, in general providence, though not yet in particular providence. But now Socrates added an enormous question: "Have they not given us in addition" our capacities for perception, and rational calculation, and "interpretation" (*hermeneia*), "through which we share all the goods and teach one another and live in community and establish laws and conduct political life?" Euthydemus replied, with a notably diminished enthusiasm, and with less than total, and rather vague, agreement: "In every way it is likely that the gods exercise much care for humans." Euthydemus may have noticed that Socrates had omitted any suggestion that the gods themselves legislate for humans, or even that they intervene to prevent and to correct human misgovernment and faulty legislation.

Socrates rushed to address at least part of the difficulty implicit in the fact that there prevails very fallible, human, all-too-human, self-government (see *Education of Cyrus*, beg.) with yet another question: "What about the fact that if we are incapable of knowing in advance what of future things are advantageous, they work at these things together with us, by expressing through the art of divination how things will turn out, to those who inquire, and by teaching how things would best come about?" Suddenly, immediately after the introduction of law and politics, and in response to Euthydemus's diminished enthusiasm in reaction, Socrates descended from his teleo-theological cosmology to conventional civic religion and its art of divination.

Euthydemus answered without mentioning civic divination, and instead brought to the fore the striking idiosyncrasy of Socrates as regards prophecy:

"With you, Socrates, they likely deal in a still more friendly fashion than with others, if indeed, even when they are not asked by you, they foretell to you what ought to be done and what not." Socrates in reply seemed unsurprised at this response, and readily followed the lead of Euthydemus, to focus on "the *daimonion*." (Euthydemus, after all, had now become a devoted and attentive follower of Socrates.) Socrates did not contest the implication drawn by Euthydemus about Socrates's special status with the gods, but he indicated an awareness that his young acolyte was not yet entirely convinced that Socrates was telling the truth in speaking of his *daimonion* (XS 104): "And that I am speaking the truth, even you *will* know, *if* you do not wait until you see the forms of the gods, but it suffices for you, when seeing their deeds, to revere and to honor the gods" (4.3.11–13). Until the introduction of the *daimonion*, Socrates had stressed the *visibility* of the evidence he presented for the gods' (general) providential care—starting with their gift of the light that makes possible visibility. Now, there was a dramatic change.

Socrates ascended, on the basis of what he termed "the gods' intimations," to teach or to preach a single deity "ordering together and holding together the whole cosmos, in which all things are beautiful and good, and which He provides always unworn and healthy and ageless for us to use, providing unerring service, quicker than thought, and whose *doing* of the greatest things is visible, but whose household management of these things is not visible to us." Socrates then implored Euthydemus to meditate also on the fact that "the Sun, while or despite seeming to be manifest to all, does not permit humans to see Him with accuracy, but even blinds anyone who irreverently attempts such gazing."[32] Socrates further implored his young listener to meditate on the fact that "the servants of the gods," the thunderbolt and the winds, are invisible—the former when coming and going, the latter simply. Last but not least Socrates implored Euthydemus to meditate on the invisible human soul, "which partakes of the divine if anything human does," ruling like a king in us. From learning about the power of these invisible things, Socrates enjoined Euthydemus, he should "honor the *daimonion*." So what exactly was Socrates implying about his own *daimonion*, in relation to the cosmic *daimonion*? Was Socrates implying that his own *daimonion* is a kind of direct emanation to him from the single, invisible deity who manages the whole cosmos as His household? Or was Socrates implying that his *daimonion* is an aspect of his own invisible soul, in its partaking of the divine? Or both? And how is the *daimonion*, in any of its possible meanings, related to the divination practiced by the civic community, and to the gods of the city—Athena, Zeus, Pluto, and so

on? Euthydemus did not ask, probably because he was so deeply moved by
Socrates's speech. "That I, oh Socrates (he said), shall not even in a small way
neglect the *daimonion*, know clearly!" (4.3.13–15).

But Euthydemus was at the same time once again moved to despon-
dency (*athumia*). For the piety that Socrates had kindled in the soul of Euthydemus was a piety of fervent gratitude;[33] and the youth declared that he
was despondent because he could not conceive how any single human being
could ever repay to the gods the gratitude they deserved for their benefits.
These are the last words we hear from Euthydemus in this conversation,
and for quite some time. This expresses the heart of his new, Socratic piety.

Socrates attempted to dispel the youth's nobly pious despair, and replace
it with civic-pious hope, by suddenly reminding of the response that is given
by "the god in Delphi," when someone asks how to gratify or to show gratitude to the gods.[34] The answer is "By the law of the city." Unlike our author, earlier (1.3.2–3), Xenophon's Socrates here gave an interpretation of this
pronouncement as referring not to practices specific to any Greek city, but
instead as referring to the "law that is presumably everywhere" (among bar-
barian nations as well as Greek cities), dictating "that it suffices to make
sacrifices to the gods according to one's capacity." Socrates further interpreted the pronouncement of "the god in Delphi" (unlike Xenophon earlier,
1.3.1, Socrates here did not name that god "the Pythia") as a "bidding of the
gods" generally. Given this universalism, Socrates of course "does not trace
this maxim to Hesiod" (XS 105), the fountainhead of sacred *Greek* religious
tradition and of the knowledge of the *Greek* gods—as Xenophon had claimed
Socrates did, when Xenophon was defending his master against the charge of
not believing in the gods of the city (1.3.3). What is more, Socrates interpreted
this pronouncement to be a commandment that one ought, while sacrificing
as much as possible and thus honoring the gods, "to take heart and to hope
for the greatest goods." And this great, sacrificial hopefulness, in obedience to
universal divine law, Socrates linked to "moderation," saying (in a curiously
complicated, negative formulation): "For one would not be moderate having
greater hopes from others than from those with the power to benefit in the
greatest way, nor otherwise rather than if one were to satisfy these."

It cannot be doubted that Socrates succeeded in inducing in Euthydemus
a profoundly awestruck piety. But as regards the *gods of the city*, did he also
make Euthydemus more pious—or did he make him only more moderate?
Xenophon does not tell us what Euthydemus's reaction was to Socrates's
final turn or half return to the Greek gods, and to the hopefully sacrificial
piety of the *nomos*. What's more, in this dialogue Socrates did not attempt,

at least explicitly, to persuade Euthydemus to return to his *praying* (recall 1.3.2 and 3.8.10).

Xenophon closes by saying that Socrates made his companions more pious and more moderate not only by "saying such things," but also by "doing them" (4.3.18). Is this a reference to Socrates's participations in the performance of the lawful, sacrificial rites and prayers offered to the civic gods—including prayers for civic victory in battle and war (recall 1.3.1–2)? But nothing like that is said here explicitly. The curious failure to specify the educative religious *deeds* of Socrates is made conspicuous by the fact that the very next sentence starts specifying at length Socrates's exemplary educative *deeds* of *justice*; by *these* deeds, Xenophon says, Socrates "did *not* hide the judgment that he had concerning the just, at least" (*peri tou dikaiou ge, ouk apekrupteto hēn eiche gnōmēn*—4.4.1).

## SOCRATES TEACHING JUSTICE

In the case of the just, Socrates's deeds do *not* hide his judgment. But they do not by themselves make his judgment clear. For the deeds need interpretation as regards their motives. This becomes starkly clear when Xenophon adduces the first specific example of Socrates's deeds of justice that evince even risky and sacrificial concern to obey the law. The example is Socrates's famous refusal, when presiding in the Assembly, to allow the populace to vote, contrary to Athenian legal procedure, on collective condemnation of the admirals from the battle of Arginusae. For we recall that Xenophon earlier adduced this same deed as exemplifying Socrates's *piety*, and specifically his worry about divine punishment of himself that would follow upon his violating his oath of office taken before the gods—a motivating piety that, Xenophon went on to explain, was based on a conception of divine supervision that differed radically from the conception held by the people of Athens (1.1.17–19). Xenophon is now entirely silent about this purported motivation (even as he was entirely silent, in that earlier account, on Socrates's being motivated by commitment to obey the law). By the same token, whereas here Xenophon says that Socrates's deliberate willingness to undergo the death penalty at his trial[35] was motivated by heroically sacrificial obedience to the law, he will soon inform us that in fact this deed of Socrates at the trial was motivated by obedience to his *daimonion's* advice, to the effect that it was in Socrates's *own best interest* to die at this time and in this way—without any reference to the motive of concern to obey the law (4.8.5–8; XS 107–8).

Contrary to the expectation that he created at 4.3.1, Xenophon does not now enable us to witness a private conversation through which Socrates attempted to make any of his companions moderate with regard to humans (recall also the charges Xenophon responded to at 1.2.9–11 and 49ff.). But maybe such a conversation is superfluous: is not the *Memorabilia* full of conversations that show Socrates teaching and exemplifying, in his words more than his deeds, moderation as well as justice in regard to humans? In any case, at this point our author treats moderation with regard to *humans* as equivalent to or replaceable by "the just," and submits (as noted above) that Socrates widely promoted and taught the just by his *deeds*, private and public, which were always lawful.[36] In addition, however, Xenophon gives an example of what he characterizes as Socrates's "frequent" speeches about justice, speeches that accorded with his deeds. But the example Xenophon chooses to give of these speeches is obviously singular: a dialogue with the alien sophist, Hippias of Elis. Xenophon thus rather conspicuously avoids, or, as it turns out, postpones (see 4.6.5–6), a private dialogue on justice between Socrates and Euthydemus; the series of their dialogues is interrupted.[37]

Hippias was "famous or notorious as a despiser of the laws," in the name of normative nature or natural right.[38] Confronted by Hippias, Socrates advances and vindicates the thesis that "the lawful (*nomimon*) is the just" (4.4.12).

At first sight, the famous specific public deeds of Socrates that Xenophon has adduced seem to exemplify adherence to this thesis—that "the one obeying" the laws "would be doing just things, and the one disobeying these, unjust things" (4.4.13). But a fly in the ointment appears when we note that one of the famous public deeds adduced is Socrates's disobedience to the Thirty when they commanded him not to speak with the young. Xenophon now says that this commandment of the Thirty was "contrary to the laws," and hence that Socrates's disobedience to the commandment was not disobedience to the laws—that it was in fact obedience to the *true* Athenian laws; but earlier, Xenophon presented Socrates himself, in dialogue with the leaders of the Thirty, speaking of their commandment as one of their "laws," and seeking to interpret it as such, and insisting to them that he would obey the(ir) laws; what's more, Xenophon himself called the command a "law," and called its formulator, Critias, a "lawgiver" (1.2.31–34). This contradiction adumbrates the fraught Socratic question, "What is law?"—which we saw so profoundly problematized in the Socratic-inspired refutation, by Alcibiades, of Pericles (1.2.40–46).[39] Xenophon's presentation of that (cogent) refutation proves that the *identification* of the legal with the just must be an *exoteric* teaching of

Socrates and the Socratics—motivated, as are all such exoteric teachings, by a sense of public responsibility or justice.[40] Such publicly responsible speech would be perhaps *the* prime example of Socratic justice in action (see Melzer 2014; Dorion 2013, 84). As Alcibiades's refutation of Pericles made clear, laws are dependent on and derivative from, are expressions of, the clashing regimes (*politeiai*) and their conflicting lawgivers.[41] Laws are more or less good or evil, more or less just or unjust, depending on the regimes. But since the rule of law is always fragile, and in almost all times and places it is more beneficial to obey and to uphold the laws (even bad or unjust laws) than to do the contrary (4.4.14), it is wise and just to veil in public speech the rare exceptions, and their complex, principled basis.[42]

The dialogue with Hippias was occasioned when the latter came upon Socrates deploring the fact that for someone seeking to learn what is the just, or to have a son or servant taught what is the just, it is difficult or impossible to find a teacher (4.4.5)—as if what is just were something perplexing and elusive (as we recall Socrates had shown Euthydemus that it is, contrary to the youth's initial convictions). "This is a strange introduction to a conversation in which Socrates proves that the just is the legal, for there are always and everywhere many who can teach the law" (XS 109; Johnson 2003, 268).

But Hippias did not find this in the least strange, because this was the aporetic way he remembered Socrates talking about justice. And Socrates here emphatically agreed with Hippias that this was indeed his characteristic, "terrible" (*deinon*), manner of speaking about justice (4.4.6; in the *Symposium* 4.1, Xenophon has Callias say to Socrates's face, and without the latter's demurral, that Socrates and his followers characteristically spend time "puzzling over what the just is," without making anyone more just; see similarly the charge by Plato's Cleitophon in the dialogue of that name).

When, after a bantering exchange, Hippias boasted that he was ready to put forward, about the just, a speech "against which neither you nor anyone else could speak," Socrates proclaimed with obvious irony (swearing by Hera) his eagerness to hear "so great a good thing," which "will put an end to jurors voting contrary to one another, and citizens contradicting one another and litigating and engaging in civil strife, and will stop the cities from disagreeing about and going to war over the just matters" (4.4.8). Socrates thus spotlighted the fact that political life is in fact riven with severe disagreement over what is just—rendering highly dubious the prospect of a teaching that gives an indisputable answer to the question, "What is the just?" Hippias warily responded by indicating emphatically his long familiarity with Socrates's accustomed ironic refutations, accompanied by his avoiding expression of his own beliefs: "But, by Zeus!—you will not hear!" Not, at

least, "until you yourself declare what you believe the just to be." Enough
of this "ridiculing others by asking and refuting everyone, while yourself
never being willing to maintain a thesis or declare your judgment about
anything!" (4.4.9). Some leading contemporary scholars are dumbfounded,
and protest: This "is such an inappropriate complaint to bring against the
*Xenophontic* Socrates, who rarely withholds his own opinion!" "The sole
interlocutor that Socrates refutes, in the *Memorabilia*, is Euthydemus," and
so "it appears purely abusive to affirm that Socrates 'refutes everyone'!"
"*Everything* happens at this point as if Hippias were formulating a reproach
which addresses itself to the Socrates in *Plato*, rather than the Socrates in
*Xenophon*!"[43] For Xenophon certainly does not have Socrates here dispute
any of Hippias's accusation. Did Xenophon forget here that he is not supposed to be writing like Plato? That his Socrates is not supposed to reproduce the Socrates of Plato?

What these scholars have failed to grasp is the most massive rhetorical-
defensive or exoteric-esoteric feature of the writing of the *Memorabilia*—
which Xenophon here for a moment makes glaring. "The typical Socratic
conversation as presented by Xenophon is greatly misleading"; Xenophon
early on declares that Socrates "was always carrying on dialogue," asking
the "What is . . ." questions (1.1.16), but Xenophon rarely presents such
dialogue—"at most 3 chapters out of the 49 chapters of the *Memorabilia*"
(XS 7–8, also 116–17, 120t); similarly, Xenophon makes clear that Socrates's
life was "blessed" by private discussion groups that studied great old books,
but Xenophon never portrays those blessed discussions. Again, Xenophon
makes it clear that Socrates taught his young followers, including not least
Alcibiades and Critias, great political and especially rhetorical skills; but Xenophon never shows us this teaching activity (the closest he comes is the
dialogues with the young cavalry commander, and the younger Pericles); and
so on. We must never forget that the massive, primary, and regulating *defensive* intention guiding the *Memorabilia* is to rebut the conviction of Socrates
on the charges that he did not believe in the gods of the city but introduced
strange, new *daimonia*, and that he corrupted the young. The most important
aspects of the life and teachings of Socrates must be ferreted out by reflection
on what is implicit and only pointed to by what is explicit. This is especially
true of the "minefield" section we are now traversing.

Socrates responded to Hippias's demand and complaint by insisting that
"I *never stop* showing" what are the just things; but when pressed by Hippias to articulate his opinion, Socrates evasively responded that he does so,
"if not by speech," then "by deed." Hippias conceded emphatically—and

all the more thoughtlessly (Strauss 1939, 519)—that deeds are more trust-worthy than speech. To this Socrates replied by getting Hippias to concede further that he had never perceived Socrates committing one or another grave injustice; and Socrates asked, "Don't you hold that refraining from in-justices is just?" (4.4.10–11).[44]

Hippias understandably saw, in this response, a dodge: "You are obvi-ously, Socrates, even now trying to avoid showing your judgment as to what you believe is the just. For what you are saying is not what the just do, but what they do *not* do!" Socrates replied: "But I for my part thought" that "the not being willing to do injustice *is* a sufficient display of the virtue of justice."[45] (The word for the *virtue* of justice, *dikaiosunē*, is here used for the first and only time in the conversation.)

Nevertheless, because Socrates saw that this display of the virtue of justice would not satisfy Hippias (among others), Socrates proceeded to offer some-thing more positive, to see how it would strike his interlocutor: "But if this is not your opinion, then consider if the following is more satisfactory to you; for I assert the lawful to be just" (4.4.12). The thesis that the lawful is the just is thus a doctrine introduced by Socrates explicitly with a view to satisfying Hippias, in reaction to the latter's dissatisfaction with Socrates's formulation of what he declared that he himself holds to be an adequate dis-play of the virtue of justice.

Hippias was amazed at what he thought he had heard: "Are you then say-ing that it is the same, Socrates—lawful and just?" When Socrates confirmed this (even though it was not precisely what he had said), Hippias still doubted that Socrates meant it, at least in its obvious sense: "Well then, I do not perceive what sort of thing you are saying is 'lawful,' or what sort 'just!'" (4.4.12–13).

Socrates proceeded patiently to explain, through question and answer, that he was referring to the "lawful" in the obvious sense: the laws of any city. Hippias took this to mean what the citizens together set down in writ-ing dictating what ought to be done and what ought not (since he speaks of the citizens and not of the multitude, or *dēmos*, his definition of law covers all republican forms—aristocracy and "plutocracy" as much as democracy [see 4.6.12], and of course Sparta as much as Athens).

Socrates accepted this, and then gained Hippias's agreement that the "law-ful person" would be one partaking of civic life in accord with those written laws, and the "unlawful" would be one who violated them, and that the former would be doing just things, and the latter, unjust; and that "therefore, the lawful person is just, the unlawful unjust." Agreeing with all this (none

of which entails the *identification* of the just with the legal), Hippias expos-
tulated: "But as for the laws (he said), oh Socrates!—how could one consider
this a serious business, or obey these, when the very ones who establish them
frequently reject and change them, upon scrutiny!?" (4.4.13–14). Precisely inasmuch as the sophist agreed that the law abiding is just, he could not take
seriously either the just in this sense or the legal, as the true norms for a wise
life (see the famous speech of Hippias in Plato's *Protagoras* 337cff.).

The rejoinder of Socrates was risibly sophistic, even demagogic—and
therefore, as a chastening lesson for the famous sophist, most instructive.
Asking (without allowing Hippias a chance to reply) if disparaging those
who obey laws because the laws are often repealed is not equivalent to blaming those who fight well in war because peace later comes to pass, Socrates
belligerently demanded: "So, are you also blaming those who with eager
spirit take the field on behalf of their fatherlands in war!?" This outrageous
imputation Hippias of course heatedly denied, swearing by Zeus (4.4.14).
And Socrates then immediately launched into an uninterrupted speech.

The monologue's first and shortest theme, expressed in two rhetorical
questions, was the glory and the benefits that the city derives from having citizens obedient to law—as exemplified above all by Lycurgus's Sparta (4.4.15).
The speech's second and somewhat lengthier theme was the public opinion
of the Greek "cities" to the effect that that "the greatest good" is "concord"
(*homonoia*) among the citizens—meaning, as interpreted by "my thinking"
(Socrates pointedly says here; cf. 4.6.14), concord that consists in obedience to
the (city's) laws. "Without concord neither would a city be well governed nor
a household nobly managed" (4.4.16). This is doubtless true; but does a household's concord *consist* in obedience to the city's laws (see the *Oeconomicus*)?

At any rate, with the mention of the private household, Socrates segued
to the third and much the longest theme of his monologue, the benefit to
the "private individual" (*idia*) of obedience to the laws, and the harm to the
private individual of disobedience to the laws (4.4.17). Socrates listed, in the
mode of anaphoric-rhetorical questions, no less than fourteen (or thirty-one,
depending on how we count) private benefits, the first and foremost being avoidance of legal punishment (no small consideration for an itinerant
foreigner like Hippias), and concluding with minimization of the number
of one's enemies (the second half of the list is much preoccupied with the
threat of and from one's enemies, and hence the need for friends and allies,
in a state of war as well as peace; the previous praise of concord in lawfulness as a great civic good is thus followed by a spotlighting of the tenuous-
ness of community; Socrates almost sounds like Hobbes).

Socrates drew his personal conclusion: "I therefore [scil. because obedience to the law is beneficial in the ways stated, especially to private individuals[46]], oh Hippias, show forth the lawful and just to be the same. But if you know things to be contrary, teach!" Of course, after this lengthy warning-reminder of the situation of individuals, including not least itinerant foreign individuals, in the cities, Hippias, vehemently swearing by Zeus, declared that he did not think that he knew anything contrary to what Socrates had been saying about the just (4.4.18; consider the public speech that Plato has Hippias report that he gives in various cities—*Hippias Major* 286a). Hippias is no fool.

So when Socrates moved to a new level, and asked, as regards the unwritten laws—which Hippias asserted to be conventionally observed in the same way in every land—if Hippias could declare that it is humans who have established these laws, Hippias of course replied no. He embraced the opinion that it is the gods who have established the unwritten laws for humans—adding, as his reason for this statement, the fact that the first of these laws among all humans is that there must be reverence for the gods. Hippias had no intention of being indicted for impiety in Athens or in any of the cities he visits. Accordingly, he made no reference, in this semipublic forum, to the causal power of nature as a source of such universal, unwritten norms, nor to any sort of normative natural right (contrast Plato, *Protagoras* 337cff.). That such was in the back of his mind, however, became visible when Socrates proceeded to ask if it is not also conventionally held everywhere that parents must be honored, but that there is to be no sexual intercourse between parents and children. For Hippias could not bring himself to agree that the latter is a "law of god," because (he explained when questioned) he perceives people who transgress this law, with impunity.[47] Was not Hippias conceiving of the truly universal human norms as being of such a character that, given human nature, human community is difficult to sustain without grave injury to itself and its members if these very minimal norms are not conventionally enforced?[48] Conflict between positive human laws and these very basic, natural-conventional (*nomikon phusikon*), norms or laws would be rare (Gray 2007, 9).

Socrates seemed to be thinking along similar lines, though of course he too expressed his view in prudently religious terminology. For he replied that "those who transgress the laws laid down by the gods pay a penalty, which is in no way possible for a human to elude" (4.4.21). When Hippias skeptically demanded to know what was the character of this *inescapable* "divine" penalty in the case of incest, Socrates adduced the purported biological fact of the likelihood that the sperm of men past or prior to their prime will produce defective offspring. "Who else (he said) would procreate badly, if these do not?!" This Socrates dared to declare "*the* greatest penalty—by Zeus!" (4.4.22–23; there is at this point in the conversation an unprecedented and never-to-be-equaled flurry of Zeus-expletives by Socrates; here we have a peak of intensity of Xenophontic comedy). Xenophon and his Socrates might seem to have forgotten the very relevant fact that at the time Socrates died, the sixty-nine-year-old and his much younger wife had "very young" children (Plato, *Apology* 34d and *Phaedo* 116b).[49]

I am inclined to judge that this passage is a most perfect exemplification of the difference between Xenophontic and Aristophanean comedy. I note again that Shaftesbury (1964, 1: 167) refers to Xenophon as the "philosophical Menander."[50]

The serious point of Xenophon's comic production would be that he shows Socrates here, together with Hippias,[51] presenting somewhat tongue in cheek a veiled version of a quite minimal, and not strict, conception of natural right (anticipating, we may note, the great Averroistic-Aristotelian conception that has played such an important role throughout the history of political philosophy since Aristotle[52]). As W. K. C. Guthrie remarks, "It is noticeable that these arguments would apply equally to a world ruled not by gods but by an impersonal nature."[53] Along these lines, Socrates went on to state the penalty for violating the universal convention dictating that one return good to those from whom one has received some benefit: the penalty is that in consequence, one becomes bereft of good friends, and has to seek out those who hate one. Swearing by Zeus, Hippias expressed his hearty agreement to "all" that Socrates had said, employing a curious formulation: "Socrates (he said), all these things befit/are *like* gods,[54] for it seems to me that the laws themselves have punishments for transgressors, better than a lawgiver in human terms." When asked, finally, if he held that the gods then legislate just things, or things other than just, Hippias, swearing again by Zeus, declared: "Not other," since "someone else would hardly legislate the just things, if not god" (4.4.24–25). This statement "implies a recognition that the just things are as such different from the legal (cf. 1.2.9–11)" (XS 113). But Socrates blithely concluded that "for the gods too, then, oh Hippias, it suffices that the just and the legal are the same."

Hippias did not demur; and he apparently no longer felt any need or desire to deliver his own speech about the just. It turns out that it was Socrates who had a speech "against which, neither you [Hippias] nor anyone else could speak!" By saying and doing such things, Socrates made Hippias and other interlocutors more just—certainly in the sense of exhibiting[55] respectful obedience to the laws everywhere (4.4.24–25).

## TEACHING HIS COMPANIONS SELF-MASTERY

From the Socratic education in "moderation" (*sophrosunē*), which we have seen consists chiefly in the proper understanding of (a) divinity and thereby piety, and then (b) justice as obedience to law including divine law, we in a sense descend: to a more basic and practical dimension of Socratic education—in self-mastery (*engkrateia*) over the pleasures of the body. This, Xenophon now says, Socrates believed to be, not itself noble, but "good (*agathon*) for one who is doing something noble (*kalon ti praxein*)" (4.5.1). We recall that Xenophon extensively showed Socrates educating to self-mastery in book 1. There, in a monologic exhortation to an audience of nameless men, Socrates proclaimed that self-mastery is the "footing" or "foundation" (*krēpis*) for virtue (1.5.4). He stressed that lack of self-mastery is unacceptable even in one's slaves, and therefore ought to be guarded against in a real man who is free—otherwise, "by Hera!" one should "pray the gods that one might happen upon good masters!" (1.5.5). Socrates never employed the term "noble" (*kalon*). Now, in explaining that Socrates turned his "companions" toward self-mastery by example and by dialogue—exemplified here by a dialogue with his recent convert Euthydemus—Xenophon of course reports Socrates speaking very differently (4.5.1–5). Socrates began by eliciting from the young man his reverence for liberty, as an especially "noble and great acquisition for a real man and a city." He then led the youth to agree that being ruled by one's bodily pleasures is the worst (*kakistēn*) enslavement, to the worst (*kakistous*) despots. This is because, Socrates submitted, "probably liberty appears to you to be doing the best things (*beltista*)," and servitude to one's bodily pleasures prevents such doings—prevents "doing the noblest things (*kallista*)," while compelling the "most shameful things" (*aichista*); prevents "the best things" (*arista*), while compelling the "worst things" (*kakista*).

This variation of superlative terminology provokes in the thoughtful hearer the question, What was Socrates understanding to be the actions that constitute the positive substance of noble liberty, beyond mere negative liberation *from* enslavement to the body? The closest Socrates got to an answer back in his early oration was his rather vague mention of "learning something good." Now, Socrates suddenly referred to "wisdom" as "the greatest good,"[56] in the course of asking Euthydemus whether it does not seem to him that lack of self-mastery draws humans into "the opposite." Before giving Euthydemus a chance to reply, Socrates shifted to a lower gear: "Or doesn't it seem to you that" lack of self-mastery "prevents attending to and learning the beneficial things, by drawing away to the pleasant?"

(4.5.6). Wisdom as the greatest good, as the transhuman goal, may transcend the beneficial—and in *this* sense, may be not only the "best," but the "noblest" (cf. XS 80–81: "The Socratic denial of the difference between reasonableness and wisdom follows from the denial of the difference between the good and the beautiful or noble things, among the latter the objects of sight standing out [II.2.3]").

From affording this momentary glimpse of the contemplative peak, Socrates quickly redescended—to "moderation," which he here assimilated to "taking care of" and "choosing" what is "fitting" or "beneficial" (4.5.7; cf. 3.9.4). Lack of self-mastery causes the opposite of this, Socrates got Euthydemus to agree; and "nothing is worse for a human." "But then isn't it likely," Socrates (sophistically) asked, "that self-mastery is for humans the cause of the opposites of what lack of self-mastery causes?" "That's likely," Euthydemus said. "Well, therefore," Socrates concluded, addressing his young companion by name, "it is likely that the very best for a human is self-mastery." Euthydemus agreed that this was indeed likely (4.5.7–8). Xenophon shows that Socrates allowed and to some extent encouraged, among some disciples, the view of himself, and of his "wisdom," that was promulgated by Antisthenes, the proto-Cynic, and that became an inspiration for (vulgar) Stoicism.[57]

But Xenophon here immediately reminds us that Socrates was no enemy of pleasure. He reports Socrates proceeding to deliver to Euthydemus what one may call the Socratic version of the speech that Virtue indignantly addressed to Vice, for the education of Heracles (Johnson 2009, 219). Socrates asked Euthydemus to ponder this paradox: that lack of self-mastery, which draws toward corporeal pleasure, actually forestalls the fullest enjoyment of the pleasures of eating, drinking, sex, and sleep, by making one incapable of postponing immediate, more tepid gratifications in these regards— whereas self-mastery "alone" enables the endurance of the postponements, and thus "alone" enables "enjoyments worth remembering, of such things" (4.5.9; recall 2.1.30 but also 3.11.13). To be sure, Socrates was here speaking not through Virtue. We may be reminded that, shortly before presenting Socrates presenting the speech of Virtue, Xenophon had presented the hedonist Aristippus agreeing with Socrates that lack of self-mastery, especially as regards sex, spells misery; and, by implication, agreeing that self-mastery is necessary for a prudently voluptuous life.[58] We may also remember that conveying this knowledge about the nature of sensual pleasure was a major part of Socrates's education of the courtesan Theodote (3.11.13).

But like Virtue, Socrates next ascended to pleasures higher than the carnal (4.5.10; recall also 1.6.1–7). He declared that those possessing self-mastery are enabled to learn, and to care for, something noble and good, through which one might nobly care for one's body and manage one's household, and become beneficial to one's friends and city, and master (*kratēseien*) one's enemies—from all of which comes not only benefits but, he concluded, enjoyment of "the greatest pleasures." He did not specify these pleasures, however—in contrast to Virtue, who had foregrounded praise of oneself as the most pleasant of all sounds, and beholding one's own noble deeds as the most pleasant of all sights (2.1.31).

Although Socrates had not mentioned virtue, and had focused on pleasure, the noble Euthydemus responded, after listening, by saying: "You seem to me, Socrates, to be saying that for a man who is weaker than the pleasures of the body, there is no virtue at all!" Socrates confirmed this in his own way, by asking, rhetorically, "What difference is there between a human lacking in self-mastery and a wild beast?" But then Socrates suddenly added: "How would someone who does not investigate the most masterful things (*kratista*),[59] but seeks in every fashion to do/make the most pleasant things, differ from mindless cattle?" No, Socrates affirmed: "Only for those with self-mastery (*engkrateia*) is it possible to investigate the most masterful of affairs (*ta kratista tōn pragmatōn*), and in speech and deed distinguishing (*dialegontas*) by kinds, choosing the good things and rejecting the bad" (4.5.11).

At this point (4.5.12) Xenophon almost insensibly glides from quoting Socrates in this particular conversation with Euthydemus to quoting rather momentous statements about dialectics that Socrates evidently made on more then one occasion: "And thus, he declared, real men become best and happiest, as well as most capable of (most powerful at) carrying on dialogue (*dialegesthai*)." "Carrying on dialogue" has been so denominated, Socrates explained, "from the coming together to deliberate in common by sorting out (*dialegontas*) affairs (*pragmata*) according to kinds (*genē*)." This "etymology is original [with Xenophon's Socrates] and is not attested in other authors" (Natali 2006, 11). Fanciful or not, this Xenophontic-Socratic etymology limns what was adumbrated in Xenophon's early, momentous statement that Socrates "was always carrying on dialogue about the human things, investigating what is piety, what is impiety, what is noble, what is base, what is just, what is unjust . . . [etc.], and also about the other things" (1.1.16). Xenophon points us to the profound connection between (a) dialectic as the art of distinguishing the beings according to their kinds (forms), including especially the kinds of the "human things," the moral and political things—an art that was not uniquely Socratic, as is evident from Plato's Eleatic Stranger

(*Sophist* 253d); and (b) the distinctively Socratic dialectic, as the art of *refu-tational* exposure and clarification of moral opinions, even of interlocutors like Euthydemus who are not potentially philosophic—and *thus* clarifying the kinds of the human things. As I have previously suggested, I believe that Xenophon indicates that the latter dialectics, or its psychological results, provides the otherwise unavailable, essential, theological foundation for the former dialectics—and indeed, for all rational science.

Dialectics, as an unorthodox kind of virtue, here suddenly emerges as the highest purpose of self-mastery (dialectics had never been mentioned in the various earlier accounts of Socratic self-mastery); and Socrates making his companions "more dialectical" suddenly becomes the crowning theme of Xenophon's presentation of Socratic tutoring. The brief passage of trans-Euthydemean pronouncements ends with a slightly but significantly altered version of the very similar immediately previous statement of Socrates: "From this, real men become best, *and most artful as leaders* as well as most dia-lectical" (4.5.12). Xenophon doubtless writes this from experience—both of being himself a successful leader of a large army through harrowing cir-cumstances (*the Anabasis*), and of being a follower of the leadership that Socrates exercised over his companions.

## MAKING HIS COMPANIONS MORE DIALECTICAL

My preceding comments on Xenophontic-Socratic dialectics have antici-pated, and have relied upon, what Xenophon next proceeds to reveal further about the meaning and status of Socratic dialectics (4.6.1). For Xenophon links Socrates's "making his companions[60] more dialectical [expert in di-alogue or conversation]" with Socrates's "never leaving off investigating, amidst[61] his companions, what each of the beings might be"—the fruits of which investigation must, Socrates held, be capable of being articulated in speech to others. The "what" that is thus ceaselessly investigated and articulated by Socrates, through dialectic, is evidently the "kind," the class character—the answer to the "What is . . ." questions. Every individual ex-istent has a more-than-individual defining *character*; to be is to exist as a par-ticular instance or instantiation of a *kind*; and the kind (though not the par-ticular as particular) can and must be articulated in speech, *logos*—nay, requires speech, *logos*, for its full existence.

Xenophon also says that Socrates "declared it not to be amazing if those who did *not* know" what each of the beings might be "were themselves tripped up (*sphallesthai*) and tripped up others"—and that *this* danger was *why* Socrates "never left off investigating, amidst his companions, what each of the beings might be." This gives the impression that Socrates's motivation in his ontology was practical; and this impression is sustained by the sequel, as Xenophon sketches the way Socrates taught followers like Euthydemus about the beings, including the heavenly or cosmic beings (after his repeated disclosures of Socrates's cosmological dialogues, Xenophon can of course no longer maintain the pretense, as he did when refuting the charge of impiety, that Socrates pursued the "What is . . ." questions only, or even chiefly, about "the human things," i.e., the moral and political things). This goes with the observation that Socrates speaks of "the beings" (*ta onta*—4.6.1) also and primarily as "the matters of action/concern" (*ta pragmata*—4.5.12), and, in the first place, as "the most masterful (*ta kratista*—4.5.11) of the matters of action." But we must not forget the theoretical signification of identifying "reality," or the "real world," with "the world of concern to us"—which is what Plato for his part signals, in a rather highfalutin way, by having his Socrates teach that the idea of the good is the cause both of the beings and of the being-known of the beings (*Republic* 509b). Humanly to know empirical reality—the only way to know, and the only reality, given to the human mind—is to know the world as shaped by the human consciousness's (mortal) neediness and concern, outside of which the human consciousness cannot ever entirely step.

Xenophon says that he will give only a small selection of examples of Socrates's defining of the beings, such as will make clear "the manner of the investigation"—first, into piety (4.6.1). But Xenophon immediately returns us to a dialogue with Euthydemus, whom we recall Socrates had decided to "disturb as little as possible," but to deliver "very simple and very clear" explanations of what he believed Euthydemus "needed to know and that would be best for him to pursue" (4.2.40). Accordingly, Socrates did not ask this young follower, "What is piety?" but instead, "What sort of thing do you believe piety to be?"—and was satisfied when Euthydemus replied, with some passion, "Most noble, by Zeus!" Socrates then turned from piety to the pious person, and again asked "what sort" he is—and was satisfied when Euthydemus replied, "One honoring the gods." Socrates then reminded Euthydemus of the stern civic truth that it is not permitted to honor the gods as one wishes, but only in accordance with what the laws command. (The Greek polis had no "freedom of religion," no "separation of church and state.") When Socrates proceeded to ask: "So, one who knows these laws" (including, of course their sanctions, even capital, for being disobeyed) "would know how he must/should honor the gods?" Euthydemus replied with a slightly hesitant affirmative—"I at least *think* so (he said)" (*oimai egōge, ephē*). And when Socrates asked, "Would anyone honor the gods otherwise than as he knew he must/should?" the young man again replied, "I don't *think* so" (4.6.2–3). But the youth was not made uneasy enough to ask the question that he should have asked, if he had been a good dialectician. He should have demanded clarification of how Socrates meant the highly ambiguous (and thus sophistic) key term "must/should" (*dei*). And we begin to see that Socrates was teaching dialectics not so much to Euthydemus as to onlookers, among whom was of course Xenophon, our witness.

On this slippery basis, Socrates elicited from his inexpert dialectician Euthydemus agreement that since "one lawfully honoring honors as he must/should," and since "he who honors as he must/should, is pious," it follows that "one who knows the lawful customs about the gods would correctly be defined, for us, as pious" (4.6.4). There is no sign that Euthydemus noticed that piety was thus slyly defined, "for us," as a virtue that requires no knowledge of the gods and no knowledge of the truth or falsehood of what the laws command us to believe. This conversation no doubt aided in bringing Euthydemus back to lawful worship. But still no mention was made of personal prayer.

When Socrates descended from asking about honoring gods, or piety, to asking about dealing with humans, he did not ask what justice is, or even what sort of thing it is, or even what sort the just are. Instead, he more quickly elicited Euthydemus's agreement that "also as regards humans" there are laws, and those who deal with one another in accordance with them deal as they must/should. But in proceeding from this to gain Euthydemus's assent to the propositions that "those knowing the lawful conventions about humans do the just things," hence *are* the just, and therefore "we correctly define the just to be those knowing the lawfully just things" (4.6.5–6), Socrates did not reproduce, rely on, or refer back to his argumentation with Hippias (cf. XS 118, 108–9). He said nothing about the good, or the benefit, especially to private individuals, of obedience to law, or about the harm of disobedience. Instead, he first got the noble young Euthydemus to agree heartily that "those who deal with one another as they must/should deal *nobly* (*kalōs*)"; then he leapt to ask if these "do not enact nobly human affairs" altogether. "That's likely, at least," said the perhaps slightly dazzled Euthydemus. In the glow of this evocation of comprehensive nobility, Socrates proceeded to introduce justice, asking (in quite a jump), "Then don't those who obey the laws do the just things?"—"Entirely so, he said" (4.6.5). (Enormous questions are thus mooted, beginning with "Is justice as obedience to law always noble?") Then Socrates asked, "And the just things: do you know what sort of things they are *called*?" On this basis—

the sort of things that are "called" just, by common opinion—Socrates was enabled to conclude that those doing what the laws command "do the just things and what they should/must." So, Socrates concluded, Aren't they "the just?" "I at least *think* so" (4.6.5–6). Euthydemus seems again to have dimly sensed something problematic about the argumentation.

From justice, Socrates turned abruptly to wisdom, as distinct from justice (4.6.7). We readers are reminded that earlier, in the culminating sections of his account of Socrates's critical inquiry into the noble, Xenophon taught us that Socrates identified justice not with knowledge of the laws, but with wisdom (which displaced piety from the virtues): "He declared justice and all the rest of virtue to be wisdom," and further declared that those who are not wise are unable to do what is just, or anything noble and good (3.9.5). But our looking forward to the present account of dialectics helped us, back then, to see the incompleteness and hence distortion in that earlier characterization of *wisdom*: in stressing that Socrates entwined wisdom with moderation, Xenophon indicated that the term "wisdom" was there being used to designate *practical* wisdom, prudence or *phronēsis* (XS 80b–81t); Xenophon was eclipsing or abstracting from *theoretical* wisdom, from science or scientific knowledge (*epistēmē*). Now, Socrates, following Euthydemus, allowed exaggeration in the opposite direction (thereby protecting the definition here of justice as obedient knowledge of law). Socrates now concluded, from Euthydemus's premises, that "the wise are wise by scientific knowledge"—and that such knowledge "is wisdom." And there suddenly came to the fore the grave theoretical limitations, the theoretical imperfection, of the virtue of wisdom so understood. "Does it seem to you possible for a human being to have scientific knowledge of all the beings?" "No, by Zeus! Not, in my opinion, even of a small part of them!" "So as regards all things, it is not possible for a human to be wise?" "By Zeus! No indeed!" Then "each," or "a human,"[62] is wise, Socrates asked in conclusion, only as to that of which he has scientific knowledge? Yes—that is the concluding opinion of Euthydemus (4.6.7). The repeated expletive "By Zeus!" points to the abyss this opens up under the feet of rational science and philosophy. If human wisdom, as scientific knowledge, is so limited, then how can rational science have confidence that the universe is not decisively governed by a mysterious, commanding divinity, to whose commanding appearances, especially to select prophets and poets, we have abundant written testimony, starting at least with Hesiod? How does the philosophic scientist have grounds for confidence even in his scientific knowledge of any *particular* realm of the beings, if he does not know whether that seemingly stable realm may not be miraculously transformed at any time? Let us not forget that Socrates has confessed that "it is not amazing if those who do not know what each of the beings might be themselves are tripped up, and trip up others" (4.6.1). At the very least it would seem that true wisdom, as awareness of these limits and questions, would include precisely that alternative dimension that was rejected by young Euthydemus when he replied: "How could anyone, as regards what he does *not* know scientifically, be wise?" (4.6.7). But when Euthydemus answered that human beings cannot have scientific knowledge of even a small part of the beings, he overlooked something of the very greatest importance: the scientific knowledge Socrates achieves of the human things, through dialectics—which, I believe, Xenophon has indicated is the dispositive Socratic response to the abysmal problem science confronts.

Xenophon reminds of this Socratic knowledge by having Socrates say, immediately after getting agreement that each human is wise in what he knows scientifically: "Well, therefore (*ar' oun*), Euthydemus,[63] also as regards the *good*, is this the way it should be sought?" "How? (he said)." Socrates proceeded to secure the agreement of Euthydemus to what has been a pervasive Socratic theme: the good is the beneficial (and its contrary, the bad, is the harmful); and as such, the good and the bad are relative, to the various beings and their differing needs (4.6.8).

Immediately, however, Socrates raised a question: But can the noble/beautiful (*kalon*) be spoken of in some other way, somehow? (4.6.9). Can you name anything noble/beautiful which you know to be such in relation to *everything*? Swearing again by Zeus, Euthydemus declared that he could not. Socrates then asked a question (to which Euthydemus replied strongly in the affirmative) that subtly embodied and introduced something that is universally beautiful—a specific truth: "Well, then—does it hold, *in beautiful fashion*, that each thing should be used for that for which each would be useful?" Socrates concluded by asking, not if the noble/beautiful is the useful, but rather, "Is the useful then noble/beautiful in relation to that for which it is useful?" Euthydemus assented. By his questioning, Socrates certainly problematized the noble/beautiful, in its relation to the good as the beneficial and the useful; but he did not reduce the beautiful to the good as the useful or beneficial. Socrates pointed to truth, to knowledge, and thus to wisdom as a theoretical virtue—to *being* wise—as good, "the greatest good," in a sense that transcends (though does not leave behind) the good as the useful and even as the beneficial.

The irreducibility of the noble/beautiful to the useful appeared in another, less "Socratic" and more "Euthydemean," way when Socrates next said (4.6.10): "But *courage*, oh Euthydemus, do you then believe (*nomizeis*) it to be among the noble/beautiful things?" Euthydemus replied: "For my part, it is the *most* noble/beautiful!" (Euthydemus had earlier characterized piety as "most noble/beautiful, by Zeus!"—4.6.2: piety and courage stand together at the peak of the noble/beautiful for Euthydemus; recall that the questions "What is pious?" and "What is noble/beautiful?" stand together at the top of the list of the Socratic questions—1.1.16.) Socrates responded by engaging in some "Socratizing": "So, is it *useful*, therefore—not with a view to the least things, is that what you believe courage to be?" Euthydemus answered: "By Zeus! (he said) with a view to *the greatest* things, indeed!" Socrates did not directly pursue what these "greatest things" might be, in his noble young interlocutor's mind. Instead, Socrates got agreement on the uselessness of ignorance of "what is," in regard to the "terrible and risky" things; and hence, agreement that those with such ignorance, and hence incorrectly either fearless or fearing, are not courageous—"No, by Zeus!" (We have here the greatest concentration of Euthydemus's oaths by Zeus. Is not the greatest of the terrible and risky things the possibility that the answer to the question, "What is god?" is Zeus, or some such being?) "So then," Socrates next asked, "it is those who are the good (*tous agathous*) in regard to the terrible and risky things that you hold to be courageous; and the bad, the cowardly?" "By all means." And, "those who are the good, in regard to such things, do you believe to be other than those able to make use of them, *in a noble/beautiful fashion*?" "None other than these!" Socrates then secured agreement that "those unable to make use, *in a noble/beautiful fashion*," must not "know how one ought to make use." And he finally concluded that Euthydemus understood "those then who *have scientific knowledge* of using, *in a noble/beautiful fashion*, the terrible and risky things are the courageous, and those who err in this are the cowards" (4.6.10–11). "*In a noble/beautiful fashion*" would obviously be otiose redundancy here if Euthydemus really understood the noble as reducible to the useful. Once again, as we have seen him do so often, Socrates provoked in thoughtful onlookers and readers the question, *What is the noble*? What exactly makes courage "more" than good, in the sense of beneficial, useful, needed? Until one answers this question, one cannot have courage, or be courageous—one must be a coward, however "brave" one looks or acts—according to Socrates, and according to Euthydemus insofar as he understands what he has been saying in agreeing with Socrates. For if one does not know what the noble means, then one cannot know what "in a noble/beautiful fashion" means, and so one cannot know how one ought to use the terrible and risky things.

Whether these radical dimensions of the Socratic teaching on courage and the noble and the good ever sank in for Euthydemus we cannot say: this is the last we hear of or from him in Xenophon. Strange![64] For prior to proceeding to his own conclusion of his account of Socrates teaching dialectics, Xenophon now (4.6.12) gives a short statement of Socrates's definitions of the various political regimes (in much more conventional terms than what Xenophon reported Socrates teaching at 3.9). And this definition of regimes, including democracy, would seem to have been a very appropriate subject for Xenophon to continue to present in the form of a dialogue with Euthydemus, since it was the refutation of the young man's conception of the regime of democracy that had been the final, crushing stage in his initial, crucial refutations by Socrates. Why not now show how Socrates reconstituted Euthydemus's understanding of, and support for, the democratic regime, even as we have seen how Socrates reconstituted Euthydemus's piety, and so on—especially since Socrates now defines democracy in rather flattering terms, as the regime in which "the ruling offices are from everybody"? Or does the Socratic conception of political regimes as here sketched indicate, upon careful scrutiny, why it would be rash of Xenophon to depict such a dialogue with Euthydemus (see XS 121–22)?

Xenophon concludes his account of how Socrates made his companions more dialectical by explaining that Socrates spoke in two massively different manners, with two massively different sorts of interlocutors or audiences (4.6.13–15). With interlocutors who challenged Socrates, by speaking against what he said (something the docile Euthydemus never did, unlike Xenophon—recall 1.4.10–12), but did so without clarity or demonstrative reasoning, Socrates responded by questioning in such a way as to lead the argument up to the key universal premises; and the "truth" of the matters thus became "evident even to the contradictors." Xenophon gives as examples objectors disputing Socrates's praise of some *particular individual* as wisest, or as the most skilled statesman, or as the most courageous, or as the best citizen. Xenophon is silent (even as he fell silent about the "good natures," immediately after highlighting them—recall 4.1.2–3) about challengers who contradicted Socrates with clarity, and demonstrative reasoning. *Their* challenging doubts are likely to have been about nonindividual matters (that is, their challenges are likely to have been about the "What is . . ." questions).

On the other hand, when Socrates went through some matter with those who did not challenge him at all with contradictions, he proceeded (as we have seen him proceed with Euthydemus in his positive teachings) through the opinions that were most agreed to: he did not lead the discussion up to the premises, but left the premises unexplored—and so of course the truth did not become evident.[65] He argued thus out of caution, "believing this to be safety of speech." At this point Xenophon interjects a strong expression of his admiring wonder at this latter rhetorical skill of the master: "Indeed of those whom I know, he was much distinguished, when he spoke/argued, in bringing about agreement in the audience." Then Xenophon tells us how Socrates himself characterized this skill of his: "He declared that Homer attributed to Odysseus being 'the safe orator,' on the grounds that Odysseus was able to lead speeches/arguments with human beings through their opinions" (4.6.15). There is a manifest, close connection between this Socratic rhetorical skill and the oratorical skill of a good public speaker (as BD observe ad loc.).

What Xenophon does not make explicit here, but what we have seen in action throughout the *Memorabilia*, is that Socrates—followed by his student-memorialist Xenophon—was able to weave into "the safe" (the exoteric) speech plenty of indications of the underlying (the esoteric), thus leading those listener-readers who are capable of challenging critically up toward the universals that are the premises. Xenophon points to this by the following transitional and somewhat ironical sentence: "I believe it is clear, then, from the things said, that Socrates disclosed his judgment simply [*haplōs*—recall *haploustata*, "very simply," at 4.2.40 end[66]], with a view to those who associated with him" (4.7.1).

## TEACHING HIS ASSOCIATES SELF-SUFFICIENCY IN DEEDS

In the last (most exposed) segment dealing with Socrates as tutor, Xenophon broadens the scope, from Socrates teaching his "companions" (*tous sunontas*—literally, "those who are with [him] or have intercourse with [him]"—4.6.1) to his attending to "those who associated with him" (*tous homilountas autō*—4.7.1).[67] The "companions," Socrates himself made "more dialectical" in their speech (4.6.1); the "associates," Xenophon now says, Socrates was concerned should become "self-sufficient in the fitting *deeds*" (4.7.1). "For while of all those I know," Xenophon says, Socrates "was distinguished in caring that he *himself* know *whatever* one of his *companions* might have knowledge of," he "was most *eager* in spirit to *teach* whatever he himself knew of the things that it is fitting for a *gentleman* to know." And as regards any such matter concerning which Socrates himself was "rather inexperienced," adds Xenophon, "he sent them to those who do know."[68]

This last introduces what turns out to be defining of the theme of this chapter—which speaks mostly of subjects of learning that Socrates did *not himself* impart. All that Socrates "taught," in these matters, was "*how far* one who has been correctly educated should be experienced in each subject" (4.7.2). Any Socratic engagement in the subjects in question—mathematics and especially astronomy, which might be thought to be the peak of philosophic science, above and beyond dialectics—is very much in need of a defensive explanation (recall 1.1.11ff.; Xenophon of course excludes profane oaths from this chapter).

Xenophon recollects Socrates "teaching" that "for a real man who is a gentleman" (*andri kalō k'agathō*) what is "fitting" (*prosēkei*) in order for him to be "correctly educated" (*orthōs pepaideumenon*) is that he should confine his study of geometry to the easiest, and strictly practical, aspects: only as much as is useful for surveying land with a view to transactions—a part of geometry that one can learn by oneself, through practice (no need to keep company with geometers or teachers of geometry).[69] Similarly as regards the study of the stars (*astrologia*): only as much as is useful for recognizing times, and directions—which can be learned, Socrates pointed out, from hunters and pilots (no need to go to any astronomers or teachers of astronomy). For Socrates declared that he saw no benefit in the practically useless, difficult dimensions of geometry, and, what is more, warned that such study takes up an enormous amount of time, and hinders many other beneficial studies. Even stronger was Socrates's turning of his gentlemen associates away from "astronomy" (*astronomia*) and its study of the complex relative motions of "the beings" aloft. Socrates declared again that he saw no benefit in this study, and again warned that it absorbs an enormous amount of time and hinders many other beneficial studies. (Yet Socrates himself, Xenophon parenthetically but repeatedly notes, was an experienced student of these difficult and life-exhausting studies that are devoid of benefit;[70] here we have lightning flashes that momentarily illuminate the landscape of the life and thought of Socrates—an environment of Socrates's life that Xenophon otherwise keeps enshrouded in night.) Socrates further warned the gentleman away from "becoming a thinker" and a "worrier"[71] about "the way in which the god contrives each of the things in the heavens." Socrates gave two very different reasons for this warning. The first was that he believed that no such contriving was discoverable by humans. The second was that "one would not be pleasing to the gods, inquiring into what they did not wish to make clear."[72] This must have raised some eyebrows among the companions of Socrates. Does this mean that Socrates, through his very time-consuming inquiries into astronomy and cosmology, experienced divine displeasure? But if so, why did he continue these exhausting inquiries, to the extent of developing and teaching to the young, such as Euthydemus, his teleological cosmology, in which he spelled out the "household management" of the universe by the supreme god, and the subordinate roles of the sun, stars, thunderbolt, and winds? What's more, Xenophon now discloses that Socrates went even further than this in his astronomical and cosmological investigations. Socrates studied the theories of Anaxagoras,[73] to the point where he was confident that they were "crazy," as least as stated; and he showed in two cases that he could prove them to be so, on the basis of empirical observations (in this context Socrates spoke of the "noble/beautiful" growth of the plants without any reference to their serving a purpose— nor did he refer to any purpose for the sun in discussing the nature of the sun). Although Socrates declared that one "worrying" (*merimnōnta*[74]) about astronomical contrivances "ran the risk of becoming crazy, no less than Anaxagoras," Socrates himself obviously overcame that risk, as well as the risk of the displeasure of the gods (4.7.2–7). Given what soon follows, we may be led to wonder if this is connected to his *daimonion*, which we recall (4.3.12) was adduced as evidence that the gods "dealt in a more friendly fashion" with him "than with others."

Before returning thematically to the *daimonion*, however, Xenophon descends: first, to saying that Socrates urged also the (much less controversial) learning of numerical calculations (*logismous*). Here, "similarly," Socrates warned that "*others*" should guard against "vain activity" (presumably the *theoretical* sciences of number and calculation, *arithmetikē* and *logistikē*[75]). "But up to the point of what was beneficial, Socrates himself studied and went through all, *with the companions*" (4.7.8).

Having brought Socrates's teaching of the "companions" suddenly back to the fore, in regard to the inoffensive study of practical numerical calculations, Xenophon proceeds to explain that the study Socrates was "vehement" in urging upon his "companions" was not calculations, or (even practical) astronomy, or (even practical) geometry, or even dialectic, but rather the study of each one's personal health as achieved through proper diet and exercise (4.7.9).

How in the world could such a fervent health-guru be thought to corrupt his young companions?!

Xenophon adds: "And if anyone" (not necessarily a companion) "should wish to be benefited more than in accord with human wisdom," Socrates "advised attending to the art of divination" (4.7.10). Xenophon makes no reference now to Socrates's radically unorthodox theological doctrine regarding the divine law that governs recourse to conventional divination (recall 1.1.9). Indeed, Xenophon will say presently, in his eulogizing conclusion to the *Memorabilia*, that Socrates, "being such as I have shown, was so pious that he *did nothing* without the advice of the gods" (4.8.11).[76]

How in the world could a man who was thus constantly urging others to rely upon, and was always himself relying upon, the employment of conventional divination be thought to disbelieve—and to lead others to disbelieve—in the gods of the city?!

At the end of the *Memorabilia*, as at the outset, Xenophon strives to make the charges upon which Socrates was convicted appear preposterous.

But what about the *daimonion* claimed by Socrates? In his conclusion, Xenophon turns back to that fraught topic.

At the end of the *Memorabilia* Xenophon returns to a defense of Socrates's "much talked about" claim that he was given unique "guidance by an uncanny divine thing *(daimonion)*." This, we recall, Xenophon thought was "especially" the reason "they charged him with carrying in strange/new, divinely uncanny things *(daimonia)*" (1.1.2). But now Xenophon does not bother to defend the conformity to lawful belief of Socrates's *daimonion*—he takes this for granted, as having been previously established. Here, as an immediate sequel to his saying that Socrates advised people to attend to the art of divination in order to get beneficial advice from the gods concerning the otherwise unknowable future (Gigon 1946, 133), Xenophon entertains the following animadversion. Someone may "think" that by his being condemned to death by the jurors, Socrates was "refuted, shown to be lying about the *daimonion* signaling to him beforehand what he ought and ought not to do" (4.8.1).

The suspicious doubter would seem to be suggesting that if Socrates were telling the truth about his *daimonion*, then it would have told him how to avoid the condemnation by the jurors. But what action could it have advised? Illegal flight? An illegal, sophistic, untruthful, defense speech (cf. *Apology* 8)? We recall that a few pages earlier (4.4.4), Xenophon said that Socrates could have "easily secured release by the jurors" if he had "gratified them and flattered them and begged them, *contrary to the laws*." Xenophon does not here, however (as we might expect), respond to the skeptic by adducing the obedience to law of Socrates and his *daimonion*, and hence the ineligibility of such recourses.

Instead, Xenophon responds on the basis of what seem to be the premises of the doubter—a preeminent concern with the nobly advantageous, and especially fame (like Virtue addressing Heracles—recall her silence on law and justice). Xenophon asks the doubter to "give thought in the first place" to the fact that Socrates was of such an age that he had little time left to live in any case; and that he missed only that part of life that is most burdensome, and in which *"everybody's"* mind declines. "And, in place of this," Socrates "acquired additional good *fame*, by *displaying* the strength of his soul"—both through his supremely truthful, free, and just courtroom speech, and through his bearing the death sentence in the most gentle and courageous[1] fashion. "For it is agreed that no human being in memory has borne death more nobly." During the thirty days that Socrates had to wait on death row (so to speak), he was witnessed by "all" his customary associates passing his time no differently than he always had before; and he always had been "most admired of all humans for living in good spirits and tranquillity." (So there was no sign of any incipient decline in Socrates, nor of any special concern on his part to make a display). "How would anyone die more nobly than thus?" And "what sort of death would be happier than the noblest?" "Or what sort more beloved by the gods than the happiest?"[2]

One can wonder how an admirer of Achilles or of Heracles or of any war hero would answer these anaphoric-rhetorical questions. Nonetheless, Xenophon might seem at this point to have responded adequately to the skeptic, doing so in terms that remind of, though they do not quite match, Virtue's address to Heracles. But we next learn that these were not the terms in which Socrates himself spoke about his life and death.

For Xenophon continues to tell of Socrates's last days, despite the fact that he was evidently not himself a witness of them. He reports what he heard from Hermogenes—a gentlemanly follower of Socrates (1.2.48) whom Xenophon earlier quoted Socrates praising very highly for his virtues as an assistant (2.10).

True to this form, Hermogenes told Xenophon that he urged Socrates to prepare a defense speech, when he saw the master neglecting to do so. Socrates responded by explaining to Hermogenes that his life as a whole was "the noblest preparation for a defense speech," inasmuch as he had spent it "doing no other thing except thoroughly investigating the just things and the unjust, and doing the just things and refraining from the unjust."[3]

When Hermogenes replied to this high-minded declaration with the down-to-earth admonition that the Athenian jurors had killed many who were innocent, from annoyance[4] at their defense speeches, Socrates, swearing by Zeus, suddenly confessed that he had in fact tried to think about an effective defense speech, but had been opposed by the *daimonion*! Hermogenes understandably expressed his astonishment at this. But Socrates explained that he had reasoned his way to a comprehension of the prudential wisdom of the *daimonion*'s intervention, interpreted by Socrates as expressing the opinion that "it is better for me to end life now" (4.8.5–6).

The first part of the reason for this judgment was that Socrates held that he had already lived out such a good life: "I would not yield to any human being as having lived a better or a more pleasant life than me." And now Xenophon gives us a most revealing and thought-provoking glimpse (if through the veil of Hermogenes's report) of how Socrates evaluated his own life. Socrates declared that he thought that "those live best who best attend to becoming best, and those live most pleasantly who especially perceive that they are becoming better"—which, he said, he had perceived about himself until this time, in part by continuously comparing himself favorably with the other humans whom he encountered. And he found reinforcement of this deeply gratifying, ever increasing self-esteem in the similar esteem from his friends, a judgment brought about not on account of their love for him but because they thought themselves becoming better by their companionship with him (4.8.6–7). Socrates did not mention, as an ingredient in the greatest good or in the greatest pleasure, any love or praise from the friends, let alone from others. The contrast with Xenophon's immediately previous stress, in his response to the imagined skeptic, on Socrates's acquisition of fame is striking.

Of course, what Socrates is reported to have said thus far did not yet explain why it was good for him now to die. In the second part of the explanation Socrates enunciated his own version of Xenophon's gloomy observations on the burdensomeness and mental decline of the old age that he saw in prospect for himself. In contrast to Xenophon, however, Socrates spoke of his future mental decline as only *"perhaps (isōs) necessary"* (see also *Agesilaus* 11.14). If he were to perceive his own decline, he asked, "how would life not be worse, and also more unpleasant?" Socrates did not say such life would be altogether without the greatest pleasure. It is only if he were to become *unaware* of his own decline that Socrates judged "life would be not worth living" (4.8.8). Does this not imply that, for Socrates, life would still be worth living so long as he possessed self-awareness, even of his own decline? Did he not indicate by these words that he embraced some substantial sacrifice in choosing not to avoid or to flee the death penalty (XS 126)?[5] Socrates certainly had not yet given a fully cogent account of why it was good for him to die at this time.

The third part of the explanation—which Xenophon says was delivered not only to Hermogenes but also to others (4.8.9–10)—was Socrates's version of the main theme of Xenophon's immediately previous response to the skeptic: concern for reputation, fame. But Socrates's focus, unlike Xenophon's, was on the negative, on shame; he insisted that if or since he was to die unjustly, it was those killing him unjustly who would incur shame. We see that he was confronting the very common tendency to think that dying unjustly, without being avenged, is ignominious—a sign of weakness, of being a "loser," or even of a lack of divine favor (one observes the power of this common opinion every day and everywhere in the passionate calls for retribution for victims of yet unpunished criminality, which victims, it is said, will in the absence of such vindication lose or lack their full dignity). In all likelihood, some such evaluation of Socrates's victimhood would have been a major consideration in the doubt about the *daimonion* expressed by the skeptic Xenophon conjured.

Socrates protested this common opinion. Almost plaintively he asked, "Why is it shameful for me, if others are incapable of recognizing or doing just things by me?" He said that he saw that the repute of men of the past, among those who come after, is not the same for those who have done injustice and for those who have suffered it. This truism does not deny the tincture of pitiful, inglorious victimhood that common opinion attaches to many of the latter victims of injustice. Socrates declared that he "knew" that he too "would draw the attention of humans, and that if" he "died now, it would be an attentiveness that was different from that given to those who killed him." The reason he gave was the following: "For I know that it will always be witnessed of me that I never did any injustice to any human being, nor made any worse, but that I tried always to make better my companions" (4.8.10). None of this explains the unambiguous goodness for him, even for his repute, of his undergoing now the death penalty.

These are the last words of Socrates in the *Memorabilia*. Xenophon takes over, and closes the book with a brief eulogy. He stresses first Socrates's benefiting his companions, especially by the memory of himself that he left behind. He then extols, at greater length, the virtues of Socrates, including his justice as benefiting to the greatest extent "those who made use of him" (4.8.11).

Why does Xenophon present Socrates delivering what on close inspection is an inadequate explanation for the asserted goodness, especially in terms of repute, of his undergoing the death penalty—right after Xenophon has presented his own, stronger (if less purely Socratic) explanation? A clue is given by Xenophon's stressing, in his own explanation, the "fame" Socrates acquired by the "display" of his strength of soul, both in the way he bore the death sentence, and in his defense speech itself—of whose actual words Xenophon tantalizingly affords no sample. If we are to experience those words, we must turn (with now whetted appetites) to another Socratic writing of

Xenophon's: to the *Apology of Socrates to the Jury*, and its unforgettable depiction and explanation of Socrates's vauntingly proud "grandiloquence" (*megalēgoria*). Xenophon quietly indicates that it was his own Socratic writings (as well as the Socratic writings of other followers) that completed and vindicated the otherwise incomplete Socratic project, transfiguring the trial and death of Socrates into something proudly and gloriously shining and beneficial to humanity, for as long as written history of the Greeks lasts. It is hard to believe that Socrates was not enjoying (in moderation) the prospect of that possibility during his final days.

INTRODUCTION

1. Judged by Nietzsche to be "the most attractive book of Greek literature" (Das anziehendste Buch der griechischen Litteratur): posthumous fragment 41 [2], from 1879 (Nietzsche 1967–2006, IV-3: 442). See also Nietzsche's letter to Gersdorff of May 26, 1876, in Nietzsche 1975–2004, II-5: #525.

2. "*Weisheit voller Schelmenstreiche*"; Nietzsche's italics. When this passage of Nietzsche's is quoted by contemporary scholars, these crucial words are sometimes omitted or excised, thus obscuring or misunderstanding the key point of Nietzsche's appraisal: see, e.g., BD 1: XCVII n3; Brisson and Dorion 2004, 138.

3. The success with which Xenophon's manner of writing captivates earnest readers is seen in Gray's perseveringly ingenuous endeavor to rescue the "transparency" of Xenophon's "innocent" and "positive" teachings (2007; 2011, esp. 2, 25, 117–18; cf. Cawkwell 1972, 26: "Though plain, he is never transparent"). Gray does sometimes concede, when she focuses closely on a specific point in the text, that "Xenophon's thought is not obvious"; that his Socrates discovers an allegorical "inner meaning" in Homer, a "hidden meaning" that expresses a "hidden intention" whose "subverting" force is hidden from "non-perceptive readers": "Xenophon can read between poetic lines in some weird ways." But Gray stubbornly insists that Xenophon did not write in the way he read Homer to have written (2011, 85, 121, 126–31). For a detailed, appreciative but critical, assessment of Gray's approach, see Buzzetti 2001. Machiavelli characteristically rips off Xenophon's veil, celebrating Xenophon's presentation of Cyrus as a master of fraud and deception and theft: *The Prince*, chaps. 14–16; *Discourses on the First Ten Books of Titus Livy* 2.13.

4. For a thorough introduction, see Melzer 2014; as regards Xenophon in particular, see Higgins 1972, esp. 293–94; 1977, pref. and chap. 1; Weil 1983, 473; Proietti 1987, ix-xxii; Vander Waerdt 1993, 26–27; Tuplin 1996; Humble 2004; Buzzetti 2001; 2014, 7–29. Flower (2012, 41 and 169) recognizes that the interpreter of the "deceptively simple" Xenophon needs to be able to "read against the grain or between the lines." See similarly Pucci 2002, 4: "Is then the 'simple' and 'garrulous' Xenophon in reality a sort of perverse writer?"; and Cartledge 2009, 347: "The limpidity of his style masks a sophistication that

requires his text to be read between as well as on the lines." Gray (2004, 173) notes "une influente école de pensée qui trouve beaucoup d'ironie et de subversion dans les ouvrages de Xénophon," citing OT and Nadon 2001, as well as Higgins 1977. In her book of 2011 Gray develops her criticism of "subversive" and "ironical" interpretations of Xenophon, and extends this critique also to Tatum 1989 and Tuplin 1993 and 2004.

5. For awareness of Xenophon's comedic art, see Bassett 1917, 565: "Fondness for hearty laughter was shared by Xenophon," who "never grew old in this respect if one is to judge by his writings"; Kronenberg 2009; on Xenophon's irony, see Higgins 1977, 12ff. and 72–73, as well as Huss 1999a and 1999b and Halliwell 2008, 139–54. Tuplin (2004, 29) notes that Xenophon is coming to be seen more and more as "a sophisticated faux-naif manipulator of the written word, a man with a straight face and a glint in the eye"; Hobden and Tuplin (2012, 14, 33) characterize "Xenophon at play" as "a masterly narrator stimulating audience inquisition through spoudaiogelastic dissonance"; "we must acknowledge the author's wish to make the reader uneasy." Shaftesbury (1964, 1: 167) characterizes Xenophon as "the philosophical Menander"; similarly, L. Strauss likens Xenophon's style and wit to that of Jane Austen (OT 185)—indirectly and all the more deliciously comic without vulgarity or boisterousness.

6. The late-modern incomprehension of Xenophon is initiated by Schleiermacher (1818), who led the way in demoting Xenophon from the rank of philosopher. As Pomeroy (1994, 21–22) observes, "Greek and Roman" authors "did not hesitate to call him a philosopher"; Dorion 2013, 11 n. 38: "À mon connaissance, Schleiermacher est le premier auteur moderne à contester le titre de philosophe que les Anciens décernaient unanimement à Xénophon"; see also Münscher 1920; Long 1988, 152–54, 162–63; Giannantoni 1990, I H 1–3, 5–7, 12, 17; on the estimation of Xenophon as a philosopher in Byzantine political theory, see Barker 1957, 66, 74; Montaigne did not hesitate to call Xenophon a "philosopher" (Essays 1.6). For the deleterious influence of Schleiermacher's essay, see BD 1: XII–XIV; for sharp criticism, see Dorion 2013, 1–26; Brisson and Dorion 2004, 138 ("critiques éculées, inlassablement et paresseusement répétées par tous les détracteurs de Xénophon depuis le début du XIXᵉ siècle"); see also Goldhill 1998; Gray 1998. Prior to Schleiermacher, and indeed throughout the nineteenth century, Xenophon was generally considered the most reliable and trustworthy guide to Socrates: see Zeller 1885, 102–3, also 182–87; and BD 1: VII–XIV, referring esp. to Bruckner 1742–44, the translation of which into English (in 1791) was used as a guide by Jefferson and other American founders. Bruckner writes (1742–44, 1: 174): "The Memoires of Socrates, written by Xenophon, afford, however, a much more accurate idea of the opinions of Socrates, and of his manner of teaching, than the Dialogues of Plato, who everywhere mixes his own conceptions and diction, and . . . those of other philosophers, with the ideas and language of his master"; see also Meiners 1781–82, 2: 420; Neschke and Worms 1992. The superior authenticity of Xenophon's over Plato's presentation of Socrates was insisted on by Hegel (1971, 2006), and predominated in the nineteenth century—see, e.g., Hurndall 1853; Talbot 1859, intro.; Labriola 1871; A. Döring 1891–92; Boutroux 1897; a major dissenting voice was Kierkegaard (1989, 221–22), who complained of Hegel's trust in Xenophon. The superior authenticity of Xenophon's Socrates continued to have strong defenders among conventionally respectable scholars in the early twentieth century: Chavanon 1903; Weissen-

born 1910; Baker 1917; Brochard 1923, 22; Arnim 1923. A useful selection of some of the preceding cited texts is available in Montuori 1992.

7. *The Wanderer and His Shadow*, opening and closing dialogues, and aphorisms 1–17 (esp. 6 end), 87, 171, 189, 191.

8. See esp. the second aphorism of *Human, All-Too-Human*.

9. See the first part of the title of the last chapter of Baur 1837: "Sokrates, bei aller Idealität, als blos menschliche, nichte als übermenschliche Erscheinung gedacht."

10. References without a title will be to book, chapter, and paragraph-subsection of the *Memorabilia*, as divided originally by Edward Wells (1690–96; see BD 1: CCXCI), whose edition gave us the subdivisions now commonly used to cite all of Xenophon's writings. The gross division, into (four) books, of the *Memorabilia* is from antiquity, probably from scholars of the Alexandrian era. Diogenes Laertius (2.6.13) suggests that in the case of the *Anabasis*, Xenophon himself made the book divisions, since they are each marked by lengthy initial summaries of the preceding book. Høeg (1950, 164) points us also and especially to the end of book 5 and beginning of book 6 of the *Anabasis*.

11. Cf. L. Strauss 1939, 531: in Xenophon we find "a remarkable document of Attic taste: it represents a higher type of comic speech than does classical comedy." The growing recognition among classical and literary scholars of Xenophon's subtle comedic genius is catalogued in Kronenberg 2009, "Introduction."

12. *The Wanderer and His Shadow*, aph. 72.

13. See esp. *Human, All-Too-Human*, vol. 1, chap. 3 ("The Religious Life"); and *The Wanderer and His Shadow*, aphs. 72–86, as well as *Beyond Good and Evil*, aphs. 210–13.

14. See esp. 3.3–5 and 4.4.1–4, as well as Xenophon's *Economist* (*Oeconomicus*) in toto.

15. Hadot 1995, 103–4: "To the same extent that the philosophical life is equivalent to the practice of spiritual exercises, it is also a tearing away from everyday life. It is a conversion, a total transformation of one's vision, life-style, and behavior. . . . We ought not to underestimate the depth and amplitude of the shock that these changes could cause, changes which might seem fantastic and senseless to healthy, everyday common sense."

16. XSD 86 and context; see also T. Pangle 1996, 2010.

17. Foucault (1984) refers to Xenophon as authoritative over fifty times, citing eight of his works.

18. Hadot 1995, 157; contrast Foucault (1984), who never refers to Kierkegaard in connection with his many references to Xenophon and Socrates.

19. *The Wanderer and His Shadow*, aph. 86.

20. Contrast O'Connor 1994, 180, with D. Morrison 1994, 181.

21. Compare and contrast Nietzsche's suggestion of the Xenophontic Socrates as a model and thus guide for morals and reason with Kant's evocation of the Platonic-Stoic ideal of the wise man: *Critique of Pure Reason* A567–70 = B595–98.

22. Franklin 1964, 64–65, 148 and context; Ralph Waldo Emerson, in his *Journals* (1909, 1: 375–76), went so far as to say that Franklin's genius "seemed a Transmigration of the Genius of Socrates" as presented by Xenophon; see similarly Giorgiana Shipley's letter to Franklin, February 11, 1777, in Franklin 1959–, 23: 303–6.

CHAPTER ONE

An earlier version of this chapter was published as T. Pangle 2015.

1. *Apomnēmoneumata*; the Latin rendering *Memorabilia*, or *Memorabilia Socratis*, originated with the edition of Levvenklaius 1569 (see Marsh 1992), and has become in modern times the most common way to refer to the work. On the conundrum posed by the one-word title *Apomnēmoneumata*, or "Recollections," and the clues to its solution, as a playfully intended puzzle, see XS 3 and XSD 84. But Strauss presumes that the "genuine title" does not include the word "Socrates," even though he concedes that "it has sometimes been *quoted* by both ancient and modern writers *as if it were* entitled *Memorabilia Socratis*." Now while it is true that some lesser good manuscripts ("Z" = Vatican 1950, and "L" = Laurentian LXXX.13) have as the title only "Xenophon the Rhetorician's Recollections," our oldest complete (and best) MS ("B" = Paris 1740, from the second half of the thirteenth century) has as a title of the first book, in a handwriting that so far as I can tell appears later than the rest of the text, "Xenophon's Recollections of Socrates. Book alpha"; this title is repeated similarly at the head of books 2, 3, and 4 (as books beta, gamma, and delta). An almost equally authoritative MS ("S" = Ambrosian 1012, from the end of the fourteenth century, replacing "M" = Venice 511; see Bandini's discussion in BD 2: X–XII) has as a title for the first book, according to the apparatus of BD, "Xenophon the Rhetorician's Recollections of Socrates"; and for the second, third, and fourth books, "Recollections of Socrates." Our oldest MS ("A" =Paris 1302, from the second half of the thirteenth century), contains only books 1 and 2, and is in very poor condition—I was unable, from inspecting a digitized photo of the crowded, torn, stained, overwritten opening pages, to discern what if any title the MS has—but according to the apparatus in BD, Bandini was able to discern a title, "Xenophon's Recollections" (with a curious misspelling: *hupomnēmoneumata*—no such word is listed in Liddell and Scott 1953). Diogenes Laertius (2.57) lists the title as simply "Recollections"; but the same list has "Anabasis" instead of "Anabasis of Cyrus," and L. Strauss (1983, 105; XSD 84) understands the latter to be "the authentic title," implying that Strauss regards Diogenes Laertius as unreliable in this matter of the titles.

2. Many earnest conventional scholars assure us that they have not been able to discern trickery or irony in Xenophon's portrait of Socrates: see, e.g., Taylor 1932, 21; Vogel 1962; Burnet 1964, 103n12; Vlastos 1980, 1 (partially self-corrected in 1991, 30–31); Long 1988, 152; Canto-Sperber 1996, 814; BD 1: LXVI, CXVII, and 102–3, 170; but contrast CIV n1. Kronenberg 2009, 17 quotes Booth 1974, 44: "The critic who asks us to ironize our straight readings may seem to be corrupting a beloved object and repudiating our very souls"; and Thomas 2000, 382: "The identification of ambiguity has always evoked anger, particularly from those who see themselves as guardians of language and of the meaning that language conveys, and particularly in the areas of philosophy and rhetoric."

3. See also 4.4.4; Nietzsche 2001, 150. But see *Apology* 25.

4. Diogenes Laertius (2.40) quotes the original formal indictment, which concludes with a demand for the death penalty, from Favorinus of Arles (ca. AD 80–150), who "says that it is still available" for inspection in the Metroon, the shrine to the mother of the gods in the Agora where the Athenian archive was kept (Mensching 1963, frag. 51). Strycker and Slings (1994, 84–85) find it "hard to believe" that the archive was still intact and

think Favorinus was himself quoting some other witness, but they find evidence to support the accuracy of the quotation.

5. This is reported to have happened: Diodorus Siculus 14.37.7; Suidas s.v. "Meletus"; Plutarch, *On Envy* 538; Diogenes Laertius 2.43; Themistius, *Orations* 20.23; Tertullian, *Apologetic* 14; St. Augustine, *City of God* 8.3; Maximus of Tyre, *If Socrates Did Nobly in Not Making a Defense* 2 (end), 8; Libanius, *Apology of Socrates* 173-77 (for the last two, see Calder et al. 2002).

6. On Xenophon's condemnation and banishment from Athens, see Higgins 1977, 22-24.

7. See XS 3-4 for the way in which Xenophon's slight misquotation of the wording of the official indictment (see note 4 above), when compared with the much greater alteration in Plato's *Apology of Socrates*, playfully signals the difference between Xenophon's and Plato's presentations of Socrates (Xenophon stays closer to what is historically accurate, but with clowning twists, at least some of which point off to the liberties Plato has taken).

8. Liddell and Scott 1953, s.v. *nomizō*; Fahr 1969, esp. 96-97, 113-20, 160-62; Burkert 1985, 275. See also Tate 1936, 1937; Snell 1975, 30ff.; Beckman 1979, 55-56; Parker 1996, 201n8; Pucci 2002, 26; BD ad loc. Contrast Taylor 1911, 7-8; and Burnet 1924, ad Plato, *Euthyphro* 3b3, and *Apology* 18c3, 24c1, 26c2 (both Taylor and Burnet are refuted by Plato, *Laws*, bk. 10, as Tate [1936, 1937] points out).

9. Our advocate does not explain how these private rituals were "manifest"; in *Apology* 11, Xenophon has Hermogenes report that Socrates in his defense speech declared only that he manifestly sacrificed at the *public* festivals and altars, without a word about his sacrificing at home. We do have evidence for Socrates's private religious rituals of worship—and it is indeed highly vivid evidence—in Aristophanes's *Clouds*; surely our advocate does not want us to think of that?!

10. XS 18; cf. 1.2.64 and also *Apology* 24. BD ad loc.: "Dans sa defense de Socrate, Xénophon insiste surtout sur l'observance extérieure des principals pratiques religieuses"; cf. Burkert 1975, 317; Hadot 1995, 123: "All that mattered was one's inner attitude; therefore the sage conformed to 'life,' i.e. to the opinions of non-philosophers"; "but he did so with" an "inner freedom" (and see again Hadot, 103-4).

11. Cicero translates as "divinum quiddam" (*On Divination* 1.122: "in libris Socraticorum saepe dicitur: 'esse divinum quiddam,' quod *'daimonion'* appellat"). Burnet's claim (1924, ad *Euthyphro* 3b5 and *Apology* 24c1, followed by Vlastos 1991, 280) that "there is no such noun-substantive as *daimonion* in classical Greek"—*that* "makes its first appearance in the Septuagint"—is refuted by Plato, *Apology* 40a4 (with which Burnet ad loc. struggles), as well as *Theages* 128e5, and what Burnet has to admit are "quasi-substantival" usages at *Theaetetus* 151a4 and *Euthyphro* 3b5. Burnet refers us approvingly to MacNaghten 1914, but there we find the conclusion (187): "Xenophon, as we have seen, always uses the word as a substantive." See also Riddell 1867, 102; Rudhardt 1958, 105; and Strycker and Slings 1994, 154n6: "From Herodotus onwards (ii 120.5 etc.), the adjective *daimonios* can be used substantively, to denote, like *to theion*, a divine agent whom one does not want to name." See Dorion 2013, 277 for a list of such usages (to these add *On Horsemanship* 11.13). For every single usage of *daimōn* and *daimonios* in Xenophon's Socratic writings, see López and García 1995, s.v.

12. The idea of a personal *daimōn* was not uncommon in Greek piety; but the way Socrates spoke about divination through his *daimonion* was radically new (although in Plato's *Apology* 27c, Socrates refutes Meletus by linking the two). Burnet 1924, ad *Euthyphro* 3b5: Socrates's "'sign' is never called a *daimōn*, though the idea of the *daimōn* as a guardian spirit was quite familiar (cf. my note on *Phaedo* 107d6 with Rep. 617e1 and 620db)." See also Tambornino 1909; François 1957. Burkert goes so far as to say that this "unique experience" of the *daimonion* not only opened Socrates to suspicion of "a secret cult," but "drove Socrates into isolation": 1985, 181 and 317, which refers us to Plato, *Phaedo* 107d as well as to *Euthyphro* 3b-c, *Apology* 31c-d, *Lysis* 223a, *Republic* 617d-e, 620d, and *Laws* 877a (to which add *Laws* 732c). See also Mary R. Lefkowitz, as quoted in O'Connor 1995, 166n19: "It was revolutionary (and dangerous) . . . in saying that the god sends him frequent, but private negative signs that no one else hears or sees, Socrates implies that he has a closer relationship to the gods than even the sons of the gods and goddesses in ancient myth." Taylor therefore certainly overstates when he writes (1932, 22): "Xenophon's apologetic purpose absolutely requires him to suppress, as far as he can, any feature in the character of his hero which is original, and therefore disconcerting to a dull and conventionally-minded reader."

13. We later learn that the *daimonion* also gave directions to Socrates himself (4.3.12, 4.8); but in accord with the overall intention of the *Memorabilia*—aiming to demonstrate Socrates's *justice* (XSD 85)—Xenophon (in marked contrast to Plato, though see *Theages* 128e) foregrounds how Socrates benefited others, rather than himself, by way of the *daimonion* (BD 1: 55).

14. 1.1.4; Dorion (2013, 279), following Jackson (1874, 235), insists that this means that the *daimonion* "cannot itself be the signal," as many commentators have mistakenly thought; but this seems blurred by what Xenophon reports Socrates saying in *Apology* 12: "How would I be carrying in strange *daimonia* in saying that of/from a god (*theou*) a voice (*phōnē*) to me becomes manifest, signaling what ought to be done?" This statement could be taken to mean that the *daimonion* is the voice (*phōnē*; *Memorabilia* 1.4.12 suggests that this word, in this context, means *linguistic* articulation and not merely a sound or cry; see also Liddell and Scott 1953 s.v.).

15. In *Apology* 12–14, Xenophon has Hermogenes report that Socrates spoke of his *daimonion* in a more blatantly unorthodox way, saying that his experience was of a "voice," from "a god," or "the god"—provoking the jurors to shout out, in outraged incredulity, or envy, that Socrates should receive greater and different things from the gods than they all did. Dorion (2013, 279–80n11) reminds us of "the celebrated fragment of Heraclitus" (Diels and Kranz 1951, frag. 93): "The Lord, to whom the oracle in Delphi belongs, neither speaks nor hides, but gives signs." Socrates "nowhere indicates the particular deity from whom he believed it to emanate" (Jackson 1874, 232, quoting Butler 1856, 1: 375).

16. Aristotle indites (*Rhetoric* 1398a15): "The *daimonion* is either god or deed of god," referring to Socrates's refutation of Meletus in Plato's *Apology*, where Socrates says (26c): "I am unable to learn whether you are saying that I teach belief that *certain* gods exist"—"*not indeed those of the city, but others*, and this is what you charge me with, belief in *others*, or if you are asserting that I myself do not in any way believe in gods, and teach these things to others."

17. Burnyeat 1997; Hegel 2006, 150. See also, on Socrates's disbelief in the gods of the city, Lactantius, *Divine Institutes* 3.20 and *Epitome of the Divine Institutes* 37; Tertullian, *Ad Nationes* 1.4 and 1.12. Consider John Locke, *Reasonableness of Christianity*, chap. 14: "The Rational and thinking part of Mankind, 'tis true, when they sought after him, found the One, Supream, Invisible God: But if they acknowledged and worshipped him, it was only in their own minds. They kept this Truth locked up in their own breasts as a Secret, nor ever durst venture it amongst the People. . . . There was no part of Mankind, who had quicker Parts, or improved them more; that had a greater light of Reason, or followed it farther in all sorts of Speculations, than the *Athenians*: And yet we find but one Socrates amongst them, that opposed and laughed at their Polytheism, and wrong Opinions of the Deity; And we see how they rewarded him for it."

18. BD 1: 55–56; Maréchal 1833, 274–75; Fahr 1969, 117–20; contrast Guthrie 1971, 84. At the end of his response to the indictment, Xenophon goes so far as to misquote significantly the official indictment, so as to change manifestly its meaning (1.2.64; cf. Hartman 1887, 130).

19. This will prove a favored trope of "Xenophon the rhetorician" (as he is often identified in the MSS): Gautier 1911, 126.

20. Montée 1869, 254: "Il n'est pas nécessaire d'admettre que Socrate ait cru à l'intervention d'une puissance surnaturelle pour ajouter foi au témoinage de Xénophon, qu'assez souvent il avertissait ses amis de ce que'ils devaient ou ne devaient pas faire suivant les inspirations de son Génie, et que ceux qui l'ont cru s'en sont fort bien trouvés, comme au contraire ceux qui ont negligé ses avis n'ont pas manqué de s'en repentir. Tout cela s'explique assez par les conseils de cette prudence dont Gabriel Naudé écrivait [1625, 312–13]." See similarly Fraguier 1746, 368–69; cf. Jackson 1874, 237.

21. 1.1.4–5; as L. Strauss points out (XS 7), Xenophon soon has Socrates use the adjectival form of *daimonion* to mean "almost the same as what is called 'natural' by others; perhaps Socrates' *daimonion* was in an outstanding manner something natural." See similarly Montaigne, *Essays* 1.11 ["Des Pronostications"] end, as well as Patin 1709, 286; Fraguier 1746, 366–68; Griffiths 1782, 441; Montée 1869, 253–56; Hegel 2006, 147–48; Zeller 1885, 95–97; cf. Long 2006, who refers us to Plutarch's dialogue *On the Divine Sign of Socrates*, esp. 580F (Galaxidorus speaking) and 588B and ff. (Simmias speaking). Riddell 1867, 106: "All Xenophon's notices of it encourage the view that it was the quick exercise of a judgment informed by knowledge of the subject, trained by experience, and inferring from cause to effect without consciousness of the process." L. Strauss directs us (1983, 47) to Aristotle, *On Prophecy in Sleep* 463b12–13: "On the whole, since some of the other animals dream, dreams in sleep would not be god-sent, not coming into being for this purpose; but they are *daimonia*—for nature is *daimonia*, but not divine (*theia*)."

22. 4.3.12; XS 5–6; see also Long 2006.

23. As is limned in the *Oeconomicus*, Socrates did not engage in "managing households and cities in noble fashion" (XSD 182, 185)—in striking contrast to Xenophon himself. Accordingly, Xenophon, in striking contrast to Socrates, not only made use of conventional divination (e.g., *Anabasis* 6.1.22–23), but was urged by Socrates to consult the Delphic oracle (ibid. 3.1.5–6). Was this last in order to remedy the deficiency of Socrates's *daimonic* prophetic knowledge, or was it in order to project the requisite, conventionally noble and pious, image before the city (XS 5; L. Strauss 1983, 112)?

24. 1.1.9: this curious formulation of Socratic doctrine would seem to entail that someone who judged all practical affairs to be guided solely by practical reason, holding that there is nothing of the *daimonion* in such affairs, could be said to be possessed by the *daimonion*. Bassett (1917, 568) points to this passage as paradigmatic of Xenophon's slyly witty paronomasia. Cf. O'Connor 1994, 167.

25. Even the Socratic doctrine concedes that "the gods give signs [only] to those to whom they are gracious" (1.1.9). See also 4.7.6 and Aristotle, *Metaphysics* 982b29–83a3.

26. Taylor 1911, chap. 4; Burnet 1924, ad *Euthyphro* 3b2; Beckman 1979, 57; Burkert 1985, 181; BD ad loc., referring us to Libanius, *Apology of Socrates* 114–16 (but see also esp. ibid. 36).

27. See esp. 1.6.14, 3.10–11, 4.2.8. Diogenes Laertius 2.45: "It seems to me that Socrates carried on dialogues about physics—when he converses about providence, according even to Xenophon, even though the latter says that he made speeches only about ethics."

28. "Grew by nature" (*ephu*) instead of "holds" (*echei*) is the intriguing reading found in a rather late MS ("F" = Paris 1794, from the mid-sixteenth century) and a major early MS ("L" or "Laur." = Laurentian LV 21, from the first half of the fourteenth century); see stemma of Bandini in BD), and this reading is followed by L. Dindorf 1826, G. Sauppe 1834, L. Breitenbach 1857, and Marchant 1923 (following G. Sauppe 1865–67, but contra Marchant 1921); unlike Hude 1934, BD fail even to register this very important alternative MS reading in their apparatus. But Hude wrongly claims that the reading in the MS Laur. LV 21 is written in a correction by a later hand; I have inspected a clear photo of the MS, and there is no sign of any "correction" at this point: see top of second column of second page.

29. See also Plato's *Apology*, and Aristophanes's *Clouds*, as well as Aristotle, *Metaphysics* 982b29–83a3 and Plutarch, *Pericles* 32.2 and *Nicias* 23.1–4—"Rational discourse about the phases of the moon . . . was still kept secret and for the few, and proceeded with a certain caution rather than trust; because they did not tolerate the studiers of nature and what were called 'chatterers about the things aloft,' on the grounds that they reduced the divine to causes without speech, and powers without providence, and necessitated effects"; see also Derenne 1930; Montuori 1974, 230ff.; 1981, 14–15; Parker 1996, 210–12; Janko 2006; BD ad loc.; Stokes 2012, 261–64; Waterfield 2012, 279–80; and—more philosophically— Ahrensdorf 1994 and Melzer 2014.

30. Stokes 2012, 248: "The word for 'think about' here [*phrontizontas*] recalls, doubtless deliberately, the 'Thinkery' [*Phrontisterion*] of Socrates in Aristophanes's *Clouds*. So, e.g. Classen 1984: 158." See also Taylor 1911, chap. 4; Luccioni 1953, 27n.

31. Sextus Empiricus, *Adversus Mathematicos* 9.92ff.; Diogenes Laertius 2.45; Fouillée 1874, vol. 1 passim; Gigon 1953, ad loc.; Theiler 1965; Long 1988, 162–63; DeFilippo and Mitsis 1994, 255–61; Gray 1998, 183; Brisson and Dorion 2004; Sedley 2008; Powers 2009; BD ad 1.4.1 and 1.4.8, as well as 4.3.18.

32. 4.5.12–4.6.1. Consider Plato's *Phaedo* 97c-99e and *Philebus* 16c-e. For further helpful elaboration, see XSD 147–50; L. Strauss 1953, chap. 4 beg. There is a curious irregularity to Xenophon's listing of the sorts of madness of the pre-Socratics. The extremes express three facets of the opposition between, on one hand, a quasi- "Eleatic" or "Parmenidean" outlook, and, on the other hand, an atomistic or a quasi-"Heraclitean"

outlook (BD ad loc.). But in the first pairing of forms of madness, the "Parmenidean" is mentioned first, whereas in the second and third pairings the atomistic or "Heraclitean" comes first. Could this be a signal that Socrates's ontology inclines slightly but significantly to the first in each pairing—plurality and mutability are more massively evident throughout nature than are limit and permanence; yet there is an important sense in which being, as what exists, is, after all, the whole, and thus one and immovable?

33. XS ad loc.: L. Strauss goes so far as to add that "the typical Socratic conversation as presented by Xenophon" stands "in the same relation to his conversations about the 'what is' of the human things," as "those 'what is' questions stand to his cosmology." See also XSD 150.

34. Xenophon thus indirectly indicates that Socrates's social or civic moderation did not entail social or civic passivity.

35. For "Baconian" expressions by ancient philosophers, see Empedocles in Diels and Kranz 1951, frag. B111 and reports A1, sec. 60 and A14; see also Athenaeus 267e.

36. Xenophon thus allows us to see that "the intention of the *Memorabilia*" is "not to show explicitly what" Socrates's "private views were. In the main it openly states his public views, i.e., the opinions which he uttered in public and in private conversations with people who were merely members of the public. Their not quite serious nature is indicated between the lines" (L. Strauss 1939, 518–19).

37. Burnet 1924, 133: the statement that Socrates was presiding "only makes its appearance in the *Memorabilia*," and "it is hard to believe that, if it were true, the fact could have been passed over in silence both in the *Apology* and the *Hellenica*."

38. *Hellenica* 1.7.14–15; Hatzfeld (1940, 169n5) highlights the significant civic-legal implications of the difference in the verbs employed in the two accounts—*prosthēsein* in the *Hellenica*, and *epipsēphisai* in the *Memorabilia*; see also BD 1: 65–67; Krentz 2009.

39. 1.1.19; cf. Powers 2009, 250.

CHAPTER TWO

An earlier version of this chapter was published as T. Pangle 2014.

1. As D. Morrison (1994, 182n3) points out, 1.2.35 shows that the term "the young" (*neoi*) could be stretched to include anyone under thirty. See, e.g., *Oeconomicus* 20.18 and *Symposium* 2.4.

2. The word *karterikōtatos* does not appear elsewhere and is a superlative form of the rare word *karterikos*, with which Socrates's chorus of followers salute him in the comedy about him by Ameipsias, the *Konnos* (frag. 9), which was produced at the same time as Aristophanes's *Clouds* (where also, of course, Socrates and his followers are depicted as extremely ascetic and impoverished).

3. Nietzsche, *Twilight of the Idols*, "The Problem of Socrates," #5; OT chap. 3a, note 27 and context (comparing *Memorabilia* 1.1.16 with *Oeconomicus* 6.12ff. and 11.1ff.) and chap. 6, note 50 and context, as well as the last para. of chap. 7.

4. Contrast Aristotle, *Nicomachean Ethics* 1117b23–19b18; and compare the speech of Cyrus, *Education of Cyrus* 1.5.8–10.

5. 1.2.3; Luccioni 1953, 32n3: "Jamais Xénophon ne parle des *mathētai* de Socrate. Il emploie toujours des termes comme *hoi sunontes*."

6. Contrast 1.2.3 and 1.2.8 with 1.2.18, 1.6.3 (and BD ad loc.), 1.6.14–15, and 4.7.1; see XS 11; D. Morrison 1994, 203–5. BD ad loc. are baffled by the puzzle of the surface contradiction; Luccioni (1953, 36n6) ascribes it to Xenophon's "inadvertance."

7. Compare Aristotle, *Nicomachean Ethics* 1155a23–27.

8. Gigon 1953, 4 and 25; Chroust 1955, 6.

9. Many scholars, starting with Cobet (1858, 665ff.)—also, e.g., Schenkl 1875; Hartman 1887, 104ff.; Birt 1893; Boutroux 1897; Mesk 1910; Baker 1917, 295; Busse 1930; Chroust 1955, 1957; Delebecque 1957, 223; Erbse 1961, 262–63; and more recently, Giannantoni 1992; Vander Waerdt 1993; and BD ad loc.—have tried to identify the unnamed, cursing incriminator with an Athenian sophist named Polycrates, who is known to have published an *Accusation of Socrates* (see Isocrates, *Busiris* 4; Diogenes Laertius 2.38–39). But no part of this work has come down to us. This has led recent scholars to become quite skeptical about this attribution: "What do we *know* of Polycrates's broadside? In truth we *know* very little. Many scholars have believed that Libanius, writing centuries later, made use of Polycrates; that is far from certain" (Stokes 2012, 245; see also Hansen 1995; Parker 1996, 206). Taylor (1911, 4) preferred Friedrich Blass's identification of the unnamed accuser as Meletus, on the basis especially of Libanius's *Apology of Socrates* (see Calder et al. 2002); while Hansen (1995, 11) suggested Anytus; and Luccioni (1953, 17–18) thought it could be Anytus or Meletus, and maybe also Lycon. These speculative suggestions have no basis in Xenophon's text, and distract from the needed careful (and wryly appreciative) interpretation of Xenophon's teaching as he has presented it, with his dramatic artfulness (see Gray 1998, 60–68, 73, 84).

10. BD ad loc. are characteristically baffled by the "strange" echo of comedy. This exhibits what L. Strauss (1939, 511n) identifies as a characteristic obtuseness of conventional Xenophon scholars: "They do not take into consideration the Aristophanean inclinations of Xenophon."

11. This is the first mention of Zeus. Xenophon, in his forensic defense of Socrates against the charges of impiety and corrupting the young, of course does not present the philosopher as ever uttering any such profane expletives. In Greek literature, such colloquial oaths are a characteristic only of comedy (including our one surviving satyr play), and the dialogues of Plato and Xenophon—along with Demosthenes (and a bit in Isaeus) among the ten canonical orators (Dover 1997, 62–63: "In the historical works of Xenophon [including *Cyr.*, *Ages.*, and *Lac.*] there are 86 occurences in all, of which no less than 76 are in the portrayal of dialogue; of the remaining ten, eight are in speeches and only two [*HG* v.1.4, *Lac.* 14.1] are the writer's intensification of his own statement"). Dover is greatly mistaken in claiming that the oaths in Aristophanes, Plato, and Xenophon serve merely as "intensification or on occasion almost as particles" (Dover 1997, 62, following Dover 1987, 50). They are important signals of (often comical) conversational tone or undertone, the emotions of speakers, and the more or less hidden theological (often irreverent but sometimes reverent) implications of the conversations (XSD 123, 170, 194–95). Naturally, the significance of each occurence of a profane oath must be determined by considering the speaker and dialogic context. For the importance for Socrates of the precise gods by whom he swears, see *Apology* 24.

12. See also 3.1.3–4: Socrates said that anyone who tried to become elected to the Athenian civic office of "general" without having acquired the requisite knowledge justly

deserved being punished by the city, while one who lacked the knowledge could not ever really be general, even if elected unanimously; and 3.9.10–13: Socrates "said that the kings and the rulers" are "not those elected by whoever might vote," but "those who have the knowledge of ruling." Even commentators as guileless as BD are compelled to remark (ad 3.1.4) that "the affirmation of Socrates remains subversive to the extent that he refuses to recognize the authority of the suffrage." (For the ironic meaning of this Socratic teaching, see OT chap. 3a, note 32: "It is ironic for the following reason: From Xenophon's point of view, the wise teacher of the royal art" is "not a potential ruler in the ordinary sense of the term, because he who knows how to rule does not necessarily wish to rule.")

13. "Xenophon does not even attempt to defend Socrates against the charge that he made subversive speeches to his companions; he only tries to show that men like Socrates do not favor violence and do not make others violent" (XS ad loc.; see also OT chap. 4, note 54 and context, as well as chap. 2, note 6 and context; Smith ad loc.; Freret 1736, 83; Vlastos 1983, 497; Stone 1988, 64; Vander Waerdt 1993, 43–44; O'Connor 1994, 156–57; Johnson 2003, 274). Xenophon allows some readers who do notice his silence, but have failed to catch on to his puckish wit, to think that he has blundered: e.g., Marchant 1923, xix–xx; Gigon 1953, ad loc.; Chroust 1957, 58.

14. Compare 1.2.31 and BD ad 1.2.15.

15. Plato of course executes his *Apology* without any reference to Critias or to Alcibiades.

16. See the baffled, critical questions and animadversions in BD ad 1.2.17–18, 27, 31.

17. See, e.g., Aeschines, *Against Timarchus* 173; Vlastos 1983.

18. Conventional scholarly bewilderment at the idea that Socrates's dialogic art could be a crucial source of political power is summed up by BD ad 1.2.31: "One will never insist enough on the fact that the dialectic is a technique or argumentation that has no utility in the public sphere. . . . In fact, since refutation is a technique of argumentation which lends itself well to private exchanges, it is hard to see what use it could be to a politician who needs to convince a crowd." But Socrates held that, for those who possess self-mastery, "it is possible to examine the most important matters, and, having distinguished them according to their kinds through dialogues in speech and in action, to choose the good things and to avoid the bad"; and it is "from this," Socrates insisted, that "men become best, and most artful as leaders/hegemonical (*hegemonikōtatous*), as well as most skilled in dialectics" (4.5.12; see also 3.7.4 and 4.6.15). Accordingly, Socrates characterized the activity of a democratic politician as "carrying on dialogue with the city" (*tou tē polei dialegesthai*—3.7.7), and Xenophon characterizes courtroom defense speeches as "carrying on dialogue with the jurors" (4.4.4). In the central passage of the dialogue *Hiero, or One Skilled in the Art of Tyranny* (5.1), Xenophon has a great tyrant disclose that tyrants have a fear of wise dialecticians, for their uncanny capacity to "contrive something"; at the start of the same dialogue (1.3), the tyrant, who has come to know his poet-interlocutor Simonides as an expert dialectician, indicates his awareness that the poet, with such wisdom, could well succeed in replacing Hiero, as the new tyrant. Commenting on this, Alexandre Kojève, a theorist with great personal experience in politics (helping to design and bring about the European Common Market), indites (OT 148–49; and see the context): "In point of fact, governmental action within an already constituted

State is purely *discursive* in its origin, and the philosopher who is past master of discourse or 'dialectic' can just as well become master of the government. If Simonides . . . was able to 'maneuver' Hiero as he pleased, there is no reason at all why he could not beat him and outmaneuver him in the domain of politics; and, in particular, there is no reason why he could not replace him at the head of the government—should he ever feel the desire. If a philosopher took power by means of his 'dialectic,' he would exercise it better than any 'uninitiate' whatsoever." Conventional scholars have not reckoned with the political power entailed in the liberation from illusions, and in the profound understanding of human psychology—not least the psychology of the politically ambitious and hence of one's political rivals as well as of oneself—that is essential to authentic Socratic dialectical refutations (cf. 2.1.3–4, and see OT chap. 3a, note 35 and 3b, esp. para. 17 end). We will witness a sample of this when we follow Alcibiades's devastating refutation of Pericles. Xenophon's massive exposition of the political education provided by Socrates is found in his autobiographical *Anabasis*, which, as its best interpreter says, "contains an analysis of how an outstanding student of Socrates"—Xenophon himself—"became, through the Socratic education, better able to rule human beings" (Buzzetti 2014, 2).

19. XS ad loc.; BD ad loc.: "Alcibiades and Critias were then justified in frequenting Socrates in order to acquire a competence in the political domain. . . . They both equally received a political formation that survived the separation from Socrates." Cf. Gigon 1953, ad loc.

20. 1.2.16 and 1.2.39; see also 1.2.47; Hartman 1887, 125–26; Gigon 1953, 44 ("Ein Widerspruch im strengsten Sinne"); BD ad 1.2.17–18, 39.

21. Hadot 1995, 104–5: "Philosophy in antiquity was a spiritual exercise"; "Although every written work is a monologue, the philosophical work is always implicitly a dialogue. The dimension of the possible interlocutor is always present within it. This explains the incoherencies and contradictions which modern historians discover with astonishment in the works of ancient philosophers."

22. See OT chap. 5, note 8 and context.

23. As has been noted by Foucault (1984, 84–85), Devereux (1992, 782n25), O'Connor (1994, 156), and BD ad loc., Xenophon's nuanced understanding of the Socratic thesis contradicts the rather simpleminded "intellectualist" conception of virtue that conventional scholars generally attribute to Socrates, on the basis of a misunderstanding of Plato. For the needed corrective, see L. Pangle 2013 and 2014, as well as Benjamin Franklin's dialogue between "Socrates" and "Crito," entitled "A Man of Sense" (1959–, 2: 15–18; for analysis, see L. Pangle 2007, 84–85).

24. See similarly the Platonic Socrates's praise of the poet Cydias in *Charmides* 155d.

25. See also L. Pangle 2013, 21–23.

26. See Plato's *Charmides* for a dramatic portrait of exactly where Critias wound up on the range of genuine understanding of Socratic teachings. See also Hadot 1995, 107: "We ought not to forget that many a philosophical demonstration derives its evidential force not so much from abstract reasoning as from an experience which is at the same time a spiritual exercise."

27. As Macleod notes (2008, 131), "This is one of the rare passages in Greek literature with an extended use of the dual form."

28. Cf. Nails 2002, 108–9.

29. Smith ad 1.2.31; Nails 2002, 110.

30. Xenophon ironically speaks as if he has never heard of Aristophanes's *Clouds*, and as if it was the Thirty who were the source of the "slander" that Socrates taught the art of speaking. As is observed by BD ad loc., if Critias, who was well informed as to Socrates's educational activity, took the trouble to formulate a law targeting Socrates through forbidding the teaching of the art of speaking, one may justifiably assume that Socrates was indeed engaged in such teaching.

31. Socrates's first quoted words in the *Memorabilia* are "I for my part (he said) am prepared to obey the laws." Only much later (4.4.3) does Xenophon disclose that Socrates in this case was lying; Socrates in fact proceeded to disobey the law in question (Buzzetti 2001, 16; see also Johnson 2003, 276; Gray 2004, 151).

32. L. Strauss 1983, 172–73; OT chap. 3a, note 29 and context; Stone 1988, 158–60.

33. XS ad loc.; OT chap. 3a, notes 14 and 29 and contexts.

34. XS 14; O'Connor 1994, 156; Buzzetti 2001, 22–23; Telemann's opera *Der geduldige Socrates* (libretto by Johann Ulrich von König) presents Alcibiades teamed with Xenophon and Plato as the three leading students of Socrates, singing together in choruses, and has Alcibiades sing an aria that concludes: "Nel saper sta la fortuna; niente v'é, che vaglia più."

35. See similarly Plato *Republic* 492aff. and *Alcibiades I*.

36. BD ad 1.2.39–40 (see also ad 1.2.30, 1.2.47, 1.3.14; and Gigon 1953, 57): "Pour mieux convaincre son lecteur que Socrate et Alcibiade n'eurent entre eux que des rapports éphémères et superficiels," Xenophon "évite soigneusement de mettre Alcibiade et Socrate en presence l'un de l'autre et de les faire converser ensemble." BD concede for once that "il serait peut-être naïf, en effet, de prendre le texte au pied de la letter."

37. Busse (1930, 221) remarks: "Das Gespräch zwischen Perikles und Alkibiades hängt sehr lose mit dem Zweck der Schutzschrift zusammen." Dorion, in BD 1: CLXI–CLXIII, is still more disconcerted, and judges that Xenophon has here written "fort maladroitment." See also O'Connor 1994, 157.

38. Gigon (1953, 68) speaks of "des fein und planmässig geführten Dialoges" (see also Gigon 1956, 137: "der gewandte Dialektiker Alkibiades"); BD ad loc. (and see also 1: CLX–CLXI) comment: "Cette réfutation est très bien structurée et elle est fort habiliment menée . . . irréprochablement conduit." See also Smith ad 1.2.45; D. Morrison 1995, 332.

39. Consider what we later hear from Socrates (2.1); and see Buzzetti (2001, 22–23), who stresses that Xenophon speaks of Critias as a "lawgiver" and the commands of the the Thirty as "law" (1.2.31–34).

40. See also Plato, *Alcibiades I* 124e-27e; *Laws* 712e-13a, 714b-15a; Buzzetti 2001, 19–23; Johnson 2003, 277–79.

41. 1.2.48; what is so strange about this list is that it names at its center—according to the two major MSS "A" (Paris 1303) and "B" (Paris 1740), as well as the (second-century) papyrus PBEROL 21108—the great Syracusan statesman-general Hermocrates (d. 407 BC), who led the defeat of Athens at Syracuse, and is otherwise unmentioned in Xenophon's Socratic writings, though he is a prominent personage in the *Hellenica* and a familiar of Socrates in Plato's *Timaeus* and *Critias*, as well as a leading figure in Thucydides. I am inclined to follow, with almost all editors and commentators, Groen van Prinsterer's (1823, 225–26) emendation of the text to read, instead of "Hermocrates,"

"Hermogenes"—the name of a close follower of Socrates in his last years, a man who did not have a political career, and who is a prominent figure in Xenophon's Socratic writings. The major dissenter is Burnet (1911, xviii–xix); but his argument in defense of retaining the MSS reading "Hermocrates" is based on a shallow reading of Xenophon. In accepting the emendation, we presume a slip in copying that goes back—given the fact that the "slip" is also in the papyrus—to antiquity, or before AD 200. There is, however, this complicating puzzle: in the set of secondary (fourteenth- and fifteenth-century) MSS that are independent of A and B, and designated by the symbol Φ by BD, there is *no name* in the text (no "Hermocrates," but also no "Hermogenes"—and no blank, as I have found by inspection of Laur. LXXX.13). What might have caused this? Was there a difficulty in reading, at this point, the MS that was being copied—the hypothesized ancient archetype ("α") from which all our MSS supposedly descend (deduced by Schenkl 1875, 18 [102])? See BD 1: CCLXIff., esp. CCLXVII–CCLXIX, CCLXXIII (the stemma in BD 1: CCLXXVIII is corrected in BD 2: XI). If "Hermocrates" is retained, then Xenophon would be quietly indicating that Socrates was the teacher of the man who inspired and led Syracuse in inflicting upon Athens, in its prime, its worst single defeat.

42. The accuser's language again echoes prominent passages in Aristophanes's *Clouds*: see Smith ad 1.2.49, referring us to *Clouds* 1321ff.; and BD ad loc., referring us to *Clouds* 1405ff.

43. "When the soul, in which alone there comes to be intellect (*phronēsis*) exits, they then as quickly as possible carry away the body of the most closely related human, and make it disappear (*aphanizousin*)" (1.2.53); see Joël 1893–1901, 2: 1133. Contrast the words of Cyrus, on his deathbed, about his burial: "What could be more blessed than this, to be mingled with Earth, which brings forth and nourishes all the beautiful things, and all the good things? I became philanthropic also in other ways, and now I believe that I would with pleasure enter into community with that which does good deeds to humans" (*Education of Cyrus* 8.7.25).

44. As we learn from *Hiero* (1.27–2.1, 3 entire, 6.12–13, 7.1–10, 8.1, 10.1, 11.8–11), the concern with being loved is more characteristic of the political man than of the philosophic, while the concern with being honored is more characteristic of the philosophic than of the political man (see OT passim, and esp. chap. 5, note 58 and context; "The desire for praise and admiration as distinguished and divorced from the desire for love is the natural foundation for the predominance of the desire for one's own perfection").

45. See also *Apology* 20–21. Commenting on these passages, Hegel expostulates (1971, 508): "Ist es also zu verwindern, dass Sokrates schuldig befunden wurde?" BD comment here: "Pour les Grecs, le manque de respect aux parents constitue une offense très grave (cf., entre autres, Platon, *Crito* 51c; *Lois* 930e; Aristophanes, *Oiseaux* 755 sq. et 1347 sq.)." See also BD ad 1.2.55, criticizing Gigon 1953, 80. Smith ad 1.2.49 helpfully draws our attention to Aristophanes, *Clouds* 1321ff.

46. The famous investigative reporter I. F. Stone, who is more suspiciously alert than most conventional scholars, finds the line from Hesiod to be "so irrelevant we can only conclude that it is dragged in" by Xenophon "as a diversionary tactic" (1988, 30).

47. L. Strauss (OT chap. 3a, note 46) suggests that "why Socrates liked" these verses of Homer, "or how he interpreted them, is indicated in 4.6.13–15."

48. Stone 1988, 30–32; see also O'Connor 1994, 157–58; cf. Dresig 1738, 110–11; XS 17.

49. This does not rule out that one may teach the superiority in principle of governance by a wise monarch while embracing actual democracy in certain circumstances: OT chap. 4; O'Connor 1994, 158; Johnson 2012, 132.

50. Recall 1.2.6; see Gray 1998, 44.

51. 1.3.1; see also 4.1.1 and *Apology* 26 as well as *Oeconomicus* 11.2.

52. Edelstein 1935, 92; XSD 85; Vander Waerdt 1993, 44n120.

53. BD 1: CLXXXIII: "At the end of the nineteenth century, most commentators were in agreement" that the *Memorabilia* was a work "lacking unity and obeying no precise plan"; see similarly Chroust 1957, 5; Gigon protests (1956, 1): "Die memorabilien sind nicht, wie es vor allem H. Maier (*Sokrates* 25 f.) und Wilamovitz (*Platon* I, 265) gemeint haben, eine 'ordnungslose Materialsammlung' und eine 'ungefüge Masse.'" In the twentieth century, conventional scholarship made modest progress in deciphering the puzzle, building on A. Döring 1891–92: see Hornstein 1915–16; Arnim 1923, 93–127; Edelstein 1935, 78–137; Erbse 1961; Fritz 1965, 275ff.; and Gray 1998, 123–58, esp. 127: "The image of Socrates cannot be fully appreciated until the structure of the entire *Memorabilia* is understood." But the entry "Xenophon" in the *Oxford Classical Dictionary*, 3rd ed., still characterizes the *Memorabilia* as "a collection of conversations, *probably not planned as a coherent whole.*" See similarly Macleod 2008, 58–60. As regards the once-fashionable attempts to dissolve the puzzles by dreaming up purported, posthumous interpolations by unknown writers other than Xenophon, see the aptly scorching critique by BD 1: CCXXIV n2.

54. In fact, "the positive part of the *Memorabilia* [I, 32 to end] consists of 37 chapters of which only the first, or, perhaps, the first three, are devoted to 'deed,' whereas almost all the rest is devoted to 'speech'" (L. Strauss 1939, 519, referring us to *Memorabilia* 3.3.11 and Plato, *Apology* 32a); see also *Crito* 52d; "the 'deed-speech' antithesis" (Strauss continues) is "an ironical expression of the antithesis between practical or political life and theoretical life"; see also Plato, *Gorgias* 450–51; Hornstein 1915–16, 37: 63.

55. XS 17–18; see also 39, 43, 91–92, 94.

56. 1.2.48, 2.1.19, 3.6.2, 3.7.9, 4.4.17, 4.5.10.

57. See again 1.2.48, 2.1.19, 3.6.2, 3.7.9, 4.4.17, 4.5.10. See also OT chap. 6, note 33 and context. We note that the statement of Xenophon's that we have already treated in 1.2.61, about Socrates's adorning the city, is pretty much the last mention for a long time (until 4.4) of Socrates's direct service to his own city.

## CHAPTER THREE

1. "Wir setzen bei dieser Betrachtung allerdings voraus, dass die von den Alexandrinern geschaffene Buchgrenze (zwischen 1,7,5 und 2,1,1) einen als Einheit konzipierten Zusammunghang ohne Berechtigung zerreisst" (Erbse 1961, 273, following A. Döring 1891–92, 47ff.); see also Delatte 1933, 85, Edelstein 1935, 100ff., esp. n41; Kühn 1954, 520.

2. XS 18, 21; see also Gigon 1953, 95 and 122, as well as Gigon 1956, 1; Gray 1995, 67; 1998, 33–35; BD ad 1.3.1, 1.3.5, 1.4.2, 1.4.19, 1.5.1.

3. 1.3.1. Montée (1869, 276) comments: "Ainsi Socrate, on ne peut en douter, n'a jamais voulu, même en matière religieuse, se mettre en opposition ouverte avec les lois

de la patrie, dont il fut toujours le plus fidèle observateur et dont il devait être le martyr;
mais cela suffit-il pour nous faire croire qu'il avait les mêmes opinions religieuses que la
foule? En aucune façon." See the context, Montée, chap. 11, "Socrate et la religion de son
temps," and esp. 277–78, 290. See also XS 18.

4. XS 19. Xenophon limits himself to saying that "if" Socrates "was of the opinion
that he had been signaled something by the gods," he prioritized compliance with the
signal (1.3.4).

5. As BD remark here in baffled surprise, this Socratic teaching on prayer "is in contradiction with all those passages where Xenophon describes, with an undissimulated
approbation, generals who pray or who offer sacrifices before a battle (Oec. 5.19–20; Cyr.
1.5.14; 1.6.1; 1.6.44–45; 3.3.21–22; 34; 57; 6.4.1; 6.4.13; 6.4.19; 7.1.1; An. 7.8.9–10, etc.)."
We add that the consummate gentleman Ischomachus taught Socrates the very different,
more conventional, understanding of prayer: Oeconomicus 11.8. Xenophon himself
teaches a version of this more conventional gentlemanly view of prayer at the outset and
in the conclusion of his treatise The Skilled Cavalry Commander.

6. BD ad loc., referring us to Plato, Republic 362b-c; see also 364b-365a.

7. Commentators protest in bafflement the obvious economic exaggeration here (especially if one thinks of Socrates's poor wife and children!): Gigon 1953, 101 ("eine fast
grotesque enkomiastische Uebertreibung"); BD ad loc. These commentators fail, as usual,
to appreciate Xenophon's tongue-in-cheek, deliberately comic, mild alazoneia (comic
boasting) on behalf of his hero: contrast XSD 100–106 (Xenophon is somewhat more forthcoming in his Oeconomicus).

8. 1.3.6–8; Smith ad loc. suggests that we translate: "jestingly but with an earnest
inner meaning," and refers us to 4.1.1 ("For even when jesting, no less than when in earnest, he benefited those who spent time with him"); Macleod (2008, 142) notes the parallels with Aristophanes's Frogs 389–90, as well as Symposium 1.1 and 4.28.

9. Odyssey 10.303 and context; for the significance of this Homeric passage, see the
interpretation in L. Strauss 1987, 2–3.

10. Compare the beginning of Spinoza's Preface to his Theologico-political Treatise.

11. With Hude 1934 and Marchant 1921 as well as other editors I follow the MSS in
this passage: BD rely on a hitherto unused third-century papyrus fragment (Heidelberg
206) "qui différe notablement du texte transmis par les manuscrits médiévaux," although,
they concede, "cela ne veut pas dire que son texte soit toujours meilleur," especially
since they conclude "que les manuscrits médiévaux descendent recta via d'une édition
établie entre le Ier et le IIe sièle après J.-C.," which is likely to derive from an influential
critical edition prepared by Alexandrian scholars (see BD's apparatus, their commentary
ad loc., and 1: CCLIV–CCLX, CCLXXVII, as well as vol. 2, "Histoire du Texte [Supplé-
ment]," n1).

12. Compare 1.6.13 (and Gigon 1953, 161: "Eine Inkohärenz ist vorhanden"), 2.1.5
(and BD ad loc.), 2.2.4, 2.6.28, 3.11, 4.1.2, 4.5.9; also Symposium 4.23–28—"mixing the
playful and serious"—as well as 8.2; XS 156.

13. 1.3.14; contrast Plato, Charmides 155d.

14. 1.3.15; Hindley (1999, 83ff.; 2004, 127, 139) finds an "apparently irreconcilable
conflict" between 1.3.8 and 1.3.14, leading to his "hypothesis" that "the latter is an interpolation." Consider also 1.4.12, which BD ad loc. and Gigon (1953, 137) see as a bafflingly

flagrant contradiction of the present passage. Schenkl (1875, 32–33) finds so unacceptable the indication that Socrates *did* have *some* pain in these regards that he insists this must be an interpolation.

15. XS 21; cf. L. Pangle 2013, 24–25, and for illuminating reflections on precisely why Socrates may have always needed a measure of continual self-mastery, see 31–32.

16. Buzzetti 2001, 6–7, who refers us also to 4.5.1.

17. 1.4.2; see similarly Plato, *Symposium* 173b; Nails 2002, 52.

18. Plato, *Symposium* 173a-b, 218b; BD ad loc. refer us to the ancient testimonies to Aristodemus collected in Giannantoni 1990, VI B 8–10. See also Nails 2002, 52–53.

19. With Bonnette 1994, ad loc., against most editors, I accept the reading of the two major MSS, A and B (Paris 1302 and 1740); the family of MSS designated Φ reads "contriving" (*mēchanōmenon*) instead of "fighting in battle" (*machomenon*); by the latter, I understand Xenophon to be indicating that Aristodemus was not so flagrant as to fail to participate with his fellow soldiers in battlefield sacrifices.

20. BD ad loc. express bewilderment: "The conclusion that ought to follow is that he mocked Socrates equally. This conclusion seems altogether counterfactual because Aristodemus is one of the most fervent admirers of Socrates."

21. We are not surprised to hear Aristodemus engaging in profane expletives more than anyone has previously (three times; the runner up is Xenophon himself, with his two profane oaths in the immediately preceding dialogue: 1.3.12).

22. 1.4.2–3. As L. Strauss points out (XS 22), Aristodemus's conception of who are the truly wise accords with the fact that he is the faithful recollector of every word and significant action in the sole dialogue that the Platonic Socrates had with great poets.

23. Throughout his dialogic writings, Xenophon makes artful use of the insertion "he said" to direct the reader's attention to preceding parts of sentences: see OT chap. 3b, note 41.

24. Erbse 1961, 275n2; Powers 2009, 254.

25. 1.6.10; commenting on these passages, Guthrie remarks (1971b, 230–31): "Belief in the self-sufficiency of the deity leads naturally to doubts about the reality of any divine providence or care for mankind." See also Gigon 1953, ad loc.; BD ad 1.4.10 and 1.4.18.

26. Richter 1893, 69: "Diese ganze Erörterung des Sokrates von #11 an gar kein Beweis für die Fürsorge der Götter um die Menschen, wie es Aristodem verlangt hatte."

27. XS 24–25 refers us to *Symposium* 8.4 for similar indication of disbelief evinced by Socrates's follower Antisthenes, who makes it clear that he thinks that Socrates uses talk of his *daimonion's* prohibitions as an excuse to avoid having to do things, even rather trivial things, that he prefers not doing.

28. 1.4.16–17; as L. Strauss points out (OT chap. 3b, note 40), Socrates thus does not seem to consider the divine to be incorporeal—referring us also to 4.3.13–14.

29. Conventional scholars, deaf to Xenophon's "roguishness" and "Attic irony," see in his repeated raising and then failing to respond adequately to this criticism a pervasive "maladroitness": Macleod (2008, 148–49, 153) sententiously pronounces that "a better way for Xenophon to prove the point he tries to make . . . would have been to concentrate not on Socrates's words and example, but on results, viz. instances of improved behaviour by Aristodemus and other associates." See similarly Luccioni 1953, 83–84n5; and BD 1: cxxv–CXLIV and ad 1.7.1, referring also to 1.2.64, 2.1.1, 3.3.15, 4.5.1, and 4.8.11 (one may

add 1.7.1 compared with 1.7.5; a reader surveying all these passages may be forced to wonder whether Xenophon is not himself one of those whose "writings," he says, lead people to make the criticism!—see Gray 1998, 80–81). BD rightly dismiss the attempts by other scholars (Gigon 1953, 166; Gray 1998, 81–82) to erase the "contradiction" (as BD call it). BD ad 4.8.11 are especially perturbed by Xenophon's closing eulogy of Socrates: "One is astonished that Xenophon contents himself with affirming, when concluding his final eulogy of Socrates, that the latter was capable (*hikanos*) of putting others to the test (*dokimasai*), of refuting them (*elengxai*), and of exhorting them to virtue and to excellence . . . , as if Socrates was not up to rendering them effectively virtuous."

30. *Oeconomicus* 12–14; recall *Memorabilia* 1.1.16: only those who can give knowledgeable answers to the Socratic questions are truly gentlemen (noble and good), while those who cannot do so are justly to be designated slavish.

31. BD ad loc.: "La progression de l'argumentation, depuis le début du #1, est tout à fait remarquable."

32. Sommerstein 2009, 18: "The great majority" of "oaths were used exclusively by men or exclusively by women. Over time, too, there seems to have been a tendency for this sexual segregation of oaths to become more complete." Bonnette 1994, ad loc. refers us to Aristophanes's *Assembly of Women* 155–56 and 189–90, "where women attempting to disguise themselves as men are chastized for continuing to use" the oath "By Hera!" (Weirdly, the 1996 supplement to Liddell and Scott 1953, in referring to our passage, *Memorabilia* 1.5.5, deletes the 1953 edition's correct statement, s.v. Hera, that this was an Athenian woman's oath.) For the importance to Socrates of which god or goddess one swears by, see *Apology* 24: "I manifestly never, in place of Zeus and Hera and the gods with these, either sacrificed to strange divine things (*daimosin*), or *swore by*, or named, other gods." See also Smith and BD ad loc.; Calder (1983) submits that the oath "By Hera!" is generally used by Plato's Socrates for ironical and feigned admiration. Sommerstein's attempt (2008) to explain the oath "By Hera!" as some sort of peculiarity of the deme from which Socrates came is a tenuous and implausible speculation that ignores the artfully playful rhetoric of Socrates, Xenophon, and Plato.

33. Richter 1893, 77n: "Die Überleitung zu den *hēdonai dia tōn chrēmatōn* is ganz überraschend." Schenkl (1875, 33) finds this so astonishing that he insists it must be the work of an interpolator.

34. Consider *Oeconomicus* 12.20 and context, esp. 13.5; XSD 170.

35. Xenophon's making this rather lengthy encounter devoid of any profane oaths is a sign of the comparatively greater seriousness of the theme.

36. *kakodaimonia*; as L. Strauss points out (XS 28 and 31–32), the term, along with the whole challenge, is evocative of Aristophanes's critique of Socrates in the *Clouds* (referring esp. to lines 102–4 and 503–4).

37. *sunousiastas*; for this meaning of the term, see Plato, *Minos* 319e; J. Morrison 1953, 4–5; Nails 2002, 33–34.

38. Gigon 1953, 153; BD ad loc.

39. 1.6.5; in the *Symposium* (4.41), it is the tactless, dour, and shallow Antisthenes who makes this claim; contrast Xenophon's wise Simonides in *Hiero* 1.20 (and context), and Xenophon's own irony in *Education of Cyrus* 1.2.11.

40. In *Apology* 18, Xenophon reports Socrates saying: "Others procure for themselves expensive delights from the market, but I contrive for myself, without expense, delights from the soul more pleasant than those." For an elaboration of the subtler Socratic reasons why the ordinary pleasures must be seen as impediments to the enjoyment of the greater pleasures and goods, see L. Pangle 2013, 26–27.

41. The ancient lexicographer called Suidas, in his entry "un-needy," has preserved the fragment: "Antiphon in the first book of *Truth*: 'on account of this, it is in need of nothing and receives nothing at all in addition, but is infinite and un-needy'"; Diels and Kranz 1951, s.v. "Antiphon der Sophist," B10. See XS 28–29; BD ad loc.; Guthrie 1971b, 230–31.

42. OT chap. 3a, note 26 and context; Gigon 1953, ad loc.; J. Morrison 1953, 5; 1955; pace Dodds 1951, 132–33; and Dodds's rather frivolous 1954.

43. It has been thought for a long time, on the basis originally of the testimony of David Ruhnken's notes in the fifth edition of Ernesti (1772, orig. 1737; see also Ruhnken 1811), that there was an excellent MS owned by the famous seventeenth-century book collector and scholar Isaac Vossius, but since lost, in which the word "beneficial" was read instead of the word "friends" at this point. This plausible alternate MS reading was accepted by Marchant 1921 (in the 1919 "corrigenda" to his 1901 ed.) and 1923, following several earlier major editors. It is noted as an alternative reading in the apparatus of Hude 1934, and thus enters as a footnote in Bonnette 1994, ad loc. Bandini, however, has convincingly shown (1994, 73–74; cf. 1992, following a suggestion of Bornemann 1824) that there never was such a MS, and that what were in fact merely plausible conjectures of Vossius were mistaken or misrepresented by Ruhnken as MS readings. No doubt, there is something strange about the MS reading we have at this point, which makes understandable the tempting emendation; but I believe by this strangeness Xenophon has Socrates indicating that what brings Socratic friendships to completion is the activity of learning together from the study of wise old books. See similarly Smith ad loc.; and XS 44.

44. 1.6.14: *kalok'agathian*, literally, "being-noble-and-good"; this may be the first occurrence in Greek literature of this abstract noun, formed from the two-word term for "gentleman" or "one noble and good" (*kalos k'agathos*; "rarely with words between," e.g., *Education of Cyrus* 4.6.3; and not written as a single word—Liddell and Scott 1953, s.v.); at any rate, it is apparently in Xenophon's writings that this term first appears; see Jüthner 1930, 99–100. For the ten other appearances in Xenophon's Socratic writings, see López and García 1995, s.v.; see also *Agesilaus* 10.3 and *Regime of the Lacedaimonians* 10.1 and 10.4; the term does not appear in Plato except in the academic definitions at 412e8; by the next century the term had become common enough to appear in surviving public inscriptions at Ithaca and Olympia: Dittenberger 1915–24, nos. 558 and 649.

45. If this "is anything like a true picture," Burnet comments (1924, 84), "it furnishes ample ground for the Aristophanic caricature of the *phrontisterion*."

46. Xenophon is silent "on the bliss of Socrates's hearers as distinguished from the bliss of Socrates himself" (XS 59): to share in Socrates's wisdom is not to share in it fully.

47. "Xenophon is damaging his own case when he incidentally betrays in one passage the fact that Socrates had at some date been something very like the head of a group of scientific students (*Mem.*, I. vi. 14)" (Taylor 1932, 23).

48. 1.6.15, contradicting 1.2.16, 31, 39, 47–48; baffled conventional scholars, who fail to appreciate Xenophon's roguishly tricky rhetoric, and the problems with which it adroitly contends, "hastily blame, incorrectly," what they see as the awkwardness of this little sequel to the previous, eloquent, Socratic speech, and propose that this section must be an interpolation by someone else, or a late addition that Xenophon "maladroitly" failed to integrate (e.g., Gilbert 1888, xxv; Gigon 1953, ad loc.; J. Morrison 1955, 8n6; BD ad loc.; Tamiolaki 2012, 583–86).

49. As is stressed by BD ad loc., following Gray 1998, 127.

50. The *alazōn* is a stock central or "hero" character of Attic Old Comedy. The character's hubristic boastfulness takes on a specially impious hue in the comedies of Aristophanes (e.g., Strepsiades in *Clouds*, Peisthetairos in *Birds*, Trugaeus in *Peace*, Chremylos and Cario in *Wealth*; see Ambler and Pangle 2013). The epithet "boaster" is applied to Socrates and his followers in the *Clouds*, first by Pheidippides (103–5) and eventually by Strepsiades (1492). On the basis of the *Clouds*, BD comment at this point: "Il semble que Socrate fut assez tôt en butte à une accusation d'imposture (*alazoneia*)."

51. See also the explicit "boasting talk" (*megalēgoria*) that Socrates engaged in at his trial, not least as regards his *daimonion*: *Apology to the Jury* as a whole and esp. 2, 13–14, 32; see XS 31–32.

52. Benjamin Franklin, the American founder who studied the *Memorabilia* most closely, and who looked to its Socrates as a model, drew up a catalogue of moral virtues in which he defined "Sincerity" as "Use no hurtful Deceit" and "Humility" as "Imitate Jesus and Socrates" (1964, 148 and context). For illuminating discussion of Franklin's Xenophontic practice of "sincerity," see L. Pangle 2007, 12, 60–62 (regarding "sincerity" in speech about religion), 72, 123–24, 164–65, 206–7 (religion again).

53. A slightly different version of this section was published as T. Pangle 2016; that online publication includes reproductions of the artworks referred to in the endnotes here.

54. In order to present the political life in its best (while still realistic) light, Xenophon must have his Socrates fall almost silent on the superior, transpolitical life. Xenophon acts, we may say, much as a choral director, who in order to allow the beauty of a weaker voice to be heard, may require the strongest voice to fall silent or to hum for a time. Misunderstanding Xenophon's art, commentators (Gigon 1956; Fritz 1965; Narcy 1995; BD ad loc.) label the Aristippus section a gross blunder by Xenophon, in that he appears to present Socrates as having forgotten his own way of life! For the reasons given by BD, the attempt by Erbse (1980) to save Xenophon from this criticism is unconvincing and obscures rather than reveals. Note that Socrates argues for the life of political rule by deploying *seventeen* questions; see Buzzetti 2014, appendix 2.

55. So Athenaeus 12.63; Gigon 1956, 12–13.

56. XS 38–39 and 75 (a "futile effort"); Grant 1871, 109 ("Nothing could have been less qualified to produce an impression on a man of the world like Aristippus"); BD ad 2.1.34. Yet from what Xenophon says in reintroducing him later, Aristippus seems to have felt pained by the fact that he was here "refuted" (as he had to admit—3.8.1); we cannot rule out the possibility that Aristippus eventually took to heart some of the first part of Socrates's teaching here, and educated himself to become more cagey politically, if not more self-restrained carnally and monetarily. Xenophon would not violate historical

verisimilitude by leaving open this possibility: the historical Aristippus is said to have been able to adjust himself well to places, times, and men, and thus to have become a favorite of the tyrant Dionysius of Syracuse (Diogenes Laertius 2.65–66). Compare OT chap. 6, note 45 and context: "It is not impossible that the historical Aristippus has served to some extent as a model for Xenophon's Simonides."

57. Mannebach 1961, 120n2 ("verba non ad Aristippum ipsum pertinere videntur"); K. Döring 1988, 63; O'Connor 1994, 159; countered by Narcy 1995, 78; and BD ad 2.1.1.

58. Consider *The One Skilled in Hunting with Dogs* 1 and Aristophanes, *Clouds* 1050.

59. XS 20: "It is easy to see how Socrates could correspond to Virtue, but how could Xenophon correspond to Vice? 'Unless indeed the care bestowed upon virtue is corruption' (I.2.8)."

60. BD ad loc. refer us to numerous passages in Xenophon's other works where he speaks of his own and other commanders' self-restraint in these regards.

61. Cf. BD ad loc., who also point us to the Platonic Socrates's striking statement at *Republic* 345e.

62. Some scholars express shock: see BD ad 2.1.10, 19; Narcy 1995, 79–80.

63. Conventional scholars are bewildered by, or see a Socratic "sophism" or a grave error of Xenophon as author in, the fact that Socrates never explicitly speaks of the pleasures of rule, and the pains of being ruled, for *individuals*, in *domestic* politics, especially in republics and democracies, but switches to speaking solely of the pleasures and pains for collective peoples, in international relations. BD ad 2.1.10 point out that in *Hiero* 8–9 and 11 Xenophon has Simonides portray in eloquent and attractive detail the great specific pleasures of domestic rule for the individual (and by obvious implication, the severe pains, for the individual, of not ruling *within* one's own city): BD ask in complaint, why couldn't Xenophon have put something similar in the mouth of Socrates here? The answer emerges if one reflects on the context, and the implications for republicanism, of Simonides's articulation of these great pleasures and severe pains (see OT, esp. chaps. 2, 4, and 5 end). We note that Aristippus recognizes that Socrates identifies the political art, in its pleasure and happiness of ruling, with "the *kingly* art" (2.1.17).

64. Scholars' expressions of scandalized disapproval of, or need to explain away, Socrates's political theory here (Gigon 1956, ad loc.; Fritz 1965, 259, 264; Narcy 1995; Gray 2004; Johnson 2009; BD ad 2.1.1, 10, 13;) exhibit an all-too-typical scholarly political naiveté. Recall the lesson about all regimes and in particular democracy conveyed by Alcibiades's refutation of Pericles (1.2.41–46). In his *Symposium* (4.30–32), Xenophon has Charmides present a lively first-person description of the pains suffered by individual, nonslave citizens stuck among the minority that is ruled and dominated under a democracy—and, conversely, the pleasures enjoyed by individuals who belong to the democracy's ruling and dominating majority; see also the discussion of this passage in Montesquieu's *Spirit of the Laws* 8.2; and see Tocqueville's sustained discussion, in *Democracy in America*, of the "tyranny of the majority" at the heart of American democracy.

65. Richter (1893, 154): "Also Xenophon ein wandernder Sophist? Ja!"

66. See the *Hiero* as a whole, and OT chap. 5, especially at the beginning: the wise "Simonides proves to be a stranger in the most radical sense."

67. See 2.2.2, *Hiero* 4.3–4, and *Ways and Means* as a whole. Adam Smith, *Lectures*

*on Jurisprudence 1762–63* III.101–2 (see also 3.114): "It is indeed almost impossible that it [slavery] should ever be totally or generally abolished. In a republican government it will scarcely ever happen that it should be abolished. The persons who make all the laws in that country are persons who have slaves themselves." Rousseau, *Social Contract* 3.15: "What! Liberty can only maintain itself through the support of servitude? Perhaps." See also Montesquieu, *Spirit of the Laws* 15.13 and 15.15–19.

68. With Bonnette 1994, ad loc. I follow the MSS here (see the apparatus in BD); most editors and translators adopt, in place of the word "thinking" (*phronōn*), a reading found in a quotation in Stobaeus and in a marginal conjecture by the Renaissance scholar Marcus Musurus on the MS Vatican 1336: "may delight in *laboring* (*ponōn*) with a view to good hope."

69. This second employment of hunting as illustrative reminds us of the first, and what it suggested about the political life (2.1.4). As Xenophon's apologetic opening of his treatise on the subject makes plain, hunting was not a pursuit that was in good repute among gentlemen.

70. Why does Xenophon have Socrates first adduce hunting, and then apologize for doing so? Could there be a distinctive kind of Socratic "hunting," of and with good friends of a peculiar sort, that normal gentlemen are likely to view as an indulgence or even a sort of "vice"—a Socratic "hunting" activity that is far removed from "the kingly art"? See Xenophon's apologetic—and very playful—*The One Skilled in Hunting with Dogs*.

71. Epicharmus flourished in Syracuse under the same tyrant, Hiero, with whom Xenophon depicts the poet Simonides conversing in the dialogue *Hiero*; Epicharmus initiated a tradition of comedies satirizing Heracles; Galinsky 1972, 85.

72. Xenophon through his Socrates here pays a tribute to Prodicus; in this respect, as in so many others, Xenophon follows in the track of Aristophanes (*Clouds* 360–63). Dorion 2013, 242: "Prodicos est le seul sophiste, dans l'œuvre de Xénophon, qui soit qualifié de sage." But Robin (1910, 31) expresses his disconcertment "de voir, dans Xénophon, ce même Socrate, qui chez Platon combat sans cesse des sophistes, faire état pour une de ses démonstrations d'un discours de Prodicus!" See also OT chap. 6, note 46 and context. Prodicus was reputed an atheist: Diels and Kranz 1951, s.v. "Prodicus," B5; Fahr 1969, 98; Dorion 2013, 241.

73. 2.1.34; Kuntz 1994, 166; Diels and Kranz 1951, s.v. "Prodicus," B1 note: "Der Stil ist sicher xenophontisch."

74. Kuntz (1994, 168; see also 174, 179) goes so far as to say: "All of his celebrated adventures are implicitly attached to the story," and "there is a suggestion that the famous twelve labors arise out of the youthful choice described here."

75. *aporounta*; the word is used repeatedly here: 2.1.22 beg., 23 mid.; Cicero translates (*De officiis* 1.118) "secum multumque *dubitasse*."

76. 2.1.22; of the many paintings of this drama, the one that perhaps best captures Xenophon's text in its description of the contrasting looks and demeanor of Virtue and Vice is Emmanuel Benner's "Hercules between Virtue and Vice," held in a private collection and available for viewing at http://www.wikigallery.org/wiki/painting_88035/Emmanuel-Benner/Hercules-Between-Virtue-And-Vice and at https://www.facebook.com/thomas.pangle.7. Shaftesbury might protest that this exemplifies his "fear, lest the painter should overdo" the portrait of Virtue's opponent, "and express the affection too

much to the life": this figure "is of a relish far more popular, and vulgarly engaging, than that other opposed to it" (1969, 59). Shaftesbury's essay elaborates his advice for painting the scene, advice that was followed closely in the work he commissioned from Paolo di Matteis; the painting can be viewed at http://www.niceartgallery.com/Paolo-di-Matteis /The-Choice-of-Hercules-1712.html; the drawings at http://www.louvre.fr/en/oeuvre -notices/choice-hercules and at https://www.facebook.com/thomas.pangle.7.

77. As Bonnette 1994, ad loc. points out, at this point (2.1.26) Socrates ceases to speak through indirect discourse (paraphrasing Prodicus), and begins to speak through direct discourse, thus making the narrative his own, until he explicitly brings Prodicus back in at 2.1.29.

78. See *Hiero* 2.1–2 and 7.1–4. Tatum (1989, 150) assimilates the way of life offered by Vice with that of the wife of Croesus, which Croesus thinks is "the happiest of all lives, because she shares all his wealth and happiness, but not his worries or misfortunes" (*Education of Cyrus* 7.2.27–28; see also 8.7.11–12). Cicero (*De officiis* 1.118) simplifies, and thus circumscribes the complexity of, Xenophon's account by substituting "Pleasure" (*Voluptas*; see also *De natura deorum* 2.61) for Xenophon's "Vice" (*Kakia*). Cicero's simplified version is followed by Silius Italicus, Petrarch, and Coluccio Salutati, as well as Shaftesbury—even though the latter claims to be following Xenophon; but Shaftesbury is providing advice to a painter of this scene, and the demands of designing a painting (see Shaftesbury 1969, 51, 54) apparently require that the figure Vice be supplanted by the more easily visible figure of Pleasure.

79. *Hiero* 1.26–2.2. In his advice to a painter of this scene, Shaftesbury (1969, 35; also 37, 39, 40) goes so far as to speak of the need to represent Heracles in "agony, or inward conflict, which indeed makes the principal action here: as it would do in a poem, were this subject to be treated by a good poet."

80. Consider *Hiero* 2.1–2; and OT, chap. 1, para. 2. The comic refraction of this deficiency inherent in the effeminate portrayal of Vice is seen in that she is here associated with indulgence in luxuriously delicate gourmet meals with rare, expensive wines, while Xenophon remains archly silent about the gross form of gluttony in which Heracles (as well as other warrior heroes like Odysseus) was notorious for actually indulging: "Heracles also was a glutton. Almost all the poets and historians make this plain. Epicharmus, for example, says in *Busiris*: 'First, if you should see him eating you would die; / His gullet thunders inside, his jaw rattles, his molar crackles, / He wheezes, his gum and his canines gnash, / His nostrils sizzle, and he wiggles his ears!' " (Athenaeus 411a, who also quotes several other great poets; see also Athenaeus 164, as well as the grossly gluttonous role played by Heracles in Aristophanes's *Birds*). Ben Jonson highlights this dimension of the mythic Heracles in his droll masque that takes off on this scene: *Pleasure Reconciled to Virtue* (1619).

81. See OT as a whole, starting with chap. 1, para. 2. "Xenophon pays a great compliment to Hiero's education by entrusting to him the only elaborate presentation of the gentleman's view of tyranny which he ever wrote" (OT chap. 3a, note 44).

82. "While Vice had not mentioned any benefit accruing to her from Heracles' joining her, Virtue expects from it a considerable increase of her prestige" (XS 37).

83. Further simplifying with a view to painting, Shaftesbury insists that while "the historian whom we follow represents Virtue to us as a lady," in a *painting* of this scene the

two allegorical figures need to be represented as divinities, with Virtue portrayed on the model of Athena, and Pleasure on the model of Aphrodite/Venus (1969, 33, 39, 43); Shaftesbury thus draws attention to the fact that Xenophon's Socrates does *not* present Virtue as one of the Olympians, or even as a goddess; unlike "our philosophical historian," Shaftesbury says, the artist errs in going too far "to create a double meaning, or equivocal sense in painting"; "the moral part" must, "of right," in "painting be far differently treated, from what it naturally is, either in the history, or poem" (1969, 48, 52, 54–55).

84. Vice is so purely atheistic that even in referring to sexual pleasure she (unlike Virtue) does not employ the usual Greek term *ta aphrodisia*, "the things of Aphrodite" (contrast 2.1.24 with 30). Compare Simonides, in speaking of the sexual pleasures of the tyrant: *Hiero* 1.26.

85. The striking reference to acquiring wealth through cattle evokes Pindar's famous fragment 169, on how the cattle rustling of Heracles exemplifies the blurred distinction between injustice and lawful justice:

Convention/Law (*nomos*), the king of all,
Of Mortals and of Immortals,
Drives on, making the greatest violence into justice
With a high hand. I bring to witness
The deeds of Heracles: for the cattle of Geryon
To the Cyclopean gate of Eurystheus,
Without asking permission or paying, were by him driven.

86. It is this point in the drama that seems to be represented in Andrea Appiani's painting, "Hercules at the Crossroads," available for viewing at http://commons.wikime dia.org/wiki/File:Andrea_Appiani_-_Hercules_at_the_crossroads.jpg and at https://www .facebook.com/thomas.pangle.7.

87. Smith ad loc.: "Observe the elaborate antithesis in the two clauses, and note that Vice usurps the nobler word *happiness*, conceding to Virtue only *pleasures* as the reward of toil and self-denial."

88. Smith ad loc.: "That Virtue has not been previously mentioned by name is a refinement of the allegory."

89. If it is the case that the subject of Albrecht Dürer's celebrated and debated woodcut, which he entitled simply "Hercules," is correctly identified as "the choice of Heracles," then this is the moment in the drama that Dürer has chosen to portray, with comic exaggeration: Heracles has to raise his club to stop Virtue from belaboring Vice with a tree branch! The woodcut has also become popularly known as "Envy," ascribing to Virtue this passion as the psychological source of Her fury. A print is available for viewing, with useful discussion, at www.albrecht-duerer-apokalypse.de/herkules-als -hahnrei/. One is reminded of the opening stage in the debate between the Just and the Unjust Discourses presented by Socrates in Aristophanes's *Clouds*.

90. Compare Cyrus's speech on virtue, corrupting the elite of the virtuous Persian citizenry: *Education of Cyrus* 1.5.7–12; see OT 194.

91. Cf. *Hiero* 1.14–16, 5.1–2, 7.1–5.

92. OT chap. 6, note 3: "Compare *Hiero* 1.11–14 with *Memorabilia* II 1. 31: Hiero does not mention one's own virtuous actions as the most pleasant sight."

93. "In this particular part of our history," Shaftesbury counsels (1969, 42), the painter "must of necessity" portray Virtue "speaking with all the force of action, such as would appear in an excellent orator, when at the height, and in the most affecting part of his discourse," that is, "in the very heat and highest transport of speech."

94. Shaftesbury (1969, 37, 40) wants the painter to make this still more expressive, by showing in the listening hero's face that "the decision he is about to make in favour of virtue, cost him not a little"; that it "may shew itself in pity and tenderness, moved in our hero by the thought of those pleasures and companions of his youth, which he is going for ever to abandon"; "Hercules remaining still in a situation expressive of suspense and doubt, would discover nonetheless that the strength of this inward conflict was over, and that victory began now to declare herself in favour of virtue"; yet "there ought to be some hopes yet remaining for this latter goddess Pleasure, and some regret apparent in Hercules." The scholiast on Aristophanes, *Clouds* 361, summarizing the original writing of Prodicus, writes: "He made Heracles incline to Virtue, and to choose Her toils over the fleeting pleasures of Vice."

95. BD ad 2.1.33 aptly refers us to Xenophon's republican political hero Aegisilaus: "And he was always in-fearful-awe-of-the-divine (*deisidaimōn*), believing that while those who are living nobly are not yet happy, those who have died gloriously are then blessed" (*Aegisilaus* 11.8); see also Narcy 1995, 87; and the deathbed speech of Cyrus to his sons: "You must, when I shall be dead, speak and do everything about me as one who is happy. . . . In time past I thus fared even as I prayed; but fear accompanying me, lest in time to come I might either see or hear or suffer something harsh, did not allow me to think myself completely great nor to take transported delight; but now, if I shall die, I leave you living, children, whom the gods granted me to have; and I leave fatherland and friends happy—and as a consequence, how would I not, justly being blessed, obtain memory for all time? . . . Have reverence for gods and for the race of humans that comes into being in succession forever; for the gods do not hide you in obscurity, but necessarily your deeds are forever plain to all" (*Education of Cyrus* 8.7.6–9).

96. Handel's *Choice of Heracles*, #11 (Solo Virtue with Chorus): "So shalt thou gain immortal praise. / The golden trump of fame, / Its loudest notes shall raise, / And 'mid the gods enroll thy name. / So shalt thou gain immortal praise!" (drawn from a poem by Robert Lowth and adapted by Handel's librettist Thomas Morell).

97. See *The One Skilled in Hunting with Dogs* 1.3. In a diary entry of January 1759 the young John Adams stressed the overwhelming impact on him of the "choice of Heracles" in Xenophon: the passage moved him to rewrite it so as to make it apply personally to himself, while lamenting his having been "seduced into the Course of unmanly Pleasures, that Vice describes to Hercules, forgetful of the glorious Promises of Fame, Immortality, and a good Conscience, which Virtue, makes to the same Hero"; "I swear I will renounce the Contemplative, and betake myself to an active roving Life by Sea or Land, or else I will attempt some uncommon unexpected Enterprize in Law!" (Adams 1961, ms. pp. 25–26). Years later, as a member of the congressional committee charged with designing the seal of the new United States, Adams proposed Simon Gribeline's engraving of the "Choice of Heracles," which was modeled on the painting and drawings by Paolo de Matteis that were commissioned and meticulously supervised by Shaftesbury. (See letter of John to Abigail Adams, August 14, 1776, in Butterfield 1975, 156; to view Gribeline's

engraving, see Fine Arts Museums of San Francisco website: https://art.famsf.org/simon
-gribelin/hercules-rejects-pleasure-and-chooses-virtue-19633012264).

98. 4.8.11; see L. Pangle 2013, 32–33.

## CHAPTER FOUR

1. See the expression of puzzlement by Richter (1893, 89), who here, as elsewhere, and like so many nineteenth- and twentieth-century scholars, dissolves the provocations to thought, by proposing that Xenophon failed to edit his own work.

2. See Plato, *Apology* 28e; *Laches* 181b; *Crito* 56b; *Symposium* 220dff.

3. Cf. *Symposium* 1.2.10; Gray (1998, 130) alertly notes another comic dimension of this sequence: "The story of the young Heracles ends with a reference . . . to himself and his illustrious parents (*O pai tokeōn agathōn*). . . . The thought association may be mildly humorous. Heracles' father was Zeus. The father of the young man who is next introduced is Socrates himself." Could Xenophon be blasphemously suggesting that Socrates took better care of his son's education than Zeus did of his son's?

4. See esp. *Hiero* 3.7–8; Millett 1991, 113 (see also 116–18, 127–28): "From the viewpoint of comparative sociology, to say nothing of our own experience, the all-inclusive quality of Greek friendship is anomalous"—referring us to the article "Friendship" in *The International Encyclopedia of the Social Sciences*; see also Benveniste 1973, 3.4; Azoulay 2004, 327; BD ad loc.

5. 2.2.7; Lamprocles cannot of course express thanks for *his* father's expenditures upon *him*!—recall 1.3.5; indeed, we have to admire (and, if we share Xenophon's sense of humor, chuckle at) the youth's uncomplaining silence and forbearance, in this regard, as Socrates pours over him this disquisition on paternal monetary sacrifice for children.

6. Edelstein 1935, 102; BD ad loc.; consider the summary comment by Smith ad loc.

7. We recall that Xenophon had Socrates begin the second part of the *Memorabilia* by teaching that "as regards friends and strangers and the rest of life, 'to *sacrifice*, in accordance with one's capacity,' is noble advice" (1.3.3).

8. BD ad loc. comment that "one ought perhaps to be astonished at the fact that Socrates speaks with approbation of the prayers of Xanthippe, who asks of the gods numerous goods for her son, given that Socrates himself abstained, in his prayers to the gods, from asking them for any specific good whatsoever (cf. I 3, 2)."

9. Nietzsche, *Genealogy of Morals* 3.7: "A married philosopher belongs *in comedy*, this is my proposition: and that exception, Socrates—the roguish Socrates, it would appear, married *ironically*, precisely in order to demonstrate *this* proposition."

10. Diogenes Laertius 2.29 says that Socrates "turned his son Lamprocles from being angry at his mother, as Xenophon has said somewhere."

11. Contrast the deathbed speech of Cyrus: *Education of Cyrus* 8.7.14–16.

12. XS 46: Whereas "reference to the gods or the god occurred as a matter of course in the section on relatives," there is only a single passage (2.6.8) in the section on friends beyond the family "where the gods or the god are mentioned" (disregarding the profane oaths). What is more, "piety is not mentioned among the qualities which a man desirable as a friend must possess" (2.6.1–5).

13. Compare *Hiero* 3.7–8: "Surely the strongest friendships (*philiai*) are opined to be

of parents toward children and children toward parents and brothers toward brothers and wives toward husbands and comrades toward comrades." XS 42: for Socrates, "blood relations, as distinguished from friends, are 'the necessary ones' (II.1.14); they are not freely chosen." See also OT chap. 6, note 26, referring us to *Anabasis* 7.7.29, where "necessity" is opposed to "friendship."

14. For the connotations of the Greek terms *chrēstos* and *ktēma*, see Redard 1953, 89–90, 98; Azoulay 2004, 288–89; Danzig 2010, 176; BD ad 2.4.1 and 2.4.5.

15. In political life, of course, the ruler, who seeks to be loved by the mass of mankind, needs to guide himself to some extent by this uncritical vision of the good friend, since this is the vision that will be held by those over whom he rules—as Cambyses teaches Cyrus (*Education of Cyrus* 1.6.24); Xenophon teaches through the *Education of Cyrus* as a whole that the powerfully successful ruler who enters uncritically into this vision winds up creating a world of servitude for everyone.

16. Gigon 1956, 121; XS 44, 46, 65; BD ad loc.

17. The oddity is further highlighted by the corresponding oddity in the way Xenophon introduces the next episode: he says that he "once heard him give also another *speech*"; but what follows is a *dialogue*!

18. In saying that "Critobule est singulièrement dépourvu d'*engkrateia*" and has "désespérément besoin d'amis authentiques" BD (ad 2.6.1) are a bit moralistically extreme, sounding somewhat like the ponderously censorious and humorless Hermogenes in *Symposium* 4.23.

19. See BD ad 2.6.1, who refer us to the quotation from Aeschines in Athenaeus 220a.

20. The serious target and in a sense addressee of this preeminent Socratic discourse, presented in the *Oeconomicus*, is the onlooker and reporter Xenophon, and others like him. As is acutely remarked by BD 1: CLXXXV, "One of the principal ways in which the *Memorabilia* is original, in comparison with the dialogues of Plato, is that the principal beneficiaries are often the listeners, and not the interlocutors of Socrates." See also 1: CXLVII–CXLVIII.

21. For the first time in the *Memorabilia*, Socrates (joining Critobulus) repeatedly uses profane expletives in this especially lighthearted and somewhat rakish conversation.

22. XS 46–47: here, in seeking a friend for Critobulus, "reasonableness (*phronesis*) or an equivalent is not mentioned among the qualities of a potential friend as he should be, although this quality is indispensable in a friend according to Socrates (1.2.52–53)."

23. Xenophon's short treatise *On Horsemanship* shows that he, unlike Socrates, was an expert in this activity.

24. XS 46: "Kritoboulos would regard the gods' ambiguous silence as unambiguous approval."

25. Plato, *Symposium* 216a-b. Commentators stress that traditionally the Sirens and their singing were regarded as a corrupting menace (see esp. the scholiast on *Odyssey* 12.39 in W. Dindorf 1855, 531; also Gigon 1956, 136); BD ad loc. go so far as to suggest an association here of the Sirens and their song with Vice and Her voluptuousness, as presented in the earlier dialogue with Aristippus.

26. The perfect gentleman in the *Oeconomicus* teaches that rule culminates in monarchy—in sharp contrast to tyranny (see esp. the closing chap. 21). Consider Plutarch's classic and deeply ambiguous account (*Pelopidas* 4.1–3) of the paragon of noble friendship

achieved between Pelopidas and Epaminondas, the pair of statesmen-generals who led Thebes to its acme: "Those who have intelligence will consider nothing to be so great as the goodwill and friendship which they maintained from the start until the end. . . . For if one regards the regime activity of Aristides and Themistocles, and Cimon and Pericles, and Nicias and Alcibiades, filled with so many mutual dissensions, and envying, and jealousies, and then looks again at the honor and favor that Pelopidas evinced for Epaminondas, he will correctly and justly proclaim that not those others, but these two, were the fellow rulers and fellow generals—who *ceaselessly struggled in competition more to get the better of one another than of their enemies.* And the true cause was their *virtue*, on account of which they did not aim, in their activities, at reputation or wealth, which naturally induce harsh and strife-ridden envy, but were both impassioned from the beginning with a divine *eros* to see the fatherland become most shining and greatest through themselves, and indeed treated their successes in this regard as personal (*idiois*)." See also Aristotle, *Nicomachean Ethics* 1162b6–13; for a penetrating analysis of the underlying problem, see L. Pangle 2003, 123ff.

27. See similarly Plato, *Laws* 678c; Aristotle, *Politics* 1278b18–20; Cicero, *Republic* 1.39–41 and *De finibus* 2.78, 109–10.

28. If it were not for the silence on divinity throughout the sections on extrafamilial friendship, this personifying expression could well be taken to refer to the divinity Philia, finding Her way through the obstacle course posed by human nature; here, once again, the silence on divinity in these sections is quietly brought to our attention. The extrafamilial friendship that Xenophon's Socrates promotes does not rely on, is independent of, divinity and providence.

29. BD ad loc. express (politically naive) shock at the "*assez mesquin*" character of this reasoning. As a matter of fact, it is by contrasting this reasoning with that of Machiavelli that the most important difference between the political theories of Xenophon and Machiavelli comes to sight.

30. Gigon 1956, 149–51; BD ad loc.

31. Contrast *Symposium* 4.27–28 and context (cf. XS 156).

32. BD ad loc.: "It is indeed remarkable that Socrates does not condemn kissing, in this passage, for reasons eminently moral," but "rather out of care for amorous efficaciousness." See also Gigon 1956, 153.

33. Critobulus would seem to be an all-around incompetent—and even laughably so when it comes to household management and care for property. Consider the light this sheds on the (comic) drama of the *Oeconomicus* (XS 51).

34. BD ad loc.: "The conclusion of this encounter is remarkable in that it constitutes one of the rare cases" where "one knows what is the reaction of the interlocutor." But BD add erroneously that of "the forty encounters reported in the *Memorabilia*, there are only three where Xenophon indicates how the interlocutor of Socrates reacts to the discourse" (the other cases BD refer to are 2.10.6 and 4.2.39–40; they overlook the very next encounter, as well as 2.9).

35. Here and in the *Oeconomicus* Xenophon and his Socrates treat the themes of friendship and economics together; as Socrates leads Critobulus to see, friends are a major part of one's "wealth," or "property"—in that term's wide range of meaning (*Oeconomicus* 1.15; XSD 91, 101–5).

36. Proust (1971, 297) has a character of his, who loves Xenophon, say of this tableau: "Never again will there be such writing. It is perfectly simple and nevertheless everything is said. That was an age when one did not develop ideas, one presented them, without laboring them, without making all that they contained become explicit."

37. See BD ad loc.; and *Hellenica* 2.3–4; Nails (2002, 46) specifies the date as 404. The specific circumstances that would likely have impoverished this friend, despite his extensive holdings, are succinctly explained by Mossé (1999, 224). The name Aristarchus, a rather common one (Fraser and Matthews 1987–2013, s.v.), means "best at ruling"; this particular Aristarchus would seem to be otherwise unknown: the prominent figure with this name was probably executed as a "destroyer of the democracy" in 406 (*Hellenica* 1.2, 1.7.28, 2.3.46; and Nails 2002, 46–47).

38. "Un véritable atelier de fabrication de vêtements . . . un véritable atelier artisanale" (Mossé 1999, 225, 227).

39. The singularity of this is marked by Mossé (1999, 225): "Nous ne connaisons d'exemples d'emprunts à finalité 'economique' que dans le monde du commerce maritime." Figueira (2012, 670) suggests "relatively advanced managerial ideation" in that Xenophon presents Aristarchus with "two levels of willingness to borrow: he is reluctant to borrow for subsistence without the reasonable expectation of being able to repay, but does indeed borrow for the raw material."

40. Mossé 1999, 226–27 points out the distinction between the unheard-of Socratic transformation and the much less radical, though unconventional, measures to which free Athenian women had to resort after the defeat in the Peloponnesian War according to Demosthenes's *Against Euboulides*.

41. Aristarchus swears three of his oaths by Zeus: in each case he uses the oath to emphasize the difference between slaves and his free relatives (Shulsky, forthcoming), indicating his slightly scandalized surprise at Socrates's line of advice, to replace slave labor by the work of free women within the home.

42. XSD 203: "Karl Marx speaks of Xenophon's 'characteristic bourgeois instinct'" (*Capital*, pt. 1, chap. 14 near the end).

43. XSD 204; in *Spirit of the Laws* bk. 20 (the book on commerce and commercialism), Xenophon is the sole classical philosopher whom Montesquieu praises. Consider also Doty 2003 and Jansen 2007, though they focus narrowly on Xenophon's *Ways and Means*.

44. The financially ruined old "comrade" (*archaion hetairon*) makes emphatic (2.8.1) his proud refusal to ask anyone for a handout or even a loan (since he has no collateral). This would explain why Socrates does not make any attempt to introduce some other Socratic associate who might loan some funds. See also BD ad 2.7.1, n10 end.

45. There are no other attestations of this name in classical Attica or Greece, though there are a couple in Asia Minor (Fraser and Matthews 1987–2013, s.v.). BD remark ad 2.7.6, in regard to otherwise unfamiliar names in these tragicomedic incidents, "It is possible that Xenophon has borrowed these names in the fashion of comedy, where evocative names are particularly frequent." See also Azoulay 2004, 293n74. In the *Anabasis*, Xenophon is quite freewheeling in his comic playfulness with names: Buzzetti 2014, 21–26.

46. Recall 2.1.8–9. With rather amazing political naiveté, BD protest ad loc.: "The politician disposes of the power by himself alone, and receives orders from no other person, while in contrast the supervisor is at the same time governor and governed."

47. We note that Xenophon here presents Socrates as having given considerable em-
pathetic thought to the conditions of hired day labor. Has Socrates had to contemplate
supporting himself by such employment?

48. The reading of the major MS A (Paris 1302); see the apparatus of BD ad loc.

49. For an authoritative, succinct account of the living conditions in Athens at this
time, see B. Strauss 1987, 42–69.

50. Pace Gigon 1956, ad loc.; see BD ad 2.7.2 and 2.8.1; Delebecque 1957, 230; Mossé
1999, 224; Nails 2002, 46.

51. *Oeconomicus* 20.15; see similarly Xenophon himself, in *The Skilled Cavalry
Commander* 8.8: "One must either work or be nourished from what others have worked
on. Otherwise, it is not at all easy either to stay alive or to obtain peace." Is Socrates a
*voyou*? See Queneau 1951; Souchier 1992; Kojève 2013, 155; cf. Aristophanes, *Clouds*
177–79. See also Gigon 1953, 101.

52. XSD 103; see also Diogenes Laertius 2.121, and BD ad 2.9, n5. In *Oeconomicus*
2.3 Socrates estimates Critobulus's household worth as being about 100 times that of
Socrates; in Plato's *Apology* (33a), Critobulus is among those who offer to pay a substantial fine for Socrates.

53. "Ruler in/of the *Demos*" (a common name, and not only in Attica; Fraser and
Matthews 1987–2013, s.v.): could this possibly be the same Archedemos whom Xenophon
describes in the *Hellenica* (1.7.2) as the leader of the *dēmos* at the time of the trial of the
admirals after the battle of Arginusae, a year or more before the present conversation?
(The possibility shocks some commentators who notice it: BD ad loc.—*that particular*
Archedemos could have been a friend of Socrates?!—XS 54.)

54. Some shocked conventional commentators have gone so far as to ask, "L'écrivain
présenterait-il dès lors, entre les lignes, un Socrate plein d'ironie, proposant à son ami
d'utiliser cyniquement un sycophante pour éloigner d'autres sycophantes?" (Azoulay 2004,
295; see also 297: "une grossière stratégie").

55. Fraser and Matthews 1987–2013, s.v.; BD ad loc. refer us to Nails 2002, 126;
Giannantoni 1990, VI B 54; and Azoulay 2004, 293n74, who remarks: "The name has
resonances oddly well-suited to the role Xenophon gives him in the dialogue—without
one being able to know if this is a deliberate play on the part of the author."

CHAPTER FIVE

1. BD ad 3.10.6; Maier 1913, 306; Azoulay 2004, 289.

2. Commentators who notice the "roguish" practical joke are shocked: Delatte 1933,
10, 13; BD ad loc.

3. XS 56–57; see also OT chap. 3a, note 32: "From Xenophon's point of view, the wise
teacher of the royal art" is "not a potential ruler in the ordinary sense of the term, because
he who knows how to rule does not necessarily wish to rule." Recall 2.1.9–10 and 2.8.5. The
playful exaggeration in Socrates's stress on knowledge, allowing it to eclipse the requirements of hard labor and practice, as well as the need to display to the ruled "that one is better then they are, in doing everything one exhorts and advises them to do," is corrected by
Xenophon's *Skilled Cavalry Commander*, esp. 6.4 and 9.2: "Of all these reminders it seems
to me the best is this: take care that everything one knows to be good gets done. Things that

are correctly known do not bear fruit in farming, managing a ship, or ruling, unless someone takes care that they are also carried out thoroughly." See Ambler, forthcoming.

4. 3.1.6; the piling up here of adjectives ending in -*ikos* (signifying expertise) echoes Aristophanean comedy: see Peppler 1910.

5. BD comment ad loc.: "One can legitimately be astonished at the fact that Socrates openly recognizes that a good general ought to practice several vices. The obligation that he finds himself under to practice these vices is clearly explicated in the parallel passage in the *Education of Cyrus*" (i.e., 1.6.27–28). See Machiavelli's most prominent, grateful acknowledgments of being a student of Xenophon: *The Prince*, chaps. 14–15, as well as *Discourses on the First Ten Books of Titus Livy* 2.13; see also XS 57.

6. XS 58; see Cicero, *Orator* 50 and *De Oratore* 2.314.

7. 3.1.11: the consensus reading of the set of related MSS designated Φ; BD accept the reading "leading" (*agein*) instead of "speaking" (*legein*) found in the major MS B (Paris 1740) as well as in a marginal notation (by a later hand, it appears to me) on Laur. LXXX.13 (the text itself reads "speaking") and in a quotation in Stobaeus.

8. BD ad loc.; Richter 1893, 112–18; Maier 1913, 32; Arnim 1923, 186–91; Delatte 1933, 7–25; H.-R. Breitenbach 1967, col. 1805; Gera 1993, 61–64.

9. According to the somewhat playful Socratic principle that truly knowing general-ship makes one the true general, we may say that if Socrates "possessed the knowledge which a general *needs*, he was a general"—"without ever having learned generalship"; and "without even having desired to be a general," as well as "without ever practicing generalship" (XS 58, my italics). The episodes that now follow help us to understand the full significance of this jesting. See also L. Strauss 1939, 536..

10. For important contributions, see Newell 1983; Bruell 1987; Ambler 2001, "Intro-duction"; Nadon 2001; Bartlett 2015; L. Pangle 2015, 2017.

11. This and the following episodes thus show Socrates pursuing his "What is . . ." questions, though in an oblique and mediated manner.

12. With BD, Hude 1934, and Marchant 1921, I follow MSS other than the leading one—B (Paris 1740)—which has a slightly but significantly different reading (*monou* instead of *monon*) meaning "not if he presided nobly over his own life alone." Bonnette 1994, ad loc. accepts this reading from B, without explanation, but probably following L. Strauss (XS 59) who paraphrases, "with a view, not to the happiness of himself alone," and who interprets Socrates as concluding "at the end" that "the good leader forgets his own happiness," adding that "the final silence on the happiness of the general cor-responds to the silence on his knowledge," and then going so far as to say: "The final silence corresponds also to the silence on the bliss of Socrates's hearers as distinguished from the bliss of Socrates himself (I.6.14)."

13. See *Hiero* 11.5–7: a tyrant, if he were to follow the advice of a wise poet, might aspire to make the city he leads the "happiest," and, through succeeding, become "victo-rious in the most noble and magnificent contest among human beings" (OT chap. 4, note 37 and context; contrast, however, XS 59; and see the even greater contrast with Lorch 2010, 196). The virtue of a good (monarchic—recall 1.2.58) leader as taught by Homer, inter-preted by Socrates, makes no reference to law; contrast the next episode: 3.3.11.

14. Recall that in the list of the "What is . . ." questions that constitute the agenda of Socrates's preoccupation with "the human things," the question "What is noble/beautiful?"

comes immediately after the lead questions, "What is pious, what impious?" (1.1.16). For the centrality of the question "What is noble/beautiful?" to the commencement of Socratic dialectics in Xenophon, see *Oeconomicus* 6.13–17 and 11.1–7; in Plato, see *Phaedo* 100b and *Republic* 538d. See also Nietzsche's *Beyond Good and Evil*, final chap.

15. Unlike Xenophon, Socrates does not, however, speak as someone who has much personal experience with horses, and does not make that experience the proof of his knowledgeable authority in the art generally (see *The Skilled Cavalry Commander* 1.16 and above all 5.4).

16. Maier 1913, 32; Delebecque 1973, 10; BD ad 3.3.1.

17. Lorch 2010, 199: "Socrates leads the cavalry commander to realize that he wants not merely to receive honor, but to earn it by performing valuable services for Athens."

18. Xenophon's own treatise begins altogether differently, laying down as the first essential the securing of the favor of the gods through making sacrifices: *The Skilled Cavalry Commander* 1.1. Socrates's silence on this essential is underlined by his profane expletive invoking Zeus.

19. This question Xenophon himself does not explicitly answer, or even raise, in his *Skilled Cavalry Commander* (see esp. 1.24 and consider 5.4ff.); he treats it implicitly, however, in his repeated grappling with the challenge of instilling obedience, especially in the face of mortal danger; and he points to a kind of answer by repeatedly enjoining religious worship and piety as a duty of the commander, while exhibiting his own piety, indicating that this is a key virtue of one seriously teaching the art (3.1, 3.2, 3.4, 5.11, 5.14, 6.1, 6.6, 7.1, 7.3, 7.4, 7.14, 9.3, and last but not least, 9.7–9: "If someone is surprised at how often the writing has referred to working with god, let him know well, that when he is often in danger his surprise will diminish"). Divinity fills the gap left gaping by Socrates in his theoretical and hence rather playful "teaching" here of the art of command (consider the opening of the first speech of Xenophon as he takes over command of the Ten Thousand: *Anabasis* 3.2.8–10). See Ambler, forthcoming.

20. "I.e. what one is impelled by his own taste to learn"; Smith ad loc.

21. 3.3.11. As noted before, Socrates taught that from "examining the most important matters, and having distinguished them according to their kinds, through dialogues," men "become best, and most hegemonical/artful-at-leading" (*hēgemonikōtetous*, 4.5.12; see also 3.7.4 and 4.6.15).

22. For the meaning of this term, unfortunately misdefined in Liddell and Scott 1953 (a mistake that remains uncorrected in the 1996 Supplement, despite having been pointed out by scholars), and almost always mistranslated, see the lexicons of Harpocration and of Suidas; Andocides 4.62; Aristotle, *Athenian Constitution* 60.3; Athenaeus 565f; and BD ad loc.; as well as H. Sauppe 1896, 220–21 and Crowther 1985. In the parallel passage in *The Skilled Cavalry Commander* (1.26), Xenophon speaks of the emulation seen in Athenian choruses, but of course does not adduce the male beauty contests—for *The Skilled Cavalry Commander* is a more serious, or at least a much less comical, work than the *Memorabilia*.

23. Xenophon devotes the third chapter of his treatise on the skilled cavalry commander to elaborating innovative cavalry processions and evolutions at major religious festivals, the choreographing and leading of which he makes a major duty of the skilled commander.

24. The Greek (*dia* plus the accusative) can also mean "for the sake of" (as at, e.g., 3.6.1); was this alternative meaning noticed by our young cavalry commander?

25. This question is implicitly posed by *The Skilled Cavalry Commander* 8.7–8. Recall the peroration of Virtue in Her victory over Vice.

26. There is no other attestation to this name in classical Attica, though there are numerous attestations to the kindred "Nicomachus" or "Victorious Fighter" (Fraser and Matthews 1987–2013, s.v.). This particular Nicomachides is unknown beyond this vignette.

27. A common Attic name, meaning "Defensive Strength": this particular "Antisthenes" is otherwise unknown (Nails 2002, 35, refuting Delatte [1933, 48], who had already pointed out the implausibility of Joël's [1893–1901, 2.1: 1074] identification of this wealthy Antisthenes as identical to the follower of Socrates who has that name). This may be another example of Xenophon imitating comedy by employing appropriate names for fictional characters.

28. BD ad loc. correctly observe that Antisthenes "is the sole politician, elected or aspiring to get himself elected, whose competence Socrates recognizes."

29. Given the importance here of this term, I have to remark that Bonnette 1994, ad loc. notes that the MSS have at this point the spelling *philoneikos* rather than *philonikos*—which latter is added in a suprascript by the original hand in the best MS, "B" (Paris 1740), and as a marginal variant in the MS Laurentian LXXX.13; Bonnette translates "lover of victory," and says that *philoneikos* has a different meaning: "lover of contention." But Liddell and Scott (1953, s.v.), in a lengthy entry, characterize *philoneikos* as merely an alternate form for *philonikos* ("In codd. the forms occur without any distinction of meaning"), and define the single word, with its two forms or spellings, as meaning both "love of victory" and "love of contention." They adduce MSS readings of Pindar, Plato, Thucydides, Lysias, Aristotle, and Isocrates, as well as Xenophon, *Hellenica* 3.16.

30. The incredulity has lasted down through the ages: the gentleman-commentator Sir Alexander Grant exclaims (1871, 111): "The paradox here is so great that we can hardly help disbelieving that the conversation actually took place."

31. Plato is more reserved than Xenophon, and assigns this conception most prominently to his Eleatic Stranger (*Statesman* 258e-259d5); Plato has his Socrates briefly indicate this conception of rule in such places as *Charmides* 171e, 172d, *Symposium* 209a-b, and *Lovers* 138c. This is the conception of statesmanship and of the political that Aristotle launches his *Politics* by attacking as ignoble (for an analysis, see T. Pangle 2013, chap. 1).

32. The veteran was disgusted with the electoral outcome and with the Athenians as electors, while Socrates defended at least the former.

33. This appears supererogatory: Socrates asked this as a question, and the veteran's affirmative answer was notably less emphatic than his previous affirmative responses; consider *Hiero*, esp. 11.12 and context.

34. It was very common for Greek generals to die in battle: in the words of Hanson (1996, 603), "in defeat," the generals in Greek phalanx warfare "normally perished." For instance, the general Tolmides died in the battle at Lebedeia, and the general Hippocrates died in the battle at Delium (in which Socrates himself fought)—both of which defeats, and dying generals, are mentioned prominently in the next dialogue (3.5.4).

35. See esp. *Anabasis* 1.6.7, 1.9.8, 2.5.13 and 3.2.23; Gomperz 1902, 50–52; to understand the further implications of the linkage Xenophon makes between Socrates and the Mysians, see Buzzetti 2008, 3–5.

36. In this conversation no mention is made of the predominant institutions in the Athenian democracy (cf. Johnson 2003, 271): the popular assemblies and juries—who within a short time after this conversation would murder Pericles, over the protests of Socrates (*Hellenica* 1.5.16, 1.6.24–38, 1.7.1–35), and then, a few years later, would murder Socrates.

37. Compare L. Strauss's suggestion as to the true, very limited, practical purpose of the dialogue Xenophon depicts Simonides conducting with Hiero: "The more specific advice—the giving of which may have been *the only purpose* of Simonides starting a conversation with Hiero" is "that a tyrant should not compete with private men in chariot races and the like, but rather should take care that the greatest number of competitors come from his city" (OT, chap 3b end; see the context).

38. With Bonnette 1994, ad loc. I follow the reading of the MSS; other editors have adopted an unnecessary emendation of Weiske (1802, 358): "athletes" instead of "others"; Weiske judges "others," the reading of the MSS, "*obscure et inepta*," but his inept emendation obscures the political point Socrates is making.

39. 3.5.5–6; see similarly Montesquieu, *Spirit of the Laws* 8.5.

40. 3.6.1. François Andrieux (1818, 214–16) made this conversation into a poem, ending: "Glaucon sut se connaitre; / Il devint raisonnable; et, depuis ce jour-là,/ Il écouta, dit-on, bien plus qu'il ne parla." The poet, seeking to make the conversation applicable to contemporary French politics of his time, evidently felt the need to make the episode seem more serious; he changed Glaucon's age to thirty and turned him into an experienced orator.

41. The only mention of Plato in Xenophon's writings (Smith ad loc.).

42. In this connection, we observe that Socrates makes no appeal to piety in this exhortation, and the divine is never mentioned. Charmides for his part appeals to what "is implanted by nature in humans" (3.7.5; Xenophon employed almost the same term in his own name at 1.2.23).

43. BD ad loc. judge that "certes, cette façon de voir heurte nos sensibilités modernes."

44. Smith ad loc.: Charmides is "a man who is thoroughly acquainted with public affairs," and who "has not hesitated in private to give advice which was accepted by the most experienced statesmen"; contrast XS 72–73.

45. 3.7.3: "nobly advises" vs. "correctly censures"; Socrates hints that Charmides's knowledge of the pitfalls or errors of politicians has somewhat more validity than his "fine" positive projects, which Socrates has indicated are aimed at the city's "increase" or "enlargement" (3.7.2); the ambiguity, not to say dubiousness, of the latter goal has become evident from Socrates's treatment of the great Pericles in the previous conversation.

46. With a few exceptions (Narcy 2004, 223–26; 2008, esp. 250), conventional scholars have been bewildered by Xenophon's sinuous ordering of the episodes here, and have been led to blame the structure of book 3 as incoherent: BD ad loc. and 1: CCXXIV–CCXXVIII; Edelstein 1935, 115.

47. For what is known of the life and writings of Aristippus, see Diogenes Laertius 2.65–85; Mannebach 1961; Giannantoni 1990 IV A; Nails 2002, 50–51; Plato puts him among the followers of Socrates at the time of the *Phaedo* (59c).

48. Burnet 1924, 133: Xenophon "certainly read up the Socratic dialogues of Plato before writing the *Memorabilia*."

49. Rossetti 2008, 116n; see also Hartman 1887, 142; Narcy 1995; Johnson (2009, 205, 215–16) characterizes Socrates here as "choosing to avoid Aristippus' question by means of Protagorean relativism," referring us to Plato's *Protagoras* 334a-c.

50. Contrast Socrates's accounts of the noble and the good at *Oeconomicus* 6.12–7.3 and 11.3–8; Aristotle's gentleman of greatness of soul prefers to possess beautiful but useless things (*Nicomachean Ethics* 1125a11).

51. BD ad loc., following Delatte (1933, 96), refer us to Socrates's boast and then defeat in the beauty contest in the *Symposium*, chap. 5.

52. Socrates says not a word about a house's "magnificence" (*megaloprepeia*), the quality that the wise poet Simonides, in dialogue with a tyrant, says makes tyrants' houses envied by most people: *Hiero* 2.2. The cultivation and achievement of magnificence, in housing as well as in other matters, is a major moral virtue of the serious gentleman according to Aristotle's *Ethics* (1122a17ff.)

53. Consider XS 77b–78t. Following Delatte (1933, 102–4), BD ad loc. remark that Socrates uses the word "pleasant" here seven times. We add that the central occurrence is when Socrates speaks of the pleasure enjoyed by the dweller "himself." In striking and subtly comical contrast to this Socratic emphasis on the criterion of pleasure is what Ischomachus taught Socrates to be the gentlemanly criteria for a well-built house (*Oeconomicus* 9.2–5; cf. Johnson 2009, 218): the gentleman's primary stress is on the fact that "the rooms of the house have been constructed with a view to this very thing—that they would be the most advantageous containers for the items that are to be in them"; first and foremost, "the bedroom, being secure, calls to it the most valuable items"; then "the dry rooms, the grain; the cool rooms, the wine," etc. Unlike Socrates, the gentleman also stresses that the house is well designed to *prevent* sexual pleasure through intercourse among the slaves. The gentleman does not mention pleasure as a criterion for good house design, though he points out that "the rooms for the daily use of humans [i.e., especially household slaves at their work] are beautifully designed to be cool in summer and warm in winter." We observe that Xenophon himself differs (characteristically) from both the gentleman and Socrates in stressing the essential importance of a house's lowly foundations (*themelioi*): "There would be no benefit from a house if the parts above were very beautiful, but the foundations were not as they should be" (*On Horsemanship* 1.2).

54. See Heidegger, *Nietzsche*, vol. 1, "Six Fundamental Facts from the History of the Aesthetic," including esp. the references to Hegel's Lectures on Aesthetics.

55. XS 76, referring us to II.2.3; III.5.28; II.6.30 [there is a typographical error in the L. Strauss text at this point, which reads Roman numeral III]; *Oeconomicus* VI.15–16, VII.15, VIII.18–20. Of unrivaled importance is *Oeconomicus* 6.15–16 and the context. See also *Apology* 29, 34 and *On Horsemanship* 10.17, 11.6–12.

56. See similarly Plato, *Phaedo* 100 and *Republic* 538c-d.

57. XS 78; conventional scholars with the exception of Narcy (2004, 223) have made heavy weather that obscures rather than illuminates Xenophon's artful ordering of these chapters: BD ad loc. and 1: CCIV n1, CCXXVIII–CCXXXI; Hartman 1887, 144–45; Delatte 1933, 173; Edelstein 1935, 115; Erbse 1961, 280–83; Gray 1998, 142–43.

58. The weightiness of the teachings of Socrates that now follow precludes Xenophon's permitting any profane oaths to be heard.

59. Recall Xenophon's rejoinder to "many" among "those claiming to philosophize" (1.2.19–23), and our analysis in chapter 2 above.

60. XS 78; courage is not included among the virtues that Xenophon, in his closing eulogy, attributes to the wise Socrates: 4.8.11 (XS 126).

61. Scythians and Thracians: these are "often cited by Greek writers as examples of half-savage daring" (Smith ad loc.); see also Hartman 1887, 144–45.

62. Delatte 1933, 124: "Le fou, aux yeux de Socrate, court les rues, les hommes qui se connaissent eux-mêmes étant très rares." The common or sub-Socratic conception of madness "s'applique à un tout autre domaine que le domaine moral, qui est propre à la conception socratique."

63. "Invidiae definitionem hic inseri nemo, ut opinor, non miretur" (Hartman 1887, 145).

64. The leading MS B (Paris 1740) reads "always" (aei); the set of MSS designated Φ reads "ought to" (dei).

65. XS 80; Education of Cyrus 3.1.38–39; Apology 20; Hartman 1887, 129; Buzzetti 2014, 116–18.

66. "Absurdius etiam est, quod ab invidia ad otium transitur" (Hartman 1887, 145).

67. Leaving open the possibility of election by fellow knowers of ruling, i.e., a true aristocracy.

68. Note that here, in "the explicit definition of rule," the "term 'wisdom' is studiously avoided" (OT chap. 5, note 37).

69. Cf. Plato, Statesman 259a-b; for rare exceptions, see Anabasis 2.2.5; Education of Cyrus 1.1.2–3; Oeconomicus 21.5; BD ad loc.

70. Cf. Vlastos 1983, 502 and 510; Narcy 1995, 76; BD ad loc.

71. Consider the Hiero as a whole, and especially the tyrant's "polite silence" at the end (OT chap. 3b, note 78 and context; contrast Luccioni 1953, 159).

72. OT chap. 4, note 47 and context; L. Strauss quotes Edmund Burke (1884, 39), identifying "tyranny" as "the unwise or unwarrantable use" of powers "which are most legal," in contradistinction to "usurpation" as "the assumption of unlawful powers."

73. Consider the Hiero as a whole and esp. 11.10–11; see OT chap. 4, notes 47 and 50 and context; and Richter 1893, 107, on the precisely Socratic character of Simonides's advice to the tyrant ("genau die des Sokrates"); XS 82.

74. BD ad loc. remark that "one may be astonished that Socrates establishes this opposition."

75. Ischomachus taught Socrates that the gods "grant only to some of the prudent and diligent to be happy, and not to others"; the contradiction between this teaching of Ischomachus in the Oeconomicus (11.8) and Socrates's thesis here is highlighted by Delatte (1933, 128–30), H.-R. Breitenbach (1967, col. 1815.33), and BD ad loc.—the last of whom refer us back also to 1.1.7–9 (see also XS 83).

76. "Above all things, it was a boast with him that he had sprung from the lineage of Apollo, and that he had painted his Hercules, a picture now at Lindos, just as he had often seen Him in his sleep (qualem sese in quiete vidisset)" (Pliny the Elder's history of Greek painters, in Natural History 35.36.71). Similarly Athenaeus 12.62, 543f-544a: Parrhasius

"said, speaking of a miracle (*terateuomenos*), that when he was painting the Heracles that is in Lindos, the god, appearing to him, gave to Himself that form best adapted for being painted; on which account he inscribed on the picture: 'In the form in which He appeared, as He often at night visited/Parrhasius in his sleep—so He is to be seen here.'" For the general importance and significance of Parrhasius, see Brunn 1889, 2: 66–82, 84, 121–23, 125–26, 183–84; W. Klein 1905, 2: 174–82; Pfuhl 1923, 2: 689–95; Bianchi-Bandinelli 1943, 59–76; Rumpf 1951.

77. Rumpf 1951, 7: "Brunn [1889] was quite right in saying that Socrates showed a fine knowledge of the artist by directing the discussion to that point in which the artist's chief strength lay." Rumpf's article includes sketches (from Zervos 1934, nos. 300–302) of vase paintings that Rumpf speculates are from Parrhasius and that were judged by Winckelmann to be worthy of Raphael. Of a pair of the figures, Rumpf writes (7): "If one reads the famous passage in Xenophon's *Memorabilia*, it seems to be a contemporary's explanation of our two *lekythoi*. They really do represent the 'character of the soul,' and in fact 'imitate it in the eyes.' One youth is *skuthrōpos*, the other *phaidros*, one with magnificance, the other prudence." Grant (1871, 115) complains of the presumption of Socrates: "The teacher seems to have been a little carried away by the lust of giving advice, when he lectured these artists." Brancacci (2004, 204) finds this to be part (along with the *Symposium*) of what he most felicitously expresses as "une réponse raffinée, gaie et subtile à la représentation de Socrate par Aristophane, une réponse qui n'est ni hargneuse ni hostile, mais légère dans le ton comme dans le contenu."

78. XS 84; Delatte (1933, 140) points out that according to Pliny (*Natural History* 35.36.71), Parrhasius painted smaller pictures of a prurient nature (*pinxit et minoribus tabellis libidines*); and Suetonius (*Tiberius* 44) reports that Tiberius kept one of them hanging in his bedchamber.

79. So Fouillée 1874, 2: 190; Jaeger 1943, 2: 45–46; and Sörbom 1966, 90–91; see also Rouveret 1989, 133; and Brunn 1889, 2: 74; contrast Delatte 1933, 138; Rumpf 1951, 7; Preisshofen 1974; BD ad loc.

80. Consider the association of magnificence with manliness or courage in Plato, *Laws* 802e, as well as 709e, 710c, 795e, 837c; also *Republic* 490c, 494b, 536a. We are compelled to note, however, that our impish Xenophon ascribes the virtue of magnificence to outstanding horses, but never to Socrates: *On Horsemanship* 10–11; cf. *Oeconomicus* 11.3–4.

81. Consider Machiavelli's *Prince*, chaps. 15–16, where liberality substitutes for justice in a purported complete list of the virtues or "things men praise."

82. Though consider "Julian the Apostate Presiding at a Conference of Sectarians," by Edward Armitage, available for viewing at https://commons.wikimedia.org/wiki/File:Edward_Armitage_-_Julian_the_Apostate_presiding_at_a_conference_of_sectarian_-_1875.jpg and at https://www.facebook.com/thomas.pangle.7.

83. One might suggest, as candidates, not only Rembrandt's mature and elderly self-portraits but above all his "Aristotle Contemplating a Bust of Homer," available for viewing at https://en.wikipedia.org/wiki/Aristotle_with_a_Bust_of_Homer.

84. XS 84t. Recall Shaftesbury's stress (1969, 48, 52, 54–55) on the limitations of painting, in his advice for portraying Xenophon's contest between Virtue and Vice for the soul of Heracles. Erasmus says (*Apophthegmata* 3.70) that Socrates once "said to a boy: 'So speak (he said), lad, so that I may see you' (*loquere igitur, inquit, adolescans, ut te*

*videam*): thus signifying that the character of a human being (*ingenium hominis*) comes to light not so much in the countenance as in the speech, because the latter is most certain."

85. The name Cleiton means "Fame, Glory": a rare name (only two other attestations in Fraser and Matthews 1987–2013, s.v.; Fraser and Matthews fail, however, to list this instance, which is also missing from Osborne and Byrne 1996); Nails 2002, 102; commentators are baffled by the contrast between the famous painter and the unknown sculptor: see BD ad loc.; and esp. Brancacci 1995.

86. Following the MSS, with Sörbom 1966, 87, against most editors and translators.

87. So conspicuous is the absence that most recent editors and translators (but not Watson 1854, Levien 1872, or Smith, who follows L. Breitenbach 1857), without support in any MS or in Stobaeus, shoehorn the word "beautiful" into the text, making room for it by erasing a word that *is* in the MSS. The MSS and Stobaeus have, as Socrates's opening sentence, "That, Cleiton, you make runners and wrestlers and pugilists and pancratists *differently* [*alloious*; "of various appearances and postures"—Smith ad loc.], I see and I know." For this, most editors substitute: "That, Cleiton, you make runners etc. *beautiful*, I see and I know." The original source of this emendation is Wilhelm Dindorf (1824, ad loc.), who was soon followed (without acknowledgment) by his brother (or pseudonym?) Ludwig August Dindorf (1831, ad loc.); contrast the latter's earlier note in Schneider and L. Dindorf 1826, ad loc. (The two brothers—or the name and the curious pseudonym?— and their editions are confused in the bibliography and apparatus of BD, as well as in other scholars' citations.) See the comment by G. Sauppe (1834, ad loc.): "Ingeniosissima coniectura L. [*sic*] Dindorfi est *kaloi hous*. Retinui tamen *alloious*, quod diversam statuarum figuram et formam significare recte dicit Schneiderus." (But later, in G. Sauppe 1871, s.v. *alloious*, the MS reading is flagged as "suspecta.")

88. XS 87 and BD ad loc. stress the need to keep in mind the difference between a courtesan (*hetaira*), who, as Xenophon says here, sells her favors only when persuaded (or makes her "living by providing emotional and intellectual companionship as well as sexual favors in return for payment"; Pomeroy 1994, 220), and a prostitute (*pornē*), who, as Xenophon had Socrates say back at 1.6.13, "sells for money to whomever wishes" ("where there is no pretense of anything other than quick sex for money"; Pomeroy 1994, 220). For fuller explanation, see Pomeroy 1975 as well as Narcy 2004, 214, and Azoulay 2004, 404.

89. Delatte (1933, 151), who continues by inditing: "One is above all astonished that Xenophon would have presented Socrates in this light in the book consecrated to defending his memory!" Kierkegaard (1989, 24) goes much further: "We are even more disgusted, because we cannot perceive the possibility of Socrates ever having been capable of it!" BD ad loc. provide an amusing assortment of other commentators' "virtuous protestations"— in order that "the reader can give himself a more precise idea of the indignation aroused by this chapter of the *Memorabilia*," which scholars have judged "non seulement licencieux, immoral et choquant, mais aussi [*sic*] indigne de Socrate." On the other side, speaking in the minority, we have the knightly judgment of Sir Alexander Grant (1871, 115): "The story of his visit to Theodota, a beautiful courtesan, is perhaps best told of all the tales in the 'Memorabilia,' and if we make certain allowances for the manners and ideas of the age, it gives most idea [*sic*] of the Socratic grace and versatile politeness."

90. In Plato's *Apology* 30d-e, Socrates calls himself "gift of god." According to Athenaeus (12, 535c, 13, 574e), Theodote was the name of an "Attic" courtesan who accompa-

nied Alcibiades everywhere he campaigned, and, when he died, arranged the burial of his remains at Melissa in Phrygia. But Xenophon makes no explicit allusion to this connection (and it is possibly a later legend, even growing in part out of the present passage; Plutarch in his life of Alcibiades identifies the courtesan who buried him as one Timandra; "Theodote" was a rather common name given girls in Attica: Fraser and Matthews 1987–2013, s.v.). The name Theodote is obviously an echo of the name of the beautiful "heroine" of Xenophon's *Education of Cyrus,* Panthea ("Wholly Divine" or "Goddess of All"—a name unattested in Attica but attested in the Aegean islands: Fraser and Matthews 1987–2013, s.v.).

91. 3.11.1: this may hold of the ugly as well as the beautiful: Thucydides (2.50) applies the same expression to the plague, saying that its look or form (*eidos*) was "beyond speech."

92. L. Strauss comments (OT chap. 5, note 60): "Socrates's temperance is the foundation for his ability and willingness to look at the beautiful and to admire it"—in striking contrast to Xenophon's Cyrus, whose "temperance is combined with inability or unwillingness to look at the beautiful or to admire it"—"Cyrus does not dare to look at the beautiful Panthea" (*Education of Cyrus* 5.1.7ff.). "To use the Aristotelian terms, whereas Cyrus is continent, Socrates is temperate or moderate."

93. Could Socrates have led his contingent to behold Theodote partly in order to provoke their thought by means of this question?

94. Obviously, then, BD ad loc. are wrong in saying that Socrates is "showing himself indifferent to the charms of Theodote."

95. Recall the conversation with Critobulus; see Xenophon's intricately allegorical treatise *The One Skilled in Hunting with Dogs*; the culminating peak of liberal-civic education as elaborated in Plato's *Laws* is hunting, by night as well as day, including "a hunting for humans that is worth reflection" (*Laws* 822–24).

96. With Bonnette 1994, ad loc. I follow the reading of the MSS; most editors, unalive to Xenophon's subtlety and irony, adopt an emendation by Schneider and L. Dindorf (1826): "sufficient" (*arestoi*) instead of "best" (*aristoi*).

97. Since Theodote was already manifestly very wealthy, it would seem that it was not her need and thirst for monetary gain that made her so attracted to a partnership with Socrates; did Socrates stir up in her a longing for more substantial "friendships" than she was already enjoying?

98. Xenophon leaves us to guess "how Theodote knew Socrates's name" (XS 89b), and how she was acquainted with his absent close followers, Simmias and Cebes, and how Socrates could assume such an acquaintance on her part; can we surmise that this is implicit testimony to the range and activity of Socrates's "hunting dogs"?

99. 3.12.8; on the connection between this episode and the depiction of the tutoring of Euthydemus, see Danzig 2010, in the chapter entitled "Xenophon's Socratic Seductions"; also BD ad loc.

100. In Plato's *Apology* (33e), Socrates identifies Epigenes, who is present with his father, as a youth who has been shaped by Socratic education; in Plato's *Phaedo* (59b), Epigenes is mentioned as one of the company present during Socrates's final hours.

101. XS 180: from a survey of the very few contexts in which the pregnant term *patris* (fatherland) occurs in the *Memorabilia* "we understand Socrates' using *patris* in III.12.4 to signify that his conversation with Epigenes is emphatically political."

102. BD ad loc. alertly point out that "Socrates seems here more reserved" as to the *positive* intellectual consequences of physical fitness.

103. *opsophagistatos*; this superlative occurs nowhere else in classical Greek; for the Aristophanean-comic connotation of this idiosyncratic term of moral disapprobation, see what follows.

104. Consider the Socratic-Xenophontic Shaftesbury's "Essay on the Freedom of Wit and Humor" (Treatise 2 of 1964).

105. 3.13.2 (recall 1.3.5); Smith ad loc. notes that the same "cure" was prescribed by Mark Twain.

106. *Clouds* 519; L. Strauss 1966, 236.

107. Aristophanes, *Peace* 810; in *Knights* (313, 353–54, 361, 929–40, 1030–34) *opsophagia* is conflated with political corruption and bribery. See the quotations from the comic poet Diphilos in Kock 1880–88, 2: 549–50, and from other comic poets in Athenaeaus: 108d (Eubolus), 125e (Sophilos), 342e (Antiphanes); at 343c-d, Athenaeus reports comic gossip that "Aristippus the Socratic" was an *opsophagos*, who was blamed by Plato himself for the vice; see also 344b; Aeschines, *Against Timarchus* 42 and 95–96; and Davidson 1997, 21–35, 289.

108. Recall the rather obviously comical 1.3.5–8, and the end of chapter 2 and the beginning of chapter 3 above. Xenophon does not quite "bookend," because he only glancingly (3.14.3) returns to the theme with which chapter 3 of book 1 began—Socrates's piety, the most deeply problematic Socratic moral "abnormality." It is to be noted, however, that the conversations on dining that conclude book 3, like the conversation with Epigenes, are untainted by any profane oaths—a purity made more conspicuous by the density of profane expletives emitted by the interlocutor who was a worn-out traveler (3.13.6).

CHAPTER SIX

1. L. Dindorf (1831, Praef. xi) was so bewildered by this opening that he proposed that it be struck, as the addition of a later hand, and that book 4 be made to begin at *kai gar paizōn*. Schenkl (1875, 40–41) responded by saying that this proposed remedy made no sense to him, but, sharing in the bewilderment, proposed treating the entire first chapter as suspect—especially the opening: "Sodann ist der ganze erste Paragraph ein müssige Gerede, das man einem Xenophon nicht verzeihen könnte."

2. Recall esp. 1.2.3 and 1.2.8, and BD ad loc., as well as Luccioni 1953, 32–36.

3. As BD alertly observe ad loc., "This is the first time, since 1.3.1 (*diamnēmoneusō*), that Xenophon employs the vocabulary of recollection in regard to Socrates."

4. It is an overstatement to say that "what Xenophon says" here "of the recollection of Socrates" extends "to *all* the readers of the *Memorabilia*"; nevertheless, for that *minority* of readers who are *truly* "receptive" to Xenophon and to his Socrates, it can be said that the study of this work "will benefit," if not "equally," then substantially, "those who come to know Socrates by the intermediary of the *Memorabilia*" (BD ad loc.).

5. Xenophon provocatively uses the word for "house" (*oikia*), not the word for "household" or "estate" (*oikos*): for the distinction, see *Oeconomicus* 1.5. This requires that the verb *oikeō* have here its primary meaning, "to dwell in," or "to inhabit," *not*

its secondary meaning, "to *manage* a house*hold or estate*" (see Liddell and Scott 1953, s.v.). Hirschig (1849, 365) was so troubled by this that he proposed—without any basis in the MS tradition—an emendation: "*oikein*, si additur *oikia*, significat *habitare*, si *oikos*, *administrare*. Sensum autem facilis et hanc significationem requiri manifestum. Quare repone *oikon* pro *oikian*." Editors and translators share the puzzlement enough that they generally note, if they do not adopt, this emendation. The explanation for the provocative original text is indicated in XS 92b–93t; see also 72t.

6. Smith ad loc.: "*achtheisas* (*agō*): the usual term for training hunting dogs."

7. *Oeconomicus* 12–13; see also *Education of Cyrus* 1.1.2; *The One Skilled in Hunting with Dogs; On Horsemanship; The Skilled Cavalry Commander*; recall *Memorabilia* 3.3.3–4.

8. *thumoeidetic*; this is the adjectival form of the Platonic term for that part of the soul that predominates in the auxiliary class according to the psychology developed by Socrates in the *Republic. Thumos* in a positive sense appears only here, and nowhere else, in the *Memorabilia*.

9. BD, vol. 1, Annexe 4, p. 233n (criticizing Effe 1971, 199): "La mention de la beauté d'Euthydème est pleinement justifiée. Xénophon cherche en effet à opposer l'attitude de Socrate à l'endroit du bel Euthydème à la façon, vulgaire et indigne, dont Critias se comportait avec lui (cf. I 2, 29–30)."

10. Smith ad loc.: "filled with conceit of fancied wisdom"; Powers 2009, 259: "an aggravatingly conceited know-it-all"; see also XS 94, 98, 100–101, 108; and Buzzetti 2001, 7–8.

11. "Socrates, seeing that young Xenophon was a good nature, asked him if he knew where in the agora the fish were; and when the latter said, 'Yes,' asked him again, 'And what about the vegetables?' And when he said he knew also about this and the other things, Socrates asked him in general, if he knew where the gentlemen [noble and good men] spent their time. When Xenophon was silent, Socrates rebuked him, and left him. And from that occasion Xenophon turned to beginning to philosophize" (Stobaeus 2.31.101); see also Diogenes Laertius 2.48; and Higgins 1977, 21–22. Cf. Delebecque 1957, 17; Erbse 1961, 274.

12. The puzzle is only evaded by scholars who suppose that Xenophon means to use Euthydemus as a stand-in for someone else—such as Xenophon himself (Delebecque 1957, 17; Erbse 1961, 273–74n2, referring to A. Döring 1891–92, 56: "ein sinnvolles Pseudonym fur—den jungen Xenophon") or Alcibiades (Ditmar 1912, 97ff., 124ff.; Gigon 1953, 40, 121; Chroust 1957, 11, 179, 305n1223, 307nn1239 and 1241; BD, vol. 1, Annexe 4) or "for any of his followers" (Waterfield 1990, 53). As for falling back on the catch-all explanation that Socrates carried on his refutation of Euthydemus for the benefit of onlookers, Xenophon is careful to specify that for the crucial refutational dialogue Socrates "went alone" (4.2.8) to meet Euthydemus—and this is re-underlined by Xenophon when he stresses that the very next conversation, in contrast, is one that Xenophon was present at, and was of a type that Socrates generally carried on before an audience: 4.3.2.

13. 4.2.8–9; the profane oath on the part of Socrates is the first we have heard since his flurry of such in his obviously comic dialogue with Theodote, teaching her about his art of seduction. In the dialogues with Euthydemus, Socrates utters four such oaths and Euthydemus no less than twenty-seven.

14. 4.2.1; BD ad loc.: "It was bad form for young people to frequent the agora (cf. Aristophanes *Knights* 1373; Isocrates *Areopagiticus* 48)."

15. O'Connor 1994, 177: "Xenophon implicitly reminds us here of the Antiphon passage, where Socrates reported that his erotic intercourse with his associates involved *picking out* the treasures (*thēsauroi*) *from* the books of the wise men of the past (*Mem.* 1.6.14)—the word *thēsauroi* appears in the *Memorabilia* only in the two passages." Socrates did not say that he himself owned any books, or that ownership of books (as opposed to study of them) was of any importance to him.

16. Smith ad loc.: "an example of *kakourgein.*"

17. Xenophon's editorial expression at this point (4.2.24), "*kai ho Socrates*: . . . ," indicates a slight pause, I believe.

18. Smith ad loc.: "*eis Delphous de*: the *de* seems to oppose its sentence to the preceding: 'You say you have no other road to travel; have you ever gone to Delphi?'"

19. See OT, chap. 1, note 5 and context.

20. Socrates said nothing here about the justice or injustice of the enemies.

21. "He does not say that justice is indisputably good (cf. *Symposium* 3.4) because he has come to see how disputable justice is" (XS 99; see also 149–50; and OT chap. 3a, note 28 and context). We add that Euthydemus also does not say that piety is indisputably good—a silence that is tacitly circumscribed by his and Socrates's profane invocations of Zeus at this point.

22. Socrates did not affirm in his own name that the goodness of wisdom is qualified or disputable; he limited himself to posing questions reminding of what tradition "sings"; scholars have read Socrates as speaking affirmatively, ignoring the context of playfully ironic, tutorial dialectic (BD ad loc.; Johnson 2005, 68; 2009, 216–17); some commentators, humorlessly and with inadvertent self-travesty, have expressed their disapproval of Xenophon for presenting Socrates as betraying wisdom here: Joël 1893–1901, I: 414–18; Kahn 1996, 396–97. Contrast L. Strauss's tongue-in-cheek comment (XS 99): "Euthydemos had perhaps never heard of the wise men who were kidnapped so that they would be slaves of the king of Persia; the two mythical examples suffice for convincing him of his error." See also OT chap. 5, note 32. In his account of Daedalus, Socrates inventively departs, rather radically, from known tradition: BD ad loc.; Grimal 1986, s.v. "Daedalus." In *The One Skilled in Hunting with Dogs* 1.11, Xenophon himself contradicts his Socrates's account here of Palamedes being killed, out of envy for his wisdom, by Odysseus. Xenophon's own account is based on the assumption that Odysseus was virtuous or wise (see OT chap. 5, note 25 and context). BD ad loc. for once discern Socrates's educative deceptions here and throughout the interrogation of Euthydemus: "S'il semble y adhérer, c'est probablement à des fins aporétiques, c'est-à-dire pour tester la prétention d'Euthydème." The sole affirmation Socrates uttered here was that "everybody sings this: how through being envied for wisdom Palamedes was destroyed by Odysseus" (XS 99: "That Socrates perished could be traced to the fact that he was envied on account of his wisdom—*Education of Cyrus* III.1.38–39"; see also OT chap. 3a, note 25 and context).

23. O'Connor 1994, 178–79: "The mention of prayer reinforces the connection between 'the disputable things,' which reveal Euthydemus's ignorance, and 'the hidden things,' which are the objects of divination."

24. See similarly *Regime of the Athenians* 1.2, 4–5; *Ways and Means* 1.1.

25. 4.2.40: the subject of the verb "he believed" is probably Socrates, but it could be Euthydemus; the sentence is ambiguous.

26. Surely Xenophon could not (could he?) be referring us to the account published by Aristophanes in the *Clouds* (251ff.), of Socrates striving to make his "initiates" ritual worshippers of the new goddesses the Clouds, along with "Master and Lord Air," and "bright Aether"? In the natural theology that Xenophon proceeds to have Socrates present to Euthydemus, the fourth element, air, is so conspicuously passed by in silence that what is in all likelihood an interpolation was put into the text (at 4.3.7 end) in order to remedy the deficiency: the addition is found in the MS Vatican 95. BD ad loc. comment: "Le passage a été jugé authentique par plusieurs philologues de la fin du XVIII et du début du XIX s. (Ruhnken [1811], Zeune [1781], Schneider [with L. Dindorf 1826], Schaefer [1811], Korais [1825]), mais il s'agit là, trés probablement, d'une interpolation due à une grammairien byzantin de la fin du XIII s., qui a voulu ajouter au texte de Xénophon le quatrième élément, l'air, après la mention des trois autres éléments (terre, #5; eau, #6; feu, #7)." For a full textual discussion, see Bandini 2006. Commenting on the "silence on the fourth element," L. Strauss wryly observes (XS 103) that "'air' occurs in Xenophon only in the compound 'measuring the air,' an activity which is comically ascribed to Socrates (*Oeconomicus* XI.3)"—referring, of course, to the famous depiction of Socrates in Aristophanes's *Clouds*.

27. Natali 2005, 677: "ogni volta la discussione prende un andamento diverso a seconda delle caratteristi che dell'interloctore."

28. BD ad 4.3.5 and 4.3.7; Burkert 1985, 188–89 and 274–75.

29. BD ad loc.: "It is without a doubt revelatory that Socrates, in this paragraph, passes agriculture by in silence. If the nourishment furnished by the gods were truly as abundant and easy of access as Socrates affirms, how come humans have to practice agriculture?" (consider the biblical account of Adam and the origin of agriculture). In this major respect the teleo-theology that Xenophon here reports Socrates teaching is even more extreme than that taught by Aristotle in his *Politics* 1256a19ff.

30. XS 102–3; BD ad loc.; Bonnette 1994, ad loc. alertly notes "the change of verb here from 'to provide' (*parechein*) to 'to procure' (*porizein*)"—Socrates thus slyly reminds of the traditional account of the theft of fire from the gods, for humanity, by Prometheus. Xenophon thus also of course arouses in his demanding readers the question, What makes the philosopher think that he *knows*—rather than merely assumes, believes, hopes, wishes—that the poet Hesiod, who claims divine inspiration and revelation, is wrong in his revealed report?

31. See above all Hesiod, *Works and Days* 42ff. and *Theogony* 507ff.; and Aeschylus, *Prometheus Bound*.

32. XS 104: "Exact observation and reverence seem to be incompatible."

33. See Nietzsche, *Beyond Good and Evil*, aph. 49; and also Cyrus in his deathbed speech, *Education of Cyrus* 8.7.3, 8.7.7–8.

34. The leading conventional commentator (BD ad loc.) declares that here we see how "much more superstitious and conformist is the Socrates of Xenophon" than the one depicted in Plato's *Alcibiades II*.

35. Xenophon (4.44) now suddenly delivers the momentous and deeply thought-provoking news that at his trial Socrates could have "easily been let off by the jurors, if he had only to a measured degree" followed custom, and departed from strict adherence to the law.

36. Xenophon says that "in *private*" Socrates "used/dealt with everyone in a lawful *and beneficial* way"; he does not say that in his *public* deeds Socrates was beneficial— "Public life does not permit one's being helpful, to all, especially to the public enemies; and acting lawfully is not the same as acting helpfully" (XS 107). Here and only here, in Xenophon's entire corpus, does he mention, very briefly (in three words), the fact that Socrates served on military campaigns (Gigon 1946, 152; H.-R. Breitenbach 1967, col. 1830; Pontier 2006, 195n1).

37. Dorion 2013, 78–79: "Chapter 4 resembles, in many respects, a kind of meteorite, come from nowhere, that arrives unexpectedly to interrupt the series of conversations between Socrates and Euthydemus (IV 2–3 and IV 5–6). The present placement of chapter 4 seems so incongruous that several commentators have put forward the hypothesis that it has been accidentally displaced." (See Marchant 1923, xix.) Dorion himself is baffled: BD 1: CCXXXIff. As Dorion stresses (2013, 78–79, following XS 108), this conversation occupies the center of book 4; or as L. Strauss observes more precisely, it takes the place of, totally eclipses, what would have been the central of the series of conversations with Euthydemus (4.2–6).

38. XS 108; BD ad loc.: Hippias "condemned the positive law, 'tyrant of humans,' which 'opposes its constraint to nature' ([Plato's] *Protagoras* 337d)"; Untersteiner 1954, 280–83; Pradeau and Fronterotta 2005, 216–17.

39. XS 15 and 107; Buzzetti 2001, 22–23.

40. "We must be thankful to Xenophon that his Euthydemos did not answer in the elenctic conversation that the just is the legal" (XS 109).

41. XS 107 and 179; OT chap. 4, para. 13; *Education of Cyrus* 1.1.1; *Ways and Means* 1.1; *Agesilaus* 1.37; *Regime of the Athenians* 1.1; *Regime of the Lacedaimonians* 15.1.

42. Johnson 2003, 271–73, 276–80; Dorion 2013, 84, 86, 88–89; *Education of Cyrus* 1.3.16–67; and Buzzetti 2001, 10ff.

43. BD ad loc. and 1: CLV–CLXVI; Waterfield 2004, 109; see also Lacey 1971, 39; Beckman 1979, 16; Gera 1993, 34; Vlastos 1991, 105; Gray 2011, 334.

44. At 4.6.14, Xenophon will report Socrates suggesting that "the work of a good *citizen*" is making the city wealthier, making it superior to its adversaries in war, making its enemies into friends by diplomacy, and, through public speaking, putting an end to civil strife and bringing about concord—all without any mention of law (OT, chap. 5, note 1 and context). As for Socrates's civic activities, recall 1.6.15 (OT, chap. 5, note 37). L. Strauss points out that Socrates does not mention manliness or courage (*andreia*) as needed for justice, and that Xenophon, while referring briefly to Socrates's military service, does not attribute to him manliness or courage; in this connection Strauss notes the absence of courage (or manliness) from all of Xenophon's lists of the virtues of Socrates: see OT chap. 3c, note 6 and context.

45. 4.4.12; how in the world can this be, for Socrates, the whole meaning of justice? Has not Xenophon been showing us how Socrates "never stopped" practicing—through speeches—justice in the sense of actively benefiting others? Yes, but these actively just speeches go far beyond obedience to the law, and in this semipublic conversation, Socrates is preparing to advance and defend the very conservative doctrine that the just is obedience to the law.

46. Failing to follow the subtlety of the action that Xenophon is having his Socrates

carry out here, commentators have reacted with puzzlement or censoriousness to the fact that Socrates in his monologue said nothing that logically implies that the legal, or obedience to the law, is the same as the just, but contended only that obedience to the law is beneficial in many ways: Striker 1987, 89; D. Morrison 1995, 337; Johnson 2003, 263 and 272; Danzig 2009, 282; Dorion 2010–11, ad loc.

47. 4.4.19–20; BD ad loc. point out that Greeks understood the Persians to practice incest regularly (citing Herodotus 3.31; Euripides, *Andromache* 173–76; Diogenes Laertius 9.83; Sextus Empiricus 1.152). In Xenophon's *Regime of the Lacedaimonians* 1.9, 2.13, and 6.2 (taken together) it is implicitly made clear that incest must be practiced regularly, if inadvertently, among the Spartans: see L. Strauss 1939, 511.

48. Dupréel 1948, 218; Untersteiner 1954, 297n38; Johnson 2003, 268–69.

49. Grotius (*De jure belli ac pacis* 2.5.12.4) expresses his "surprise at the comment of Socrates"; "if disparity of age" were "the only reason opposed to such a marriage, the marriage would surely not be void or unlawful, any more than a marriage between other persons, one of whom is as much older than the other as parents ordinarily are older than children."

50. In their dialogue, Socrates and Hippias let loose with eleven profane expletives, six by Hippias and five by Socrates.

51. A number of commentators have gone so far as to suggest that Xenophon has here put into the mouth of Socrates a major part of the doctrine of Hippias on unwritten laws and natural right: Dümmler 1889, 251–56; Zuretti 1916; Bignone 1938, 132n1; Levi 1942, 447; Dupréel 1948, 216–19; Untersteiner 1954, 280–83.

52. See Averroes's commentary on Aristotle's *Ethics* ad 1134b18ff.—this Averroistic interpretation of Aristotle is followed by Marsilius of Padua in his *Defensor pacis* 1.19.13 and esp. 2.12.7–8, and by John Locke in his *Questions Concerning the Law of Nature* I (folio 13); see similarly Montesquieu's *Spirit of the Laws* 1.1; for helpful analysis, see L. Strauss 1952, chap. 4 beg.; 1953, chap. 4 end.

53. Guthrie 1971b, 119; see also Johnson 2003, 265; and Danzig 2009, 284–85.

54. *theois eoike*: the reading of all the MSS and Stobaeus. Many editors accept an emendation of Brodaeus 1559, "befit/are *like* divine things (*theiois eoike*)." Marchant 1921 ad loc. attributes this reading to the purported MS "Vossianus"—which, as we have previously noted, probably never existed (see again Bandini 1994, 73–74).

55. In Plato's *Hippias Major* 286a-b, Hippias is presented as boasting about a speech he gives to great success in various cities (including Sparta), which—in the words of Dorion (2013, 87n105)—"subscribes entirely to the lawful conventions."

56. This "is the only statement ever made by Socrates on what is the greatest good" (XS 114); recall our interpretation of 4.2.33. In the *Apology* (21), Socrates says that education is the greatest good *for humans*: "Education cannot be the greatest good simply, because gods do not need education. Education, i.e., the most excellent education, which is education to wisdom, is the greatest good for human beings, i.e., for human beings as such, for men in so far as they do not transcend humanity by approaching divinity: God alone is simply wise" (OT chap. 5, para. 13; see similarly XS 133).

57. See the speeches of Antisthenes, and of Socrates to Antisthenes, in the *Symposium*. Cf. the rather overstated views of Joël (1893–1901, 1: 561ff.), Chroust (1957, chap. 2), and Brancacci (1990).

58. 2.1.5: BD ad loc. speak of "cet hédonisme de *l'enkrateia*"; and refer to Cyrus's similar "ascétisme hédoniste" in *Education of Cyrus* 1.5.9.

59. Socrates plays on the root (*krat*) shared by the word for "self-mastery" and the word for "most masterful," a word that also can be translated "best," "strongest," "most dominating," and, perhaps most accurately, "most superior/supreme" (see 1.4.13). For clarification of the meaning and etymology of this important root, see Benveniste 1973, 357–67.

60. Xenophon "does not speak here, as he did when introducing the conversation on continence, of 'all companions'—IV.5.2" (XS 116).

61. The reading of the best MS B (Paris 1740); editors tend to follow the family of MSS Φ, which has "with" (*sun*) in place of "amidst" (*en*): see XS 116b–117t: "Perhaps Socrates never ceased considering what each of the beings is silently 'in the midst of his companions' (the reading of B)."

62. The reading of the best MS B is "human"; editors tend to follow the reading of Φ, "each."

63. 4.6.8; Socates had not addressed the young man by name since the start of this particular conversation.

64. BD ad loc.: "Some have been justly astonished at the situating and the raison d'être of #12 (cf. Arnim 1923, p. 151–52; Edelstein 1935, p. 128 n. 66)."

65. See the similar procedure of Aristotle in his *Nicomachean Ethics* 1095a30–b13, 1098b1–8.

66. BD ad loc.: "La première phrase du chapitre 7 renvoie tres clairement à IV 2, 40."

67. 4.7.1; recall the shift in 1.1.4–6 from "the companions" to "the serviceable associates" (*tous epitēdeious*): the former benefited from the *daimonion*, while the latter Socrates advised to employ conventional divination.

68. BD ad loc. note the difficulty here: "It follows from this that Socrates does not possess all the kinds of knowledge that it is fitting for a gentleman to possess, even though he is himself a gentleman (cf. I 2, 18; 48; Banq. I 1)." The most important and massive gentlemanly matter and "deed" in which Socrates lacked experience is farming (including rule over slaves), and increasing one's wealth in a noble manner by farming; not unconnected is his inexperience in horsemanship and the cavalry. Of course Xenophon does not in his *Memorabilia*, and especially at its close, highlight these massive gaps in Socrates's gentlemanly experience: Xenophon reserves that for his *Oeconomicus*. There we learn that, paradoxically, and despite his total lack of experience, Socrates did teach farming; in fact, we are made witnesses to his doing so at great length—in his own distinctive manner, to be sure. Recall also Socrates's rejoinder at 1.6.15.

69. 4.7.1–2; BD ad loc. point out that here Socrates is said to view geometry along the same lines as does Aristophanes's character Strepsiades in the *Clouds*—in contrast to Socrates and his students as depicted in that play.

70. Commenting on the *eirōneia* of this passage, Burnet writes (1924, 82–83): Socrates as "the *hetairos* of Archelaus must have known all there was to be known about such things." But "we may be sure that he never talked about these matters in public. Plato is consistent on this point." It is "practically only in such things as the myth of the *Phaedo* that" Socrates "is made to betray his knowledge of contemporary science," and "it is from Xenophon that we get our only direct statement."

71. The terms "thinker" (*phrontistēs*) and "worrier" (*merimnōnta*) echo Aristophanes's terms for Socrates in the *Clouds* 94, 227–34, 266, 489–90; as O'Connor observes (1994, 169n22), "Aristophanes coined *merimnophrontistēs* (anxious brooder) as a comic word for Socrates." Xenophon has used the term *merimnōnta* to characterize philosophic students of the nature of all things in 1.1.14. See also Plato's *Apology* 18b7, commenting on which, Burnet (1924, ad loc.) suggests that *phrontistēs* became "a regular nickname of Socrates"; see also *Symposium* 6.6 and 7.2. BD ad loc.: "There can be no doubt as to the apologetic intention of this passage."

72. 4.7.6; see Aristotle, *Metaphysics* 982b29–83a2.

73. One of the specific Anaxagorean theories that Socrates attacks—the suggestion that the sun is glowing stone—was by one major account the basis for Anaxagoras being tried and convicted for impiety at Athens: Diogenes Laertius 2.12. As BD ad loc. put it, "Anaxagoras is pretty clearly depicted, in this passage, as a thinker" whose extravagant theories "run the risk of leading to atheism." And "the critique of Anaxagoras" has "doubtless a defensive dimension inasmuch as Socrates" was said to be "the student of Anaxagoras" (see Plato's *Phaedo* 96ff. and Diogenes Laertius 2.19 and 2.45).

74. The word echoes Aristophanes's *Clouds* 100: O'Connor 1994, 169n22; Vander Waerdt 1994a, 82n91; BD ad loc.

75. For the precise divisions of the mathematic sciences as conceived by the Greeks, see J. Klein 1968.

76. The contradiction between this and what Xenophon laid out in 1.1.7–9 is pointed out by Halévy (1896, 94). O'Connor (1994, 167) sees "the tension," but submits that Socrates's *daimonion* "allows the reconciliation"; if so, this would entail Socrates hearing from the *daimonion* on an everyday and even all-day basis.

CONCLUSION

1. BD ad loc.: "C'est le seul passage, dans les *Mémorables*, où Xénophon fait mention du courage de Socrate."

2. 4.8.1–3; the Greek word for "happiness," *eudaimonia*, has *daimōn* as its root and means literally "having a good *daimon*" (Narcy 2005, 119).

3. 4.8.4; recall in contrast 4.4.11–12. Contrast also the *Oeconomicus* (11.2), where Xenophon presents Socrates asking the perfect gentleman Ischomachus whether *he* ever feels the need to make any preparations for defending himself. The gentleman replies: "Well, don't I seem to you, Socrates, to be continually practicing my defense, inasmuch as I do injustice to no one, but rather benefit as many people as I can? And don't I seem to you to practice myself in lodging accusations against people, by keeping a watchful eye out for certain persons who commit injustice against many, in private dealings, and also against the city, while they do no good to anyone?" Socrates did not engage, "thumotically," in policing and law enforcement (see also Plato's *Laws* 730d-31a).

4. With Bonnette 1994, ad loc. I follow the MSS and not the emendation most editors accept from Bornemann (1824, ad *Apology* 4) in his misguided attempt to harmonize the text of the *Memorabilia* at this point with the text of Xenophon's very differently intended *Apology*.

5. Burnet 1924, 146: "It would be easy to show that, from all we know of his physical constitution, there was no reason why Socrates should not have looked forward to another ten years of activity." Consider what Xenophon has his great Cyrus say on his deathbed, as a "very old man": "I never perceived even my old age becoming weaker than my youth" (*Education of Cyrus* 8.7.6). Still, in criticism of Burnet, Shero (1927, 109) aptly comments: "But it would seem that even a person with as hardy a constitution as his might look forward to the time of life beyond three score years and ten with some questionings, and would think it likely that his vision would become less perfect, his hearing less keen, his mind less alert, and his memory less retentive, as Socrates is represented as forecasting to Hermogenes."

# WORKS CITED

Citations from primary sources are by standard pagination, or section and subsection, of critical editions. Specific editions of primary sources are listed for cases where references have made peculiarities or page numbers of the editions significant. All translations are my own unless otherwise noted.

Photos of some of the original manuscripts whose variant readings are discussed in the notes are available for inspection online and may be accessed through the portal of the Princeton University Library at: http://library.prince ton.edu/byzantine/search/site/xenophon.

Photos of works of pictorial art referenced and discussed may be found collected for viewing at https://www.facebook.com/thomas.pangle.7.

Abbreviations for Works Frequently Cited

BD  *Xénophon, Mémorables.* Text established by Michele Bandini and translation by Louis-André Dorion, with textual essays by the former and introduction, commentary, and notes by the latter, 3 vols. (Paris: Budé, 2010–11). Now the standard critical edition.

OT  Leo Strauss, *On Tyranny.* Revised and expanded edition, including the Strauss-Kojève correspondence (New York: Free Press, 1991).

Smith  *Xenophon, Memorabilia.* Edition and commentary by Josiah Renick Smith, on the basis of the 1889 edition of L. Breitenbach and Mücke (Boston: Ginn, 1903).

XS  Leo Strauss, *Xenophon's Socrates.* Ithaca, NY: Cornell University Press, 1972.

XSD   Leo Strauss, *Xenophon's Socratic Discourse*. Ithaca, NY: Cornell
University Press, 1970.


Adams, John. 1961. *Diary and Autobiography of John Adams, 1755–1770*. Vol. 1. Ed.
    L. H. Butterfield. Cambridge, MA: Harvard University Press.
Ahrensdorf, Peter. 1994. "The Question of Historical Context and the Study of Plato."
    *Polity* 27: 113–32.
Ambler, Wayne, ed. and trans. 2001. *Xenophon: The Education of Cyrus*. Ithaca, NY:
    Cornell University Press.
_____. 2008. *Xenophon: The Anabasis of Cyrus*. With introd. by Eric Buzzetti. Ithaca,
    NY: Cornell University Press.
———. Forthcoming. "On The Skilled Cavalry Commander." In McBrayer, forthcoming.
Ambler, Wayne, and Thomas L. Pangle, eds. and trans. 2013. *Birds, Peace, Wealth: Aris-
    tophanes' Critique of the Gods*. Philadelphia: Paul Dry.
Andrieux, François-Guillaume-Jean-Stanislas. 1818. "Socrate et Glaucon: Dialogue tiré
    de Xénophon." In *Oeuvres*, 3: 214–16. Paris: Nepveu.
Arnim, Hans Friedrich August von, ed. 1923. *Xenophon's Memorabilien und Apologie des
    Sokrates*. Copenhagen: Ost.
Azoulay, Vincent. 2004. *Xénophon et les grâces du pouvoir: De la charis au charisme*.
    Paris: Sorbonne.
Baker, William W. 1917. "An Apologetic for Xenophon's *Memorabilia*." *Classical Journal*
    12: 293–309.
Bandini, Michele. 1992. "Nota critica a Xenophon, *Memorabilia* II 9.4." *Studi Classici e
    Orientali* 41: 465–66.
———. 1994. "La costituzione del testo dei Commentarii Socratici di Senofonte dal Quatro-
    cento ad oggi." *Revue d'Histoire des Textes* 24: 61–91.
———. 2006. "Senofonte nella prima età paleologa: Il testo di Memor. IV 3, 7-8 nel codice
    Urb, gr. 95." *Néa Rhomi* 3: 305–16.
Barker, Ernest. 1957. *Social and Political Thought in Byzantium: From Justinian I to the
    Last Palaeologus; Passages from Byzantine writers and Documents*. Oxford: Claren-
    don Press.
Bartlett, Robert C., ed. 1996. *Xenophon, The Shorter Socratic Writings: "Apology of Soc-
    rates to the Jury," "Oeconomicus," and Symposium."* Ithaca, NY: Cornell University
    Press.
———. 2015. "How to Rule the World: An Introduction to Xenophon's *The Education of
    Cyrus*." *American Political Science Review* 109: 143–54.
Bassett, Samuel E. 1917. "Wit and Humor in Xenophon." *Classical Journal* 12: 565–74.
Baur, Ferdinand Christian. 1837. *Das Christliche des Platonismus oder Sokrates und
    Christus*. Tübingen: Fues.
Beckman, James. 1979. *The Religious Dimension of Socrates' Thought*. Waterloo, ON:
    Canadian Corporation for Studies in Religion.
Benveniste, Emile. 1973. *Indo-European Language and Society*. London: Faber.
Bianchi-Bandinelli, Ranuccio. 1943. *Storicità dell'arte classica*. Florence: Sansoni.
Bignone, Ettore. 1938. *Studi nel pensiero antico*. Naples: Loffredo.

Birt, Theodor. 1893. *De Xenophontis commentariorum Socraticorun compositione.* Marburg: Elwert.

Bonnette, Amy L., ed. and trans. 1994. *Xenophon, Memorabilia.* Ithaca, NY: Cornell University Press.

Bornemann, Friedrich Augustus, ed. 1824. *Xenophontis Convivium et Socratis Apologia.* Leipzig: Hartmann.

Booth, Wayne C. 1974. *A Rhetoric of Irony.* Chicago: University of Chicago Press.

Boutroux, Emile. 1897. "Socrate: Fondateur de la science morale." In *Études d'histoire de la philosophie.* Paris: Alcan.

Brancacci, Aldo. 1990. *Oikeios logos: La filosofia del linguaggio di Antistene.* Naples: Bibliopolis.

———. 1995. "Ethos e pathos nella teoria delle arti: Una poetica socratica della pittura e della scultura." *Elenchos* 16: 101–27.

———. 2004. "Socrate, La musique et la danse: Aristophane, Xénophon, Platon." *Les Études Philosophiques* 2: 193–211.

Breitenbach, Hans-Rudolph. 1967. "Xenophon von Athen." In Georg Wissowa et al., eds., *Paulys Realencyclopädie der classischen Altertumswissenschaft,* 2nd ser., vol. 9.2, cols. 1569–2052. Stuttgart: J. B. Metzler.

Breitenbach, Ludwig, ed. 1857. *Xenophon's Memorabilien.* 2nd ed. Berlin: Weidmann.

———, ed. 1889. *Xenophon's Memorabilien.* 6th ed. by Dr. Rudolf Mücke. Berlin: Weidmann.

Brisson, Luc, and Louis-André Dorion. 2004. "Pour une relecture des écrits socratiques de Xénophon." *Les Etudes Philosophiques* 69: 137–40.

Brochard, Victor. 1923. *Les sceptiques grecs.* Paris: Vrin.

Brodaeus, Johannes [a.k.a. Jean Brodeau]. 1559. *Adnotationes in omnia Xenophontis opera.* Basel: Nicolaum Brylingerum.

Bruckner, Johann Jakob. 1742–44. *Historia critica philosophiae.* 5 vols. Reprint. Olms: Hildesheim, 1975.

———. 1791. *The History of Philosophy, from the Earliest Times to the Beginning of the Present Century; Drawn up from Brucker's Historia Critica Philosophiae.* Trans. William Enfield. 2 vols. London: Johnson.

Bruell, Christopher. 1987. "Xenophon." In Leo Strauss and Joseph Cropsey, eds., *History of Political Philosophy.* 3rd ed. Chicago: University of Chicago Press.

Brunn, Heinrich. 1889. *Geschichte der griechischen Künstler.* 2 vols. 2nd ed. Stuttgart: Ebner & Seubert.

Burke, Edmund. 1884. "Speech on a Motion Made in the House of Commons by the Right Honorable C. J. Fox for Leave to Bring in a Bill to Repeal and Alter Certain Acts Respecting Religious Opinions, upon the Occasion of a Petition of the Unitarian Society; May 11, 1792." In *Works,* 7: 39–58. London: Nimmo.

Burkert, Walter. 1985. *Greek Religion.* Cambridge, MA: Harvard University Press.

Burnet, John, ed. 1911. *Plato's Phaedo.* Oxford: Clarendon Press.

———, ed. 1924. *Plato: Euthyphro, Apology, Crito.* Oxford: Clarendon Press.

———. 1964. *Greek Philosophy: Thales to Plato.* London: Macmillan.

Burnyeat, Miles F. 1997. "The Impiety of Socrates." *Ancient Philosophy* 17: 1–12.

Busse, Adolf. 1930. "Xenophons Schutzschrift und Apologie des Sokrates." *Rheinisches Museum für Philologie* 79: 215–29.

Butler, William Archer. 1856. *Lectures on the History of Ancient Philosophy*. Ed. W. Hepworth Thompson. 2 vols. Cambridge: Macmillan.

Butterfield, Lyman Henry, ed. 1975. *The Book of Abigail and John: Selected Letters of the Adams Family, 1762–1784*. Cambridge, MA: Harvard University Press.

Buzzetti, Eric. 2001. "The Rhetoric of Xenophon and the Treatment of Justice in the *Memorabilia*." *Interpretation: A Journal of Political Philosophy* 29: 3–33.

———. 2008. "The Political Life and the Socratic Education." Introduction to Ambler 2008.

———. 2014. *Xenophon the Socratic Prince: The Argument of the Anabasis of Cyrus*. New York: Palgrave Macmillan.

Calder, William M. III. 1983. "The Oath by Hera in Plato." In *Mélanges Édouard Delebecque*. Aix-en-Provence: Publications de l'Université de Provence.

——— et al., eds. and trans. 2002. *The Unknown Socrates: Translations, with Introductions and Notes, of Four Important Documents in the Late Antique Reception of Socrates the Athenian*. Wauconda, IL: Bolchazy Carducci.

Canto-Sperber, Monique. 1996. "Socrates." In J. Brunschwig and G. E. R. Lloyd, eds., *Le savoir grec: Dictionnaire critique*. Paris: Flammarion.

Cartledge, Paul. 2009. "Appendix E: Spartan Government and Society." In Robert B. Strassler, ed., *The Landmark Xenophon's "Hellenica."* New York: Pantheon.

Cawkwell, George. 1972. "Introduction" to Rex Warner, trans., *Xenophon: The Persian Expedition*. London: Penguin.

Chavanon, Albert. 1903. *Étude sur les sources principales des "Mémorables" de Xénophon*. Paris: Bibliothèque de l'École des Hautes Études.

Chroust, Anton-Hermann. 1955. "Xenophon, Polycrates, and the Indictment of Socrates." *Classica et Mediaevalia* 16: 1–77.

———. 1957. *Socrates, Man and Myth: The Two Socratic Apologies of Xenophon*. London: Routledge.

Classen, J. 1984. "Xenophons Darstellung der Sophistik und der Sophisten." *Hermes* 112: 154–67.

Cobet, Carel G. 1858. *Novae lectiones quibus continentur observationes criticae in scriptores graecos*. Lugduni-Batavorum: Brill.

Crowther, Nigel B. 1985. "Male 'Beauty' Contests in Greece: The *Euandria* and *Euexia*." *L'Antiquité Classique* 54: 285–91.

Danzig, Gabriel. 2009. "Big Boys and Little Boys: Justice and Law in Xenophon's *Cyropaedia* and *Memorabilia*." *Polis* 26: 271–95.

———. 2010. *Apologizing for Socrates: How Plato and Xenophon Created Our Socrates*. Lanham, MD: Lexington.

Davidson, James N. 1997. *Courtesans and Fishcakes: The Consuming Passions of Classical Athens*. Chicago: University of Chicago Press.

DeFilippo, Joseph G., and Phillip T. Mitsis. 1994. "Socrates and Stoic Natural Law." In Vander Waerdt 1994b.

Delatte, Armand. 1933. *Le troisième livre des "Souvenirs" socratiques de Xénophon: Étude critique*. Paris: Droz.

Delebecque, Édouard. 1957. *Essai sur la vie de Xénophon*. Paris: Klincksieck.

———, ed. and trans. 1973. *Xénophon: Le commandant de cavalrie*. Paris: Budé.

Derenne, Eudore. 1930. *Les procès d'impiété intentés aux philosophes à Athènes au Vme et au IVme siècles avant J.-C.* Liège: Vaillant-Carmanne.

Devereux, Daniel T. 1992. "The Unity of the Virtues in Plato's *Protagoras* and *Laches*." *Philosophical Review* 101: 765–89.

Diels, Hermann, and Walther Kranz, eds. 1951. *Die Fragmente der Vorsokratiker.* 6th ed. Zurich: Hildesheim.

Dindorf, Ludwig August [believed by some to be a pseudonym for the next, but usually thought to be a brother], ed. 1831. *Xenophontis Commentarii.* Leipzig: Teubner.

Dindorf, Wilhelm [a.k.a. Karl Wilhelm Dindorf], ed. 1824. *Xenophontis Commentarii.* Leipzig: Teubner.

———, ed. 1855. *Scholia graeca in Homeri Odysseam.* Oxford: Oxford University Press.

Ditmar, Heinrich. 1912. *Aischines von Sphettos: Studien zur Literaturgeschichte der Sokratiker.* Berlin: Weidmann.

Dittenberger, Wilhelm. 1915–24. *Sylloge inscriptionum graecarum.* 3rd ed. Leipzig: Hirzelium.

Dodds, Eric Robertson. 1951. *The Greeks and the Irrational.* Berkeley: University of California Press.

———. 1954. "The Nationality of Antiphon the Sophist." *Classical Review* 4: 94–95.

Döring, August. 1891–92. "Die Disposition von Xenophons *Memorabilien* als Hülfsmittel positiver Kritik" and "Nachträge zur Disposition der *Memorabilien* (Archiv IV.1)." *Archiv für Geschichte der Philosophie* 4: 34–60 and 5: 61–66.

Döring, Klaus. 1988. *Der Sokratesschuler Aristipp und die Kyrenaïker.* Wiesbaden: Steiner.

Dorion, Louis-André. 2013. *L'autre Socrate: Études sur les écrits socratiques de Xénophon.* Paris: Les Belles Lettres.

Doty, Ralph, ed. 2003. *Xenophon, Poroi: A Translation.* Lewiston, NY: Edwin Mellen.

Dover, Kenneth. 1987. *Greek and the Greeks.* Oxford: Oxford University Press.

———. 1997. *The Evolution of Greek Prose Style.* Oxford: Oxford University Press.

Dresig, Sigismund Frederick. 1738. *De Socrate iuste damnato.* Leipzig: Langenheim. In Montuori 1981.

Dümmler, Ferdinand. 1889. *Akademia: Beiträge zur Literaturgeschichte der sokratischen Schulen.* Giessen: Ricker.

Dupréel, Eugène. 1948. *Les sophistes: Protagoras, Gorgias, Prodicus, Hippias.* Neuchâtel: Griffon.

Edelstein, Emma. 1935. *Xenophontisches und platonisches Bild des Sokrates.* Berlin: Ebering.

Effe, Bernd. 1971. "Platons *Charmides* und der *Alkibiades* des Aeschines von Sphettos." *Hermes* 99: 198–208.

Emerson, Ralph Waldo. 1909. *The Journals of Ralph Waldo Emerson.* Vol. 1. Boston: Houghton Mifflin.

Erbse, Hartmut. 1961. "Die Architektonik im Aufbau von Xenophons *Memorabilien*." *Hermes* 89: 257–87.

———. 1980. "Aristipp und Sokrates bei Xenophon (Bemerkungen zu *Mem.* 2,1)." *Würzburger Jahrbücher für die Altertumswissenschaft* 6: 7–19.

Ernesti, Johann August, ed. 1772. *Apomnemoneumata (Commentarii) seu Memorabilium Socratis dictorum libri IV.* 5th ed. Leipzig: Fritsch.

Fahr, Wilhelm. 1969. *Theous nomizein: Zum Problem der Anfänge des Atheismus bei den Griechen.* Berlin: Olms.

Figueira, Thomas J. "Economic Thought and Economic Fact in the Works of Xenophon." In Hobden and Tuplin 2012.

Flower, Michael A., ed. and trans. 2012. *Xenophon's Anabasis, or the Expedition of Cyrus.* Oxford: Oxford University Press.

Foucault, Michel. 1984. *Histoire de la sexualité.* Vol. 2, *L'usage des plaisirs.* Paris: Gallimard.

Fouillée, Alfred. 1874. *La philosophie de Socrate.* 2 vols. Paris: Ladrange.

Fraguier, Claude-François. 1746. "Dissertation sur l'ironie de Socrate, sur son pretendu Démon et sur ses moeurs." *L'Histoire et des Mémoires de L'Académie royale des inscriptions et belles lettres* 4: 360–79.

François, Gilbert. 1957. *Le polythéisme et l'emploi au singulier des mots theos, daimon dans la littérature grecque d'Homère à Platon.* Paris: Les Belles Lettres.

Franklin, Benjamin. 1959–. *The Papers of Benjamin Franklin.* Ed. Leonard Labaree et al. 41 vols. New Haven, CT: Yale University Press.

———. 1964. *Autobiography.* Ed. Leonard Labaree. New Haven, CT: Yale University Press.

Fraser, Peter Marshall, and Elaine Matthews, et al. 1987–2013. *A Lexicon of Greek Personal Names.* 7 vols. Oxford: Clarendon Press.

Freret, Nicola. 1736. *Observations sur les causes at sur les circonstances de la condemnation de Socrate.* In Montuori 1981.

Fritz, Kurt von. 1965. "Das erste Kapitel des zweiten Buches von Xenophons *Memorabilien* und die Philosophie des Aristipp von Kyrene." *Hermes* 93: 257–79.

Galinsky, G. Carl. 1972. *Herakles Themes.* Oxford: Blackwell.

Gautier, Léopold. 1911. *La langue de Xénophon.* Geneva: Georg.

Gera, Deborah Levine. 1993. *Xenophon's Cyropaedia: Style, Genre, and Literary Technique.* Oxford: Oxford University Press.

Giannantoni, Gabriele, ed. 1990. *Socratis et socraticorum reliquae.* 4 vols. Naples: Bibliopolis.

———. 1992. "Pour une édition des sources antiques sur Socrate." In Konstantinos Boudouris, ed., *The Philosophy of Socrates: Elenchus, Ethics, and Truth.* Athens: Center for Greek Philosophy and Culture.

Gigon, Olof. 1946. "Xenophontea." In *Eranos Rudbergianus: Opuscula philologica Gunnaro Rudberg a. d. XVI Kal. Nov. anno MCMXLV dedicata. Eranos: Acta Philologica Suecana, vol. XLIV.* Uppsala: Eranos.

———. 1953. *Kommentar zum ersten Buch von Xenophons "Memorabilien."* Schweizerische Beiträge zur Altertumswissenschaft 5. Basel: F. Reinhardt.

———. 1956. *Kommentar zum zweiten Buch von Xenophons "Memorabilien."* Schweizerische Beiträge zur Altertumswissenschaft 7. Basel: F. Reinhardt.

Gilbert, Walter, ed. 1888. *Xenophontis Commentarii.* Leipzig: Teubner.

Goldhill, Simon. 1998. Review of Vivienne Gray, *The Framing of Socrates.* Bryn Mawr Classical Review. http://bmcr.brynmawr.edu/.

Gomperz, Theodor. 1902. *Griechische Denker.* Vol. 2. Leipzig: Von Veit.

Grant, Sir Alexander. 1871. *Xenophon.* London: Blackwood.

Gray, Vivienne J. 1995. "Xenophon's Image of Socrates in the *Memorabilia.*" *Prudentia* 27: 50–73.

———. 1998. *The Framing of Socrates: The Literary Interpretation of Xenophon's "Memorabilia."* Stuttgart: Steiner.

———. 2004. "Le Socrate de Xénophon et la démocratie." *Les Études Philosophiques* 69: 141–76.

———. 2007. *Xenophon on Government.* Cambridge: Cambridge University Press.

———. 2011. *Xenophon's Mirror of Princes: Reading the Reflections.* Oxford: Oxford University Press.

Griffiths, Ralph. 1782. Review of Robert Nares, *Essay on the Demon or Divination of Socrates. The Monthly Review, or, Literary Journal* 67: 440–43.

Grimal, Pierre. 1986. *The Dictionary of Classical Mythology.* Oxford: Blackwell.

Groen van Prinsterer, Guillaume. 1823. *Prosopographia Platonica.* Lugduni-Batavorum: Hazenberg.

Guthrie, William Keith Chambers. 1971a. *Socrates.* Cambridge: Cambridge University Press.

———. 1971b. *The Sophists.* Cambridge: Cambridge University Press.

Hadot, Pierre. 1995. *Philosophy as a Way of Life: Spiritual Exercises from Socrates to Foucault.* Oxford: Blackwell.

Halévy, Elie. 1896. "Travaux récents relatifs à Socrate." *Revue de Metaphysique et de Morale* 4: 86–117.

Halliwell, Stephen. 2008. *Greek Laughter: A Study of Cultural Psychology from Homer to Early Christianity.* Cambridge: Cambridge University Press.

Hansen, Mogens Herman. 1995. *The Trial of Sokrates—from the Athenian Point of View.* Historisk-filosofiske Meddelelser 71. Copenhagen : Kongelige Danske Videnskabernes Selskab.

Hanson, Victor Davis. 1996. "Appendix F: Land Warfare in Thucydides." In Robert Strassler, ed., *The Landmark Thucydides.* New York: Simon & Schuster.

Hartman, Jacobus Johannes. 1887. *Analecta Xenophontea.* Lugduni-Batavorum: Van Doesburgh.

Hatzfeld, Jean. 1940. "Socrate au procès des Arginuses." *Revue des Études Anciennes* 42: 165–71.

Hegel, Georg W. F. 1971. *Vorlesungen über die Geschichte der Philosophie.* Ed. R. E. Moldenhauer and K. M. Michel. Vol. 1. In *Werke,* vol. 18. Frankfurt am Main: Suhrkamp.

———. 2006. *Lectures on the History of Philosophy, 1825–26.* Trans. R. F. Brown and J. M. Stewart. Vol. 2. Oxford: Clarendon Press.

Higgins, William Edward. 1972. "The Concept and Role of the Individual in Xenophon." *Harvard Studies in Classical Philology* 76: 289–94.

———. 1977. *Xenophon the Athenian: The Problem of the Individual and the Society of the Polis.* Albany: SUNY Press.

Hindley, Clifford. 1999. "Xenophon on Male Love." *Classical Quarterly* n. s. 49: 74–99.

———. 2004. "*Sophron Eros*: Xenophon's Ethical Erotics." In Tuplin 2004.

Hirschig, Rudolph Bernard [confused with Guillelmus Adrianus Hirschig in BD]. 1849. "Xenophontis opusculi, quod inscribitur *Memorabilia,* loci quidam emendantur." *Philologus* 4: 362–66.

Hobden, Fiona E., and Christopher J. Tuplin, eds. 2012. *Xenophon: Ethical Principles and Historical Inquiry.* Leiden: Brill.

Høeg, Carsten. 1950. "*Xenophontos Kurou Anabasis*: Oeuvre anonyme ou pseudonyme ou orthonyme?" *Classica et Mediaevalia* 11: 151–79.

Hornstein, Franz. 1915–16. "Komposition und Herausgabe der Xenophontischen *Memorabilien.*" *Wiener Studien: Zeitschrift für klassische Philologie und Patristik* 36: 122–139 and 37: 63–87.

Hude, Charles, ed. 1934. *Xenophontis Commentarii*. Stuttgart: Teubner.

Humble, Noreen. 2004. "The Author, Date, and Purpose of Chapter 14 of the *Lakedaimonion Politeia*." In Tuplin 2004.

Hurndall, William F. 1853. *De philosophia morali Socratis*. Heidelberg: Mohrii.

Huss, Bernhard. 1999a. "The Dancing Socrates and the Laughing Xenophon, or the Other Symposium." *American Journal of Philology* 120: 381–409.

———. 1999b. *Xenophons Symposium: Ein Kommentar*. Stuttgart: Teubner.

Jackson, Henry. 1874. "The *diamonion sēmeion* of Socrates." *Journal of Philology* 5: 232–47.

Jaeger, Werner. 1943. *Paideia: The Ideals of Greek Culture*. Trans. Gilbert Highet. Vol. 2. Oxford: Oxford University Press.

Janko, Richard. 2006. "Socrates the Freethinker." In S. Ahbel-Rappe and R. Kamtekar, eds., *A Companion to Socrates*. Malden, MA: Blackwell.

Jansen, Joseph N. 2007. *After Empire: Xenophon's "Poroi" and the Reorientation of Athens' Political Economy*. PhD diss., University of Texas at Austin.

Joël, Karl. 1893–1901. *Der echte und der xenophontische Sokrates*. 3 vols. Berlin: Gaertner.

Johnson, David M. 2003. "Xenophon's Socrates on Law and Justice." *Ancient Philosophy* 23: 255–81.

———. 2005. "Xenophon's Socrates at His Most Socratic (*Mem.* 4.2.)." *Oxford Studies in Ancient Philosophy* 29: 39–73.

———. 2009. "Aristippus at the Crossroads: The Politics of Pleasure in Xenophon's *Memorabilia*." *Polis* 26: 204–22.

Jüthner, Julius. 1930. "Kalokagathia." In *Charisteria Alois Rzach zum achtzigsten Geburtstag dargebracht*. Rechenberg: Stiepel.

Kahn, Charles H. 1996. *Plato and the Socratic Dialogue: The Philosophical Use of a Literary Form*. Cambridge: Cambridge University Press.

Kierkegaard, Soren. 1989. *The Concept of Irony, with Continual Reference to Socrates*. Trans. H. V. Hong and E. H. Hong. Princeton: Princeton University Press.

Klein, Jacob. 1968. *Greek Mathematical Thought and the Origin of Algebra*. Cambridge, MA: MIT Press.

Klein, Wilhelm. 1905. *Geschichte der griechischen Kunst*. 3 vols. Leipzig: Velt.

Kock, Karl Theodor. 1880–88. *Comicorum atticorum fragmenta*. 3 vols. Leipzig: Teubner.

Korais, Adamantios, ed. 1825. *Xenophōntos Apomnēmoneumata*. Paris: Didot.

Krentz, Peter. 2009. "Appendix A: The Arginusae Affair." In Robert Strassler, ed., *The Landmark Xenophon's "Hellenika."* New York: Pantheon.

Kronenberg, Leah. 2009. *Allegories of Farming from Greece and Rome: Philosophical Satire in Xenophon, Varro, and Virgil*. Cambridge: Cambridge University Press.

Kühn, Joseph H. 1954. Review of Gigon, *Kommentar zum ersten Buch von Xenophons "Memorabilien."* *Gnomon* 26: 512–21.

Kuntz, Mary. 1994. "The Prodikean 'Choice of Herakles': A Reshaping of Myth." *Classical Journal* 89: 163–81.

Labriola, Antonio. 1871. *La dottrina di Socrates secondo Senofonte, Platone, ed Aristotele*. Naples: Regia Università.

Lacey, Alan Robert. 1971. "Our Knowledge of Socrates." In Gregory Vlastos, ed., *The Philosophy of Socrates: A Collection of Critical Essays*. Notre Dame: University of Notre Dame.

Levi, Adolfo. 1942. "Ippia di Elide e la corrente naturalistica della Sofistica." *Sophia* 9: 441–50.

Levien, Edward, ed. and trans. 1872. *Memoirs of Socrates*. London: Low.

Levvenklaius, Johannes [a.k.a. Leuunklavius, Leunclavius, Lenklau], trans. 1562 [also 1569, 1572, 1594]. *Xenophontis Opera*. 2 vols. Basel: Guarinum.

Liddell, Henry George, and Robert Scott. 1953. *A Greek-English Lexicon*. 9th ed. Rev. aug. Henry Stuart Jones. Oxford: Clarendon Press.

Long, Anthony Arthur. 1988. "Socrates in Hellenistic Philosophy." *Classical Quarterly* n. s. 38: 150–71.

———. 2006. "How Does Socrates' Divine Sign Communicate with Him?" In S. Ahbel-Rappe and R. Kamtekar, eds., *A Companion to Socrates*. Malden, MA: Blackwell.

López, Alfredo Róspide, and Francisco Martín García. 1995. *Index Socraticorum Xenophontis operum*. Hildesheim: Olms-Weidmann.

Lorch, Benjamin. 2010. "Xenophon's Socrates on Political Ambition and Political Philosophy." *Review of Politics* 72: 189–211.

Luccioni, Jean. 1953. *Xénophon et le socratisme*. Paris: Presses universitaires.

Macleod, M. D., ed. 2008. *Xenophon, Apology and Memorabilia I*. Oxford: Oxbow.

MacNaghten, R. E. 1914. "Socrates and the *Daimonion*." *Classical Review* 28: 185–89.

Maier, Heinrich. 1913. *Sokrates: Sein Werk und seine geschichtliche Stellung*. Tübingen: Mohr.

Mannebach, Erich, ed. 1961. *Aristippi et Cyrenaicorum fragmenta*. Leiden: Brill.

Marchant, Edgar Cardew, ed. 1921. *Xenophontis Opera omnia*. 5 vols. 2nd and rev. ed. Oxford: Clarendon Press.

———, ed. and trans. 1923. *Xenophon in Seven Volumes*. Vol. 4. Loeb Classical Library. Cambridge, MA: Harvard University Press. [Oddly, Marchant indicates on p. xxix that he does not follow his own Oxford Classical Text, but the text of G. Sauppe, 1865.]

Maréchal, Sylvain. 1833. *Dictionnaire des athées anciens et modernes*. 2nd ed. Brussels: Balleroy.

Marsh, David. 1992. "Xenophon." In Virginia Brown et al., eds., *Catalogus translationum et commentariorum*. Medieval and Renaissance Latin Translations and Commentaries 7. Washington, DC: Catholic University of America Press.

McBrayer, Gregory, ed. Forthcoming. *Xenophon: The Shorter Writings*. Ithaca, NY: Cornell University Press.

Meiners, Christoph. 1781–82. *Geschichte des Ursprungs, Fortgangs und Verfalls der Wissenschaften in Griechenland und Rom*. 2 vols. Lemgo: Meyer.

Melzer, Arthur. 2014. *Philosophy between the Lines: The Lost History of Esoteric Writing*. Chicago: University of Chicago Press.

Mensching, Eckart, ed. 1963. *Favorin von Arelate: Der erste Teil der Fragmente; Memorabilien und Omnigena historia.* 3 vols. Berlin: De Gruyter.

Mesk, Josef. 1910. "Die Anklagerede des Polykrates gegen Sokrates." *Wiener Studien* 32: 56–84.

Millett, Paul. 1991. *Lending and Borrowing in Ancient Athens.* Cambridge: Cambridge University Press.

Montée, Pierre. 1869. *La philosophie de Socrate.* Paris: Durand and Pédone-Lauriel.

Montuori, Mario. 1974. *Socrate: Fisologia di un mito.* Florence: Sansoni.

———. 1981. *De Socrate iuste damnato: La nascita del problema socratico nel XVIII secolo.* Rome: dell'Ateneo.

———, ed. 1992. *The Socratic Problem: The History—the Solutions from the 18th Century to the Present Time; 61 Extracts from 54 Authors in Their Historical Context.* Amsterdam: Gieben.

Morrison, Donald R. 1994. "Xenophon's Socrates as Teacher." In Vander Waerdt 1994b.

———. 1995. "Xenophon's Socrates on the Just and the Lawful." *Ancient Philosophy* 15: 329–47.

Morrison, J. S. 1953. "*Memorabilia* I.6: The Encounters of Socrates and Antiphon." *Classical Review* 3: 3–6.

———. 1955. "Socrates and Antiphon." *Classical Review* 5: 8–12.

Mossé, Claude. 1999. "Le travail des femmes dans l'Athènes de l'époque classique." *Saitabi* 49: 223–28.

Münscher, Karl. 1920. *Xenophon in der griechisch-römischen Literatur.* Leipzig: Dieterich'sche.

Nadon, Christopher. 2001. *Xenophon's Prince: Republic and Empire in the "Cyropaedia."* Berkeley: University of California Press.

Nails, Debra. 2002. *The People of Plato: A Prosopography of Plato and Other Socratics.* Indianapolis: Hackett.

Narcy, Michel. 1995. "Le choix d'Aristippe (Xénophon, *Mémorables* II 1)." In G. Giannantoni et al., eds., *La tradizione socratica.* Naples: Instituto italiano per gli studi filosofici.

———. 2004. "La meilleure amie de Socrate: Xénophon *Mémorables*, III, 11." *Les Études Philosophiques* 2 (May): 213–34.

———. 2008. "Sur la composition du livre III des *Mémorables* de Xénophon." In Michèle Broze et al., eds., *Mélanges de philosophie et de philologie offerts à Lambros Couloubaritsis.* Paris: Vrin.

Natali, Carlo. 2005. "La religiosità in Socrate secondo Senofonte." *Humanitas* 60: 670–91.

———. 2006. "Socrates' Dialectic in Xenophon's *Memorabilia.*" In L. Judson and V. Karasmanis, eds., *Remembering Socrates.* Oxford: Oxford University Press.

Naudé, Gabriel. 1653. *Apologie pour tous les grands personnages qui ont été faussement soupçonnez de Magie.* The Hague: Vlac.

Neschke, Ada, and Anne-Lise Worms. 1992. "Le degré zéro de la philosophie platonicienne: Platon dans l'*Historia critica philosophiae* de J. J. Brucker (1742)." *Revue de Métaphysique et de Morale* 97: 377–400.

Newell, Waller R. 1983. "Tyranny and the Science of Ruling in Xenophon's *Education of Cyrus.*" *Journal of Politics* 45: 889–906.

Nichols, James H., Jr. 1979. "On the Proper Use of Ancient Political Philosophy: A Comment on Stephen Taylor Holmes's 'Aristippus in and out of Athens.'" *American Political Science Review* 73: 129–33.

Nietzsche, Friedrich. 1967–2006. *Werke: Kritische Gesamtausgabe.* Ed. Giorgio Colli and Mazzino Montinari. 24 vols. Berlin: De Gruyter.

———. 1975–2004. *Nietzsche Briefwechsel: Kritische Gesamtausgabe.* Ed. Giorgio Colli and Mazzino Montinari. 25 vols. Berlin: De Gruyter.

———. 2001. *The Pre-Platonic Philosophers.* Trans. Greg Whitlock. Urbana: University of Illinois Press.

O'Connor, David K. 1994. "The Erotic Self-Sufficiency of Socrates: A Reading of Xenophon's *Memorabilia.*" In Vander Waerdt 1994b.

Osborne, Michael J., and Sean G. Byrne. 1996. *The Foreign Residents of Athens: An Annex to the Lexicon of Greek Personal Names; Attica.* Leuven: Peeters.

Pangle, Lorraine Smith. 2007. *The Political Philosophy of Benjamin Franklin.* Baltimore: Johns Hopkins University Press.

———. 2013. "Virtue and Self-Control in Xenophon's Socratic Thought." In Ann Ward and Lee Ward, eds., *Natural Right and Political Philosophy: Essays in Honor of Catherine and Michael Zuckert.* Notre Dame: University of Notre Dame Press.

———. 2014. *Virtue Is Knowledge: The Moral Foundations of Socratic Political Philosophy.* Chicago: University of Chicago Press.

———. 2015. "Moral Indignation, Magnanimity, and Philosophy in the Trial of the Armenian King." In Andrea Radasanu, ed., *In Search of Humanity: Essays in Honor of Clifford Orwin.* Lanham, MD: Lexington.

———. 2017. "Xenophon on the Psychology of Supreme Political Ambition." *American Political Science Review* 111: 308–21.

Pangle, Thomas L. 1996. "On the *Apology of Socrates to the Jury.*" In Bartlett 1996.

———. 2010. "Socratic Political Philosophy in Xenophon's *Symposium.*" *American Journal of Political Science* 54: 140–52.

———. 2013. *Aristotle's Teaching in the "Politics."* Chicago: University of Chicago Press.

———. 2014. "Xenophon on Whether Socratic Political Theorizing Corrupts the Young." *Kronos* 3: 41–57.

———. 2015. "Humanity and Divinity in Xenophon's Defense of Socrates." In Andrea Radasanu, ed., *In Search of Humanity: Essays in Honor of Clifford Orwin.* Lanham, MD: Lexington.

———. 2016. "Socrates' Argument for the Superiority of the Life Dedicated to Politics." *Interpretation* 42: 437–62.

Parker, Robert. 1996. *Athenian Religion: A History.* Oxford: Clarendon Press.

Patin, Guy. 1709. *L'esprit de Guy Patin: Tiré de ses conversations, de son cabinet, de ses lettres, et de ses ouvrages.* Ed. Antoine Lancelot and Laurent Bordelon. Amsterdam: Schelten.

Peppler, Charles W. 1910. "The Termination *-kos,* as Used by Aristophanes for Comic Effect." *American Journal of Philology* 31: 428–44.

Pfuhl, Ernst. 1923. *Malerei und Zeichnung der Griechen.* 3 vols. Munich: Bruckmann.

Pomeroy, Sarah B. 1975. *Goddesses, Whores, Wives, and Slaves.* New York: Schocken.

————. 1994. *Xenophon, Oeconomicus: A Social and Historical Commentary*. Oxford: Clarendon Press.

Pontier, Pierre. 2006. *Trouble et ordre chez Platon et Xénophon*. Paris: Vrin.

Powers, Nathan. 2009. "The Natural Theology of Xenophon's Socrates." *Ancient Philosophy* 29: 249–66.

Pradeau, Jean-François, and Francesco Fronterotta, eds. and trans. 2005. *Platon: Hippias majeur, Hippias mineur*. Paris: Flammarion.

Preisshofen, Felix. 1974. "Sokrates im Gesprach mit Parrhasios und Kleiton." In K. Döring and W. Kullman, eds., *Studia Platonica: Festschrift für Hermann Gundert zu seinem 65. Geburtstag*. Amsterdam: Grüner.

Proietti, Gerald. 1987. *Xenophon's Sparta: An Introduction*. Leiden: Brill.

Proust, Marcel. 1971. *Jean Santeuil*. Paris: Gallimard.

Pucci, Pietro. 2002. *Xenophon, Socrates' Defense: Introduction and Commentary*. Amsterdam: Hakkert.

Queneau, Raymond. 1951. "Philosophes et voyous." *Les Temps Modernes* 63: 1193–1205.

Redard, Georges. 1953. *Recherches sur chrē, chrēsthai: Étude sémantique*. Paris: Champion.

Richter, Ernst. 1893. "Xenophon-Studien." In Alfred Fleckeisen, ed., *Jahrbucher für classische Philologie* 19: 57–155. Leipzig: Teubner.

Riddell, James. 1867. *The Apology of Plato*. Oxford: Oxford University Press.

Robin, Léon. 1910. "Les 'Mémorables' de Xénophon et notre connaisance de la philosophie de Socrate." *Année philosophique* 21: 1–47.

Rossetti, Livio. 2008. "Savoir imiter c'est connaître: Le cas de *Mémorables*, III 8." In Michel Narcy and Alonso Tordesillas, eds., *Xénophon et Socrate, Actes du colloque d'Aix-en-Provence (6–9 novembre 2003)*. Paris: Vrin.

Rouveret, Agnès. 1989. *Histoire et imaginaire de la peinture ancienne (Ve siècle av. J.-C.—Ier siècle ap. J.-C.)*. Rome: École Française.

Rudhardt, Jean. 1958. *Notions fondamentales de la pensée religieuse et actes constitutifs du culte dans la Grèce classique*. Geneva: Droz.

Ruhnken, David. 1811. "Davidis Ruhnkenii Animadversiones in Xenophontis *Memorabilia*, in edit. quinta Ernnestiana anni 1772." *Classical Journal* 6: 444–60.

Rumpf, Andreas. 1951. "Parrhasios." *American Journal of Archaeology* 55: 1–12.

Sauppe, Gustav Albert, ed. 1834. *Xenophontis Commentarii*. Leipzig: Wienbrack.

————. 1865–67. *Xenophontis Opera*. Leipzig: Tauchnitz.

————. 1871. *Lexilogus Xenophonteus sive Index Xenophontis Grammaticus*. Leipzig: Teubner.

Sauppe, Hermann. 1896. *Ausgewählte Schriften*. Berlin: Weidmann.

Schaefer, Gottfried Heinrich, ed. 1811. *Xenophontis Commentarii*. Leipzig: Tauchnitz.

Schenkl, M. Karl. 1875. "Xenophontische Studien," Heft 2, "Beiträge zur Kritik der Apomnemoneumata." *Sitzungsberichte der Akademie der Wissenschaften 80*. Vienna: K. Gerold's Sohn.

Schleiermacher, Friedrich. 1818. "Über den Werth des Sokrates als Philosophen." *Abhandlungen der philosophischen Klasse der Königlich-preussischen Akademie der Wissenschaften aus den Jahren 1814–1815*, 50–68.

Schneider, Johann Gottlob, and Ludwig August Dindorf, eds. 1826. *Xenophontis Memorabilia Socratis*. Oxford: Clarendon Press.

Sedley, David. 2008. "Socrates' Place in the History of Teleology." *Elenchos* 29: 317–34.

Shaftesbury, Anthony Ashley Cooper, 3rd Earl of. 1964. *Characteristics of Men, Manners, Opinions, Times*. 2 vols. in 1. Indianapolis: Bobbs-Merrill.

———. 1969. *A Notion of the Historical Draught or Tablature of the Judgment of Hercules according to Prodicus, Lib. II. Xen. de Mem. Soc.; Treatise II of Second Characters or the Language of Forms*. Ed. Benjamin Rand. New York: Greenwood.

Shero, L. R. 1927. "Plato's *Apology* and Xenophon's *Apology*." *Classical Weekly* 20: 107–11.

Shulsky, Abram. Forthcoming. "On the *Ways and Means*." In McBrayer, forthcoming.

Snell, Bruno. 1975. *Die Entdeckung des Geistes: Studien zur Entstehung des europäischen Denkens bei den Griechen*. 4th ed. Göttingen: Vandenhoeck & Ruprecht.

Sommerstein, Alan H. 2008. "Swearing by Hera: A Deme Meme?" *Classical Quarterly* 58: 326–31.

———. 2009. *Talking about Laughter; and Other Studies in Greek Comedy*. Oxford: Oxford University Press.

Sörbom, Güron. 1966. *Mimesis and Art: Studies in the Origin and Early Development of Aesthetic Vocabulary*. Stockholm: Svenska Bokförlaget.

Souchier, Emmanuël. 1992. "Philosophes et voyous ou 'l'engagement' mis entre parenthèses." *Littérature* 86: 15–21.

Stokes, Michael. 2012. "Three Defences of Socrates: Relative Chronology, Politics, and Religion." In Hobden and Tuplin 2012.

Stone, I. F. 1988. *The Trial of Socrates*. Boston: Little, Brown.

Strauss, Barry. 1987. *Athens after the Peloponnesian War: Class, Faction, and Policy, 403–386 BC*. Ithaca, NY: Cornell University Press.

Strauss, Leo. 1939. "The Spirit of Sparta or the Taste of Xenophon." *Social Research* 6: 502–36.

———. 1952. *Persecution and the Art of Writing*. Glencoe, IL: Free Press.

———. 1953. *Natural Right and History*. Chicago: University of Chicago Press.

———. 1958. *Thoughts on Machiavelli*. Glencoe, IL: Free Press.

———. 1966. *Socrates and Aristophanes*. New York: Basic Books.

———. 1983. *Studies in Platonic Political Philosophy*. Chicago: University of Chicago Press.

———. 1987. "Introduction." In Leo Strauss and Joseph Cropsey, eds., *History of Political Philosophy*. Chicago: University of Chicago Press.

———. 1989. *The Rebirth of Classical Political Rationalism: An Introduction to the Thought of Leo Strauss*. Ed. Thomas L. Pangle. Chicago: University of Chicago Press.

Striker, Gisela. 1987. "Origins of the Concept of Natural Law." *Proceedings of the Boston Area Colloquium in Ancient Philosophy* 2: 79–94.

Strycker, Emile de, and Simon R. Slings. 1994. *Plato's Apology of Socrates: A Literary and Philosophical Study with a Running Commentary*. Leiden: Brill.

Talbot, Eugène, ed. and trans. 1859. *Oeuvres complètes de Xénophon*. 2 vols. Paris: Hachette.

Tambornino, Julius. 1909. *De antiquorum daemonismo*. Giessen: Töpelmann.

Tamiolaki, M. 2012. "Virtue and Leadership in Xenophon: Ideal Leaders or Ideal Losers?" In Hobden and Tuplin 2012.

Tate, J. 1936. "Greek for 'Atheism.'" *Classical Review* 50: 3–5.

———. 1937. "More Greek for 'Atheism.'" *Classical Review* 51: 3–6.

Tatum, James. 1989. *Xenophon's Imperial Fiction: On the Education of Cyrus.* Princeton, NJ: Princeton University Press.

Taylor, Alfred E. 1911. *Varia Socratica.* Oxford: Parker.

———. 1932. *Socrates: The Man and His Thought.* London: Davies.

Theiler, Willy. 1965. *Zur Geschichte der teleologischen Naturbetrachtung bis auf Aristoteles.* Berlin: De Gruyter.

Thomas, Richard F. 2000. "A Trope by Any Other Name: 'Polysemy,' Ambiguity, and *Significatio* in Virgil." *Harvard Studies in Classical Philology* 100: 381–407.

Tuplin, Christopher. 1993. *The Failings of Empire: A Reading of Xenophon, Hellenika 2.3.11–7.5.27.* Stuttgart: Steiner.

———. 1996. "Xenophon." In *Oxford Classical Dictionary*, pp. 1628–31. 3rd ed. Oxford: Oxford University Press.

———, ed. 2004. *Xenophon and His World: Papers from a Conference Held in Liverpool in July 1999.* Stuttgart: Steiner.

Untersteiner, Mario. 1954. *The Sophists.* Oxford: Blackwell.

Vander Waerdt, Paul A. 1993. "Socratic Justice and Self-Sufficiency: The Story of the Delphic Oracle in Xenophon's *Apology of Socrates.*" *Oxford Studies in Ancient Philosophy* 11: 1–48.

———. 1994a. "Socrates in the Clouds." In Vander Waerdt 1994b.

———, ed. 1994b. *The Socratic Movement.* Ithaca, NY: Cornell University Press.

Vlastos, Gregory. 1980. "The Paradox of Socrates." In Gregory Vlastos, ed., *The Philosophy of Socrates: A Collection of Critical Essays.* Notre Dame: University of Notre Dame Press.

———. 1983. "The Historical Socrates and Athenian Democracy." *Political Theory* 11: 495–516.

———. 1991. *Socrates: Ironist and Moral Philosopher.* Ithaca, NY: Cornell University Press.

Vogel, Cornelia Johanna de. 1962. "Who Was Socrates?" *Journal of the History of Philosophy* 1: 143–61.

Waterfield, Robin, ed. and trans. 1992. *Xenophon: Conversations of Socrates (Socrates' Defence, Memoirs of Socrates, The Dinner-Party, The Estate-Manager).* London: Penguin.

———. 2004. "Xenophon's Socratic Mission." In Tuplin 2004.

———. 2012. "Xenophon on Socrates' Trial and Death." In Hobden and Tuplin 2012.

Watson, John Selby, trans. 1854. *The Anabasis or Expedition of Cyrus, and the Memorabilia of Socrates.* London: Bohn.

Weil, Raymond. 1983. "Socrate au début des *Helleniques.*" In *Mélanges Édouard Delebecque.* Aix-en-Provence: Publications de l'Université de Provence.

Weiske, Benjamin, ed. 1802. *Xenophontum Atheniensis Scripta.* Vol. 5. Leipzig: Fritsch.

Weissenborn, Hermann, ed. 1910. *De Xenophontis in Commentariis scribendis fide historica.* Jena: Neuenhahni.

Wells, Edward, ed. 1690–96. *Xenophontis Opera: Graece et Latine.* Trans. Johannes Levenklaius. 8 vols. Oxford: Oxford University Press. (This is the edition from which originates the division of all of Xenophon's writings into chapters and paragraph-subsections.)

Zeller, Eduard. 1885. *Socrates and the Socratic Schools.* Trans. Oswald J. Reichel. 2nd ed. London: Longmans, Green.

Zervos, Christina. 1934. *L'art en Grèce, des temps prehistoriques au début du XVIIIe siècle.* Paris: Cahiers d'art.

Zeune, Johann Carl, ed. 1781. *Xenophontis Memorabilium Socratis.* Leipzig: Fritsch.

Zuretti, Carlo Oreste. 1916. "Xenophontis Memor. IV 4." *Rivista di Filologia e d'Instruzione Classica* 54: 114–27.

# INDEX OF NAMES

The following names have not been indexed because they are referred to pervasively: Michele Bandini, Louis-André Dorion, Josiah Renick Smith, Leo Strauss, Socrates, Xenophon (except for the works of the last).

Kronenberg, Leah, 15, 218n5, 219n11, 220n2
Kühn, Joseph H., 231n1
Kuntz, Mary, 238n73

Labriola, Antonio, 218–19n6
Lacey, Alan Robert, 260n43
Laches, 68
Lactantius, 223n17
Lamprocles, 80–85, 242n5, 242n8, 242n10
Lefkowitz, Mary R., 222n12
Levi, Adolfo, 261n51
Levien, Edward, 254n87
Levvenklaius, Johannes (a.k.a. Leuunklavius, Leunclavius, Lenklau), 220n1
Libanius, *Apology of Socrates*, 221n5, 224n26, 226n9
Locke, John, *Questions Concerning the Law of Nature*, 261n52; *Reasonableness of Christianity*, 223n17
Long, Anthony Arthur, 218n6, 220n2, 223nn21–22, 224n31
López, Alfredo Róspide, 221n11, 235n44
Lorch, Benjamin, 113, 247n13, 248n17
Lowth, Robert, 241n96
Luccioni, Jean, 224n30, 225n5, 226n6, 226n9, 233–34n29, 252n71, 256n2
Lycis, 161
Lycon, 226n9
Lycurgus, 194
Lysias, 249n29

Machiavelli, Niccolò, 3, 107, 116, 217n3, 244n29; *Discourses on the First Ten Books of Titus Livy*, 217n3, 247n5; *The Prince*, 83, 217n3, 247n5, 253n81
Macleod, M. D., 228n27, 231n53, 232n8, 233–34n29
MacNaghten, R. E., 221n11
Maier, Heinrich, 231n53, 246n1, 247n8, 248n16
Mannebach, Erich, 237n57, 250n47
Marchant, Edgar Cardew, 224n28, 227n13, 232n11, 235n43, 247n12, 260n37, 261n54
Maréchal, Sylvain, 223n18
Marsh, David, 220n1
Marsilius of Padua, *Defensor Pacis*, 261n52
Marx, Karl, 107; *Capital*, 245n42
Matteis, Paolo di, 238–39n76, 241–42n97
Matthews, Elaine, 153, 245n37, 245n45, 246n53, 246n55, 249n26, 254n85, 254–55n90

Maximus of Tyre, *If Socrates Did Nobly in Not Making a Defense*, 221n5
Meiners, Christoph, 218–19n6
Meletus, 221n5, 222n12, 222n16, 226n9
Melzer, Arthur, 20, 191, 217n4, 224n29
Menander, 196, 218n5
Mensching, Eckart, 220n4
Mesk, Josef, 226n9
Millett, Paul, 106, 242n4
Mitsis, Phillip T., 224n31
Montaigne, Michel de, 218–19n6, 223n21
Montée, Pierre, 223nn20–21, 231–32n3
Montesquieu, *Spirit of the Laws*, 135, 237n64, 237–38n67, 245n43, 250n39, 261n52
Montuori, Mario, 218–19n6, 224n29
Morell, Thomas, 241n96
Morrison, Donald R., 219n20, 225n1, 226n6, 229n38, 260–61n46
Morrison, J. S., 234n37, 235n42, 236n48
Mossé, Claude, 245nn37–40, 246n50
Münscher, Karl, 218–19n6
Muses, the, 71
Musurus, Marcus, 238n68

Nadon, Christopher, 217–18n4, 247n10
Nails, Debra, 228n28, 229n29, 233nn17–18, 234n37, 245n37, 246n50, 246n55, 249n27, 250n47, 254n85
Narcy, Michel, 236n54, 237n57, 237n62, 237n64, 241n95, 250n46, 251n49, 251n57, 252n70, 254n88, 263n2
Natali, Carlo, 199, 259n27
Naudé, Gabriel, 223n20
Neschke, Ada, 218–19n6
Newell, Waller R., 247n10
Nichols, James H., Jr., 69
Nicias, 68, 243–44n26
Nicomachides, 124–30, 249n26
Nietzsche, Friedrich, 1–3, 6, 83, 217n1, 220n3; *Beyond Good and Evil*, 219n13, 247–48n14, 259n33; *Genealogy of Morals*, 242n9; *Human, All-Too-Human*, 219n13; *Twilight of the Idols*, 225n3; *The Wanderer and His Shadow*, 1–3, 217n2, 219n7, 219nn12–13, 219n19, 219n21

O'Connor, David K., 219n20, 222n12, 224n24, 227n13, 228n23, 229n34, 229n37, 230n48, 231n49, 237n57, 258n15, 258n23, 263n71, 263n74

Printed and bound by CPI Group (UK) Ltd, Croydon, CR0 4YY

09/06/2025

14685683-0003